Renault Espace
Service and Repair Manual

John S. Mead

Models covered

(3197-256)

Renault Espace models with 4-cylinder petrol & diesel engines, including special/limited editions

2.0 litre (1995 cc) & 2.2 litre (2165 cc) petrol engines

2.1 litre (2068 cc) Turbo-diesel engine

Does not cover 2849 cc Z7W V-6 petrol engine, automatic transmission, or Quadra (four-wheel-drive) models

© Haynes Publishing 1996

A book in the **Haynes Service and Repair Manual Series**

ISBN **1 85960 197 9**

British Library Cataloguing in Publication Data
A catalogue record for this book is available from the British Library.

ABCDE
FGHIJ
KLMN

Printed in the USA

Haynes Publishing
Sparkford, Nr Yeovil, Somerset BA22 7JJ, England

Haynes North America, Inc
861 Lawrence Drive, Newbury Park, California 91320, USA

Editions Haynes S.A.
Tour Aurore - La Défense 2, 18 Place des Reflets,
92975 PARIS LA DEFENSE Cedex, France

Haynes Publishing Nordiska AB
Box 1504, 751 45 UPPSALA, Sweden

Contents

LIVING WITH YOUR RENAULT ESPACE

MAINTENANCE

Routine Maintenance and Servicing

Contents

REPAIRS & OVERHAUL

REFERENCE

The Renault Espace range was introduced in 1984 as a five-door, five- or seven-seat multi-purpose vehicle. It quickly established itself as a trend setter and leader in what would become a very competitive sector of the market. Originally available with 2.0 litre carburettor petrol engine and 2.1 litre turbocharged diesel engine, a more powerful fuel-injected version of the 2.0 litre petrol engine was added to the range in 1989. This also marked the first facelift of the Espace range, with reshaped grille and various styling and mechanical revisions. If the first two versions can be considered as "Phase 1" and "Phase 2", then the next change came in 1991, when the range received major engineering and styling revisions. For the purpose of this manual, this major change will be referred to as the "Phase 3" version. Also introduced at this time was the 2.2 litre fuel-injected petrol engine, together with enhanced emission control equipment and numerous vehicle safety features.

All engines are based on the aluminium block wet-liner J-series which is similar in construction in both petrol and diesel forms. These engines are all of four-cylinder overhead camshaft design, mounted longitudinally at the front of the vehicle, together with the transmission and final drive. All models covered by this manual have front-wheel drive with a five-speed manual transmission.

Suspension is fully independent at the front, with upper and lower wishbones and coil springs, while at the rear, a semi-independent, coil-sprung, rigid axle is used. Power steering is standard on all models.

A wide range of standard and optional equipment is available within the Espace range to suit most tastes, including central locking, electric windows, an electric sunroof, an air bag and unrivalled interior layout flexibility. An anti-lock braking system and air conditioning system are available as options on certain models.

Provided that regular servicing is carried out in accordance with the manufacturer's recommendations, the Espace should prove reliable and very economical. The engine compartment is well-designed, and most of the items requiring frequent attention are easily accessible.

Renault Espace RXE

The Renault Espace Team

Haynes manuals are produced by dedicated and enthusiastic people working in close co-operation. The team responsible for the creation of this book included:

Author	John S. Mead
Sub-editor	Carole Turk
Editor & Page Make-up	Bob Jex
Workshop manager	Paul Buckland
Photo Scans	John Martin Paul Tanswell
Cover illustration & Line Art	Roger Healing

We hope the book will help you to get the maximum enjoyment from your car. By carrying out routine maintenance as described you will ensure your car's reliability and preserve its resale value.

Your Renault Espace Manual

The aim of this manual is to help you get the best value from your vehicle. It can do so in several ways. It can help you decide what work must be done (even should you choose to get it done by a garage), provide information on routine maintenance and servicing, and give a logical course of action and diagnosis when random faults occur. However, it is hoped that you will use the manual by tackling the work yourself. On simpler jobs it may even be quicker than booking the car into a garage and going there twice, to leave and collect it. Perhaps most important, a lot of money can be saved by avoiding the costs a garage must charge to cover its labour and overheads.

The manual has drawings and descriptions to show the function of the various components so that their layout can be understood. Then the tasks are described and photographed in a clear step-by-step sequence.

Acknowledgements

Thanks are due to Champion Spark Plug, who supplied the illustrations showing spark plug conditions. Certain illustrations are the copyright of the Renault (UK) Limited, and are used with their permission. Special thanks to Ash Renault of Yeovil, Somerset who provided several of the project vehicles used in the origination of this manual. Thanks are also due to Sykes-Pickavant Limited, who provided some of the workshop tools, and to all those people at Sparkford who helped in the production of this manual.

We take great pride in the accuracy of information given in this manual, but vehicle manufacturers make alterations and design changes during the production run of a particular vehicle of which they do not inform us. No liability can be accepted by the authors or publishers for loss, damage or injury caused by any errors in, or omissions from the information given.

Working on your car can be dangerous. This page shows just some of the potential risks and hazards, with the aim of creating a safety-conscious attitude.

General hazards

Scalding

• Don't remove the radiator or expansion tank cap while the engine is hot.
• Engine oil, automatic transmission fluid or power steering fluid may also be dangerously hot if the engine has recently been running.

Burning

• Beware of burns from the exhaust system and from any part of the engine. Brake discs and drums can also be extremely hot immediately after use.

Crushing

• When working under or near a raised vehicle, always supplement the jack with axle stands, or use drive-on ramps. *Never venture under a car which is only supported by a jack.*
• Take care if loosening or tightening high-torque nuts when the vehicle is on stands. Initial loosening and final tightening should be done with the wheels on the ground.

Fire

• Fuel is highly flammable; fuel vapour is explosive.
• Don't let fuel spill onto a hot engine.
• Do not smoke or allow naked lights (including pilot lights) anywhere near a vehicle being worked on. Also beware of creating sparks (electrically or by use of tools).
• Fuel vapour is heavier than air, so don't work on the fuel system with the vehicle over an inspection pit.
• Another cause of fire is an electrical overload or short-circuit. Take care when repairing or modifying the vehicle wiring.
• Keep a fire extinguisher handy, of a type suitable for use on fuel and electrical fires.

Electric shock

• Ignition HT voltage can be dangerous, especially to people with heart problems or a pacemaker. Don't work on or near the ignition system with the engine running or the ignition switched on.

• Mains voltage is also dangerous. Make sure that any mains-operated equipment is correctly earthed. Mains power points should be protected by a residual current device (RCD) circuit breaker.

Fume or gas intoxication

• Exhaust fumes are poisonous; they often contain carbon monoxide, which is rapidly fatal if inhaled. Never run the engine in a confined space such as a garage with the doors shut.
• Fuel vapour is also poisonous, as are the vapours from some cleaning solvents and paint thinners.

Poisonous or irritant substances

• Avoid skin contact with battery acid and with any fuel, fluid or lubricant, especially antifreeze, brake hydraulic fluid and Diesel fuel. Don't syphon them by mouth. If such a substance is swallowed or gets into the eyes, seek medical advice.
• Prolonged contact with used engine oil can cause skin cancer. Wear gloves or use a barrier cream if necessary. Change out of oil-soaked clothes and do not keep oily rags in your pocket.
• Air conditioning refrigerant forms a poisonous gas if exposed to a naked flame (including a cigarette). It can also cause skin burns on contact.

Asbestos

• Asbestos dust can cause cancer if inhaled or swallowed. Asbestos may be found in gaskets and in brake and clutch linings. When dealing with such components it is safest to assume that they contain asbestos.

Special hazards

Hydrofluoric acid

• This extremely corrosive acid is formed when certain types of synthetic rubber, found in some O-rings, oil seals, fuel hoses etc, are exposed to temperatures above 400°C. The rubber changes into a charred or sticky substance containing the acid. *Once formed, the acid remains dangerous for years. If it gets onto the skin, it may be necessary to amputate the limb concerned.*
• When dealing with a vehicle which has suffered a fire, or with components salvaged from such a vehicle, wear protective gloves and discard them after use.

The battery

• Batteries contain sulphuric acid, which attacks clothing, eyes and skin. Take care when topping-up or carrying the battery.
• The hydrogen gas given off by the battery is highly explosive. Never cause a spark or allow a naked light nearby. Be careful when connecting and disconnecting battery chargers or jump leads.

Air bags

• Air bags can cause injury if they go off accidentally. Take care when removing the steering wheel and/or facia. Special storage instructions may apply.

Diesel injection equipment

• Diesel injection pumps supply fuel at very high pressure. Take care when working on the fuel injectors and fuel pipes.

⚠️ *Warning: Never expose the hands, face or any other part of the body to injector spray; the fuel can penetrate the skin with potentially fatal results.*

Remember...

DO

• Do use eye protection when using power tools, and when working under the vehicle.

• Do wear gloves or use barrier cream to protect your hands when necessary.

• Do get someone to check periodically that all is well when working alone on the vehicle.

• Do keep loose clothing and long hair well out of the way of moving mechanical parts.

• Do remove rings, wristwatch etc, before working on the vehicle – especially the electrical system.

• Do ensure that any lifting or jacking equipment has a safe working load rating adequate for the job.

DON'T

• Don't attempt to lift a heavy component which may be beyond your capability – get assistance.

• Don't rush to finish a job, or take unverified short cuts.

• Don't use ill-fitting tools which may slip and cause injury.

• Don't leave tools or parts lying around where someone can trip over them. Mop up oil and fuel spills at once.

• Don't allow children or pets to play in or near a vehicle being worked on.

The following pages are intended to help in dealing with common roadside emergencies and breakdowns. You will find more detailed fault finding information at the back of the manual, and repair information in the main chapters.

If your car won't start and the starter motor doesn't turn

☐ If it's a model with automatic transmission, make sure the selector is in 'P' or 'N'.
☐ Open the bonnet and make sure that the battery terminals are clean and tight.
☐ Switch on the headlights and try to start the engine. If the headlights go very dim when you're trying to start, the battery is probably flat. Get out of trouble by jump starting (see next page) using a friend's car.

If your car won't start even though the starter motor turns as normal

☐ Is there fuel in the tank?
☐ Is there moisture on electrical components under the bonnet? Switch off the ignition, then wipe off any obvious dampness with a dry cloth. Spray a water-repellent aerosol product (WD-40 or equivalent) on ignition and fuel system electrical connectors like those shown in the photos. Pay special attention to the ignition coil wiring connector and HT leads. (Note that Diesel engines don't normally suffer from damp.)

A Check that the spark plug HT leads (where applicable) are securely connected by pushing them home.

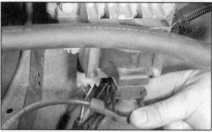

B Make sure that the HT lead to the ignition coil (where applicable) is also securely connected.

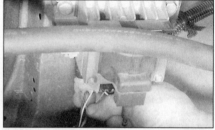

C The wiring connector at the ignition coil power module (where applicable) may cause problems if not connected securely.

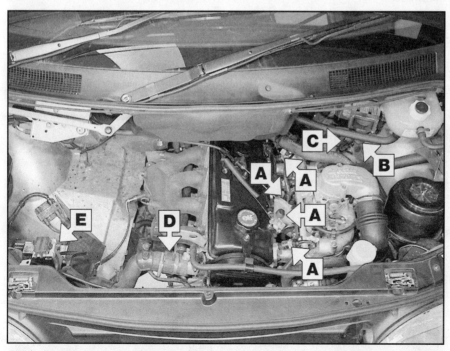

Check that electrical connections are secure (with the ignition switched off) and spray them with a water dispersant spray like WD40 if you suspect a problem due to damp

D Check the security of the wiring at the coolant temperature sensor connection. Any problems on these connections can cause a variety of starting and running problems.

E Check the security and condition of the battery connections.

Jump starting

Jump starting will get you out of trouble, but you must correct whatever made the battery go flat in the first place. There are three possibilities:

1 *The battery has been drained by repeated attempts to start, or by leaving the lights on.*

2 *The charging system is not working properly (alternator drivebelt slack or broken, alternator wiring fault or alternator itself faulty).*

3 *The battery itself is at fault (electrolyte low, or battery worn out).*

When jump-starting a car using a booster battery, observe the following precautions:

✔ Before connecting the booster battery, make sure that the ignition is switched off.

✔ Ensure that all electrical equipment (lights, heater, wipers, etc) is switched off.

✔ Make sure that the booster battery is the same voltage as the discharged one in the vehicle.

✔ If the battery is being jump-started from the battery in another vehicle, the two vehcles MUST NOT TOUCH each other.

✔ Make sure that the transmission is in neutral (or PARK, in the case of automatic transmission).

1 Connect one end of the red jump lead to the positive (+) terminal of the flat battery

2 Connect the other end of the red lead to the positive (+) terminal of the booster battery.

3 Connect one end of the black jump lead to the negative (-) terminal of the booster battery

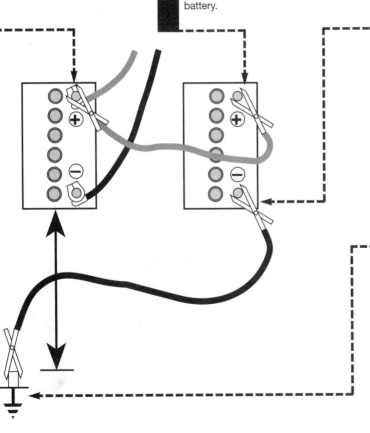

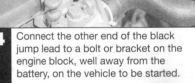

4 Connect the other end of the black jump lead to a bolt or bracket on the engine block, well away from the battery, on the vehicle to be started.

5 Make sure that the jump leads will not come into contact with the fan, drive-belts or other moving parts of the engine.

6 Start the engine using the booster battery, then with the engine running at idle speed, disconnect the jump leads in the reverse order of connection.

Wheel changing

Some of the details shown here will vary according to model. For instance, the location of the spare wheel and jack is not the same on all cars. However, the basic principles apply to all vehicles.

 Warning: Do not change a wheel in a situation where you risk being hit by other traffic. On busy roads, try to stop in a lay-by or a gateway. Be wary of passing traffic while changing the wheel – it is easy to become distracted by the job in hand.

Preparation

☐ When a puncture occurs, stop as soon as it is safe to do so.
☐ Park on firm level ground, if possible, and well out of the way of other traffic.
☐ Use hazard warning lights if necessary.

☐ If you have one, use a warning triangle to alert other drivers of your presence.
☐ Apply the handbrake and engage first or reverse gear (or Park on models with automatic transmission).

☐ Chock the wheel diagonally opposite the one being removed – a couple of large stones will do for this.
☐ If the ground is soft, use a flat piece of wood to spread the load under the jack.

Changing the wheel

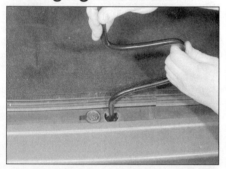

1 From inside the luggage compartment, use the wheelbrace to lower the spare wheel cradle.

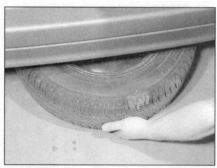

2 Slide the spare wheel out from the underside of the vehicle.

3 Remove the wheel trim from the wheel to be changed.

4 Slacken each wheel bolt on the wheel to be changed by half a turn.

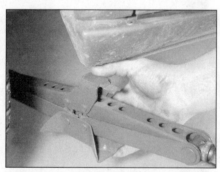

5 Locate the jack below the reinforced jacking point on firm ground (don't jack the vehicle at any other point on the sill).

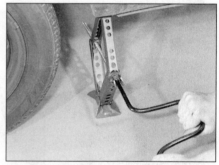

6 Turn the jack handle clockwise until the wheel is raised clear of the ground, remove the bolts and lift the wheel clear.

7 Position the spare wheel and fit the bolts. Tighten moderately with the wheel brace, then lower the vehicle to the ground.

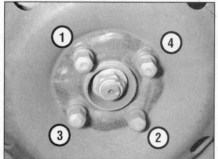

8 Tighten the wheel bolts in the sequence shown, then fit the wheel trim. Put the punctured wheel in the spare wheel cradle.

Finally...

☐ Remove the wheel chocks.

☐ Stow the jack and tools in the correct locations in the car. Secure the spare wheel cradle securely - don't leave it hanging down under the car.

☐ Check the tyre pressure on the wheel just fitted. If it is low, or if you don't have a pressure gauge with you, drive slowly to the nearest garage and inflate the tyre to the right pressure.

☐ Have the damaged tyre or wheel repaired as soon as possible.

Identifying leaks

Puddles on the garage floor or drive, or obvious wetness under the bonnet or underneath the car, suggest a leak that needs investigating. It can sometimes be difficult to decide where the leak is coming from, especially if the engine bay is very dirty already. Leaking oil or fluid can also be blown rearwards by the passage of air under the car, giving a false impression of where the problem lies.

 Warning: Most automotive oils and fluids are poisonous. Wash them off skin, and change out of contaminated clothing, without delay.

 The smell of a fluid leaking from the car may provide a clue to what's leaking. Some fluids are distinctively coloured. It may help to clean the car carefully and to park it over some clean paper overnight as an aid to locating the source of the leak.
Remember that some leaks may only occur while the engine is running.

Sump oil

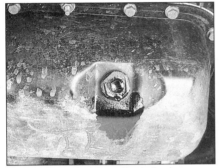

Engine oil may leak from the drain plug...

Oil from filter

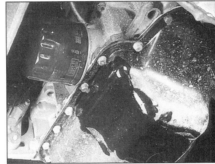

...or from the base of the oil filter.

Gearbox oil

Gearbox oil can leak from the seals at the inboard ends of the driveshafts.

Antifreeze

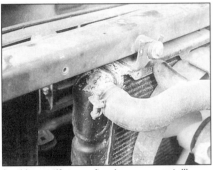

Leaking antifreeze often leaves a crystalline deposit like this.

Brake fluid

A leak occurring at a wheel is almost certainly brake fluid.

Power steering fluid

Power steering fluid may leak from the pipe connectors on the steering rack.

Towing

When all else fails, you may find yourself having to get a tow home – or of course you may be helping somebody else. Long-distance recovery should only be done by a garage or breakdown service. For shorter distances, DIY towing using another car is easy enough, but observe the following points:
□ Use a proper tow-rope – they are not expensive. The vehicle being towed must display an 'ON TOW' sign in its rear window.
□ Always turn the ignition key to the 'on' position when the vehicle is being towed, so

that the steering lock is released, and that the direction indicator and brake lights will work.
□ Only attach the tow-rope to the towing eyes provided.
□ Before being towed, release the handbrake and select neutral on the transmission.
□ Note that greater-than-usual pedal pressure will be required to operate the brakes, since the vacuum servo unit is only operational with the engine running.
□ On models with power steering, greater-than-usual steering effort will also be required.

□ The driver of the car being towed must keep the tow-rope taut at all times to avoid snatching.
□ Make sure that both drivers know the route before setting off.
□ Only drive at moderate speeds and keep the distance towed to a minimum. Drive smoothly and allow plenty of time for slowing down at junctions.
□ On models with automatic transmission, special precautions apply. If in doubt, do not tow, or transmission damage may result.

Introduction

There are some very simple checks which need only take a few minutes to carry out, but which could save you a lot of inconvenience and expense.

These "Weekly checks" require no great skill or special tools, and the small amount of time they take to perform could prove to be very well spent, for example;

☐ Keeping an eye on tyre condition and pressures, will not only help to stop them wearing out prematurely, but could also save your life.

☐ Many breakdowns are caused by electrical problems. Battery-related faults are particularly common, and a quick check on a regular basis will often prevent the majority of these.

☐ If your car develops a brake fluid leak, the first time you might know about it is when your brakes don't work properly. Checking the level regularly will give advance warning of this kind of problem.

☐ If the oil or coolant levels run low, the cost of repairing any engine damage will be far greater than fixing the leak, for example.

Underbonnet check points

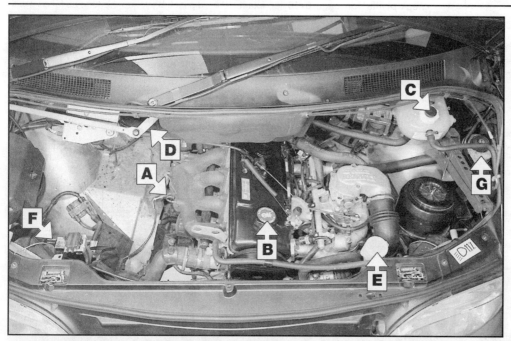

◀ Petrol models

A *Engine oil level dipstick*
B *Engine oil filler cap*
C *Coolant expansion tank*
D *Brake fluid reservoir*
E *Screen washer fluid reservoir*
F *Battery*
G *Power steering fluid reservoir*

◀ Diesel models

A *Engine oil level dipstick*
B *Engine oil filler cap*
C *Coolant expansion tank*
D *Brake fluid reservoir*
E *Screen washer fluid reservoir*
F *Battery*
G *Power steering fluid reservoir*

Engine oil level

Before you start
✔ Make sure that your car is on level ground.
✔ Check the oil level before the car is driven, or at least 5 minutes after the engine has been switched off.

HAYNES HiNT *If the oil is checked immediately after driving the vehicle, some of the oil will remain in the upper engine components, resulting in an inaccurate reading on the dipstick!*

The correct oil
Modern engines place great demands on their oil. It is very important that the correct oil for your car is used (See "Lubricants, fluids and tyre pressures").

Car Care
● If you have to add oil frequently, you should check whether you have any oil leaks. Place some clean paper under the car overnight, and check for stains in the morning. If there are no leaks, the engine may be burning oil *(see "Fault Finding")*.

● Always maintain the level between the upper and lower dipstick marks (see photo 3). If the level is too low severe engine damage may occur. Oil seal failure may result if the engine is overfilled by adding too much oil.

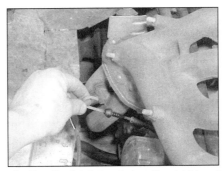

1 The dipstick is located on the right-hand side of the engine (*see "Underbonnet check points"* on page 0•10 for exact location). Withdraw the dipstick.

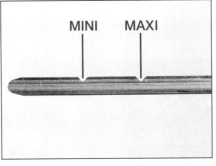

MINI   MAXI

3 Note the oil level on the end of the dipstick which should be between the upper ("MAXI") mark and lower ("MINI") mark. Approximately 0.5 to 1.0 litre of oil will raise the level from the lower to the upper portion of the hatched area.

2 Using a clean rag or paper towel remove all oil from the dipstick. Insert the clean dipstick back into the tube as far as it will go, then withdraw it again.

4 Oil is added through the filler cap. Unscrew the cap and top-up the level; a funnel may help to reduce spillage. Add the oil slowly, checking the level on the dipstick frequently. Avoid overfilling (see *"Car Care"*).

Coolant level

Warning: DO NOT attempt to remove the expansion tank pressure cap when the engine is hot, as there is a very great risk of scalding. Do not leave open containers of coolant about, as it is poisonous.

Car Care
● With a sealed-type cooling system, adding coolant should not be necessary on a regular basis. If frequent topping-up is required, it is likely there is a leak. Check the radiator, all hoses and joint faces for signs of staining or wetness, and rectify as necessary.

● It is important that antifreeze is used in the cooling system all year round, not just during the winter months. Don't top-up with water alone, as the antifreeze will become too diluted.

1 The coolant level varies with the temperature of the engine. When the engine is cold, the coolant level should be between 20 and 30 mm from the bottom of the expansion tank. When the engine is hot, the level may rise above this level.

2 If topping-up is necessary, **wait until the engine is cold.** Turn the expansion tank cap slowly anti-clockwise and wait until any pressure in the system is released. Once any pressure is released, unscrew it fully and lift it off.

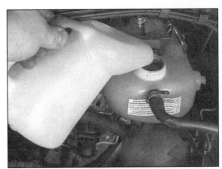

3 Add a mixture of water and antifreeze through the expansion tank filler neck until the coolant is at the correct level. Refit the cap, turning it clockwise as far as it will go to secure.

Screen washer fluid level

Screenwash additives not only keep the winscreen clean during foul weather, they also prevent the washer system freezing in cold weather - which is when you are likely to need it most. Don't top-up using plain water as the screenwash will become too diluted, and will freeze during cold weather.

Caution: On no account use coolant antifreeze in the washer system - this could discolour or damage paintwork.

1 The fluid level can be clearly seen on the translucent reservoir fitted to early models. On later models, release the cap and observe the level in the reservoir by looking down the filler neck.

2 When topping-up the reservoir, a screenwash additive should be added in the quantities recommended on the bottle.

Brake fluid level

Warning:
● *Brake fluid can harm your eyes and damage painted surfaces, so use extreme caution when handling and pouring it.*
● *Do not use fluid that has been standing open for some time, as it absorbs moisture from the air, which can cause a dangerous loss of braking effectiveness.*

HAYNES HINT

● *Make sure that your car is on level ground.*
● *The fluid level in the reservoir will drop slightly as the brake pads wear down, but the fluid level must never be allowed to drop below the "MINI" mark.*

Safety first!

● If the reservoir requires repeated topping-up this is an indication of a fluid leak somewhere in the system, which should be investigated immediately.

● If a leak is suspected, the car should not be driven until the braking system has been checked. Never take any risks where brakes are concerned.

1 The brake fluid reservoir is located on the right-hand side of the engine compartment (diesel model shown).

2 The "MAXI" and "MINI" marks are indicated on the side of the reservoir (petrol model shown). The fluid level must be kept between the marks.

3 If topping-up is necessary, first wipe the area around the filler cap with a clean rag before removing the cap.

4 Carefully add fluid; avoid spilling any on surrounding paintwork. Use only the specified fluid; mixing different types of fluid can damage the system. After filling to the correct level, refit the cap securely. Wipe off any spilt fluid.

Power steering fluid level

Before you start:

✔ Park the vehicle on level ground.
✔ Set the steering wheel straight-ahead.
✔ The engine should be turned off.

HAYNES HiNT *For the check to be accurate, the steering must not be turned once the engine has been stopped.*

Safety first!

● The need for frequent topping-up indicates a leak, which should be investigated immediately.

1 The fluid reservoir is remotely mounted in the engine compartment and various reservoir types may be fitted. If the reservoir has maximum and minimum markings on the side, these should be used for reference. If no markings are visible then with the filler cap removed, the level should be maintained just above the level of the internal grille (refer to Chapter 10 for further details).

2 Before removing the filler cap, make sure that you carefully wipe the surrounding area so that dirt does not enter the reservoir.

3 If topping-up is necessary, add a little fluid of the specified type, then check the fluid level. Look at the side of the reservoir and check that the fluid is up to the maximum mark, or look inside at the fluid level - make sure it's covering the grid, or level with the pad in the sleeve. Take care not to allow any dirt into the system and do not overfill the reservoir. When the level is correct, refit the cap.

Wiper blades

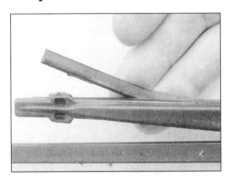

1 Check the condition of the wiper blades; if in any doubt, renew them. Wiper blades should be renewed annually.

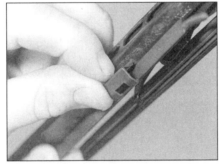

2 To remove a front wiper blade, pull the arm fully away from the glass until it locks. Swivel the blade through 90° and press the locking tab with your fingers.

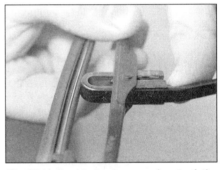

3 Slide the blade down and out of the hooked end of the arm.

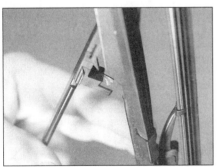

4 On the rear wiper blade, pull the arm away from the glass until it locks. Swivel the blade 90° to release the side locking tabs.

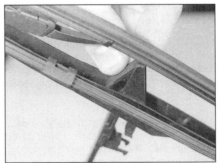

5 Disconnect the washer hose (later models). Lift up the front blade locking clip.

6 Depress the tab and withdraw the blade from the arm.

Tyre condition and pressure

It is very important that tyres are in good condition, and at the correct pressure - having a tyre failure at any speed is highly dangerous. Tyre wear is influenced by driving style - harsh braking and acceleration, or fast cornering, will all produce more rapid tyre wear. As a general rule, the front tyres wear out faster than the rears. Interchanging the tyres from front to rear ("rotating" the tyres) may result in more even wear. However, if this is completely effective, you may have the expense of replacing all four tyres at once!

Remove any nails or stones embedded in the tread before they penetrate the tyre to cause deflation. If removal of a nail does reveal that the tyre has been punctured, refit the nail so that its point of penetration is marked. Then immediately change the wheel, and have the tyre repaired by a tyre dealer.

Regularly check the tyres for damage in the form of cuts or bulges, especially in the sidewalls. Periodically remove the wheels, and clean any dirt or mud from the inside and outside surfaces. Examine the wheel rims for signs of rusting, corrosion or other damage. Light alloy wheels are easily damaged by "kerbing" whilst parking; steel wheels may also become dented or buckled. A new wheel is very often the only way to overcome severe damage.

New tyres should be balanced when they are fitted, but it may become necessary to re-balance them as they wear, or if the balance weights fitted to the wheel rim should fall off. Unbalanced tyres will wear more quickly, as will the steering and suspension components. Wheel imbalance is normally signified by vibration, particularly at a certain speed (typically around 50 mph). If this vibration is felt only through the steering, then it is likely that just the front wheels need balancing. If, however, the vibration is felt through the whole car, the rear wheels could be out of balance. Wheel balancing should be carried out by a tyre dealer or garage.

1 Tread Depth - visual check
The original tyres have tread wear safety bands (B), which will appear when the tread depth reaches approximately 1.6 mm. The band positions are indicated by a triangular mark on the tyre sidewall (A).

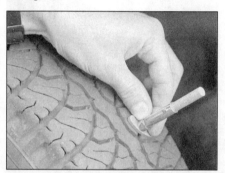

2 Tread Depth - manual check
Alternatively, tread wear can be monitored with a simple, inexpensive device known as a tread depth indicator gauge.

3 Tyre Pressure Check
Check the tyre pressures regularly with the tyres cold. Do not adjust the tyre pressures immediately after the vehicle has been used, or an inaccurate setting will result.

Tyre tread wear patterns

Shoulder Wear

Underinflation (wear on both sides)
Under-inflation will cause overheating of the tyre, because the tyre will flex too much, and the tread will not sit correctly on the road surface. This will cause a loss of grip and excessive wear, not to mention the danger of sudden tyre failure due to heat build-up.
Check and adjust pressures
Incorrect wheel camber (wear on one side)
Repair or renew suspension parts
Hard cornering
Reduce speed!

Centre Wear

Overinflation
Over-inflation will cause rapid wear of the centre part of the tyre tread, coupled with reduced grip, harsher ride, and the danger of shock damage occurring in the tyre casing.
Check and adjust pressures

If you sometimes have to inflate your car's tyres to the higher pressures specified for maximum load or sustained high speed, don't forget to reduce the pressures to normal afterwards.

Uneven Wear

Front tyres may wear unevenly as a result of wheel misalignment. Most tyre dealers and garages can check and adjust the wheel alignment (or "tracking") for a modest charge.
Incorrect camber or castor
Repair or renew suspension parts
Malfunctioning suspension
Repair or renew suspension parts
Unbalanced wheel
Balance tyres
Incorrect toe setting
Adjust front wheel alignment
Note: *The feathered edge of the tread which typifies toe wear is best checked by feel.*

Bulbs and fuses

✔ Check all external lights and the horn. Refer to the appropriate Sections of Chapter 12 for details if any of the circuits are found to be inoperative.

✔ Visually check all accessible wiring connectors, harnesses and retaining clips for security, and for signs of chafing or damage.

 HAYNES HiNT *If you need to check your brake lights and indicators unaided, back up to a wall or garage door and operate the lights. The reflected light should show if they are working properly.*

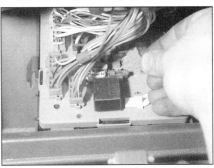

1 If a single indicator light, stop light or headlight has failed it is likely that a bulb has blown and will need to be replaced. Refer to Chapter 12 for details. If both stop lights have failed, it is possible that the stop light switch above the brake pedal needs adjusting (see Chapter 12).

2 If more than one indicator light or headlight has failed it is likely that either a fuse has blown or that there is a fault in the circuit (see *"Electrical fault finding"* in Chapter 12). The fuses are mounted in the fusebox located under or inside the glovebox.

3 To replace a blown fuse, simply prise it out. Fit a new fuse of the same rating, available from car accessory shops. It is important that you find the reason that the fuse blew - a complete checking procedure is given in Chapter 12.

Battery

Caution: Before carrying out any work on the vehicle battery, read the precautions given in "Safety first" at the start of this manual.

✔ Make sure that the battery tray is in good condition, and that the clamp is tight. Corrosion on the tray, retaining clamp and the battery itself can be removed with a solution of water and baking soda. Thoroughly rinse all cleaned areas with water. Any metal parts damaged by corrosion should be covered with a zinc-based primer, then painted.

✔ Periodically (approximately every three months), check the charge condition of the battery as described in Chapter 5A.

✔ If the battery is flat, and you need to jump start your vehicle, see *Roadside Repairs*.

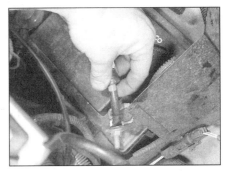

1 The battery is at the front of the engine compartment on the left-hand, or right-hand side according to model. The exterior of the battery should be inspected periodically for damage such as a cracked case or cover.

2 Check the tightness of battery clamps to ensure good electrical connections. You should not be able to move them. Also check each cable for cracks and frayed conductors.

HAYNES HiNT

Battery corrosion can be kept to a minimum by applying a layer of petroleum jelly to the clamps and terminals after they are reconnected.

3 If corrosion (white, fluffy deposits) is evident, remove the cables from the battery terminals, clean them with a small wire brush, then refit them. Automotive stores sell a tool for cleaning the battery post . . .

4 . . . as well as the battery cable clamps

Lubricants and fluids

Engine	Multigrade engine oil, viscosity SAE 10W/40 or 15W/40, to API SG/CD
Cooling system	Ethylene glycol-based antifreeze
Transmission	80W gear oil to API GL 5
Braking system	Universal brake/clutch fluid to SAE J1703 or DOT 3
Power steering	Dexron type II ATF

Tyre pressures

	Front	Rear
Phase 1 and 2 models		
Normal use	2.4 bars	2.1 bars
Fully laden or high speed	2.5 bars	2.5 bars
"Space saver" spare	2.7 bars	2.7 bars
Phase 3 models		
Normal use	2.3 bars	1.9 bars
Fully laden or high speed	2.5 bars	2.6 bars
"Space saver" spare	2.5 bars	2.5 bars

Note: *Refer to the tyre pressure data sticker on the glovebox lid for the correct tyre pressures for your particular vehicle. Pressures apply only to original-equipment tyres, and may vary if other makes or type is fitted; check with the tyre manufacturer or supplier for correct pressures if necessary.*

Chapter 1 Part A:
Routine maintenance and servicing - petrol models

Contents

Degrees of difficulty

Easy, suitable for novice with little experience	**Fairly easy,** suitable for beginner with some experience	**Fairly difficult,** suitable for competent DIY mechanic	**Difficult,** suitable for experienced DIY mechanic	**Very difficult,** suitable for expert DIY or professional

Lubricants and fluids

Refer to "Weekly checks" and relevant Chapters

Capacities

Engine oil (approximate):

Excluding filter:

2.0 litre models .... 5.0 litres

2.2 litre models .... 5.5 litres

Including filter:

2.0 litre models .... 5.5 litres

2.2 litre models .... 6.0 litres

Difference between MAX and MIN dipstick marks (approx.) .... 0.5 to 1.0 litre

Cooling system (approximate):

2.0 litre carburettor models .... 7.2 litres

2.0 litre fuel-injected models .... 8.4 litres

2.2 litre models .... 8.4 litres

Transmission .... 2.2 litres

Fuel tank .... 60 litres

Engine

Oil filter type .... Champion F104

Air filter type .... Champion W115

Fuel filter type:

Carburettor models .... Champion L101

Fuel-injected models .... Champion L206

Cooling system

Antifreeze mixture:

35% antifreeze .... Protection down to -23°C

50% antifreeze .... Protection down to -40°C

Note: *Refer to antifreeze manufacturer for latest recommendations.*

Ignition system

Spark plugs:*

2.0 litre carburettor models .... Champion S279YC

2.0 litre fuel-injected models .... Champion S6YC

2.2 litre models .... Champion S7YC or RS7YC

Spark plug electrode gap .... 0.9 mm

The spark plug types shown above are recommendations only. Consult the data label in the vehicle engine compartment for specific applications.

Brakes

Front and rear brake pad minimum thickness

(friction material and backing plate) .... 6.0 mm

Rear brake shoe minimum thickness (friction material and shoe) ..... 2.5 mm

Tyres

Tyre size .... 185/70 R 13H, 185/70 SR 13, 185/65 R 14H, 195/65 R14H, 195/65 R14 MXT according to model

Tyre pressures .... See *"Weekly checks"*

Wiper blades

All models .... Champion VX55 or X55

Torque wrench settings

	Nm
Roadwheel bolts	90
Spark plugs	25

The maintenance intervals in this manual are provided with the assumption that you, not the dealer, will be carrying out the work. These are the minimum maintenance intervals recommended by the manufacturer for vehicles driven daily. If you wish to keep your vehicle in peak condition at all times, you may wish to perform some of these procedures more often. We encourage frequent maintenance, because it enhances the efficiency, performance and resale value of your vehicle.

If the vehicle is driven in dusty areas, used to tow a trailer, or driven frequently at slow speeds (idling in traffic) or on short journeys, more frequent maintenance intervals are recommended.

When the vehicle is new, it should be serviced by a factory-authorised dealer service department, in order to preserve the factory warranty.

Every 250 miles (400 km) or weekly
- ☐ Refer to "Weekly checks"

Every 5000 miles (7500 km)
In addition to all the items listed above, carry out the following:
- ☐ Renew the engine oil (Section 3)
- ☐ Check the condition of the auxiliary drivebelt(s) (Section 4)
- ☐ Check the condition of the spark plugs (Section 5)
- ☐ Check the distributor cap, rotor arm and HT leads (Section 6)
- ☐ Check the battery and electrical equipment (Section 7)
- ☐ Check the engine for fluid leaks and the condition of the hoses (Section 8)
- ☐ Check the condition of the emission control equipment (Section 9)
- ☐ Check the engine idle speed and mixture settings - carburettor engines (Section 10)
- ☐ Check the condition of the brake pads (Section 11)
- ☐ Check the handbrake adjustment (Section 12)
- ☐ Check the condition and security of the steering and suspension components (Section 13)
- ☐ Check the condition of the driveshaft gaiters (Section 14)
- ☐ Inspect the underbody and the brake hydraulic pipes and hoses (Section 15)
- ☐ Check the condition of the fuel lines (Section 15)
- ☐ Check the condition and security of the exhaust system (Section 16)
- ☐ Check the condition of the seat belts (Section 17)
- ☐ Lubricate the locks and hinges (Section 18)
- ☐ Check the condition of the bodywork, paint and exterior trim (Section 19)
- ☐ Road test (Section 20)
- ☐ Check the operation of the air conditioning system (Section 21)

Every 10 000 miles (15 000 km)
In addition to all the items listed above, carry out the following:
- ☐ Renew the engine oil filter (Section 22)
- ☐ Renew the air cleaner filter element (Section 23)
- ☐ Check the transmission oil level (Section 24)
- ☐ Check the condition of the rear brake shoes (Section 25)

Every 40 000 miles (60 000 km)
In addition to all the items listed above, carry out the following:
- ☐ Renew the fuel filter (Section 26)
- ☐ Renew the transmission oil (Section 27)
- ☐ Renew the brake hydraulic fluid (Section 28)
- ☐ Have the front wheel alignment checked (Section 29)

Every 80 000 miles (120 000 km)
In addition to all the items listed above, carry out the following:
- ☐ Renew the timing belt (Section 30)

Note: *It is strongly recommended that the timing belt renewal interval is halved to 40 000 mies (60 000 km) on vehicles which are subjected to intensive use, ie. mainly short journeys or a lot of stop-start driving. The actual belt renewal interval is therefore very much up to the individual owner, but bear in mind that severe engine damage will result if the belt breaks.*

Every 2 years (regardless of mileage)
- ☐ Renew the coolant (Section 31).

1A

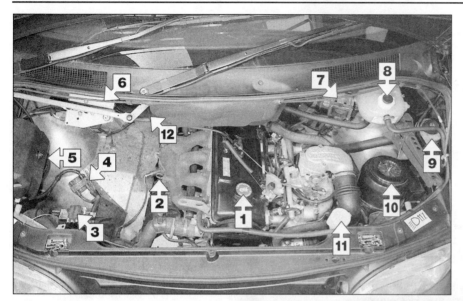

Underbonnet view of a 2.0 litre, Phase 3 model

1 Oil filler cap
2 Engine oil dipstick
3 Diagnostic socket
4 Fusible links
5 Fuel/ignition ECU case
6 Wiper motor and linkage
7 Ignition coil and power module
8 Coolant expansion tank
9 Steering fluid reservoir
10 Air cleaner
11 Washer reservoir
12 Brake master cylinder reservoir

Front underbody view of a 2.0 litre, Phase 3 model

1 Engine oil drain plug
2 Power steering pump drivebelt adjuster
3 Power steering pump
4 Suspension lower arm
5 Driveshaft inner CV joint
6 Exhaust front pipe
7 Transmission undertray
8 Engine mounting

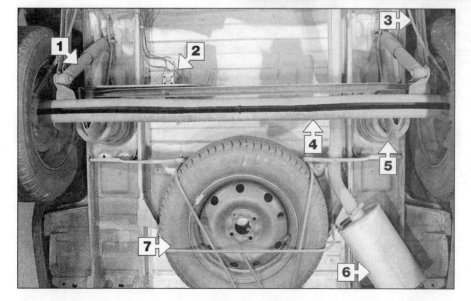

Rear underbody view of a 2.0 litre, Phase 3 model

1 Shock absorber
2 Brake compensator
3 Handbrake cable
4 Rear axle
5 Rear spring
6 Exhaust silencer
7 Spare wheel

1 Introduction

1 This Chapter is designed to help the home mechanic maintain his/her vehicle for safety, economy, long life and peak performance.
2 This Chapter contains a master maintenance schedule, followed by Sections dealing specifically with each task in the schedule. Visual checks, adjustments, component renewal and other helpful items are included. Refer to the accompanying illustrations of the engine compartment and the underside of the vehicle for the locations of the various components.
3 Servicing your vehicle in accordance with the maintenance schedule and the following Sections will provide a planned maintenance programme, which should result in a long and reliable service life. This is a comprehensive plan, so maintaining some items but not others at the specified service intervals will not produce the same results.
4 As you service your vehicle, you will discover that many of the procedures can - and should - be grouped together, because of the particular procedure being performed, or because of the close proximity of two otherwise-unrelated components to one another. For example, if the vehicle is raised for any reason, the exhaust should be inspected at the same time as the suspension and steering components.
5 The first step of this maintenance programme is to prepare yourself before the actual work begins. Read through all the Sections relevant to the work to be carried out, then make a list and gather together all the parts and tools required. If a problem is encountered, seek advice from a parts specialist or a dealer service department.

2 Intensive maintenance

1 If, from the time the vehicle is new, the routine maintenance schedule is followed closely, and frequent checks are made of fluid levels and high-wear items, as suggested throughout this manual, the engine will be kept in relatively good running condition, and the need for additional work will be minimised.
2 It is possible that there will be some times when the engine is running poorly due to the lack of regular maintenance. This is even more likely if a used vehicle, which has not received regular and frequent maintenance checks, is purchased. In such cases, additional work may need to be carried out, outside of the regular maintenance intervals.
3 If engine wear is suspected, a compression test (refer to Part A of Chapter 2) will provide valuable information regarding the overall performance of the main internal components. Such a test can be used as a basis to decide on the extent of the work to be carried out. If, for example, a compression test indicates serious internal engine wear, conventional maintenance as described in this Chapter will not greatly improve the performance of the engine, and may prove a waste of time and money, unless extensive overhaul work (Chapter 2C) is carried out first.
4 The following series of operations are those often required to improve the performance of a generally poor-running engine:

Primary operations

a) *Clean, inspect and test the battery (See "Weekly checks").*
b) *Check all the engine-related fluids (See "Weekly checks").*
c) *Check the condition and tension of the auxiliary drivebelts (Section 4).*
d) *Adjust the valve clearances (Chapter 2A).*
e) *Renew the spark plugs (Section 5).*
f) *Inspect the distributor cap, rotor arm and HT leads (Section 6).*
g) *Check the condition of all hoses, and check for fluid leaks (Section 8).*
h) *Check the condition of the air cleaner filter element and renew if necessary (Section 23).*
i) *Renew the fuel filter - fuel-injected engines (Section 26).*
j) *Check the engine idle speed and mixture settings - carburettor engines (Section 10).*

5 If the above operations do not prove fully effective, carry out the following operations:

Secondary operations

All the items listed under "Primary operations", plus the following:

a) *Check the charging system (Chapter 5A).*
b) *Check the ignition system (Chapter 5B).*
c) *Check the fuel system (Chapter 4).*
d) *Renew the ignition HT leads (Section 6).*

1A

5000 mile service - petrol

3 Engine oil renewal

Note: *A suitable square-section wrench may be required to undo the sump drain plug on some models. These wrenches can be obtained from most motor factors or your Renault dealer.*
1 Frequent oil changes are the best preventive maintenance the home mechanic can give the engine, because ageing oil becomes diluted and contaminated, which leads to premature engine wear.
2 Make sure that you have all the necessary tools before you begin this procedure. You should also have plenty of rags or newspapers handy, for mopping up any spills. The oil should preferably be changed when the engine is still fully warmed-up to normal operating temperature, just after a run; warm oil and sludge will flow out more easily. Take care, however, not to touch the exhaust or any other hot parts of the engine when working under the vehicle. To avoid any possibility of scalding, and to protect yourself from possible skin irritants and other harmful contaminants in used engine oils, it is advisable to wear gloves when carrying out this work. Access to the underside of the vehicle is greatly improved if the vehicle can be lifted on a hoist, driven onto ramps, or supported by axle stands. (see *"Jacking and vehicle support"*). Whichever method is chosen, make sure that the vehicle remains level, or if it is at an angle, that the drain plug is at the lowest point.
3 Position the draining container under the drain plug, and unscrew the plug **(see illustration)**. If possible, try to keep the plug pressed into the sump while unscrewing it by hand the last couple of turns.

3.3 Slackening the sump drain plug with a square-section wrench

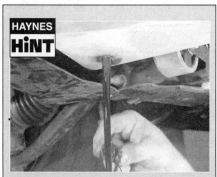

Keep the drain plug pressed into the sump while unscrewing it by hand the last couple of turns. As the plug releases, move it away sharply so the stream of oil from the sump runs into the container, not up your sleeve!

4 Allow the oil to drain into the container, and check the condition of the plug's sealing washer; renew it if worn or damaged.

5 Allow some time for the old oil to drain, noting that it may be necessary to reposition the container as the oil flow slows to a trickle; when the oil has completely drained, wipe clean the drain plug and its threads in the sump and refit the plug, tightening it securely.

6 Remove the old oil and all tools from under the vehicle, then lower the vehicle to the ground.

7 Remove the dipstick and the oil filler cap from the engine. Fill the engine with oil, using the correct grade and type of oil, (see "Weekly Checks"). Pour in half the specified quantity of oil first, then wait a few minutes for the oil to fall to the sump. Continue adding oil a small quantity at a time, until the level is up to the lower (minimum) notch on the dipstick. Adding approximately 0.5 to 1.0 litre will raise the level to the upper (maximum) notch on the dipstick.

8 Start the engine. If the oil filter has been renewed as well at this interval, the oil pressure warning light will take a few seconds to go out while the new filter fills with oil; do not race the engine while the light is on. Run the engine for a few minutes, while checking for leaks around the drain plug.

9 Switch off the engine, and wait a few minutes for the oil to settle in the sump once more. With the new oil circulated and the filter now completely full, recheck the level on the dipstick, and add more oil as necessary.

10 Dispose of the used engine oil safely and in accordance with environmental regulations (see "General repair procedures").

Note: It is antisocial and illegal to dump oil down the drain. To find the location of your local oil recycling bank, call this number free.

0800 66 33 66

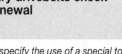

4 Auxiliary drivebelts check and renewal

Note: *Renault specify the use of a special tool (Ele. 346-04) to correctly set the drivebelt tension. If access to this tool cannot be obtained, an approximate setting can be achieved using the method described below. If the method described is used, the tension should be checked using the special tool at the earliest possible opportunity.*

1 The auxiliary drivebelts transmit power from the crankshaft pulley to the alternator, coolant pump, steering pump and air conditioning compressor (as applicable). A variety of belt arrangements and tensioning methods will be found, according to equipment and engine type.

Check

2 With the engine switched off, open and support the bonnet, then locate the auxiliary drivebelts fitted to your car (Be very careful, and wear protective gloves to minimise the risk of burning your hands on hot components, if the engine has recently been running).

3 Using an inspection light or a small electric torch, and rotating the engine when necessary with a spanner applied to the crankshaft pulley bolt, check the whole length of the drivebelt for cracks, separation of the rubber, and torn or worn ribs. Also check for fraying and glazing, which gives the drivebelt a shiny appearance. Both sides of the drivebelt should be inspected, which means you will have to twist the drivebelt to check the underside. Use your fingers to feel the drivebelt where you can't see it. If you are in any doubt as to the condition of the drivebelt, renew it.

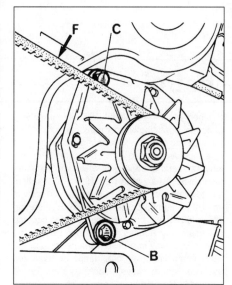

4.5 Early type alternator pivot bolts (B) and (C), and deflection checking point (F)

Note: Adjuster strap bolt is lower down, accessible from below

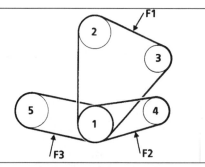

4.4 Auxiliary drivebelt arrangement

1 Crankshaft pulley
2 Coolant pump pulley
3 Alternator pulley
4 Steering pump pulley
5 Air conditioning compressor pulley
F1, F2, F3 = deflection checking points for each drivebelt

Renewal and adjustment

4 When removing a particular drivebelt, it will obviously be necessary to remove those in front of it first **(see illustration)**.

Alternator/coolant pump drivebelt

5 Slacken the alternator pivot and adjuster strap nuts and bolts **(see illustration)**.

6 Move the alternator towards the engine to release the belt tension. On later models a positive tensioning device is used: slacken the adjuster strap, then turn the tensioner bolt to move the alternator inwards **(see illustration)**.

7 Slip the belt off the pulleys and remove it.

8 When refitting, move the alternator away from the engine until the belt can be deflected 4.5 to 5.5 mm by firm thumb pressure at a point midway between the alternator and coolant pump pulleys. Tighten the pivot and adjusting strap nuts and bolts in this position and recheck the tension.

9 On models with a positive tensioning device, be careful not to overtension the belt. On models without such a device, it may be helpful to lever the alternator away from the engine to achieve the desired tension. Only use a wooden or plastic lever, and only lever at the pulley end.

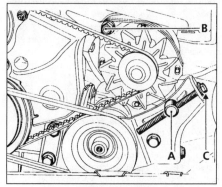

4.6 Later type alternator with positive tensioning device

A Adjuster strap bolt
B Pivot bolt   C Tensioner bolt

Steering pump drivebelt

Note: *Three different pump mounting arrangements may be encountered. Identify the type fitted then proceed according to the relevant subheading. Further details and illustrations will be found in Chapter 10.*

First version

10 Slacken the pump lower mounting nuts and bolts. Slacken the drivebelt upper adjuster nut and bolt and slip the drivebelt off the crankshaft and pump pulleys.

11 When refitting, move the steering pump away from the engine until the belt can be deflected 4.0 to 4.5 mm by firm thumb pressure at a point midway between the two pulleys. Tighten the adjuster and the mounting nuts and bolts in this position and recheck the tension.

Second version

12 At the rear of the pump, slacken the upper mounting bolt.

13 At the front of the pump, slacken the four bolts securing the mounting plate to the front of the engine. Note that one of these bolts also serves as the alternator adjuster strap retaining bolt. On some models, access to these front bolts may be easier from below. Slip the drivebelt off the crankshaft and pump pulleys.

14 When refitting, move the steering pump away from the engine until the belt can be deflected 4.0 to 4.5 mm by firm thumb pressure at a point midway between the two pulleys. Tighten the adjuster and the mounting nuts and bolts in this position and recheck the tension.

Third version

15 Slacken the steering pump front and rear mounting bolts. Slacken the positive tensioner bolt and slip the drivebelt off the crankshaft and pump pulleys. Access to these front bolts may be easier from below.

16 When refitting, turn the positive tensioner bolt to move the steering pump away from the engine until the belt can be deflected 4.0 to 4.5 mm by firm thumb pressure at a point midway between the two pulleys. Tighten the mounting bolts in this position and recheck the tension.

Air conditioning compressor drivebelt

17 Renewal of the compressor drivebelt is a complex operation requiring removal of all the other auxiliary drivebelts and the engine timing belt. The compressor drivebelt is driven by an additional crankshaft sprocket located behind the crankshaft pulley and timing belt.

18 To remove the belt, first remove the timing belt as described in Chapter 2A, Section 8. Slacken the compressor upper and lower mounting bolts, move the compressor towards the engine and slip off the belt.

19 Fit the new belt and tension it by moving the compressor until the belt can be deflected 3.5 to 4.5 mm by firm thumb pressure at a point midway between the two pulleys. Tighten the mounting bolts in this position and recheck the tension.

20 Refit the timing belt (Chapter 2A, Section 8).

All drivebelts

21 Recheck the tension of a new belt after a few hundred miles.

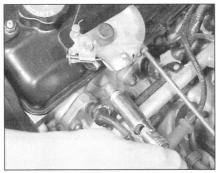

5.4a Removing a spark plug

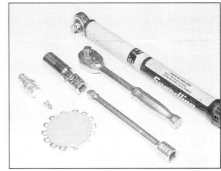

5.4b Tools required for spark plug removal, gap adjustment and refitting

5 Spark plug check and renewal

1 The correct functioning of the spark plugs is vital for the correct running and efficiency of the engine. It is essential that the plugs fitted are appropriate for the engine. If the correct type is used and the engine is in good condition, the spark plugs should provide a long service life. If the following checks indicate that the spark plugs are worn, they should be renewed. Spark plug cleaning is rarely necessary, and should not be attempted unless specialised equipment is available, as damage can easily be caused to the firing ends.

2 If the marks on the original-equipment spark plug (HT) leads cannot be seen, mark the leads "1" to "4", to correspond to the cylinder the lead serves (No 1 cylinder is at the transmission end of the engine). Pull the leads from the plugs by gripping the end fitting, not the lead, otherwise the lead connection may be fractured. Where necessary, release the leads from the support clips on the side of the camshaft cover.

3 It is advisable to remove the dirt from the spark plug recesses using a clean brush, vacuum cleaner or compressed air before removing the plugs, to prevent dirt dropping into the cylinders.

4 Unscrew the plugs using a spark plug spanner, suitable box spanner or a deep socket and extension bar **(see illustrations)**. Keep the socket aligned with the spark plug - if it is forcibly moved

to one side, the ceramic insulator may be broken off. As each plug is removed, examine it as follows.

5 Examination of the spark plugs will give a good indication of the condition of the engine. If the insulator nose of the spark plug is clean and white, with no deposits, this is indicative of a weak mixture or too hot a plug (a hot plug transfers heat away from the electrode slowly, a cold plug transfers heat away quickly).

6 If the tip and insulator nose are covered with hard black-looking deposits, then this is indicative that the mixture is too rich. Should the plug be black and oily, then it is likely that the engine is fairly worn, as well as the mixture being too rich.

7 If the insulator nose is covered with light tan to greyish-brown deposits, then the mixture is correct and it is likely that the engine is in good condition.

8 The spark plug electrode gap is of considerable importance as, if it is too large or too small, the size of the spark and its efficiency will be seriously impaired. The gap should be set to the value given in the *Specifications* **(see illustration)**.

9 To set the gap, measure it with a feeler blade, and then bend the outer plug electrode until the correct gap is achieved **(see illustration)**. The centre electrode should never be bent, as this may crack the insulator and cause plug failure, if nothing worse. If using feeler blades, the gap is correct when the appropriate size blade is a firm sliding fit.

10 Special spark plug electrode gap adjusting tools are available from most motor accessory shops, or from some spark plug manufacturers.

1A

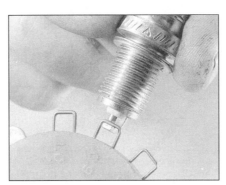

5.8 Measuring the spark plug gap with a wire gauge

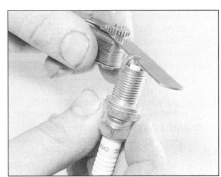

5.9 Measuring the spark plug gap with a feeler blade

It is very often difficult to insert spark plugs into their holes without cross-threading them. To avoid this possibility, fit a short length of 5/16 inch internal diameter rubber hose over the end of the spark plug. The flexible hose acts as a universal joint to help align the plug with the plug hole. Should the plug begin to cross-thread, the hose will slip on the spark plug, preventing thread damage to the aluminium cylinder head

11 Before fitting the spark plugs, check that the threaded connector sleeves are tight, and that the plug exterior surfaces and threads are clean.

12 Remove the rubber hose (if used), and tighten the plug to the specified torque (see *Specifications*) using the spark plug socket and a torque wrench. Refit the remaining spark plugs in the same manner.

13 Connect the HT leads in their correct order, and refit any components removed for access.

6 Distributor, rotor arm and HT lead check

Warning: Voltages produced by an electronic ignition system are considerably higher than those produced by conventional ignition systems. Extreme care must be taken when working on the system if the ignition is switched on. Persons with surgically-implanted cardiac pacemaker devices should keep well clear of the ignition circuits, components and test equipment.

1 The spark plug (HT) leads should be inspected one at a time, to prevent mixing up the firing order, which is essential for proper engine operation. Gain access to the leads and disconnect them as described for the spark plug check and renewal.

2 Check inside the boot for corrosion, which will look like a white crusty powder. Clean this off as much as possible; if it is excessive, or if cleaning leaves the metal connector too badly corroded to be fit for further use, the lead must be renewed. Push the lead and boot back onto the end of the spark plug. The boot should fit tightly onto the end of the plug - if it doesn't, remove the lead and use pliers carefully to crimp the metal connector inside the boot until the fit is snug.

3 Using a clean rag, wipe the entire length of the lead to remove built-up dirt and grease. Once the lead is clean, check for burns, cracks and other damage. Do not bend the lead sharply, because the conductor might break.

4 Inspect the remaining spark plug (HT) leads, ensuring that each is securely fastened at the distributor cap and spark plug when the check is complete. If any sign of arcing, severe connector corrosion, burns, cracks or other damage is noticed, obtain new spark plug (HT) leads, renewing them as a set.

 If new spark plug leads are to be fitted, remove the leads one at a time and fit each new lead in exactly the same position as the old one.

5 Undo the retaining screws and remove the distributor cap then thoroughly clean it inside and out with a dry lint-free rag.

6 Examine the HT lead segments inside the cap. If they appear badly burned or pitted renew the cap. Also check the carbon brush in the centre of the cap, ensuring that it is free to move and stands proud of its holder. Make sure that there are no sign of cracks or black "tracking" lines running down the inside of the cap, which will also mean renewal if evident.

7 Refit the cap on completion.

7 Battery and electrical equipment check

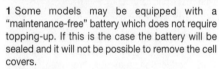

1 Some models may be equipped with a "maintenance-free" battery which does not require topping-up. If this is the case the battery will be sealed and it will not be possible to remove the cell covers.

2 On models not equipped with a "maintenance-free" battery, check the electrolyte level of all six battery cells. The level must be approximately 10 mm above the plates; this may be shown by maximum and minimum level lines marked on the battery's casing. If the level is low, unscrew the filler/vent caps, and add distilled water **(see illustration)**. Install and retighten the caps. *Caution: Overfilling the cells may cause electrolyte to spill over during periods of heavy charging, causing corrosion or damage.*

3 Periodically (approximately every three months)

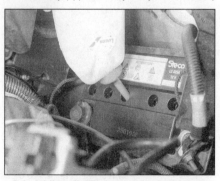

7.2 Adding distilled water to the battery

check the charge condition of the battery as described in Chapter 5A.

4 Further information on the battery, charging, and jump starting can be found in Chapter 5A, and in the preliminary sections of this manual.

5 Check the operation of all interior electrical equipment and accessories, including the courtesy lights, heater blower, instrument panel warning lights and illumination lights. Renew any blown bulbs or faulty components, referring to Chapter 12.

8 Hose and fluid leak check

1 Visually inspect the engine joint faces, gaskets and seals for any signs of water or oil leaks. Pay particular attention to the areas around the camshaft cover, cylinder head, oil filter and sump joint faces. Bear in mind that, over a period of time, some very slight seepage from these areas is to be expected - what you are really looking for is any indication of a serious leak. Should a leak be found, renew the offending gasket or oil seal by referring to the appropriate Chapters in this manual.

2 Also check the security and condition of all the engine-related pipes and hoses, and all hydraulic system pipes and hoses. Ensure that all cable-ties or securing clips are in place, and in good condition. Clips which are broken or missing can lead to chafing of the hoses, pipes or wiring, which could cause more serious problems in the future.

3 Carefully check the radiator hoses and heater hoses along their entire length. Renew any hose which is cracked, swollen or deteriorated. Cracks will show up better if the hose is squeezed. Pay close attention to the hose clips that secure the hoses to the cooling system components. Hose clips can pinch and puncture hoses, resulting in cooling system leaks.

4 Inspect all the cooling system components (hoses, joint faces etc.) for leaks.

5 Where any problems are found on system components, renew the component or gasket with reference to Chapter 3.

6 Check the security of all fuel and hydraulic hose attachments and pipe unions, and inspect the fuel hoses and vacuum hoses for kinks, chafing and deterioration.

A leak in the cooling system wil usually show up as white or rust coloured deposits on the area adjoining the leak

If no obvious leaks can be found, but coolant is still being lost, it is advisable to have the pressure cap and the entire system pressure-tested by a dealer or suitably equipped garage, as this will often show up a small leak not previously apparent. If you are keen, pressure-testing equipment similar to that shown above is available from larger car accessory shops

9 Emission control equipment check

Of the emission control systems that may be fitted, only the crankcase ventilation system and the fuel evaporative emission control systems requires regular checking, and even then, the components of this system require no attention other than to check that the hoses are clear and undamaged. Details of these checks will be found in Chapter 4D.

Should it be felt that the other systems are not functioning correctly, the advice of a dealer should be sought.

10 Idle speed and mixture check and adjustment

1 On carburettor models, the idle speed and mixture (CO content) can be adjusted, provided the necessary test equipment is available. Details of the procedure are given in Chapter 4, Part A.

2 On all other models, the only adjustment possible, is that of the idle mixture CO content on certain 2.0 litre models without catalytic converters.

3 Due to the need for special diagnostic equipment to accurately adjust the CO content it is recommended that the vehicle is taken to a suitably equipped Renault dealer for this work to be carried out.

11 Brake pad wear check

1 Jack up the front, and where applicable the rear of the vehicle in turn, and support it on axle stands (see *"Jacking and vehicle support"*).

For a quick check, the thickness of the friction material on each brake pad can be measured through the aperture in the caliper body

2 For better access to the brake calipers, remove the roadwheels.

3 If any one of the brake pads has worn down to, or below, the specified limit, *all four* pads at that end of the car must be renewed as a set (ie all the front pads or all the rear pads).

4 For a comprehensive check, the brake pads should be removed and cleaned. The operation of the brake calipers can then be checked, and the brake discs can be fully examined. Refer to Chapter 9 for details.

12 Handbrake - adjustment

Refer to Chapter 9, Section 17.

13 Steering and suspension check

Front suspension and steering check

1 Apply the handbrake, then raise the front of the vehicle and support it on axle stands. (see *"Jacking and vehicle support"*).

2 Visually inspect the balljoint dust covers and the steering gear gaiters for splits, chafing or deterioration. Any wear of these components will cause loss of lubricant, together with dirt and water entry, resulting in rapid deterioration of the balljoints or steering gear.

3 Check the steering fluid hoses for chafing or deterioration, and the pipe and hose unions for fluid leaks. Also check for signs of fluid leakage under pressure from the steering gear gaiters, which would indicate failed fluid seals within the steering gear.

4 Check for signs of fluid leakage around the shock absorber body, or from the rubber boot around the piston rod (where fitted). Should any fluid be noticed, the shock absorber is defective internally, and renewal is necessary.

5 Grasp the roadwheel at the 12 o'clock and 6 o'clock positions, and try to rock it (see

illustration). Very slight free play may be felt, but if the movement is appreciable, further investigation is necessary to determine the source. Continue rocking the wheel while an assistant depresses the footbrake. If the movement is now eliminated or significantly reduced, it is likely that the hub bearings are at fault. If the free play is still evident with the footbrake depressed, then there is wear in the suspension joints or mountings.

6 Now grasp the wheel at the 9 o'clock and 3 o'clock positions, and try to rock it as before. Any movement felt now may again be caused by wear in the hub bearings or the steering track rod balljoints. If the outer track rod end balljoint is worn, the visual movement will be obvious. If the inner joint is suspect, it can be felt by placing a hand over the steering gear gaiter, and gripping the track rod. If the wheel is now rocked, movement will be felt at the inner joint if wear has taken place.

7 Using a large screwdriver or flat bar, check for wear in the suspension mounting bushes by levering between the relevant suspension component and its attachment point. Some movement is to be expected as the mountings are made of rubber, but excessive wear should be obvious. Also check the condition of any visible rubber bushes, looking for splits, cracks or contamination of the rubber.

8 With the vehicle standing on its wheels, have an assistant turn the steering wheel back-and-forth, about an eighth of a turn each way. There should be very little, if any, lost movement between the steering wheel and roadwheels. If this is not the case, closely observe the joints and mountings previously described, but in addition, check the steering column universal joints for wear, and also check the steering gear itself.

9 The efficiency of the shock absorber may be checked by bouncing the car at each front corner. Generally speaking, the body will return to its normal position and stop after being depressed. If it rises and returns on a rebound, the shock absorber is probably suspect. Examine also the shock absorber upper and lower mountings for any signs of wear or fluid leakage.

Rear suspension check

10 Chock the front wheels, then raise the rear of the vehicle and support it on axle stands. (see *"Jacking and vehicle support"*).

11 Check the rear hub bearings for wear, using

13.5 Check for wear in the hub bearings by grasping the wheel and trying to rock it

1A

the method described for the front hub bearings (paragraph 5).

12 Using a large screwdriver or flat bar, check for wear in the suspension mounting bushes by levering between the relevant suspension component and its attachment point. Some movement is to be expected as the mountings are made of rubber, but excessive wear should be obvious. Check the condition of the shock absorbers as described previously.

14 Driveshaft gaiter check

With the vehicle raised and securely supported on stands (see *"Jacking and vehicle support"*), turn the steering onto full lock, then slowly rotate the roadwheel. Inspect the condition of the outer constant velocity (CV) joint rubber gaiters, squeezing the gaiters to open out the folds **(see illustration)**. Check for signs of cracking, splits or deterioration of the rubber, which may allow the grease to escape, and lead to water and grit entry into the joint. Also check the security and condition of the retaining clips. Repeat these checks on the inner CV joints. If any damage or deterioration is found, the gaiters should be renewed as described in Chapter 8.

At the same time, check the general condition of the CV joints themselves by first holding the driveshaft and attempting to rotate the wheel. Repeat this check by holding the inner joint and attempting to rotate the driveshaft. Any appreciable movement indicates wear in the joints, wear in the driveshaft splines, or a loose driveshaft retaining nut.

15 Underbody and fuel/brake line check

1 With the vehicle raised and supported on axle stands (see *"Jacking and vehicle support"*), or over an inspection pit, thoroughly inspect the underbody and wheel arches for signs of damage and corrosion. In particular, examine the bottom of the side sills, and any concealed areas where mud can collect. Where corrosion and rust is evident, press and tap firmly on the panel with a

14.1 Check the condition of the driveshaft gaiters

screwdriver, and check for any serious corrosion which would necessitate repairs. If the panel is not seriously corroded, clean away the rust, and apply a new coating of underseal. Refer to Chapter 11 for more details of body repairs.

2 At the same time, inspect the body panels for stone damage and general condition.

3 Inspect all of the fuel and brake lines on the underbody for damage, rust, corrosion and leakage. Also make sure that they are correctly supported in their clips. Where applicable, check the PVC coating on the lines for damage.

4 Inspect the flexible brake hoses in the vicinity of the calipers and connections to the rear axle, where they are subjected to most movement. Bend them between the fingers (but do not actually bend them double, or the casing may be damaged) and check that this does not reveal previously-hidden cracks, cuts or splits.

5 Inspect the fuel tank and filler neck for punctures, cracks and other damage. The connection between the filler neck and tank is especially critical. Sometimes a rubber filler neck or connecting hose will leak due to loose retaining clamps or deteriorated rubber.

6 Carefully check all rubber hoses and metal fuel lines leading away from the fuel tank. Check for loose connections, deteriorated hoses, crimped lines, and other damage. Pay particular attention to the vent pipes and hoses, which often loop up around the filler neck and can become blocked or crimped. Follow the lines to the front of the vehicle, carefully inspecting them all the way. Renew damaged sections as necessary.

16 Exhaust system check
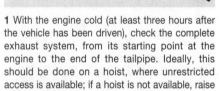

1 With the engine cold (at least three hours after the vehicle has been driven), check the complete exhaust system, from its starting point at the engine to the end of the tailpipe. Ideally, this should be done on a hoist, where unrestricted access is available; if a hoist is not available, raise and support the vehicle on axle stands (see *"Jacking and vehicle support"*).

2 Check the pipes and connections for evidence of leaks, severe corrosion, or damage. Make sure that all brackets and rubber mountings are in good condition, and tight; if any of the mountings are to be renewed, ensure that the replacements are of the correct type. Leakage at any of the joints or in other parts of the system will usually show up as a black sooty stain in the vicinity of the leak.

3 At the same time, inspect the underside of the body for holes, corrosion, open seams, etc. which may allow exhaust gases to enter the passenger compartment. Seal all body openings with silicone or body putty.

4 Rattles and other noises can often be traced to the exhaust system, especially the rubber mountings. Try to move the system, silencer(s) and catalytic converter. If any components can touch the body or suspension parts, secure the exhaust system with new mountings.

17 Seat belt check

Check the seat belts for satisfactory operation and condition. Inspect the webbing for fraying and cuts. Check that they retract smoothly and without binding into their reels.

Check the seat belt mountings, ensuring that all the bolts are securely tightened.

18 Door, tailgate and bonnet check and lubrication

Check that the doors, bonnet and tailgate close securely. Check that the bonnet safety catch operates correctly. Check the operation of the door check straps.

Lubricate the hinges, door check straps, the striker plates and the bonnet catch sparingly with a little oil or grease.

19 Bodywork, paint and exterior trim check

1 The best time to carry out this check is after the car has been washed so that any surface blemish or scratch will be clearly evident and not hidden by a film of dirt.

2 Starting at one front corner check the paintwork all around the car, looking for minor scratches or more serious dents. Check all the trim and make sure that it is securely attached over its entire length.

3 Check the security of all door locks, door mirrors, badges, bumpers radiator grille and wheel trim. Anything found loose, or in need of further attention should be done with reference to the relevant Chapters of this manual.

4 Rectify any problems noticed with the paintwork or body panels as described in Chapter 11.

20 Road test

Instruments and electrical equipment

1 Check the operation of all instruments and electrical equipment.

2 Make sure that all instruments read correctly, and switch on all electrical equipment in turn to check that it functions properly.

Steering and suspension

3 Check for any abnormalities in the steering, suspension, handling or road "feel".

4 Drive the vehicle, and check that there are no unusual vibrations or noises.

5 Check that the steering feels positive, with no excessive "sloppiness", or roughness, and check for any suspension noises when cornering, or when driving over bumps.

Drivetrain

6 Check the performance of the engine, clutch, transmission and driveshafts.

7 Listen for any unusual noises from the engine, clutch and transmission.

8 Check that the clutch action is smooth and progressive, that the drive is taken up smoothly, and that the pedal travel is not excessive. Also listen for any noises when the clutch pedal is depressed. Check that all gears can be engaged smoothly, without noise, and that the gear lever action is not abnormally vague or "notchy".

9 Make sure that the engine runs smoothly when idling, and that there is no hesitation when accelerating.

10 Listen for a metallic clicking sound from the front of the vehicle, as the vehicle is driven slowly in a circle with the steering on full lock. Carry out this check in both directions. If a clicking noise is heard, this indicates wear in a driveshaft joint, in which case, further inspection will be necessary (see Chapter 8).

Check the operation and performance of the braking system

11 Make sure that the vehicle does not pull to one side when braking, and that the wheels do not lock prematurely when braking hard.

12 Check that there is no vibration through the steering when braking.

13 Check that the handbrake operates correctly, without excessive movement of the lever, and that it holds the vehicle stationary on a slope.

14 With the engine switched off, test the operation of the brake servo unit as follows. Depress the footbrake four or five times to exhaust the vacuum, then start the engine. As the engine

starts, there should be a noticeable "give" in the brake pedal as vacuum builds up. Allow the engine to run for at least two minutes, and then switch it off. If the brake pedal is now depressed again, it should be possible to detect a hiss from the servo as the pedal is depressed. After about four or five applications, no further hissing should be heard, and the pedal should feel considerably harder.

21 Air conditioning system check

⚠️ **Warning: The air conditioning system is under high pressure. Do not loosen any fittings or remove any components until after the system has been discharged. Air conditioning refrigerant must be properly discharged into an approved type of container, at a dealer service department or an automotive air conditioning repair facility capable of handling the refrigerant safely. Always wear eye protection when disconnecting air conditioning system fittings.**

⚠️ **Warning: Be sure to wear eye protection when using compressed air!**

1 The following maintenance checks should be performed on a regular basis, to ensure that the air conditioner continues to operate at peak efficiency:

a) *Check the auxiliary drivebelt. If it's worn or deteriorated, renew it (see Section 4).*

b) *Check the system hoses. Look for cracks, bubbles, hard spots and deterioration. Inspect the hoses and all fittings for oil bubbles and seepage. If there's any evidence of wear, damage or leaks, renew the hose(s).*

c) *Inspect the condenser fins for leaves, insects*

and other debris. Use a "fin comb" or compressed air to clean the condenser.

d) *Check that the drain tube from the front of the evaporator is clear - note that it is normal to have clear fluid (water) dripping from this while the system is in operation, to the extent that quite a large puddle can be left under the vehicle when it is parked.*

2 It's a good idea to operate the system for about 30 minutes at least once a month, particularly during the winter. Long term non-use can cause hardening, and subsequent failure, of the seals.

3 Because of the complexity of the air conditioning system and the special equipment necessary to service it, in-depth fault diagnosis and repairs are not included in this manual. For more complete information on the air conditioning system, refer to the Haynes "*Automotive Heating and Air Conditioning Manual*".

4 The most common cause of poor cooling is simply a low system refrigerant charge. If a noticeable drop in cool air output occurs, the following quick check will help you determine if the refrigerant level is low.

5 Warm the engine up to normal operating temperature.

6 Place the air conditioning temperature selector at the coldest setting, and put the blower at the highest setting. Open the doors - to make sure the air conditioning system doesn't cycle off as soon as it cools the passenger compartment.

7 With the compressor engaged - the clutch will make an audible click, and the centre of the clutch will rotate - feel the inlet and outlet pipes at the compressor. One side should be cold, and one hot. If there's no perceptible difference between the two pipes, there's something wrong with the compressor or the system. It might be a low charge - it might be something else. Take the vehicle to a dealer service department or an automotive air conditioning specialist.

1A

10 000 mile service - petrol

22 Engine oil filter renewal

1 Begin by draining the engine oil, referring to the procedures in Section 3, paragraphs 1 to 5.

2 The oil filter is located on the right-hand side of the cylinder block, below the exhaust manifold.

3 Reposition the draining container under the oil filter then, using a suitable filter removal tool if necessary, slacken the filter initially, then unscrew it by hand the rest of the way; be prepared for some oil spillage **(see illustration)**. Empty the oil in the old filter into the container.

4 Using a clean, lint-free rag, wipe clean the cylinder block around the filter mounting. Check the old filter to make sure that the rubber sealing

ring hasn't stuck to the engine; if it has, carefully remove it.

22.3 Using an oil filter removal tool to slacken the oil filter

5 Apply a light coating of clean engine oil to the sealing ring on the new filter. Screw the filter into position on the engine until it seats, then tighten it firmly by hand only - **do not** use any tools.

6 Refill the engine with oil as described in Section 3, paragraph 10 onward.

23 Air cleaner element renewal

1 Release the four clips or undo the wing nut securing the air cleaner lid to the housing. **(see illustration)**.

2 Lift off the lid and remove the air cleaner element **(see illustration)**.

23.1 Unscrew the wing nut to remove the air cleaner lid

23.2 Lift the old element out of the housing

23.5 When refitting, ensure that the notch (arrowed) engages with the housing peg

24.1 Unscrewing the transmission filler/level plug

3 Wipe inside the housing and lid with a cloth. Be careful not to sweep debris into the air inlet.

4 Fit the new element, making sure it is the right way up.

5 Refit the lid; secure with the clips or wing nut. The notch on the lid engages with the peg on the housing on fuel-injected engines **(see illustration)**.

24 Transmission oil level check

1 The manual transmission does not have a dipstick. To check the oil level, raise the vehicle and support it securely on axle stands, making sure that the vehicle is level (see *"Jacking and vehicle support"*). On the left-hand side of the transmission casing you will see the filler/level plug. Wipe all around the filler/level plug with a clean rag then unscrew and remove it **(see illustration)**. If the lubricant level is correct, the oil should be up to the lower edge of the hole.

2 If the transmission needs more lubricant (if the oil level is not up to the hole), use a syringe, or a plastic bottle and tube, to add more. Stop filling the transmission when the lubricant begins to run out of the hole. Make sure that you use the correct type of lubricant (see *Specifications*).

3 Refit and tighten the filler/level plug. Drive the car a short distance, then check for leaks.

4 Regular topping-up indicates a leak, which should be found and rectified without delay.

25 Brake shoe wear check

Refer to Chapter 9, Section 6.

40 000 mile service - petrol

26 Fuel filter renewal

26.5 Fuel filter connections and retaining clamp

> ⚠ **Warning: Before carrying out the following operation, refer to the precautions given in "Safety first!" at the beginning of this manual, and follow them implicitly. Petrol is a highly-dangerous and volatile liquid, and the precautions necessary when handling it cannot be overstressed.**

1 The fuel filter is situated underneath the right-hand side of the vehicle, in front of the fuel tank on early models, or under the left-hand side of the vehicle level with the front seat on later models. To gain access to the filter, apply the handbrake, then jack up the rear of the vehicle and support it on axle stands (see *"Jacking and Vehicle Support"*).

2 Disconnect the battery negative lead.

3 Using suitable clamps, clamp the flexible fuel hoses at each side of the filter. Alternatively, be prepared to plug the hoses quickly as they are disconnected.

4 Noting the direction of the arrow marked on the filter body, release the retaining clips and disconnect the fuel hoses from the filter. Where the original Renault crimped-type clips are still fitted, cut and discard them; replace them with standard worm-drive hose clips on installation.

5 Unscrew the nut or bolt and release the retaining clamp **(see illustration)**.

6 Remove the filter from the vehicle. Dispose safely of the old filter; it will be highly inflammable, and may explode if thrown on a fire.

7 Connect the new filter to the hoses and tighten the retaining clips. Make sure that the arrow on the filter points in the correct direction (ie towards the hose which leads to the engine compartment).

8 Locate the filter in the retaining strap then insert and tighten the nut or bolt.

9 Lower the vehicle to the ground, start the engine and check the filter hose connections for leaks.

27 Transmission oil renewal

1 Raise the vehicle and support it securely on axle stands, making sure that the vehicle is level (see *"Jacking and vehicle support"*).

2 Remove the plastic undertray from the base of the transmission **(see illustration)**.

3 On the bottom of the transmission casing you will see the drain plug. Place a suitable container beneath the plug, then unscrew and remove it **(see illustration)**.

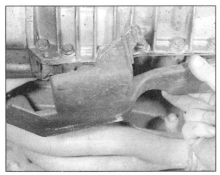

27.2 Removing the transmission undertray

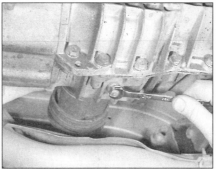

27.3 Transmission drain plug removal

for some time as it absorbs moisture from the air. Excess moisture can cause a dangerous loss of braking effectiveness.

The procedure is similar to that for the bleeding of the hydraulic system as described in Chapter 9, except that the brake fluid reservoir should be emptied by siphoning, and allowance should be made for the old fluid to be removed from the circuit when bleeding a section of the circuit.

> **HAYNES HiNT** *Old hydraulic fluid is darker in colour than the new, making it easy to distinguish between the two.*

4 When all the lubricant has drained, refit the drain plug, and tighten it securely. Refit the undertray.
5 Refill the transmission with fresh lubricant using the procedures described in Section 24.

28 Brake fluid renewal

⚠ *Warning: Brake hydraulic fluid can harm your eyes and damage painted surfaces, so use extreme caution when handling and pouring it. Do not use fluid that has been standing open*

29 Front wheel alignment check

Ideally, have this work carried out by a Renault dealer as special gauges are needed for accuracy. Details of the alignment procedure and the work involved will be found in Chapter 10.

80 000 mile service - petrol

1A

30 Timing belt renewal

Refer to Chapter 2A.

Every 2 years (regardless of mileage) - petrol

31 Coolant renewal

Cooling system draining

⚠ *Warning: Wait until the engine is cold before starting this procedure. Do not allow antifreeze to come in contact with your skin, or with the painted surfaces of the vehicle. Rinse off spills immediately with plenty of water. Never leave antifreeze lying around in an open container, or in a puddle in the driveway or on the garage floor. Children and pets are attracted by its sweet smell, but antifreeze can be fatal if ingested.*

1 With the engine completely cold, remove the expansion tank filler cap. Turn the cap anti-clockwise, wait until any pressure remaining in the system is released, then unscrew it and lift it off.
2 Position a suitable container beneath the radiator bottom hose connection.
3 Slacken the hose clip, pull off the hose and allow the coolant to drain into the container.

4 To assist draining, open the cooling system bleed screws. These are located in various places according to engine and model type. On carburettor engines there is just one bleed screw, located on the top of the automatic choke housing on the side of the carburettor. On early fuel-injected engines, there is either a filler cap, or a bleed screw on top of the radiator (open whichever is fitted). On later fuel-injected engines, there is a bleed screw in the radiator top hose next to the thermostat housing **(see illustration)**, and another one in the heater hose at its connection with the heater matrix

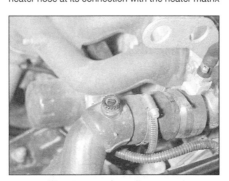

31.4 Bleed screw in radiator top hose

pipe stub. In some cases there may be a combination of all these types, so check carefully to see which are fitted to your vehicle.
5 When the flow of coolant stops, reposition the container below the cylinder block drain plug. This is located at the rear of the cylinder block on the right-hand side.

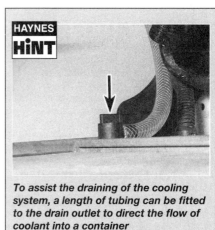

> **HAYNES HiNT**
> *To assist the draining of the cooling system, a length of tubing can be fitted to the drain outlet to direct the flow of coolant into a container*

6 Remove the drain plug, and allow the coolant to drain into the container.

7 If the coolant has been drained for a reason other than renewal, then provided it is clean and less than two years old, it can be re-used, though this is not recommended.

8 Refit the radiator bottom hose and cylinder block drain plug on completion of draining.

Cooling system flushing

9 If coolant renewal has been neglected, or if the antifreeze mixture has become diluted, then in time, the cooling system may gradually lose efficiency, as the coolant passages become restricted due to rust, scale deposits, and other sediment. The cooling system efficiency can be restored by flushing the system clean.

10 The radiator should be flushed independently of the engine, to avoid unnecessary contamination.

Radiator flushing

11 To flush the radiator, first tighten the radiator bleed screw, where applicable.

12 Disconnect the top and bottom hoses and any other relevant hoses from the radiator, with reference to Chapter 3.

13 Insert a garden hose into the radiator top inlet. Direct a flow of clean water through the radiator, and continue flushing until clean water emerges from the radiator bottom outlet.

14 If after a reasonable period, the water still does not run clear, the radiator can be flushed with a good proprietary cleaning agent. It is important that their manufacturer's instructions are followed carefully. If the contamination is particularly bad, insert the hose in the radiator bottom outlet, and reverse-flush the radiator.

Engine flushing

15 To flush the engine, first refit the cylinder block drain plug, and tighten the cooling system bleed screws.

16 Remove the thermostat as described in Chapter 3, then temporarily refit the top hose at its engine connection.

17 With the top and bottom hoses disconnected from the radiator, insert a garden hose into the radiator top hose. Direct a clean flow of water

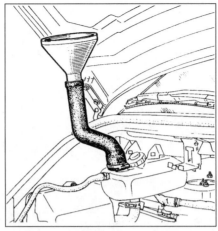

31.22 Header tank made from a hose and funnel

through the engine, and continue flushing until clean water emerges from the radiator bottom hose.

18 On completion of flushing, refit the thermostat and reconnect the hoses with reference to Chapter 3.

Cooling system filling

19 Before attempting to fill the cooling system, make sure that all hoses and clips are in good condition, and that the clips are tight. Note that an antifreeze mixture must be used all year round, to prevent corrosion of the engine components (see Chapter 3). Also check that the cylinder block drain plug is in place and tight.

20 Remove the expansion tank filler cap.

21 Open all the cooling system bleed screws (see paragraph 4).

22 Some of the cooling system hoses and components are positioned at the same level (or higher) as the top of the radiator expansion tank. To allow the system to bleed properly it is necessary to have an adequate "head" of coolant when refilling. A suitable "header tank" can be made up from a radiator hose which can be attached to the expansion tank at one end, and to a funnel at the other **(see illustration)**.

23 Fit the "header tank" to the expansion tank and slowly fill the system. Coolant will emerge from each of the bleed screws in turn, starting with the lowest screw. As soon as coolant free from air bubbles emerges from the lowest screw, tighten that screw, and watch the next bleed screw in the system. Repeat the procedure until the coolant is emerging from the highest bleed screw in the cooling system and all bleed screws are securely tightened.

24 Ensure that the "header tank" is full (at least 0.5 litres of coolant). Start the engine, and run it at a fast idle speed (do not exceed 2000 rpm) until the cooling fan cuts in, and then cuts out three times. Stop the engine. **Note:** *Take care not to scald yourself with hot coolant during this operation.*

25 Allow the engine to cool then remove the "header tank".

26 When the engine has cooled, check the coolant level with reference to *"Weekly checks"*. Top-up the level if necessary and refit the expansion tank cap.

Antifreeze mixture

27 The antifreeze should always be renewed at the specified intervals. This is necessary not only to maintain the antifreeze properties, but also to prevent corrosion which would otherwise occur as the corrosion inhibitors become progressively less effective.

28 Always use an ethylene-glycol based antifreeze which is suitable for use in mixed-metal cooling systems. The quantity of antifreeze and levels of protection are given in the *Specifications*.

29 Before adding antifreeze, the cooling system should be completely drained, preferably flushed, and all hoses checked for condition and security.

30 After filling with antifreeze, a label should be attached to the expansion tank, stating the type and concentration of antifreeze used, and the date installed. Any subsequent topping-up should be made with the same type and concentration of antifreeze.

31 Do not use engine antifreeze in the windscreen/tailgate washer system, as it will cause damage to the vehicle paintwork. A screenwash additive should be added to the washer system in the quantities stated on the bottle.

Chapter 1 Part B:
Routine maintenance and servicing - diesel models

Contents

Degrees of difficulty

| Easy, suitable for novice with little experience | | Fairly easy, suitable for beginner with some experience | | Fairly difficult, suitable for competent DIY mechanic | | Difficult, suitable for experienced DIY mechanic | | Very difficult, suitable for expert DIY or professional | |

Lubricants and fluids

Refer to "Weekly checks" and relevant Chapters

Capacities

Engine oil (approximate)

Excluding filter	5.5 litres
Including filter	6.0 litres
Difference between MAX and MIN dipstick marks (approx.)	0.5 to 1.0 litre
Cooling system (approximate)	7.2 litres
Transmission	2.2 litres
Fuel tank	60 litres

Engine

Oil filter type	Champion F105
Air filter type	Champion W132
Fuel filter type:	
Up to 1991, CAV system	Champion L132
All other models	Champion L111
Glow plug type	Champion CH137

Cooling system

Antifreeze mixture:

35% antifreeze	Protection down to -23°C
50% antifreeze	Protection down to -40°C

Note: *Refer to antifreeze manufacturer for latest recommendations.*

Brakes

Front and rear brake pad minimum thickness (friction material and backing plate)	6.0 mm
Rear brake shoe minimum thickness (friction material and shoe)	2.5 mm

Tyres

Tyre size	185/70 R 13H, 185/70 SR 13, 185/65 R 14H, 195/65 R14H, 195/65 R14 MXT according to model
Tyre pressures	See *"Weekly checks"*

Wiper blades

All models	Champion VX55 or X55

Torque wrench settings

	Nm
Roadwheel bolts	90

The maintenance intervals in this manual are provided with the assumption that you, not the dealer, will be carrying out the work. These are the minimum maintenance intervals recommended by the manufacturer for vehicles driven daily. If you wish to keep your vehicle in peak condition at all times, you may wish to perform some of these procedures more often. We encourage frequent maintenance, because it enhances the efficiency, performance and resale value of your vehicle.

If the vehicle is driven in dusty areas, used to tow a trailer, or driven frequently at slow speeds (idling in traffic) or on short journeys, more frequent maintenance intervals are recommended.

When the vehicle is new, it should be serviced by a factory-authorised dealer service department, in order to preserve the factory warranty.

Every 250 miles (400 km) or weekly
☐ Refer to *"Weekly checks"*

Every 5000 miles (7500) km
In addition to all the items listed above, carry out the following:
☐ Renew the engine oil and filter (Section 3)
☐ Drain any water from the fuel filter (Section 4)
☐ Check the security of the turbocharger components (Section 5)
☐ Check the condition of the auxiliary drivebelt(s) (Section 6)
☐ Check the battery and electrical equipment (Section 7)
☐ Check the engine for fluid leaks and the condition of the hoses (Section 8)
☐ Check the condition of the emission control equipment (Section 9)
☐ Check the condition of the brake pads (Section 10)
☐ Check the condition and security of the steering and suspension components (Section 11)
☐ Check the condition of the driveshaft gaiters (Section 12)
☐ Inspect the underbody and the brake hydraulic pipes and hoses (Section 13)
☐ Check the condition of the fuel lines (Section 13)
☐ Check the condition and security of the exhaust system (Section 14)
☐ Check the condition of the seat belts (Section 15)
☐ Lubricate the locks and hinges (Section 16)
☐ Check the condition of the bodywork, paint and exterior trim (Section 17)
☐ Road test (Section 18)
☐ Check the operation of the air conditioning system (Section 19)

Every 10 000 miles (15 000 km)
In addition to all the items listed above, carry out the following:
☐ Renew the fuel filter (Section 20)
☐ Check the engine idle speed and anti-stall speed (Section 21)
☐ Check the transmission oil level (Section 22)

Every 15 000 miles (22 500 km)
In addition to all the items listed above, carry out the following:
☐ Renew the air cleaner filter element (Section 23)
☐ Check the condition of the brake shoes (Section 24)
☐ Check the handbrake adjustment (Section 25)

Every 40 000 miles (60 000 km)
In addition to all the items listed above, carry out the following:
☐ Renew the transmission oil (Section 26)
☐ Renew the brake hydraulic fluid (Section 27)
☐ Have the front wheel alignment checked (Section 28)

Every 80 000 miles (120 000 km)
In addition to all the items listed above, carry out the following:
☐ Renew the timing belt (Section 29)

Note: *It is strongly recommended that the timing belt renewal interval is halved to 56 000 km on vehicles which are subjected to intensive use, ie. mainly short journeys or a lot of stop-start driving. The actual belt renewal interval is therefore very much up to the individual owner, but bear in mind that severe engine damage will result if the belt breaks.*

Every 2 years (regardless of mileage)
☐ Renew the coolant (Section 30)

1B

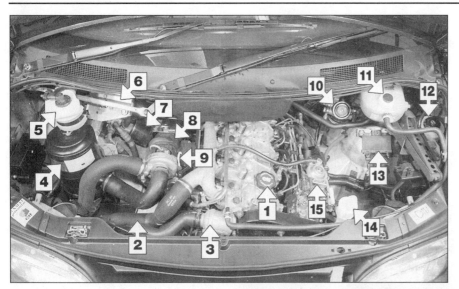

Underbonnet view of a Phase 3 model

1 Oil filler cap
2 Intercooler ducting
3 Intercooler
4 Air cleaner
5 Brake fluid reservoir
6 Wiper motor and linkage
7 Oil filter
8 Turbocharger
9 Engine oil dipstick
10 Fuel filter
11 Coolant expansion tank
12 Steering fluid reservoir
13 Preheating control unit
14 Washer reservoir
15 Injection pump

Front underbody view of a Phase 3 model

1 Engine oil drain plug
2 Power steering pump drivebelt adjuster
3 Power steering pump
4 Suspension lower arm
5 Driveshaft inner CV joint
6 Exhaust front pipe
7 Transmission undertray
8 Engine mounting

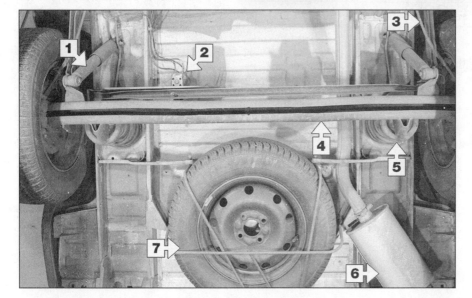

Rear underbody view of a Phase 3 model

1 Shock absorber
2 Brake compensator
3 Handbrake cable
4 Rear axle
5 Rear spring
6 Exhaust silencer
7 Spare wheel

1 Introduction

1 This Chapter is designed to help the home mechanic maintain his/her vehicle for safety, economy, long life and peak performance.

2 This Chapter contains a master maintenance schedule, followed by Sections dealing specifically with each task in the schedule. Visual checks, adjustments, component renewal and other helpful items are included. Refer to the accompanying illustrations of the engine compartment and the underside of the vehicle for the locations of the various components.

3 Servicing your vehicle in accordance with the maintenance schedule and the following Sections will provide a planned maintenance programme, which should result in a long and reliable service life. This is a comprehensive plan, so maintaining some items but not others at the specified service intervals will not produce the same results.

4 As you service your vehicle, you will discover that many of the procedures can - and should - be grouped together, because of the particular procedure being performed, or because of the close proximity of two otherwise-unrelated components to one another. For example, if the vehicle is raised for any reason, the exhaust should be inspected at the same time as the suspension and steering components.

5 The first step of this maintenance programme is to prepare yourself before the actual work begins. Read through all the Sections relevant to the work to be carried out, then make a list and gather together all the parts and tools required. If a problem is encountered, seek advice from a parts specialist or a dealer service department.

2 Intensive maintenance

1 If, from the time the vehicle is new, the routine maintenance schedule is followed closely, and frequent checks are made of fluid levels and high-wear items, as suggested throughout this manual, the engine will be kept in relatively good running condition, and the need for additional work will be minimised.

2 It is possible that there will be some times when the engine is running poorly due to the lack of regular maintenance. This is even more likely if a used vehicle, which has not received regular and frequent maintenance checks, is purchased. In such cases, additional work may need to be carried out, outside of the regular maintenance intervals.

3 If engine wear is suspected, a compression or leakdown test (refer to Part B of Chapter 2) will provide valuable information regarding the overall performance of the main internal components. Such a test can be used as a basis to decide on the extent of the work to be carried out. If, for example, a compression test indicates serious internal engine wear, conventional maintenance as described in this Chapter will not greatly improve the performance of the engine, and may prove a waste of time and money, unless extensive overhaul work (Chapter 2C) is carried out first.

4 The following series of operations are those often required to improve the performance of a generally poor-running engine:

Primary operations

a) Clean, inspect and test the battery (See "Weekly checks").
b) Check all the engine-related fluids (See "Weekly checks").
c) Check the condition and tension of the auxiliary drivebelts (Section 6).
d) Adjust the valve clearances (Chapter 2B).
e) Check the condition of all hoses, and check for fluid leaks (Section 8).
f) Check the condition of the air cleaner filter element and renew if necessary (Section 23).
g) Renew the fuel filter (Section 20).
h) Check the idle speed and anti-stall speed settings (Section 21).

5 If the above operations do not prove fully effective, carry out the following operations:

Secondary operations

6 All the items listed under "Primary operations", plus the following:

a) Check the charging system (Chapter 5A).
b) Check the preheating system (Chapter 5C).
c) Check the fuel system (Chapter 4D).

5000 mile service - diesel

3 Engine oil and filter renewal

Note: A suitable square-section wrench may be required to undo the sump drain plug on some models. These wrenches can be obtained from most motor factors or your Renault dealer.

1 Frequent oil changes are the best preventive maintenance the home mechanic can give the engine, because ageing oil becomes diluted and contaminated, which leads to premature engine wear.

2 Make sure that you have all the necessary tools before you begin this procedure. You should also have plenty of rags or newspapers handy, for mopping up any spills.

The oil should preferably be changed when the engine is still fully warmed-up to normal operating temperature, just after a run; warm oil and sludge will flow out more easily. Take care, however, not to touch the exhaust or any other hot parts of the engine when working under the vehicle. To avoid any possibility of scalding, and to protect yourself from possible skin irritants and other harmful contaminants in used engine oils, it is advisable to wear gloves when carrying out this work. Access to the underside of the vehicle is greatly improved if the vehicle can be lifted on a hoist, driven onto ramps, or supported by axle stands. (see "Jacking and vehicle support"). Whichever method is chosen, make sure that the vehicle remains level, or if it is at an angle, that the drain plug is at the lowest point.

3 Position the draining container under the drain plug, and unscrew the plug **(see illustration)**. If possible, try to keep the plug pressed into the sump while unscrewing it by hand the last couple of turns.

3.3 Sump drain plug location

HAYNES HINT

Keep the drain plug pressed into the sump while unscrewing it by hand the last couple of turns. As the plug releases, move it away sharply so the stream of oil from the sump runs into the container, not up your sleeve!

4 Allow the oil to drain into the container, and check the condition of the plug's sealing washer; renew it if worn or damaged.

5 Allow some time for the old oil to drain, noting that it may be necessary to reposition the container as the oil flow slows to a trickle; when the oil has completely drained, wipe clean the drain plug and its threads in the sump and refit the plug, tightening it securely.

6 The oil filter is remotely mounted on the right-hand side of the engine compartment bulkhead.

7 Reposition the draining container under the oil filter then, using a suitable filter removal tool if necessary, slacken the filter initially, then unscrew it by hand the rest of the way; be prepared for some oil spillage **(see illustration)**. Empty the oil in the old filter into the container.

8 Using a clean, lint-free rag, wipe clean the filter mounting. Check the old filter to make sure that the rubber sealing ring hasn't stuck to the mounting; if it has, carefully remove it.

9 Apply a light coating of clean engine oil to the sealing ring on the new filter. Screw the filter into position until it seats, then tighten it firmly by hand only - **do not** use any tools.

10 Remove the old oil and all tools from under the vehicle, then lower the vehicle to the ground.

OIL CARE

FOLLOW THE CODE

OIL BANK LINE
0800 66 33 66

Note: It is antisocial and illegal to dump oil down the drain. To find the location of your local oil recycling bank, call this number free.

11 Remove the dipstick and the oil filler cap from the engine. Fill the engine with oil, using the correct grade and type of oil, (see *"Weekly Checks"*). Pour in half the specified quantity of oil first, then wait a few minutes for the oil to fall to the sump. Continue adding oil a small quantity at a time, until the level is up to the lower (minimum) notch on the dipstick. Adding approximately 0.5 to 1.0 litre will raise the level to the upper (maximum) notch on the dipstick.

12 Start the engine. The oil pressure warning light will take a few seconds to go out while the new filter fills with oil; do not race the engine while the light is on. Run the engine for a few minutes, while checking for leaks around the drain plug.

13 Switch off the engine, and wait a few minutes for the oil to settle in the sump once more. With the new oil circulated and the filter now completely full, recheck the level on the dipstick, and add more oil as necessary.

14 Dispose of the used engine oil safely and in accordance with environmental regulations (see *"General repair procedures"*).

4 Fuel filter water draining

1 A water drain plug is provided at the base of the fuel filter housing, located at the rear of the engine compartment on the left-hand side.

2 Place a suitable container beneath the plug. To make draining easier, a suitable length of tubing can be attached to the outlet on the plug to direct the fuel flow. On some filter housings a length of tubing is already fitted to allow the water to drain out under the vehicle.

3 Loosen the fuel inlet union on the filter head, then open the drain plug by turning it anti-clockwise **(see illustration)**.

4 Allow the entire contents of the filter to drain into the container, then tighten the drain plug and the fuel inlet union.

5 Dispose of the drained fuel safely.

6 Prime and bleed the fuel system as described in Chapter 4C.

5 Turbocharger check

Check all hose and pipe connections (oil, coolant and boost pressure) for security and leaks.

Rectify any problems without delay.

6 Auxiliary drivebelts check and renewal

Note: *Renault specify the use of a special tool (Ele. 346-04) to correctly set the drivebelt tension. If access to this tool cannot be obtained, an approximate setting can be achieved using the method described below. If the method described is used, the tension should be checked using the special tool at the earliest possible opportunity.*

1 The auxiliary drivebelts transmit power from the crankshaft pulley to the alternator, coolant pump, steering pump and air conditioning compressor (as applicable). A variety of belt arrangements and tensioning methods will be found, according to equipment and engine type.

Check

2 With the engine switched off, open and support the bonnet, then locate the auxiliary drivebelts fitted to your car (Be very careful, and wear protective gloves to minimise the risk of burning your hands on hot components, if the engine has recently been running).

3 Using an inspection light or a small electric torch, and rotating the engine when necessary with a spanner applied to the crankshaft pulley bolt, check the whole length of the drivebelt for cracks, separation of the rubber, and torn or worn ribs. Also check for fraying and glazing, which gives the drivebelt a shiny appearance. Both sides of the drivebelt should be inspected, which means you will have to twist the drivebelt to check the underside. Use your fingers to feel the drivebelt where you can't see it. If you are in any doubt as to the condition of the drivebelt, renew it.

Renewal and adjustment

4 When removing a particular drivebelt, it will obviously be necessary to remove those in front of it first **(see illustration)**.

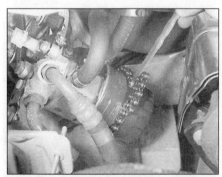

3.7 Using an oil filter removal tool to slacken the oil filter

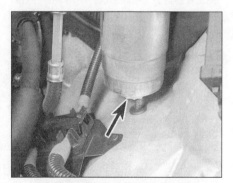

4.3 Open the fuel filter drain plug (arrowed) by turning it anti-clockwise

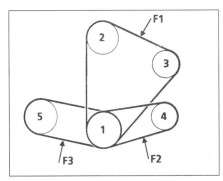

6.4 Auxiliary drivebelt arrangement

1 Crankshaft pulley
2 Coolant pump pulley
3 Alternator pulley
4 Steering pump pulley
5 Air conditioning compressor pulley
F1, F2, F3 = deflection checking points for
each drivebelt

Alternator/coolant pump drivebelt

5 Slacken the alternator pivot and adjuster strap nuts and bolts **(see illustration)**.
6 Move the alternator towards the engine to release the belt tension. On later models a positive tensioning device is used: slacken the tensioner bolt to move the alternator inwards **(see illustration)**.
7 Slip the belt off the pulleys and remove it.
8 When refitting, move the alternator away from the engine until the belt can be deflected 4.5 to 5.5 mm by firm thumb pressure at a point midway between the alternator and coolant pump pulleys. Tighten the pivot and adjusting strap nuts and bolts in this position and recheck the tension.
9 On models with a positive tensioning device, be careful not to overtension the belt. On models without such a device, it may be helpful to lever the alternator away from the engine to achieve the desired tension. Only use a wooden or plastic lever, and only lever at the pulley end.

Steering pump drivebelt

Note: *Three different pump mounting arrangements may be encountered. Identify the type fitted then proceed according to the relevant sub-heading. Further details and illustrations will be found in Chapter 10.*
First version
10 Slacken the pump lower mounting nuts and bolts. Slacken the drivebelt upper adjuster nut and bolt and slip the drivebelt off the crankshaft and pump pulleys.
11 When refitting, move the steering pump away from the engine until the belt can be deflected 4.0 to 4.5 mm by firm thumb pressure at a point midway between the two pulleys. Tighten the adjuster and the mounting nuts and bolts in this position and recheck the tension.
Second version
12 At the rear of the pump, slacken the upper mounting bolt.

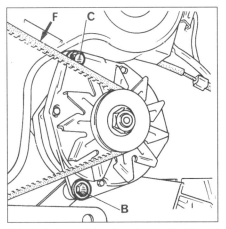

6.5 Early type alternator pivot bolts (B) and (C), and deflection checking point (F)

Note: *Adjuster strap bolt is lower down, accessible from below*

13 At the front of the pump, slacken the four bolts securing the mounting plate to the front of the engine. One of these bolts also serves as the alternator adjuster strap retaining bolt. On some models, access to these front bolts may be easier from below. Slip the drivebelt off the crankshaft and pump pulleys.
14 When refitting, move the steering pump away from the engine until the belt can be deflected 4.0 to 4.5 mm by firm thumb pressure at a point midway between the two pulleys. Tighten the adjuster and the mounting nuts and bolts in this position and recheck the tension.
Third version
15 Slacken the steering pump front and rear mounting bolts. Slacken the positive tensioner bolt and slip the drivebelt off the crankshaft and pump pulleys. Access to these front bolts may be easier from below.
16 When refitting, turn the positive tensioner bolt to move the steering pump away from the engine until the belt can be deflected 4.0 to 4.5 mm by firm thumb pressure at a point midway between the two pulleys. Tighten the mounting bolts in this position and recheck the tension.

Air conditioning compressor drivebelt

17 Renewal of the compressor drivebelt is a complex operation requiring removal of all the other auxiliary drivebelts and the engine timing belt. The compressor drivebelt is driven by an additional crankshaft sprocket located behind the crankshaft pulley and timing belt.
18 To remove the belt, first remove the timing belt as described in Chapter 2B, Section 7. Slacken the compressor upper and lower mounting bolts, move the compressor towards the engine and slip off the belt.
19 Fit the new belt and tension it by moving the compressor until the belt can be deflected 3.5 to 4.5 mm by firm thumb pressure at a point midway between the two pulleys. Tighten the mounting bolts in this position and recheck the tension.

20 Refit the timing belt as described in Chapter 2B, Section 7.

All drivebelts

21 Recheck the tension of a new belt after a few hundred miles.

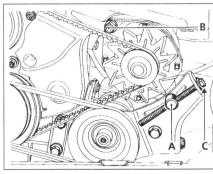

6.6 Later type alternator with positive tensioning device

A Adjuster strap bolt
B Pivot bolt   C Tensioner bolt

7 Battery and electrical equipment check

1 Some models may be equipped with a "maintenance-free" battery which does not require topping-up. If this is the case the battery will be sealed and it will not be possible to remove the cell covers.
2 On models not equipped with a "maintenance-free" battery, check the electrolyte level of all six battery cells. The level must be approximately 10 mm above the plates; this may be shown by maximum and minimum level lines marked on the battery's casing. If the level is low, unscrew the filler/vent caps, and add distilled water **(see illustration)**. Install and retighten the caps. *Caution: Overfilling the cells may cause electrolyte to spill over during periods of heavy charging, causing corrosion or damage.*

7.2 Adding distilled water to the battery

1B

3 Periodically (approximately every three months) check the charge condition of the battery as described in Chapter 5A.

4 Further information on the battery, charging, and jump starting can be found in Chapter 5A, and in the preliminary sections of this manual.

5 Check the operation of all interior electrical equipment and accessories, including the courtesy lights, heater blower, instrument panel warning lights and illumination lights. Renew any blown bulbs or faulty components with reference to Chapter 12.

8 Hose and fluid leak check

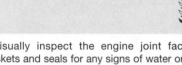

1 Visually inspect the engine joint faces, gaskets and seals for any signs of water or oil leaks. Pay particular attention to the areas around the camshaft cover, cylinder head, oil filter and sump joint faces. Bear in mind that, over a period of time, some very slight seepage from these areas is to be expected - what you are really looking for is any indication of a serious leak. Should a leak be found, renew the offending gasket or oil seal by referring to the appropriate Chapters in this manual.

2 Also check the security and condition of all the engine-related pipes and hoses, and all hydraulic system pipes and hoses. Ensure that all cable-ties or securing clips are in place, and in good condition. Clips which are broken or missing can lead to chafing of the hoses, pipes or wiring, which could cause more serious problems in the future.

3 Carefully check the radiator hoses and heater hoses along their entire length. Renew any hose which is cracked, swollen or deteriorated. Cracks will show up better if the hose is squeezed. Pay close attention to the hose clips that secure the hoses to the cooling system components. Hose clips can pinch and puncture hoses, resulting in cooling system leaks.

4 Inspect all the cooling system components (hoses, joint faces etc.) for leaks.

A leak in the cooling system will usually show up as white or rust coloured deposits on the area adjoining the leak

If not obvious leaks can be found, but coolant is still being lost, it is advisable to have the pressure cap and the entire system pressure-tested by a dealer or suitably equipped garage, as this will often show up a small leak not previously apparent. If you are keen, pressure-testing equipment similar to that shown above is available from larger car accessory shops

5 Where any problems are found on system components, renew the component or gasket with reference to Chapter 3.

6 Check the security of all fuel and hydraulic hose attachments and pipe unions, and inspect the fuel hoses and vacuum hoses for kinks, chafing and deterioration.

9 Emission control equipment check

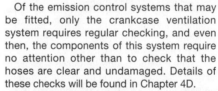

Of the emission control systems that may be fitted, only the crankcase ventilation system requires regular checking, and even then, the components of this system require no attention other than to check that the hoses are clear and undamaged. Details of these checks will be found in Chapter 4D.

Should it be felt that the other systems are not functioning correctly, the advice of a dealer should be sought.

10 Brake pad wear check

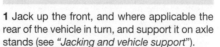

1 Jack up the front, and where applicable the rear of the vehicle in turn, and support it on axle stands (see *"Jacking and vehicle support"*).

2 For better access to the brake calipers, remove the roadwheels.

3 If any one of the brake pads has worn down to, or below, the specified limit, *all four* pads at that end of the car must be renewed as a set (ie all the front pads or all the rear pads).

4 For a comprehensive check, the brake pads should be removed and cleaned. The operation of the brake calipers can then be checked, and the brake discs can be fully examined. Refer to Chapter 9 for details.

For a quick check, the thickness of the friction material on each brake pad can be measured through the aperture in the caliper body

11 Steering and suspension check

Front suspension and steering check

1 Apply the handbrake, then raise the front of the vehicle and support it on axle stands. (see *"Jacking and vehicle support"*).

2 Visually inspect the balljoint dust covers and the steering gear gaiters for splits, chafing or deterioration. Any wear of these components will cause loss of lubricant, together with dirt and water entry, resulting in rapid deterioration of the balljoints or steering gear.

3 Check the steering fluid hoses for chafing or deterioration, and the pipe and hose unions for fluid leaks. Also check for signs of fluid leakage under pressure from the steering gear gaiters, which would indicate failed fluid seals within the steering gear.

4 Check for signs of fluid leakage around the shock absorber body, or from the rubber boot around the piston rod (where fitted). Should any fluid be noticed, the shock absorber is defective internally, and renewal is necessary.

5 Grasp the roadwheel at the 12 o'clock and 6 o'clock positions, and try to rock it **(see illustration)**. Very slight free play may be felt, but if the movement is appreciable, further investigation is necessary to determine the source. Continue rocking the wheel while an assistant depresses the footbrake. If the movement is now eliminated or significantly reduced, it is likely that the hub bearings are at fault. If the free play is still evident with the footbrake depressed, then there is wear in the suspension joints or mountings.

6 Now grasp the wheel at the 9 o'clock and 3 o'clock positions, and try to rock it as before. Any movement felt now may again be caused by wear in the hub bearings or the steering track rod balljoints. If the outer track rod end balljoint is worn, the visual movement will be obvious. If the inner joint is suspect, it can be felt by placing a hand over the steering gear gaiter, and gripping the track rod. If the

11.5 Check for wear in the hub bearings by grasping the wheel and trying to rock it

12.1 Check the condition of the driveshaft gaiters

wheel is now rocked, movement will be felt at the inner joint if wear has taken place.

7 Using a large screwdriver or flat bar, check for wear in the suspension mounting bushes by levering between the relevant suspension component and its attachment point. Some movement is to be expected as the mountings are made of rubber, but excessive wear should be obvious. Also check the condition of any visible rubber bushes, looking for splits, cracks or contamination of the rubber.

8 With the vehicle standing on its wheels, have an assistant turn the steering wheel back-and-forth, about an eighth of a turn each way. There should be very little, if any, lost movement between the steering wheel and roadwheels. If this is not the case, closely observe the joints and mountings previously described, but in addition, check the steering column universal joints for wear, and also check the steering gear itself.

9 The efficiency of the shock absorber may be checked by bouncing the car at each front corner. Generally speaking, the body will return to its normal position and stop after being depressed. If it rises and returns on a rebound, the shock absorber is probably suspect. Examine also the shock absorber upper and lower mountings for any signs of wear or fluid leakage.

Rear suspension check

10 Chock the front wheels, then raise the rear of the vehicle and support it on axle stands. (see *"Jacking and vehicle support"*).

11 Check the rear hub bearings for wear, using the method described for the front hub bearings (paragraph 5).

12 Using a large screwdriver or flat bar, check for wear in the suspension mounting bushes by levering between the relevant suspension component and its attachment point. Some movement is to be expected as the mountings are made of rubber, but excessive wear should be obvious. Check the condition of the shock absorbers as described previously.

12 Driveshaft gaiter check

With the vehicle raised and securely supported on stands (see *"Jacking and vehicle support"*), turn the steering onto full lock, then slowly rotate the roadwheel. Inspect the condition of the outer constant velocity (CV) joint rubber gaiters, squeezing the gaiters to open out the folds **(see illustration)**. Check for signs of cracking, splits or deterioration of the rubber, which may allow the grease to escape, and lead to water and grit entry into the joint. Also check the security and condition of the retaining clips. Repeat these checks on the inner CV joints. If any damage or deterioration is found, the gaiters should be renewed as described in Chapter 8.

At the same time, check the general condition of the CV joints themselves by first holding the driveshaft and attempting to rotate the wheel. Repeat this check by holding the inner joint and attempting to rotate the driveshaft. Any appreciable movement indicates wear in the joints, wear in the driveshaft splines, or a loose driveshaft retaining nut.

13 Underbody and fuel/brake line check

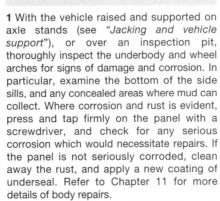

1 With the vehicle raised and supported on axle stands (see *"Jacking and vehicle support"*), or over an inspection pit, thoroughly inspect the underbody and wheel arches for signs of damage and corrosion. In particular, examine the bottom of the side sills, and any concealed areas where mud can collect. Where corrosion and rust is evident, press and tap firmly on the panel with a screwdriver, and check for any serious corrosion which would necessitate repairs. If the panel is not seriously corroded, clean away the rust, and apply a new coating of underseal. Refer to Chapter 11 for more details of body repairs.

2 At the same time, inspect the body panels for stone damage and general condition.

3 Inspect all of the fuel and brake lines on the underbody for damage, rust, corrosion and leakage. Also make sure that they are correctly supported in their clips. Where applicable, check the PVC coating on the lines for damage.

4 Inspect the flexible brake hoses in the vicinity of the calipers and connections to the rear axle, where they are subjected to most movement. Bend them between the fingers (but do not actually bend them double, or the casing may be damaged) and check that this does not reveal previously-hidden cracks, cuts or splits.

5 Inspect the fuel tank and filler neck for punctures, cracks and other damage. The connection between the filler neck and tank is especially critical. Sometimes a rubber filler neck or connecting hose will leak due to loose retaining clamps or deteriorated rubber.

6 Carefully check all rubber hoses and metal fuel lines leading away from the fuel tank. Check for loose connections, deteriorated hoses, crimped lines, and other damage. Pay particular attention to the vent pipes and hoses, which often loop up around the filler neck and can become blocked or crimped. Follow the lines to the front of the vehicle, carefully inspecting them all the way. Renew damaged sections as necessary.

1B

14 Exhaust system check

1 With the engine cold (at least three hours after the vehicle has been driven), check the complete exhaust system, from its starting point at the engine to the end of the tailpipe. Ideally, this should be done on a hoist, where unrestricted access is available; if a hoist is not available, raise and support the vehicle on axle stands (see *"Jacking and vehicle support"*).

2 Check the pipes and connections for evidence of leaks, severe corrosion, or damage. Make sure that all brackets and rubber mountings are in good condition, and tight; if any of the mountings are to be renewed, ensure that the replacements are of the correct type. Leakage at any of the joints or in other parts of the system will usually show up as a black sooty stain in the vicinity of the leak.

3 At the same time, inspect the underside of the body for holes, corrosion, open seams, etc. which may allow exhaust gases to enter the passenger compartment. Seal all body openings with silicone or body putty.

4 Rattles and other noises can often be traced to the exhaust system, especially the rubber mountings. Try to move the system, silencer(s) and catalytic converter. If any components can touch the body or suspension parts, secure the exhaust system with new mountings.

15 Seat belt check

Check the seat belts for satisfactory operation and condition. Inspect the webbing for fraying and cuts. Check that they retract smoothly and without binding into their reels.

Check the seat belt mountings, ensuring that all the bolts are securely tightened.

16 Door, tailgate and bonnet check and lubrication

Check that the doors, bonnet and tailgate close securely. Check that the bonnet safety catch operates correctly. Check the operation of the door check straps.

Lubricate the hinges, door check straps, the striker plates and the bonnet catch sparingly with a little oil or grease.

17 Bodywork, paint and exterior trim check

1 The best time to carry out this check is after the car has been washed so that any surface blemish or scratch will be clearly evident and not hidden by a film of dirt.
2 Starting at one front corner check the paintwork all around the car, looking for minor scratches or more serious dents. Check all the trim and make sure that it is securely attached over its entire length.
3 Check the security of all door locks, door mirrors, badges, bumpers radiator grille and wheel trim. Anything found loose, or in need of further attention should be done with reference to the relevant Chapters of this manual.
4 Rectify any problems noticed with the paintwork or body panels (see Chapter 11).

18 Road test

Instruments and electrical equipment

1 Check the operation of all instruments and electrical equipment.
2 Make sure that all instruments read correctly, and switch on all electrical equipment in turn to check that it functions properly.

Steering and suspension

3 Check for any abnormalities in the steering, suspension, handling or road "feel".
4 Drive the vehicle, and check that there are no unusual vibrations or noises.

5 Check that the steering feels positive, with no excessive "sloppiness", or roughness, and check for any suspension noises when cornering, or when driving over bumps.

Drivetrain

6 Check the performance of the engine, clutch, transmission and driveshafts.
7 Listen for any unusual noises from the engine, clutch and transmission.
8 Check that the clutch action is smooth and progressive, that the drive is taken up smoothly, and that the pedal travel is not excessive. Also listen for any noises when the clutch pedal is depressed. Check that all gears can be engaged smoothly, without noise, and that the gear lever action is not abnormally vague or "notchy".
9 Make sure that the engine runs smoothly when idling, and that there is no hesitation when accelerating.
10 Listen for a metallic clicking sound from the front of the vehicle, as the vehicle is driven slowly in a circle with the steering on full lock. Carry out this check in both directions. If a clicking noise is heard, this indicates wear in a driveshaft joint, in which case, further inspection will be necessary (see Chapter 8).

Check the operation and performance of the braking system

11 Make sure that the vehicle does not pull to one side when braking, and that the wheels do not lock prematurely when braking hard.
12 Check that there is no vibration through the steering when braking.
13 Check that the handbrake operates correctly, without excessive movement of the lever, and that it holds the vehicle stationary on a slope.
14 With the engine switched off, test the operation of the brake servo unit as follows. Depress the footbrake four or five times to exhaust the vacuum, then start the engine. As the engine starts, there should be a noticeable "give" in the brake pedal as vacuum builds up. Allow the engine to run for at least two minutes, and then switch it off. If the brake pedal is now depressed again, it should be possible to detect a hiss from the servo as the pedal is depressed. After about four or five applications, no further hissing should be heard, and the pedal should feel considerably harder.

19 Air conditioning system check

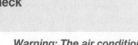 *Warning: The air conditioning system is under high pressure. Do not loosen any fittings or remove any components until after the system has been discharged. Air conditioning refrigerant must be properly discharged into an approved type of*

container, at a dealer service department or an automotive air conditioning repair facility capable of handling the refrigerant safely. Wear eye protection when disconnecting air conditioning system fittings.

Warning: Be sure to wear eye protection when using compressed air!

1 The following maintenance checks should be performed on a regular basis, to ensure that the air conditioner continues to operate at peak efficiency:
a) *Check the auxiliary drivebelt. If it's worn or deteriorated, renew it (see Section 6).*
b) *Check the system hoses. Look for cracks, bubbles, hard spots and deterioration. Inspect the hoses and all fittings for oil bubbles and seepage. If there's any evidence of wear, damage or leaks, renew the hose(s).*
c) *Inspect the condenser fins for leaves, insects and other debris. Use a "fin comb" or compressed air to clean the condenser.*
d) *Check that the drain tube from the front of the evaporator is clear - note that it is normal to have clear fluid (water) dripping from this while the system is in operation, to the extent that quite a large puddle can be left under the vehicle when it is parked.*

2 It's a good idea to operate the system for about 30 minutes at least once a month, particularly during the winter. Long term non-use can cause hardening, and subsequent failure, of the seals.
3 Because of the complexity of the air conditioning system and the special equipment necessary to service it, in-depth fault diagnosis and repairs are not included in this manual. For more complete information on the air conditioning system, refer to the Haynes "Automotive Heating and Air Conditioning Manual".
4 The most common cause of poor cooling is simply a low system refrigerant charge. If a noticeable drop in cool air output occurs, the following quick check will help you determine if the refrigerant level is low.
5 Warm the engine up to normal operating temperature.
6 Place the air conditioning temperature selector at the coldest setting, and put the blower at the highest setting. Open the doors - to make sure the air conditioning system doesn't cycle off as soon as it cools the passenger compartment.
7 With the compressor engaged - the clutch will make an audible click, and the centre of the clutch will rotate - feel the inlet and outlet pipes at the compressor. One side should be cold, and one hot. If there's no perceptible difference between the two pipes, there's something wrong with the compressor or the system. It might be a low charge - it might be something else. Take the vehicle to a dealer service department or an automotive air conditioning specialist.

10 000 mile service - diesel

20 Fuel filter renewal

Lucas/CAV filter

1 Drain the filter bowl (see Section 4).
2 Unscrew the through-bolt from the top of the filter head, then withdraw the bolt, whilst supporting the filter bowl **(see illustration)**.
3 Lower the filter bowl, taking care not to strain the coolant hoses. Recover the lower seal, and lift out the element **(see illustrations)**. (If desired, the filter bowl can be removed completely after disconnecting the coolant hoses.)
4 Recover the upper seals, noting their locations **(see illustrations)**.
5 Clean out the filter bowl.
6 Fit a new element and new seals (supplied with the filter) to the bowl, making sure that the seals are correctly located.
7 Fit the element and the bowl to the filter head, then fit and tighten the through-bolt.
8 Prime and bleed the fuel system as described in Chapter 4C.

Bosch filter

9 Drain the filter bowl (see Section 4).
10 Using a strap wrench type filter removal tool, slacken the filter initially, then unscrew it by hand the rest of the way **(see illustration)**.
11 Make sure that the seal is in position on the new filter element then screw the element into position.
12 Tighten the element moderately tightly by hand, then tighten it a further quarter turn with the removal tool.
13 Prime and bleed the fuel system as described in Chapter 4C.

21 Idle speed and anti-stall speed checking and adjustment

Refer to Chapter 4, Part C.

22 Transmission oil level check

1 The manual transmission does not have a dipstick. To check the oil level, raise the vehicle and support it securely on axle stands, making sure that the vehicle is level (see "Jacking and vehicle support"). On the left-hand side of the transmission casing you will see the filler/level plug. Wipe all around the filler/level plug with a clean rag then unscrew and remove it **(see illustration)**. If the lubricant level is correct, the oil should be up to the lower edge of the hole.
2 If more oil is needed (if the oil level is not up to the hole), use a syringe, or a plastic bottle and tube, to add more. Stop filling the transmission when the lubricant begins to run out of the hole. Make sure that you use the correct type of lubricant (see *Specifications*).
3 Refit the filler/level plug, and tighten it securely. Drive the vehicle a short distance, then check for leaks.
4 Regular topping-up indicates a leak, which should be found and rectified without delay.

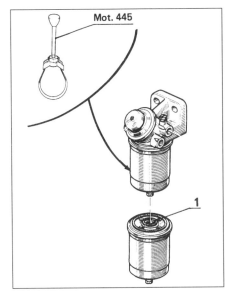

20.10 Bosch fuel filter arrangement showing removal tool and seal location (1)

1B

20.2 Unscrew the through-bolt from the top of the fuel filter head

20.3a Recover the lower seal . . .

20.3b . . . and lift out the filter element

20.4a Recover the large rubber seal . . .

20.4b . . . and the small O-ring seal

22.1 Unscrew transmission filler/level plug

15 000 mile service - diesel

23 Air cleaner element renewal

1 Unscrew the wing nut securing the air cleaner lid to the housing (see illustration).
2 Lift off the lid and remove the air cleaner element (see illustration).
3 Wipe clean inside the housing and lid with a cloth. Be careful not to sweep debris into the air inlet.
4 Fit the new element, making sure it is the right way up.
5 Refit the lid and secure it with the wing nut.

23.1 Unscrew the wing nut to remove the air cleaner lid

23.2 Lift the old element out of the housing

24 Brake shoe wear check

Refer to Chapter 9, Section 6.

25 Handbrake - adjustment

Refer to Chapter 9, Section 17.

40 000 mile service - diesel

26 Transmission oil renewal

1 Raise the vehicle and support it securely on axle stands, making sure that the vehicle is level (see "Jacking and vehicle support").
2 Remove the plastic undertray from the base of the transmission (see illustration).
3 On the bottom of the transmission casing you will see the drain plug. Place a suitable container beneath the plug, then unscrew and remove it (see illustration).

4 When all the oil has drained, refit the drain plug, and tighten securely. Refit the undertray.
5 Refill the transmission with fresh lubricant using the procedures described in Section 22.

27 Brake fluid renewal

 Warning: Brake hydraulic fluid can harm your eyes and damage painted surfaces, so use extreme caution when handling

and pouring it. Do not use fluid that has been standing open as it absorbs moisture from the air. Excess moisture can cause a dangerous loss of braking effectiveness.

The procedure is similar to that for the bleeding of the hydraulic system as described in Chapter 9, except that the brake fluid reservoir should be emptied by siphoning, and allowance should be made for the old fluid to be removed from the circuit when bleeding a section of the circuit.

HAYNES HINT Old hydraulic fluid is invariably much darker in colour than the new, making it easy to distinguish between the two.

28 Front wheel alignment check

Ideally, have this work carried out by a Renault dealer as special gauges are needed for accuracy. Details of the alignment procedure and the work involved will be found in Chapter 10.

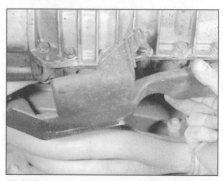

26.2 Removing the transmission undertray

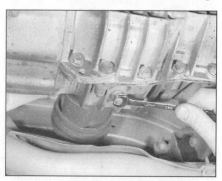

26.3 Transmission drain plug removal

80 000 mile service - diesel

29 Timing belt renewal

Refer to Chapter 2, Part B.

Every 2 years (regardless of mileage) - diesel

30 Coolant renewal

Cooling system draining

 Warning: Wait until the engine is cold before starting this procedure. Do not allow antifreeze to come in contact with your skin, or with the painted surfaces of the vehicle. Rinse off spills immediately with plenty of water. Never leave antifreeze lying around in an open container, or in a puddle in the driveway or on the garage floor. Children and pets are attracted by its sweet smell, but antifreeze can be fatal if ingested.

1 With the engine completely cold, remove the expansion tank filler cap. Turn the cap anti-clockwise, wait until any pressure remaining in the system is released, then unscrew it and lift it off.

2 Position a suitable container beneath the radiator bottom hose connection.

3 Slacken the hose clip, pull off the hose and allow the coolant to drain into the container.

4 To assist draining, open the cooling system bleed screws, if fitted. On early engines, bleed screws were not fitted, on later engines there is either a filler cap, or a bleed screw on top of the radiator (open whichever is fitted), and

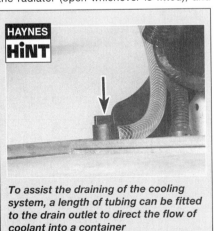

To assist the draining of the cooling system, a length of tubing can be fitted to the drain outlet to direct the flow of coolant into a container

another one in the heater hose at its connection with the heater matrix pipe stub. There may also be one in the heater hose area near the fuel injection pump. In some cases there may be a combination of all these types, so check carefully to see which are fitted to your vehicle.

5 When the flow of coolant stops, reposition the container below the cylinder block drain plug. This is located on the left-hand side of the cylinder block in front of the starter motor.

6 Remove the drain plug, and allow the coolant to drain into the container.

7 If the coolant has been drained for a reason other than renewal, then provided it is clean and less than two years old, it can be re-used, though this is not recommended.

8 Refit the radiator bottom hose and cylinder block drain plug on completion of draining.

Cooling system flushing

9 If coolant renewal has been neglected, or if the antifreeze mixture has become diluted, then in time, the cooling system may gradually lose efficiency, as the coolant passages become restricted due to rust, scale deposits, and other sediment. The cooling system efficiency can be restored by flushing the system clean.

10 The radiator should be flushed independently of the engine, to avoid unnecessary contamination.

Radiator flushing

11 To flush the radiator, first tighten the radiator bleed screw, where applicable.

12 Disconnect the top and bottom hoses and any other relevant hoses from the radiator, with reference to Chapter 3.

13 Insert a garden hose into the radiator top inlet. Direct a flow of clean water through the radiator, and continue flushing until clean water emerges from the radiator bottom outlet.

14 If after a reasonable period, the water still does not run clear, the radiator can be flushed with a good proprietary cleaning agent. It is important that their manufacturer's instructions are followed carefully. If the contamination is particularly bad, insert the hose in the radiator bottom outlet, and reverse-flush the radiator.

Engine flushing

15 To flush the engine, first refit the cylinder block drain plug, and tighten the cooling system bleed screws.

16 Remove the thermostat as described in Chapter 3.

17 With the bottom hose disconnected at the radiator, insert a garden hose into the thermostat housing. Direct a clean flow of water through the engine, and continue flushing until clean water emerges from the radiator bottom hose.

18 On completion of flushing, refit the thermostat and reconnect the hoses with reference to Chapter 3.

Cooling system filling

19 Before attempting to fill the cooling system, make sure that all hoses and clips are in good condition, and that the clips are tight. Note that an antifreeze mixture must be used all year round, to prevent corrosion of the engine components (see Chapter 3). Also check that the cylinder block drain plug is in place and tight.

20 Remove the expansion tank filler cap.

21 Open all the cooling system bleed screws (see paragraph 4).

22 Some of the cooling system hoses and components are positioned at the same level (or higher) as the top of the radiator expansion tank. To allow the system to bleed properly it is necessary to have an adequate "head" of coolant when refilling. A suitable "header tank" can be made up from a radiator hose which can be attached to the expansion tank at one end, and to a funnel at the other **(see illustration)**.

23 Fit the "header tank" to the expansion tank and slowly fill the system. Coolant will emerge from each of the bleed screws in turn, starting with the lowest screw. As soon as coolant free from air bubbles emerges from the lowest screw, tighten that screw, and watch the next bleed screw in the system. Repeat the procedure until the coolant is emerging from the highest bleed screw in the cooling system and all bleed screws are securely tightened.

24 Ensure that the "header tank" is full (at least 0.5 litres of coolant). Start the engine, and run it at a fast idle speed (do not exceed 2000 rpm) until the cooling fan cuts in, and then cuts out three times. Stop the engine.

Note: *Take great care not to scald yourself with the hot coolant during this operation.*

25 Allow the engine to cool then remove the "header tank".

26 When the engine has cooled, check the coolant level with reference to *"Weekly checks"*. Top-up the level if necessary and refit the expansion tank cap.

Antifreeze mixture

27 The antifreeze should always be renewed at the specified intervals. This is necessary not only to maintain the antifreeze properties, but also to prevent corrosion which would otherwise occur as the corrosion inhibitors become progressively less effective.

28 Always use an ethylene-glycol based antifreeze which is suitable for use in mixed-metal cooling systems. The quantity of antifreeze and levels of protection are given in the *Specifications*.

29 Before adding antifreeze, the cooling system should be completely drained, preferably flushed, and all hoses checked for condition and security.

30 After filling with antifreeze, a label should be attached to the expansion tank, stating the type and concentration of antifreeze used, and the date installed. Any subsequent topping-up should be made with the same type and concentration of antifreeze.

31 Do not use engine antifreeze in the windscreen/tailgate washer system, as it will cause damage to the vehicle paintwork. A screenwash additive should be added to the washer system in the quantities stated on the bottle.

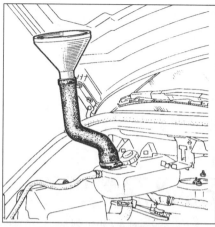

30.22 Header tank made from a hose and funnel

Chapter 2 Part A:
Petrol engine in-car repair procedures

Contents

Degrees of difficulty

Easy, suitable for novice with little experience	Fairly easy, suitable for beginner with some experience 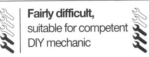	Fairly difficult, suitable for competent DIY mechanic	Difficult, suitable for experienced DIY mechanic	Very difficult, suitable for expert DIY or professional

2A

Specifications

Engine (general)

Type designation:

J6R	1995 cc, carburettor
J7R	1995 cc, fuel injection
J7T	2165 cc, fuel injection
Bore	80.00 mm

Stroke:

J6R and J7R engines	82.00 mm
J7T engines	89.00 mm

Compression ratio:

J7R 760 engines	10.0 : 1
All other engines	9.2 : 1

Compression pressure:

Overall value	9 to 11 bar
Variation between cylinders	1.4 bar maximum
Firing order	1-3-4-2 (No 1 at flywheel end of engine)
Direction of crankshaft rotation	Clockwise (viewed from front of engine)

Valve clearances (cold):

J6R engines:

Inlet	0.10 mm
Exhaust	0.25 mm

J7R and J7T engines

Inlet	0.10 to 0.15 mm
Exhaust	0.20 to 0.25 mm

Timing belt

Deflection midway between auxiliary shaft and camshaft sprockets:

Belts with square tooth profile	5.5 to 7.0 mm
Belts with round tooth profile	6.0 to 8.0 mm

Camshaft

Endfloat . . . . 0.07 to 0.13 mm

Lubrication system

Oil pressure (warm engine @ 3000 rpm) . . . . 3.0 bar minimum
Oil pump type . . . . Gear, driven from auxiliary shaft
Oil pump clearances:
    Endfloat . . . . 0.02 to 0.10 mm
    Gear teeth to body . . . . 0.05 to 0.12 mm

Torque wrench settings

	Nm
Camshaft cover nuts	5
Camshaft sprocket bolt	49
Auxiliary shaft sprocket bolt	49
Crankshaft pulley bolt:	
Bolt shank length of 45 mm	80
Bolt shank length of 55 mm or greater	125
Timing belt tensioner:	
Spring-loaded tensioner nut and bolt	25
Manually adjusted tensioner:	
Backplate nut/bolt	20
Tensioner pulley nut/bolt	50
Rocker shaft filter bolt	20
Oil pump body to crankcase	44
Oil pump cover to body	12
Sump bolts (single-piece sump):	
Steel sump	12
Aluminium sump	16
Sump bolts (two-piece sump):	
Sump pan to strengthening base	10
Strengthening base to crankcase:	
7 mm bolts	15
10 mm bolts	40
Cylinder head bolts:*	
Stage 1	20
Stage 2	Angle tighten a further 105°
Stage 3	Angle tighten a further 105°
Main bearing caps	95
Big-end bearing caps:*	
J6R and J7R engines	49
J7T engines	65
Flywheel bolts*	60
Engine mounting nuts and bolts	40

New nuts/bolts must be used

---

1 General information

How to use this Chapter

This Part of Chapter 2 describes those repair procedures that can reasonably be carried out on the engine while it remains in the vehicle. If the engine has been removed from the vehicle and is being dismantled as described in Part C, any preliminary dismantling procedures can be ignored.

Note that, while it may be possible physically to overhaul items such as the piston/connecting rod assemblies while the engine is in the vehicle, such tasks are not normally carried out as separate operations. Usually, several additional procedures (not to mention the cleaning of components and of oilways) have to be carried out. For this reason, all such tasks are classed as major overhaul procedures, and are described in Part C of this Chapter.

Part C describes the removal of the engine/transmission from the vehicle, and the full overhaul procedures that can then be carried out.

Engine description

The 1995 cc (J6R/J7R) and 2165 cc (J7T) engines are of four-cylinder overhead camshaft design, mounted longitudinally at the front of the vehicle, with the transmission mounted on the rear end of the engine.

The camshaft is driven by a toothed timing belt which also drives the auxiliary shaft. The camshaft operates the eight valves via rocker arms which are mounted on a shaft which is positioned directly above the camshaft. Valve clearances are adjusted via the screw and locknut arrangement fitted to each rocker arm. The inlet and exhaust valves are each closed by coil springs and operate in guides pressed into the cylinder head. On some J6R, and all J7R and J7T engines, the distributor is driven directly from the rear of the camshaft by means of an offset dog.

The crankshaft runs in five main bearings of the usual shell type. Endfloat is controlled by thrustwashers either side of number 2 main bearing.

The connecting rods rotate on horizontally-split bearing shells at their big-ends. The pistons are attached to the connecting rods by gudgeon pins which are an interference fit in the connecting rod small end bore. The aluminium alloy pistons are fitted with three piston rings, comprising two compression rings and an oil control ring.

The cylinder bores are formed by replaceable wet liners that are located from their bottom ends; sealing rings are fitted at the base of each liner to prevent the escape of coolant into the sump.

Lubrication is by means of a gear type oil pump which is driven by the auxiliary shaft via a worm gear. On early J6R engines the worm gear also drives the distributor which is mounted just above, on the cylinder block. The oil pump draws oil through a strainer located in the sump and then forces it through a full-flow cartridge-type filter into galleries in the cylinder block/crankcase, from where it is distributed to the crankshaft (main bearings) and camshaft. The big-end bearings are supplied with oil via internal drillings in the crankshaft, while the camshaft bearings also receive a pressurised supply. The camshaft lobes and valves are lubricated by splash, as are all other engine components.

Repair operations possible with the engine in the vehicle

The following work can be carried out with the engine in the vehicle.
 a) Compression pressure - testing.
 b) Camshaft cover - removal and refitting.
 c) Crankshaft pulley - removal and refitting.
 d) Timing belt cover - removal and refitting.
 e) Timing belt - removal and refitting.
 f) Timing belt tensioner and sprockets - removal and refitting.
 g) Camshaft and auxiliary shaft oil seals - renewal.
 h) Camshaft and rocker arms - removal and refitting.
 i) Cylinder head - removal and refitting.
 j) Cylinder head and pistons - decarbonising.
 k) Sump - removal and refitting.
 l) Oil pump - removal, inspection and refitting.
 m) Crankshaft oil seals - renewal.
 n) Engine/transmission mountings - inspection and renewal.
 o) Flywheel - removal and refitting.

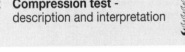

2 Compression test - description and interpretation

1 When engine performance is down, or if misfiring occurs which cannot be attributed to the ignition or fuel systems, a compression test can provide diagnostic clues as to the engine's condition. If the test is performed regularly, it can give warning of trouble before any other symptoms become apparent.
2 The engine must be fully warmed-up to normal operating temperature, the battery must be fully charged, and all the spark plugs must be removed (Chapter 1). The aid of an assistant will also be required.
3 Disable the ignition system by disconnecting the ignition coil LT feed. On fuel-injected engines, also disconnect the wiring connectors to each fuel injector to prevent fuel from contaminating the engine oil.

4 Fit a compression tester to the No 1 cylinder spark plug hole - the type of tester which screws into the plug thread is to be preferred.
5 Have the assistant hold the throttle wide open, and crank the engine on the starter motor; after one or two revolutions, the compression pressure should build up to a maximum figure, and then stabilise. Record the highest reading obtained.
6 Repeat the test on the remaining cylinders, recording the pressure in each.
7 All cylinders should produce very similar pressures; a difference of more than 2 bars between any two cylinders indicates a fault. Note that the compression should build up quickly in a healthy engine; low compression on the first stroke, followed by gradually-increasing pressure on successive strokes, indicates worn piston rings. A low compression reading on the first stroke, which does not build up during successive strokes, indicates leaking valves or a blown head gasket (a cracked head could also be the cause). Deposits on the undersides of the valve heads can also cause low compression.
8 If the pressure in any cylinder is low, carry out the following test to isolate the cause. Introduce a teaspoonful of clean oil into that cylinder through its spark plug hole, and repeat the test.
9 If the addition of oil temporarily improves the compression pressure, this indicates that bore or piston wear is responsible for the pressure loss. No improvement suggests that leaking or burnt valves, or a blown head gasket, maybe to blame.
10 A low reading from two adjacent cylinders is almost certainly due to the head gasket having blown between them; the presence of coolant in the engine oil will confirm this.
11 If one cylinder is about 20 percent lower than the others and the engine has a slightly rough idle, a worn camshaft lobe could be the cause.
12 If the compression reading is unusually high, the combustion chambers are probably coated with carbon deposits. If this is the case, the cylinder head should be removed and decarbonised.
13 On completion of the test, refit the spark plugs and reconnect the ignition system and fuel injectors.

3 Top dead centre (TDC) for number 1 piston - locating

1 Top dead centre (TDC) is the highest point in the cylinder that each piston reaches as the crankshaft turns. Each piston reaches TDC at the end of the compression stroke and again at the end of the exhaust stroke; however, for the purpose of timing the engine, TDC refers to the position of No 1 piston at the end of its

3.2 When No 1 piston is at TDC, the timing mark on the camshaft sprocket should be aligned with the pointer on the timing belt cover

compression stroke. On all engines in this manual, No 1 piston (and cylinder) is at the flywheel end of the engine.
2 When No 1 piston is at TDC, the timing mark on the camshaft sprocket should be aligned with the pointer on the outer timing belt cover (the sprocket mark can be viewed through the cut-out in the timing belt cover, above the pointer) (see illustration). Additionally, the timing mark on the flywheel should be aligned with the TDC (0°) mark on the transmission bellhousing. However, unless the engine is removed from the vehicle, it is almost impossible to see the flywheel and bellhousing marks.
3 To align the timing marks, the crankshaft must be turned. This should be done by using a spanner on the crankshaft pulley bolt. Access from above is limited but can just be managed from below.
4 Turn the crankshaft in the normal direction of rotation until No 1 piston is approaching TDC on its compression stroke. This can be established by feeling for compression being generated in No 1 cylinder (place a finger over the spark plug hole with the spark plug removed). As the piston nears TDC, check that the distributor rotor arm is nearly aligned with the No 1 cylinder HT lead segment in the distributor cap. Now continue turning the crankshaft very slowly until the mark on the camshaft sprocket is aligned with the pointer on the outer timing belt cover.
5 To keep the crankshaft in the TDC position, remove the brass plug from the crankcase, located just forward of the starter motor. Insert a dowel rod of suitable diameter to be a snug fit in the hole, to engage in the timing slot provided for this purpose in the crankshaft counterbalance weight (see illustrations). It may be necessary to move the crankshaft very slightly back and forth to check for positive engagement of the dowel rod in the crankshaft slot. Once in place it should be impossible to turn the crankshaft. If the crankshaft will still move to and fro slightly, then the dowel rod has entered a balance hole in the crankshaft, instead of the timing slot.

2A

3.5a Remove the brass plug from the crankcase . . .

3.5b . . . and insert a dowel rod (arrowed) to retain the crankshaft at TDC

4 Camshaft cover - removal and refitting

Removal

1 Refer to the relevant part of Chapter 4 and disconnect the accelerator cable from its attachment at the carburettor or pivot quadrant, and at the support bracket on the camshaft cover. On fuel-injected models, disconnect the throttle link rod from the linkage ball studs **(see illustration)**.
2 Detach the HT lead support bracket, crankcase ventilation hoses and (where applicable) the hot air inlet duct to the carburettor.
3 Undo the nuts and lift off the camshaft cover **(see illustration)**.
4 Remove the gasket, if necessary, and thoroughly clean the cover.

Refitting

5 Clean the mating face of the cylinder head and camshaft cover and if necessary locate a new gasket in position.
6 Position the cover on the cylinder head, refit the nuts and tighten them securely.
7 Reconnect the disturbed components using the reversal of removal. Adjust the accelerator cable as described in the relevant Part of Chapter 4.

5 Valve clearances - checking and adjustment

1 The importance of having the valve clearances correctly adjusted cannot be overstressed as they vitally affect the performance of the engine. That being said the check should not be regarded as routine maintenance and should only be carried out when the valve gear has become noisy, after engine overhaul, or when trying to trace the cause of power loss which may be attributed to the valve. The clearances are checked as follows noting that the engine must be cold (engine not having been started for at least two and a half hours) for the check to be accurate.
2 Access to the crankshaft pulley bolt (to turn the engine over) is extremely limited but it should just be possible to engage a socket and bar on the bolt from below. If this is not possible, then it will be necessary to remove the radiator (see Chapter 3) to gain the necessary working clearance.
3 Remove the camshaft cover as described in Section 4.
4 The procedure is now as follows according to engine type.

J6R (carburettor) engines

5 Position the engine with No 1 piston at TDC on its compression stroke as described in Section 3.

6 Turn the crankshaft clockwise (viewed from the front of the vehicle) by 90°. Looking through the viewing aperture on the timing belt rear cover (cylinder head side) check to see whether there is a mark on the camshaft sprocket rim at this point **(see illustration)**. If no mark is visible adjust the valve clearances as follows. If a mark is visible, use the procedure for the J7R/J7T engines beginning at paragraph 12.
7 It is important that the clearance of the relevant valve is checked and adjusted when the valve is fully closed and the rocker arm rests on the heel of the cam (directly opposite the peak). This can be ensured by carrying out the adjustments in the following sequence, remembering that number 1 cylinder is at the transmission end of the engine. Refer to the *Specifications* for the correct clearances, and note that the inlet valves are on the inlet manifold side of the engine and the exhaust valves are on the exhaust manifold side.

Valve fully open	Adjust valves
No 1 cyl exhaust	*No 3 cyl inlet and No 4 cyl exhaust*
No 3 cyl exhaust	*No 4 cyl inlet and No 2 cyl exhaust*
No 4 cyl exhaust	*No 2 cyl inlet and No 1 cyl exhaust*
No 2 cyl exhaust	*No 1 cyl inlet and No 3 cyl exhaust*

8 With the relevant valve fully open, check the clearances of the two valves specified. Clearances are checked by inserting a feeler blade of the correct thickness between the valve stem and the rocker arm adjusting screw, the feeler blade should be a light, sliding fit. If adjustment is necessary, slacken the adjusting screw locknut and turn the screw as necessary until the feeler blade is a light sliding fit. Once the correct clearance is obtained hold the adjusting screw and securely tighten the locknut **(see illustration)**. Recheck the valve clearance and adjust again if necessary.
9 Rotate the crankshaft until the next valve in the sequence is fully open and check the clearances of the next two specified valves.
10 Repeat the procedure until all eight valve

4.1 Disconnect the throttle link rod from the linkage ball studs (arrowed)

4.3 Undo the nuts and lift off the camshaft cover

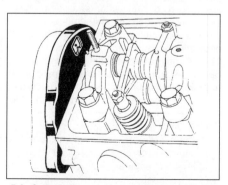

5.6 Camshaft sprocket mark aligned with pointer in timing belt rear cover

5.8 Valve clearance adjustment

clearances have been checked and, if necessary, adjusted.

11 Refit the camshaft cover as described in Section 4, and the radiator (if removed for access) as described in Chapter 3.

J7R/J7T (fuel-injected) engines

12 Position the engine with No 1 piston at TDC on its compression stroke as described in Section 3.

13 Turn the crankshaft clockwise (viewed from the front of the vehicle) by 90°. Looking through the viewing aperture on the timing belt rear cover (cylinder head side) align the mark on the rear face of the camshaft sprocket rim with the pointer in the rear cover **(see illustration 5.6)**. The clearance for No 2 cylinder inlet valve and No 4 cylinder exhaust valve can now be checked with feeler blades and, if necessary adjusted to the figures given in the *Specifications*. Note that the inlet valves are on the inlet manifold side of the engine and the exhaust valves are on the exhaust manifold side.

14 If adjustment is necessary, slacken the adjusting screw locknut and turn the screw as necessary until the feeler blade is a light sliding fit. Once the correct clearance is obtained hold the adjusting screw and securely tighten the locknut. Recheck the valve clearance and adjust again if necessary.

15 Turn the crankshaft 180° clockwise (viewed from the front of the vehicle) until the second mark on the sprocket is aligned with the pointer. Adjust the next pair of valves then continue with the procedure as shown in the table below, turning the crankshaft 180° clockwise each time.

16 Repeat the procedure until all eight valve clearances have been checked and, if necessary, adjusted.

17 Refit the camshaft cover as described in Section 4, and the radiator (if removed for access) as described in Chapter 3.

6 Crankshaft pulley - removal and refitting

Removal

1 As access to the crankshaft pulley is very limited when the engine is fitted to the vehicle, drain the cooling system (Chapter 1) then remove the radiator as described in Chapter 3.

2 Remove the auxiliary drivebelts as described in Chapter 1.

3 To prevent crankshaft rotation whilst the pulley retaining bolt is slackened, select top gear and have an assistant apply the brakes firmly. If the engine has been removed from the vehicle, lock the flywheel ring gear using the arrangement shown **(see illustration 3.5a and 3.5 b)**. **Do not** attempt to lock the crankshaft by inserting the locking pin through the cylinder block and into the crankshaft TDC slot.

4 Unscrew the retaining bolt and remove the pulley from the end of the crankshaft.

Refitting

5 Locate the pulley on the end of the crankshaft, aligning its locating holes with the sprocket roll pins, and refit the retaining bolt.

6 Lock the crankshaft by the method used on removal and tighten the pulley retaining bolt to the specified torque setting.

7 Refit the auxiliary drivebelts as described in Chapter 1.

8 Refit the radiator as described in Chapter 3.

7 Timing belt cover - removal and refitting

Removal

1 As access to the timing belt cover and its associated components is very limited when the engine is fitted to the vehicle, drain the cooling system (Chapter 1) then remove the radiator as described in Chapter 3.

2 Remove all the auxiliary drivebelts as described in Chapter 1. Note that on vehicles equipped with air conditioning and having their drivebelt situated behind the timing belt, this drivebelt can be left in position.

3 Undo the nuts and free the cable guide from the front of the timing belt cover **(see illustration)**.

4 Work around the cover and remove all the nuts and bolts along with their washers.

7.3 Undo the nuts (arrowed) and free the cable guide from the timing belt cover

5 Carefully withdraw the cover from the engine compartment and recover the collars and distance sleeves from the centre of the cover rubber mountings.

6 Examine the cover mounting rubbers for signs of damage or deterioration and renew as necessary.

Refitting

7 Ensure all the cover mounting rubbers are correctly fitted and fit the collars into position in the centre of each rubber. Also fit the distance sleeves to the relevant studs.

8 Refit the timing belt cover to the engine, taking great care not to displace the mounting rubbers or collars. Refit the washers and cover retaining nuts and bolts, tightening them securely.

9 Refit the cable guide and securely tighten its retaining nuts.

10 Refit the auxiliary drivebelts as described in Chapter 1.

11 Refit the radiator as described in Chapter 3.

8 Timing belt - removal, inspection and refitting

Removal

1 Disconnect the battery negative lead.

2 Position No 1 piston at TDC as described in Section 3 and lock the crankshaft in position with the locking pin.

3 Remove the timing belt cover as described in Section 7.

4 Remove the crankshaft pulley as described in Section 6. To prevent the possibility of the locking pin being damaged, remove the pin temporarily as the pulley retaining bolt is slackened and refit it once the bolt is slack.

5 With the crankshaft locking pin inserted, check that the camshaft and auxiliary shaft sprockets are correctly positioned **(see illustration)**. Temporarily lay the timing belt cover in position to check that the timing mark on the camshaft sprocket is aligned with the pointer in the cover upper window, and a similar mark on the auxiliary shaft sprocket is aligned with the pointer in the cover lower

Camshaft sprocket mark aligned with pointer:	Inlet valve to adjust on cylinder:	Exhaust valve to adjust on cylinder:
1st mark	2	4
2nd mark	1	2
3rd mark	3	1
4th mark	4	3

2A

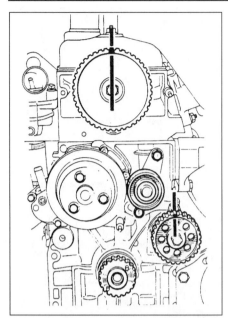

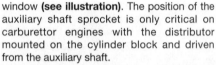

8.5a Correct alignment of camshaft and auxiliary shaft sprockets with No 1 piston at TDC

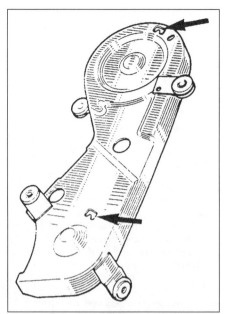

8.5b TDC pointers (arrowed) in the timing belt cover

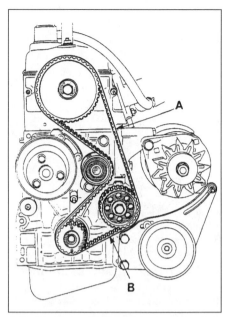

8.12 The timing belt must be taut at points A and B

window (see illustration). The position of the auxiliary shaft sprocket is only critical on carburettor engines with the distributor mounted on the cylinder block and driven from the auxiliary shaft.

6 On early engines with a spring-loaded timing belt tensioner, slacken the tensioner retaining bolt and nut, push the tensioner against spring pressure to relieve tension on the belt, and retighten the upper nut. Take care if completely removing the tensioner, that the spring and piston do not fly out of their apertures at high speed.

7 On later engines with a manually-adjusted timing belt tensioner, slacken the tensioner pulley centre nut and tensioner backplate upper bolt. Pivot the tensioner pulley and backplate away from the belt to release the belt tension.

8 Slip the timing belt off the sprockets and remove it from the engine. Store the belt on its edge while removed if it is to be re-used.

Inspection

9 Check the timing belt carefully for any signs of uneven wear, splitting or oil contamination and renew it if there is the slightest doubt about its condition. If the engine is undergoing an overhaul and has covered more than or close to 72 000 miles (115 000 km) since the original belt was fitted, renew the belt as a matter of course. If signs of oil contamination are found, trace the source of the oil leak and rectify it, then wash down the engine timing belt area and all related components to remove all traces of oil. Whilst the belt is removed examine the tensioner and sprocket components as described in Section 9.

10 Note that during the course of production, the timing belt and sprocket tooth profile has

been changed from round section to square section. Ensure that the correct type of belt is obtained if renewal is necessary.

Refitting

11 Prior to refitting the timing belt, check that the crankshaft is still positioned at TDC for No 1 piston, and locked with the locking pin. Check that the camshaft and auxiliary shaft sprockets are correctly aligned with the relevant pointers in the timing belt cover as described in paragraph 5. If the camshaft sprocket has been removed ensure that the correct timing marks are in alignment, according to engine type (see Section 9).

12 Offer up the timing belt and, starting at the crankshaft sprocket and working in an anti-clockwise direction, engage the belt with the auxiliary shaft and camshaft sprockets and then round the tensioner. Keep the belt taught as it is fed over the sprockets, ensure that the belt teeth are correctly seated centrally in the sprockets and the timing marks remain in alignment (see illustration). If a used belt is being refitted, ensure that the arrow mark made on removal points in the normal direction of rotation as before. Tension the timing belt according to tensioner type as follows.

Early engines with spring-loaded tensioner

13 Slacken the tensioner retaining nut and bolt. Check that the tensioner pulley is forced against the timing belt under spring pressure then securely tighten the retaining nut and bolt.

14 Refit the crankshaft pulley (Section 6).

15 Now turn the crankshaft two complete turns in a clockwise direction, returning to the

TDC position. **Do not** under any circumstances rotate the crankshaft anti-clockwise.

16 Refit the crankshaft locking pin and check that the camshaft and auxiliary shaft sprocket timing marks are still correctly aligned when the timing belt cover is temporarily placed in position. Remove the locking pin and refit the brass plug.

17 Release the tensioner bolt and nut about a quarter turn each, then retighten first the bolt, then the nut, to the specified torque.

18 Check that the belt deflection midway between the camshaft and auxiliary shaft sprockets is as specified, under moderate thumb pressure.

19 Refit the timing belt cover (Section 7) and reconnect the battery.

Later engines with manually adjusted tensioner

20 Pivot the tensioner backplate towards the timing belt until the upper retaining bolt is located at the mid-point of the backplate slot. Hold the backplate in this position and tighten the bolt to the specified torque.

21 The timing belt tension is set by rotating the eccentric tensioner pulley using a peg spanner fitted to the two holes in the pulley. In the absence of the special Renault peg spanner (Mot. 1135), a home-made peg spanner can be fabricated. Alternatively, obtain two suitable diameter bolts and insert these in the holes in the pulley hub; the pulley can then be rotated using a screwdriver or bar inserted between the bolts.

22 Using one of the methods described, rotate the tensioner pulley towards the belt. Tension is correct when the deflection midway between the camshaft and auxiliary

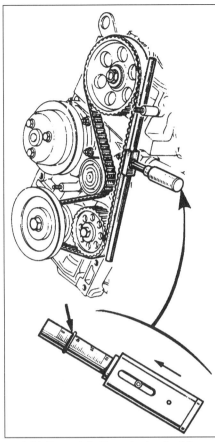

8.22 Renault belt tensioning tool for checking timing belt tension

shaft sprockets is as given in the Specifications. Ideally the Renault belt tensioning tool (Ele. 346) should be used to accurately check the tension **(see illustration)**. In the absence of this tool, an approximate setting may be achieved by measuring the belt deflection under firm thumb pressure. It must be stressed, however, that this is only an approximate check, the tension can only be accurately checked using the Renault tool.

23 With the belt correctly tensioned, hold the tensioner pulley stationary and tighten the pulley retaining nut to the specified torque.

24 Refit the crankshaft pulley (Section 6) then turn the crankshaft two complete turns in a clockwise direction, returning to the TDC position. **Do not** under any circumstances rotate the crankshaft anti-clockwise. Refit the crankshaft locking pin and check that the camshaft and auxiliary shaft sprocket timing marks are still correctly aligned when the timing belt cover is temporarily placed in position. Remove the locking pin and refit the brass plug.

25 Recheck the timing belt deflection. If the belt deflection is being checked without the Renault tool, the tension must be checked by a Renault dealer at the earliest opportunity.

26 Refit the timing belt cover (Section 7) and reconnect the battery.

9.4 Removing the crankshaft sprocket

9 Timing belt tensioner and sprockets - removal, inspection and refitting

Removal

1 Remove the timing belt as described in Section 8, then proceed as described under the relevant sub-heading.

Camshaft sprocket

2 Slacken the camshaft sprocket retaining bolt whilst holding the sprocket stationary with a suitable peg spanner which engages with the sprocket holes. A suitable home-made tool can be fabricated from two lengths of steel strip (one long, the other short) and three nuts and bolts; one nut and bolt forming the pivot of a forked tool with the remaining two nuts and bolts at the tips of the "forks" to engage with the sprocket holes.

3 Unscrew the retaining bolt and washer and remove the sprocket from the end of the camshaft, noting which way around it is fitted. If the Woodruff key is a loose fit in the camshaft end, remove it and store it with the sprocket for safe-keeping. Note that the camshaft must not be rotated whilst the sprocket is removed.

Crankshaft sprocket

4 With the crankshaft pulley removed, slide the sprocket off the end of the crankshaft.

Using a home-made tool to hold the camshaft sprocket stationary whilst the bolt is tightened (shown with cylinder head removed)

9.7 Removing the auxiliary shaft sprocket

Note which way round the sprocket is fitted to avoid confusion when refitting. Extract the Woodruff key from the crankshaft end and store it with the sprocket for safe-keeping **(see illustration)**.

5 On models not equipped with air conditioning, slide the spacer off the end of the crankshaft and store it with the sprocket.

6 On models with air conditioning, the air conditioning compressor drivebelt drive pulley is situated behind the crankshaft sprocket. Where necessary, remove the drivebelt (see Chapter 1) and slide off the drive pulley.

Auxiliary shaft sprocket

7 Using the method given in paragraph 2, slacken and remove the retaining bolt and washer and slide the sprocket off the end of the shaft **(see illustration)**. If the Woodruff key is a loose fit in the shaft, remove it and store it with the sprocket for safe-keeping.

Tensioner assembly

8 On early engines with a spring-loaded tensioner, slacken and remove the tensioner retaining nut and bolt along with their washers, whilst firmly holding the tensioner pulley. With the nut and bolt removed, slowly pivot the pulley assembly away from the spring, until all tension is relieved, then remove the tensioner pulley assembly and withdraw the plunger and spring from the housing **(see illustrations)**.

9 On later engines with a manually-operated tensioner, undo the tensioner nut and bolts and remove the assembly from the cylinder block.

9.8a Remove the timing belt tensioner pulley assembly . . .

2A

9.8b ... and withdraw the plunger and spring

Inspection

10 Thoroughly clean the relevant sprocket(s) and renew any that show signs of wear, damage or cracks. Note that during the course of production the tooth profile has been changed from round section to square section. Ensure that the correct type of sprocket is obtained if component renewal is necessary.

11 Clean the tensioner pulley but do not use any strong solvent which may enter the pulley bearings. Check that the pulley rotates freely on the backplate, with no sign of stiffness or of free play. Renew the assembly if there is any doubt about its condition or if there are any obvious signs of wear or damage. On spring-loaded tensioners, It is recommended that the tensioner spring is renewed regardless of its apparent condition, since its condition is critical.

Refitting

Camshaft sprocket

12 Refit the Woodruff key (where removed) to the slot in the camshaft end and slide on the

sprocket. Note that where the sprocket is of the type having five round holes and a single square hole, the sprocket can be fitted in either of two ways, according to engine type. With reference to the sprocket, it can be seen that there are two keyways in the sprocket hub **(see illustration)**. Adjacent to one keyway there is a square hole and two identifying bosses, adjacent to the other keyway there is a round hole and one identifying boss. On J6R and J7R engines, fit the sprocket so that the camshaft Woodruff key engages with the keyway adjacent to the round hole and single boss. On J7T engines, fit the sprocket so that the camshaft Woodruff key engages with the keyway adjacent to the square hole and two bosses. In all cases fit the sprocket so that the hub offset is towards the cylinder head **(see illustration)**.

13 Refit the sprocket retaining bolt and washer and tighten it to the specified torque setting whilst preventing rotation using the method employed on removal.

14 Refit the timing belt as described in Section 8.

Crankshaft sprocket

15 On models not equipped with air conditioning, slide the spacer onto the end of the crankshaft.

16 On models with air conditioning, where necessary, slide the drive pulley onto the crankshaft and refit the air conditioning compressor drivebelt as described in Chapter 2.

17 Refit the Woodruff key to the slot in the crankshaft, and slide on the sprocket ensuring it is fitted the correct way around. On models equipped with air conditioning, ensure that the sprocket roll pins engage correctly with the holes in the drive pulley.

18 Refit the timing belt as described in Section 8.

Auxiliary shaft sprocket

19 Refit the Woodruff key to the auxiliary shaft slot and slide on the sprocket with its

large offset inner face towards the crankcase **(see illustration)**. If the sprocket is installed incorrectly it will not be aligned centrally with the timing belt.

20 Refit the retaining bolt and washer and tighten it to the specified torque setting, using the method employed on removal to prevent rotation.

21 Refit the timing belt as described in Section 8.

Tensioner assembly

22 On early engines with a spring-loaded tensioner, fit the spring to the inside of the plunger and refit the plunger assembly to the housing. Compress the plunger and manoeuvre the tensioner pulley assembly into position. Refit the tensioner retaining nut and bolt and check that the tensioner assembly pivots smoothly and is forced towards the timing belt by the tensioner spring. Pivot the pulley fully away from the timing belt and securely tighten its retaining nut and bolt to keep it there.

23 On later engines with a manually-operated tensioner, locate the unit on the cylinder block. refit the nut and bolts and tighten the lower bolt securely. Pivot the pulley fully away from the timing belt and lightly tighten its retaining nut and bolt to keep it there.

24 On all engines, refit the timing belt as described in Section 8.

10 Camshaft and auxiliary shaft oil seals - renewal

Camshaft oil seal

1 Remove the camshaft sprocket as described in Section 9, then unbolt and remove the timing belt rear cover.

2 Punch or drill two small holes opposite each other in the oil seal. Screw a self-tapping screw into each and pull on the screws with pliers to extract the seal.

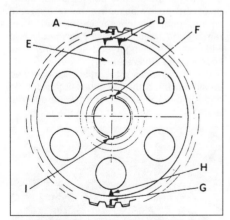

9.12a Camshaft sprocket identification
A Timing mark for J7T engines
D Identifying bosses for J7T engines
E Square hole
F Keyway for use with J7T engines
G Timing mark for J6R and J7R engines
H Identifying boss for J6R and J7R engines
I Keyway for J6R and J7R engines

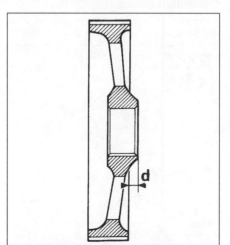

9.12b Fit the camshaft sprocket so that the hub offset (d) is towards the cylinder head

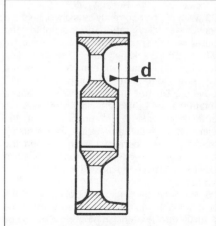

9.19 Fit the auxiliary shaft sprocket so the hub offset (d) is towards the crankcase

3 Clean the seal housing and polish off any burrs or raised edges which may have caused the seal to fail in the first place.

4 Lubricate the lips of the new seal with clean engine oil and ease it into position on the end of the shaft. Press the seal into its housing using a suitable tubular drift, such as a socket, which bears only on the hard outer edge of the seal. Take great care not to damage the seal lips during fitting and ensure that the seal lips face inwards.

5 Refit the timing belt rear cover then refit the camshaft sprocket as described in Section 9.

Auxiliary shaft oil seal

6 Remove the auxiliary shaft sprocket as described in Section 9.

7 Undo the retaining bolts and slide the auxiliary shaft cover off the end of the shaft. Recover the gasket and discard it, a new one should be used on refitting.

8 Using a suitable flat-bladed screwdriver, lever the seal out of the cover whilst taking great care not to mark the cover.

9 Position the new seal in the cover and tap it into position using a suitable tubular drift, such as a socket, which bears only on the hard outer edge of the seal. Ensure that the seal lip is facing inwards.

10 Remove all traces of gasket from the cover and cylinder block/crankcase mating surfaces and position a new gasket on the cylinder block.

11 Slide the cover into position carefully easing the seal over the end of the auxiliary shaft.

12 To prevent the possibility of oil leakage smear the shafts of the cover retaining bolts with a suitable sealant. Renault recommend the use of Loctite sealant (available from your Renault dealer); in the absence of this ensure a good quality sealant is used.

13 Ensure the gasket is correctly positioned then refit the cover retaining bolts and tighten them securely.

14 Refit the auxiliary shaft sprocket as described in Section 9.

11 Cylinder head - removal and refitting

Removal

1 Remove the camshaft cover as described in Section 4.

2 Remove the timing belt as described in Section 8.

3 If not already done, drain the cooling system as described in Chapter 1.

4 Refer to the relevant part of Chapter 4 and remove the air cleaner and inlet ducting as necessary for access.

5 Disconnect the appropriate cooling system hoses, vacuum hoses and wiring connections to the cylinder head and its associated components. Take note of and label their respective connections as they are detached to avoid confusion on refitting.

6 Disconnect and plug the fuel hoses to prevent leakage and the ingress of dirt.

7 Detach the distributor cap and HT leads and remove the rotor arm.

8 Remove the inlet and exhaust manifolds as described in the relevant Part of Chapter 4.

9 Working in the reverse of the sequence shown (**see illustration 11.26b**), progressively slacken the cylinder head bolts by half a turn at a time until all can be unscrewed by hand.

10 With the exception of the front right-hand bolt, remove each cylinder head bolt and washer.

11 With the front right-hand bolt still in position, the joint between the cylinder head and gasket and the cylinder block/crankcase must now be broken without disturbing the wet liners; although these liners are better located and sealed than some wet liner engines, there is still a risk of coolant and foreign matter leaking into the sump if the cylinder head is lifted carelessly. If care is not taken and the liners are moved, there is also a possibility of the bottom seals being disturbed, causing leakage after refitting the head.

12 To break the joint, strike the side of the head firmly at the rear using a soft-faced mallet or hammer and block of wood.

13 Once the gasket seal is broken, remove the right-hand front bolt and washer from the cylinder head. If required, the rocker shaft assembly can now be removed.

14 The cylinder head can then be lifted out of the engine compartment; use assistance if possible as it is an awkward assembly. Remove the gasket from the top of the block, noting the position of the locating dowel. If the dowel is a loose fit, remove it and store it with the head for safe-keeping.

15 Note **do not** attempt to rotate the crankshaft with the cylinder head removed, otherwise the wet liners may be displaced. Operations that require the rotation of the crankshaft (eg cleaning the piston crowns), should only be carried out once the cylinder liners are firmly clamped in position. In the absence of the special Renault liner clamping tool (Mot. 521-01), the liners can be clamped in position using large flat washers positioned underneath suitable-length bolts, or the original head bolts with suitable spacers fitted to their shanks (**see illustration**).

16 If the cylinder head is to be dismantled for overhaul, remove the camshaft as described in Section 12, then refer to the relevant Sections of Part C of this Chapter.

Preparation for refitting

17 The mating faces of the cylinder head and cylinder block/crankcase must be perfectly clean before refitting the head. Use a hard plastic or wood scraper to remove all traces of gasket and carbon; also clean the piston crowns. Take particular care as the soft aluminium alloy is damaged easily. Also, make sure that the carbon is not allowed to enter the oil and water passages - this is particularly important for the lubrication system, as carbon could block the oil supply to any of the engine's components. Using adhesive tape and paper, seal the water, oil and bolt holes in the cylinder block/crankcase. To prevent carbon entering the gap between the pistons and bores, smear a little grease in the gap. After cleaning each piston, use a small brush to remove all traces of grease and carbon from the gap, then wipe away the remainder with a clean rag. Clean all the pistons in the same way.

18 Check the mating surfaces of the cylinder block/crankcase and the cylinder head for nicks, deep scratches and other damage. If slight, they may be removed carefully with a file, but if excessive, machining may be the only alternative to renewal.

19 If warpage is suspected of the cylinder head gasket surface, use a straight-edge to check it for distortion. Refer to Part C of this Chapter if necessary.

20 Prior to refitting the cylinder head, check the cylinder liner protrusion as described in Section 13 of Part C of this Chapter. Although the measuring procedure specifies that the liners should be fitted without seals, the seals have no effect on liner protrusion. If the liner protrusion exceeds the specified limits, seek the advice of a Renault dealer prior to refitting the head.

21 When purchasing a new cylinder head gasket, it is essential that the latest type asbestos-free gasket is obtained. This has been fitted to all engines since February 1992 to overcome problems of oil leakage into the cooling system, and can be fitted retrospectively to earlier engines. Note that with this type of gasket and method of tightening the cylinder head bolts, new bolts must always be used whenever they are removed.

Refitting

22 Wipe clean the mating surfaces of the cylinder head and cylinder block/crankcase. Check that the locating dowel is in position at the front right-hand corner of the cylinder block/crankcase surface. Where necessary, remove the cylinder liner clamps.

11.15 Fabricated liner clamps

2A

11.23 Position the new gasket on the cylinder block/crankcase surface

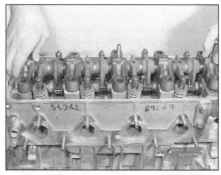

11.24 Lower the rocker arm assembly into position on the cylinder head

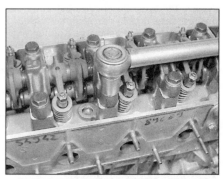

11.26a Tighten the cylinder head bolts in sequence

23 Position the new gasket on the cylinder block/crankcase surface then, with the aid of an assistant lower the head into position, engaging it with the locating dowel **(see illustration)**.

24 Lower the rocker arm assembly into position on the cylinder head, ensuring that the thrust plate engages correctly with the camshaft slot **(see illustration)**.

25 Using new cylinder head bolts, lightly lubricate the threads and underside of the bolt heads with engine oil then refit the bolts.

26 Working in the sequence shown, tighten all the head bolts to the Stage 1 torque setting given in the *Specifications* using a torque wrench **(see illustrations)**.

27 Once all the bolts have been tightened to their Stage 1 setting, working again in the given sequence, angle-tighten the bolts through the specified Stage 2 angle, using a socket and extension bar. It is recommended that an angle-measuring gauge is used during this stage of the tightening, to ensure accuracy. If a gauge is not available, use white paint to make alignment marks between the bolt head and cylinder head prior to tightening; the marks can then be used to check that the bolt has been rotated through the correct angle during tightening.

28 Finally, wait three minutes then tighten the bolts again, in the given sequence through the specified Stage 3 angle. Note that no further tightening of the cylinder head bolts will be necessary.

29 Refit the inlet and exhaust manifolds as described in the relevant Part of Chapter 4.

30 Refit the rotor arm, distributor cap and HT leads.

31 Reconnect the fuel hoses.

32 Using the notes made during removal, reconnect the appropriate cooling system hoses, vacuum hoses and wiring connections to the cylinder head and its associated components.

33 Refer to the relevant part of Chapter 4 and refit the air cleaner and inlet ducting removed for access.

34 Refit the timing belt as described in Section 8.

35 Adjust the valve clearances then refit the camshaft cover as described in Sections 5 and 4 respectively.

36 Refill the cooling system as described in Chapter 1.

12 Camshaft and rocker arms - removal, inspection and refitting

Removal

Rocker arm assembly

1 Remove the cylinder head as described in Section 11. With the cylinder head on the bench, the rocker arm assembly can be lifted out.

2 To dismantle the rocker arm assembly, unscrew the bolt from the rear end of the

rocker shaft whilst retaining the rocker pedestal to prevent it be sprung off the end of the shaft. Recover the oil filter from inside the shaft then slide off the various components, keeping all components in their correct fitted order. Make a note of each components correct fitted position as it is removed, to ensure it is positioned correctly on reassembly **(see illustration)**.

3 To separate the front pedestal and shaft, extract the roll pin from the top of the pedestal - renew this roll pin if it is not of the solid type. If necessary, the camshaft thrust plate can also be unbolted from the front of the pedestal.

Camshaft

4 Remove the cylinder head and rocker arm assembly as previously described.

5 Remove the camshaft sprocket as described in Section 9.

6 Punch or drill two small holes opposite each other in the camshaft oil seal. Screw a self-tapping screw into each and pull on the screws with pliers to extract the seal.

7 Slide the camshaft out of the front of the cylinder head.

Inspection

Rocker arm assembly

8 Examine the rocker arm bearing surfaces which contact the camshaft lobes for wear ridges and scoring. Renew any rocker arms

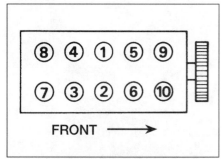

11.26b Cylinder head bolt tightening sequence

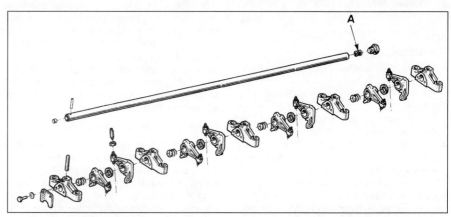

12.2 Exploded view of the rocker arm assembly. Note oil filter (A)

on which these conditions are apparent. If a rocker arm bearing surface is badly scored also examine the corresponding lobe on the camshaft for wear as it is likely that both will be worn. Renew worn components as necessary, the rocker arm assembly can be dismantled as in paragraphs 2 and 3. Renew the shaft retaining roll pin and rocker shaft oil filter regardless of its apparent condition.

9 Inspect the ends of the adjusting screws for signs of wear or damage and renew as required.

10 If the rocker arm assembly has been dismantled, examine the rocker arm and shaft bearing surfaces for wear ridges and scoring. If there are obvious signs of wear, the relevant rocker arm(s) and/or shaft must be renewed. Also check that the rocker arm oil holes are clear by passing a piece of wire through each one.

Camshaft

11 Examine the camshaft bearing surfaces and cam lobes for signs of wear ridges and scoring. Renew the camshaft if any of these conditions are apparent. Examine the condition of the bearing surfaces both on the camshaft journals and in the cylinder head. If the head bearing surfaces are worn excessively, the cylinder head will need to be renewed.

12 Examine the camshaft thrust plate for signs of wear or scoring. If worn, the thrust plate must be renewed otherwise camshaft endfloat will be excessive. The thrust plate is secured to the front of the front rocker arm pedestal by two bolts.

Refitting

Camshaft

13 Ensure the cylinder head and camshaft bearing surfaces are clean then liberally oil the camshaft bearings and lobes and slide the camshaft back into position in the cylinder head.

14 Lubricate the lips of the new seal with clean engine oil and ease it into position on the end of the shaft **(see illustration)**. Press the seal into the cylinder head using a suitable tubular drift, such as a socket, which bears only on the hard outer edge of the seal can be used to tap the seal into position. Take great

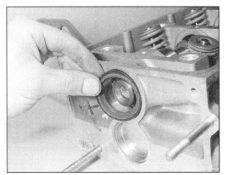

12.14 Lubricate the new oil seal with oil, and ease it into position over the camshaft

care not to damage the seal lips during fitting and ensure that the seal lips face inwards.

15 Refit the camshaft sprocket as described in Section 9.

16 Refit the rocker arm assembly as follows.

Rocker arm assembly

17 If the rocker arm assembly was dismantled, refit the rocker shaft to the front pedestal, aligning its locating hole with the pedestal threaded hole, and fit a new roll pin. Apply a smear of clean engine oil to the shaft then slide on all removed components, ensuring each is correctly fitted in its original position.

18 Once all components are in position on the shaft, compress the rear pedestal. Install the new oil filter in the shaft bore, then refit the bolt and tighten it to the specified torque setting.

19 Lower the rocker arm assembly into position on the cylinder head, ensuring that the thrust plate engages correctly with the camshaft slot.

20 Refit the cylinder head (see Section 11).

13 Sump - removal and refitting

Note: *Three different types of sump may be fitted according to model year. These will be either a single-piece steel sump, a single-piece aluminium sump or a two-piece sump comprising a small steel lower pan bolted to an aluminium strengthening base. The strengthening base is in turn bolted to the underside of the crankcase. Identify the type fitted then proceed as follows under the appropriate sub-heading.*

Removal

Single-piece steel sump

1 Disconnect the battery negative lead.

2 Referring to Chapter 1, drain the engine oil, then clean and refit the engine oil drain plug, tightening it securely. If the engine is nearing its service interval when the oil and filter are due for renewal, it is recommended that the filter is also removed and a new one fitted. After reassembly, the engine can then be replenished with fresh engine oil.

3 Chock the rear wheels then jack up the front of the vehicle and support it on axle stands (see "*Jacking and vehicle support*").

4 To gain the necessary clearance required to remove the sump, the engine must be raised slightly. To do this, from underneath the vehicle undo the nuts securing the front engine mountings to the chassis member brackets. Attach a hoist or engine support bar to the lifting bracket attached to the front of the cylinder head and raise the engine slightly. On later models with a detachable crossmember, removal of the crossmember alone may provide sufficient clearance without the need to raise the engine.

5 On later models, undo the bolts and remove the crossmember for access to the rear sump bolts. Note the location of the engine earth strap.

6 Remove the flywheel cover plate from the bellhousing.

7 Disconnect the breather hose from the sump (where fitted) then progressively slacken and remove the sump retaining bolts.

8 Break the joint by striking the sump with the palm of the hand, then lower the sump and withdraw it from underneath the vehicle. Discard the sump gasket, a new one should be used on refitting.

9 While the sump is removed, take the opportunity to inspect the oil pump strainer mesh for signs of clogging or splitting and clean/renew as necessary.

Single-piece aluminium sump

10 Carry out the operations described in paragraphs 1 to 5 above.

11 Where fitted, remove the oil level sensor from the lower left-hand side of the cylinder block.

12 Slacken and remove the three bolts securing the transmission housing to the rear of the sump.

13 Disconnect the breather hose from the sump (where necessary) then progressively slacken and remove the sump retaining bolts noting their locations and different lengths **(see illustration)**. Withdraw each bolt in turn and store it in its correct fitted order by pushing it through a clearly-marked cardboard template.

14 Break the joint by striking the sump with the palm of the hand, then lower the sump and withdraw it from underneath the vehicle. Discard the sump gasket, a new one should be used on refitting.

15 While the sump is removed, take the opportunity to inspect the oil pump strainer mesh for signs of clogging or splitting and clean/renew as necessary.

Two-piece sump

16 Carry out the operations described in paragraphs 1 to 5 above.

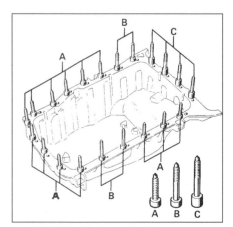

13.13 Single-piece aluminium sump bolt locations

2A

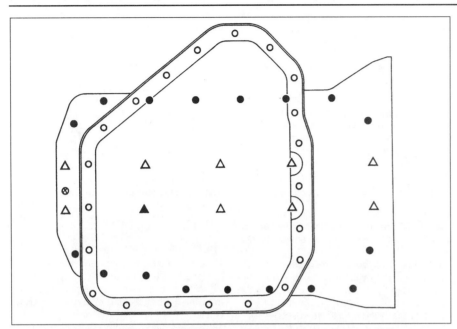

13.23 Two-piece sump and strengthening base bolt locations and sizes
White circles = 6 mm   Black circles = 7 mm   Triangles = 10 mm

17 Where fitted, remove the oil level sensor from the lower left-hand side of the cylinder block.

18 Progressively slacken and remove the bolts securing the steel sump pan to the strengthening base.

19 Break the joint by striking the sump pan with the palm of the hand, then lower the pan and withdraw it from underneath the vehicle. Discard the gasket, a new one should be used on refitting.

20 Slacken and remove the three bolts securing the transmission housing to the rear of the strengthening base.

21 Undo the four bolts and remove the oil pump cover and strainer assembly from the pump body. Collect the two pump gears.

22 Undo the remaining two bolts, remove the oil pump body and withdraw the pump driveshaft.

23 Progressively slacken the strengthening base retaining bolts. Note that there are three different bolt sizes located as shown **(see illustration)**. Withdraw each bolt in turn and store it in its correct fitted order by pushing it through a clearly-marked cardboard template.

24 Break the joint by striking the strengthening base with the palm of the hand, then lower the base and withdraw it from underneath the vehicle. Discard the gasket, a new one should be used on refitting.

Refitting

Single-piece steel and aluminium sumps

25 Clean all traces of gasket from the mating surfaces of the cylinder block/crankcase and sump, then use a clean rag to wipe out the sump and the engine's interior.

26 Position the new gasket on the sump

mating surface and manoeuvre the sump into position.

27 Refit the sump retaining bolts, ensuring that all bolts are fitted in the correct locations, and tighten them finger tight only at this stage.

28 On aluminium sumps, refit the three bolts securing the transmission housing to the sump and tighten them securely.

29 Once the transmission housing bolts are tight, evenly and progressively tighten the sump retaining bolts. Where fitted, reconnect the breather hose to the sump.

30 On steel sumps, refit the flywheel cover plate to the bellhousing.

31 Lower the engine back into position on the mounting brackets and remove the hoist/engine support bar (as applicable). Refit the nuts securing the engine mountings to the brackets and tighten them to the specified torque setting.

32 Refit the crossmember and the oil level sensor (where fitted).

33 Lower the vehicle to the ground, reconnect the battery and replenish the engine oil as described in Chapter 1.

Two-piece sump

34 Clean all traces of gasket from the mating surfaces of the cylinder block/crankcase, the strengthening base and sump, then use a clean rag to wipe out the sump and the engine's interior.

35 Position the new gasket on the strengthening base mating surface using a few drops of gasket sealer to just hold it in place.

36 Manoeuvre the base into position and refit the retaining bolts tightening them finger tight only at this stage. Make sure that all the bolts are fitted in their correct locations.

37 Refit the three bolts securing the strengthening base to the bellhousing. Tighten these bolts finger tight only at this stage also.

38 Tighten the strengthening base-to-crankcase bolts progressively, to the torque figures given in the *Specifications*.

39 Check that the circlip is securely located in the groove in the base of the oil pump driveshaft. Insert the driveshaft into position, noting that the circlip must be at the lower end of the shaft.

40 With the locating dowels in position, manoeuvre the oil pump body into position, refit the two bolts and tighten them to the specified torque.

41 Refit the two oil pump gears, liberally lubricated with clean engine oil, and the pump cover and strainer assembly. Secure the cover with the four bolts.

42 Using a new gasket, refit the steel sump pan to the strengthening base and tighten the bolts progressively to the specified torque.

43 Fully tighten the three bolts securing the strengthening base to the bellhousing.

44 Lower the engine back into position and remove the hoist/engine support bar (as applicable). Refit the nuts securing the engine mountings to the chassis brackets and tighten them to the specified torque setting.

45 Refit the crossmember and the oil level sensor (where fitted).

46 Lower the vehicle to the ground, reconnect the battery and replenish the engine oil as described in Chapter 1.

---

14 Oil pump - removal, inspection and refitting

Removal

Engines with single-piece sumps

1 Remove the sump (Section 13).

2 Slacken and remove the pump retaining bolts then lower the pump away from the base of the cylinder block/crankcase.

3 With the pump removed withdraw the pump driveshaft noting that the circlip is at the lower end of the shaft.

Engines with two-piece sumps

4 Remove the sump (Section 13). Note that it will only be necessary to remove the small sump pan; the strengthening base can be left in position.

5 Undo the four bolts and remove the oil pump cover and strainer assembly from the pump body. Collect the two pump gears.

6 Undo the remaining two bolts, remove the oil pump body and withdraw the pump driveshaft.

Inspection

Note: *No oil pump components are available separately. If the pump is worn it must be renewed as a complete unit.*

7 Undo the pump cover retaining bolts then separate the cover from the main pump body and withdraw the pump gears.

8 Clean all components in a suitable solvent and examine them for wear or damage.

9 Refit the gears to the pump housing and using feeler blades measure the clearance between each gear and the pump body.

10 Using feeler blades and a straight-edge placed across the top of the pump body and gears, measure the gear endfloat.

11 Remove the split pin and withdraw the spring cup, spring, guide and pressure relief piston from the pump body. Examine all the pressure relief valve components for signs of wear or damage. Discard the split pin a new one should be used on reassembly.

12 Compare the clearances found with the specified limits given in the Specifications at the start of this Chapter. If any clearance exceeds the specified limit, or there is obvious signs of wear or damage on any component then the pump must be renewed complete; no pump components are available separately.

13 Examine the pump driveshaft ends for signs of wear or damage and renew if necessary. If the driveshaft end(s) round off, the oil pump will cease to work, leading to a loss of oil pressure which will result in serious engine damage. Therefore the condition of the driveshaft is critical.

14 If all is well, lubricate the pump components with clean engine oil. Refit the pressure relief valve components, and secure them in position with a new split pin. Except on engines with a two-piece sump, refit the gears to the pump body and wipe clean the pump body and cover mating surfaces. Refit the cover to the body and securely tighten its bolts.

Refitting

Engines with single-piece sumps

15 Check that the circlip is securely located in the groove in the base of the driveshaft. Insert the driveshaft into position, noting that the circlip must be at the lower end of the shaft, ensuring that it is correctly engaged with its drive gear.

16 With the locating dowels in position, manoeuvre the oil pump into position, ensuring that the pump is correctly engaged with the driveshaft. Refit the pump mounting bolts and tighten them to the specified torque.

17 Refit the sump as described in Section 13.

Engines with two-piece sumps

18 Check that the circlip is securely located in the groove in the base of the driveshaft. Insert the driveshaft into position, noting that the circlip must be at the lower end of the shaft.

19 With the locating dowels in position, manoeuvre the oil pump body into position, refit the two bolts and tighten them to the specified torque.

20 Refit the two oil pump gears and the pump cover and strainer assembly. Secure the cover with the four bolts.

21 Refit the sump as described in Section 13.

15.4 Locate the new front oil seal . . .

15 Crankshaft oil seals - renewal

Front (timing belt) oil seal

1 Remove the timing belt and the crankshaft sprocket and spacer/air conditioning drive pulley (as applicable) as described in Sections 8 and 9 respectively.

2 Make a note of the correct fitted depth of the seal in its housing, then punch or drill two small holes opposite each other in the seal. Screw a self-tapping screw into each and pull on the screws with pliers to extract the seal. Alternatively, the seal can be levered out of position using a suitable flat-bladed screwdriver taking great care not to damage the crankshaft shoulder or seal housing.

3 Clean the seal housing and polish off any burrs or raised edges which may have caused the seal to fail in the first place.

4 Lubricate the lips of the new seal with clean engine oil and carefully locate the seal on the end of crankshaft noting that its sealing lip must be facing inwards **(see illustration)**. Don't damage the seal lips during fitting.

5 Press the seal into its housing until it is positioned at the same depth as the original was prior to removal. If necessary, a suitable tubular drift, such as a socket, which bears only on the hard outer edge of the seal can be used to tap the seal into position. Take great care not to damage the seal lips during fitting and ensure that the seal lips face inwards. Note that if the surface of the crankshaft was noted to be badly scored, press the new seal slightly further into its housing so that its lip is running on an unmarked area of the crank.

6 Wash off any traces of oil, then refit the crankshaft sprocket and associated components, and the timing belt as described in Sections 9 and 8.

Rear (flywheel) oil seal

7 Remove the flywheel as described in Section 16. Make a note of the correct fitted depth of the seal in its housing.

8 Renew the seal as described above in paragraphs 2 to 5 **(see illustration)**.

9 Wash off any traces of oil, then refit the flywheel as described in Section 16.

15.8 . . . and rear oil seal on the crankshaft

16 Flywheel - removal, inspection and refitting

Removal

1 Remove the transmission as described in Chapter 7.

2 Remove the clutch as described in Chapter 6.

3 Mark the flywheel in relation to the crankshaft to aid refitting.

4 The flywheel must now be held stationary while the securing bolts are loosened. To do this, locate a long bolt in one of the engine-to-transmission mounting bolt holes and either insert a wide-bladed screwdriver or bar in the starter ring gear or use a suitable locking tool.

5 Bend up the locking plate tabs (where fitted), unscrew the securing bolts and withdraw the flywheel from the crankshaft.

Inspection

6 Examine the flywheel for scoring of the clutch face and for wear or chipping of the ring gear teeth. If the clutch face is scored, the flywheel may be machined until flat, but renewal is preferable.

7 If the ring gear teeth are worn or damaged, the flywheel must be renewed.

Refitting

8 Clean the flywheel and crankshaft faces, then coat the locating face on the crankshaft with Loctite Autoform, or equivalent.

9 Locate the flywheel on the crankshaft making sure that the previously made marks are aligned. The securing bolt holes are offset, so the flywheel cannot be fitted incorrectly.

10 Apply thread locking fluid to the threads of the new retaining bolts then fit the bolts. Note that where a locking plate was originally fitted, this should be renewed and located behind the bolts. Tighten the bolts in a diagonal sequence to the specified torque. Hold the flywheel stationary as during removal. Where applicable, bend up the locking plate tabs to secure the bolts.

11 Refit the clutch and transmission as described in Chapter 6 and 7 respectively.

2A

17 Engine/transmission mountings - inspection and renewal

Inspection

1 Chock the rear wheels then jack up the front of the vehicle and support it on (see *"Jacking and vehicle support"*). Remove the front roadwheels.

2 Check the mounting rubber to see if it is cracked, hardened or separated from the metal at any point; renew the mounting if any such damage or deterioration is evident. There are four mountings; two attached to the engine and two attached to the transmission **(see illustrations)**.

3 Check that all the mounting's fasteners are securely tightened; use a torque wrench to check if possible.

4 Using a large screwdriver or a pry bar, check for wear in the mounting by carefully levering against it to check for free play; where this is not possible, enlist the aid of an assistant to move the engine/transmission back and forth or from side to side while you watch the mounting. While some free play is to be expected even from new components, excessive wear should be obvious. If excessive free play is found, check first that the fasteners are correctly secured, then renew any worn components as described below.

17.2a Front (engine) mounting

Renewal

5 To renew a mounting rubber, first attach a hoist or engine support bar to the lifting bracket attached to the front of the cylinder head and raise the engine slightly. Alternately, position a jack and interposed block of wood beneath the engine and raise the jack so that it is supporting the weight of the engine. Position the jack beneath the transmission if it is these mountings which are being renewed.

6 With the weight of the engine/transmission supported, working from underneath the vehicle, undo the nuts or bolts securing the mounting rubber to the chassis member. Then undo the nut or bolts securing the mounting to the bracket and manoeuvre the mounting rubber out of position, noting that it may be

17.2b Rear (transmission) mounting

necessary to raise the engine slightly. If necessary the mounting bracket can also be unbolted and removed from the engine/transmission.

7 On refitting, refit the mounting bracket (where removed) and tighten its retaining bolts to the specified torque setting.

8 Manoeuvre the mounting rubber into position and refit its retaining nuts/bolts, tightening them by hand only at this stage. Lower the engine back down onto its mountings and remove the hoist/engine support bar (as applicable). Rock the engine to settle the disturbed mounting in position then tighten the mounting nuts to the specified torque setting.

9 Lower the vehicle on completion.

Chapter 2 Part B:
Diesel engine in-car repair procedures

Contents

Degrees of difficulty

Easy, suitable for novice with little experience	**Fairly easy,** suitable for beginner with some experience	**Fairly difficult,** suitable for competent DIY mechanic	**Difficult,** suitable for experienced DIY mechanic	**Very difficult,** suitable for expert DIY or professional

Specifications

Engine (general)
Type designation. J8S
Bore .... 86 mm
Stroke .... 89 mm
Compression ratio .... 21.0 : 1
Capacity .... 2068 cc
Firing order .... 1-3-4-2 (No 1 at flywheel end of engine)
Direction of crankshaft rotation .... Clockwise (viewed from front of engine)

Cylinder head and valves
Valve head recess below cylinder head joint face .... 0.80 to 1.15 mm
Valve clearances (cold):
   Inlet .... 0.20 mm
   Exhaust .... 0.25 mm

Timing belt
Deflection midway between camshaft and injection pump sprockets .. 3.0 to 5.0 mm

Camshaft
Endfloat .... 0.05 to 0.15 mm

Lubrication system
Oil pressure (warm engine @ 3000 rpm) .... 3.5 bar minimum
Oil pump type .... Gear, driven from auxiliary shaft
Oil pump clearances:
   Endfloat .... 0.02 to 0.10 mm
   Gear teeth to body .... 0.05 to 0.12 mm

Torque wrench settings

	Nm
Crankshaft pulley bolt	98
Camshaft sprocket bolt	50
Injection pump sprocket nut	50
Auxiliary shaft sprocket bolt	50
Rocker shaft:	
Shaft end bolt	20
Rocker arm pedestal bolts	30
Cylinder head bolts:	
Stage 1	30
Stage 2	50
Stage 3	105

Start the engine, allow it to run for 20 minutes then switch it off and allow it to cool for at least two and half hours. Slacken each bolt in turn and tighten to:

	Nm
Retightening torque	105
Oil pump body to crankcase	44
Oil pump cover to body	12
Sump bolts (single-piece sump):	
Steel sump	12
Aluminium sump	16
Sump bolts (two-piece sump):	
Sump pan to strengthening base	10
Strengthening base to crankcase:	
7 mm bolts	15
10 mm bolts	40
Flywheel bolts*	60
Engine mounting nuts and bolts	40
Transmission housing to engine bolts	54
Main bearing cap bolts	95
Big-end bearing cap bolts*	65
Piston oil jet nozzle bolts	14

*New bolts must be used

1 General information

How to use this Chapter

This Part of Chapter 2 describes those repair procedures that can reasonably be carried out on the engine while it remains in the vehicle. If the engine has been removed from the vehicle and is being dismantled as described in Part C, any preliminary dismantling procedures can be ignored.

Note that while it may be possible physically to overhaul items such as the piston/connecting rod assemblies while the engine is in the vehicle, such tasks are not usually carried out as separate operations. Usually, several additional procedures (not to mention the cleaning of components and of oilways) have to be carried out. For this reason all such tasks are classed as major overhaul procedures and are described in Part C of this Chapter.

Part C describes the removal of the engine/transmission from the vehicle and the full overhaul procedures that can then be carried out.

Engine description

The 2068 cc (J8S) engine is of four-cylinder overhead camshaft design, mounted longitudinally at the front of the vehicle, with the transmission mounted on the rear end of the engine.

The camshaft is driven by a toothed timing belt. The camshaft operates the eight valves via rocker arms which are mounted on a shaft which is positioned directly above the camshaft. Valve clearances are adjusted via the screw and locknut arrangement fitted to each rocker arm. The inlet and exhaust valves are each closed by coil springs and operate in guides pressed into the cylinder head.

The toothed timing belt also drives the fuel injection pump and auxiliary shaft. The coolant pump is driven by the same drivebelt as the alternator.

The crankshaft runs in five main bearings of the usual shell type. Endfloat is controlled by thrustwashers either side of number 2 main bearing.

The connecting rods rotate on horizontally-split bearing shells at their big-ends. The pistons are attached to the connecting rods by fully floating gudgeon pins which are retained by circlips. The aluminium alloy pistons are fitted with three piston rings, comprising two compression rings and an oil control ring.

The cylinder bores are formed by replaceable wet liners that are located from their bottom ends; sealing rings are fitted at the base of each liner to prevent the escape of coolant into the sump.

Lubrication is by means of a gear type oil pump which is driven by the auxiliary shaft via a worm gear. It draws oil through a strainer located in the sump and then forces it through a full-flow cartridge-type filter into galleries in the cylinder block/crankcase, from where it is distributed to the crankshaft (main bearings) and camshaft. The big-end bearings are supplied with oil via internal drillings in the crankshaft, while the camshaft bearings also receive a pressurised supply. The camshaft lobes and valves are lubricated by splash, as are all other engine components.

The turbocharger bearings also receive a pressurised oil supply, the turbocharger being linked to the cylinder block oil galleries by a feed and return hose. The pistons are also cooled by oil sprayed onto the underside of each assembly by the jets (one for each cylinder) mounted on the cylinder block.

An oil cooler is fitted to keep the oil temperature constant under extreme use. The cooler is mounted on the right-hand side of the engine compartment and is linked to the right-hand side of the cylinder block/ crankcase by a feed and return hose. The oil is forced from the pump directly to the oil cooler before returning to the cylinder block to circulate around the engine components as described above.

Repair operations possible with the engine in the vehicle

The following work can be carried out with the engine in the vehicle.

a) *Compression and leakdown pressure - testing.*
b) *Cylinder head cover - removal and refitting.*
c) *Crankshaft pulley - removal and refitting.*
d) *Timing belt cover - removal and refitting.*
e) *Timing belt - removal and refitting.*
f) *Timing belt tensioner and sprockets - removal and refitting.*
g) *Camshaft and auxiliary shaft oil seals - renewal.*
h) *Camshaft and rocker arms - removal and refitting.*
i) *Cylinder head - removal and refitting.*
j) *Cylinder head and pistons - decarbonising.*
k) *Sump - removal and refitting.*
l) *Oil pump - removal, inspection and refitting.*
m) *Oil cooler components - removal and refitting*
n) *Crankshaft oil seals - renewal.*
o) *Engine/transmission mountings - inspection and renewal.*
p) *Flywheel - removal and refitting.*

2 Compression and leakdown tests - description and interpretation

Compression test

Note: *A compression tester specifically designed for diesel engines must be used for this test.*

1 When engine performance is down, or if misfiring occurs which cannot be attributed to the fuel system, a compression test can provide diagnostic clues as to the engine's condition. If the test is performed regularly, it can give warning of trouble before any other symptoms become apparent.

2 A compression tester specifically intended for diesel engines must be used, because of the higher pressures involved. The tester is connected to an adapter which screws into the glow plug or injector hole. On these models, an adapter suitable for use in the injector holes will be required, due to the limited access to the glow plug holes. It is unlikely to be worthwhile buying such a tester for occasional use, but it may be possible to borrow or hire one - if not, have the test performed by a garage.

3 Unless specific instructions to the contrary are supplied with the tester, observe the following points:

a) *The battery must be in a good state of charge, the air filter must be clean, and the engine should be at normal operating temperature.*
b) *All the injectors or glow plugs should be removed before starting the test. If*

removing the injectors, also remove the flame shield washers, otherwise they may be blown out.
c) *The stop solenoid must be disconnected, to prevent the engine from running or fuel from being discharged.*

4 There is no need to hold the accelerator pedal down during the test, because the diesel engine air inlet is not throttled.

5 The actual compression pressures measured are not so important as the balance between cylinders. Values are given in the *Specifications*.

6 The cause of poor compression is less easy to establish on a diesel engine than on a petrol one. The effect of introducing oil into the cylinders ("wet" testing) is not conclusive, because there is a risk that the oil will sit in the swirl chamber or in the recess on the piston crown instead of passing to the rings. However, the following can be used as a rough guide to diagnosis.

7 All cylinders should produce very similar pressures; any difference greater than that specified indicates the existence of a fault. Note that the compression should build up quickly in a healthy engine; low compression on the first stroke, followed by gradually-increasing pressure on successive strokes, indicates worn piston rings. A low compression reading on the first stroke, which does not build up during successive strokes, indicates leaking valves or a blown head gasket (a cracked head could also be the cause). Deposits on the undersides of the valve heads can also cause low compression.

8 A low reading from two adjacent cylinders is almost certainly due to the head gasket having blown between them; the presence of coolant in the engine oil will confirm this.

9 If the compression reading is unusually high, the cylinder head surfaces, valves and pistons are probably coated with carbon deposits. If this is the case, the cylinder head should be removed and decarbonised (see Part C).

Leakdown test

10 A leakdown test measures the rate at which compressed air fed into the cylinder is lost. It is an alternative to a compression test, and in many ways it is better, since the escaping air provides easy identification of where pressure loss is occurring (piston rings, valves or head gasket).

11 The equipment needed for leakdown testing is unlikely to be available to the home mechanic. If poor compression is suspected, have the test performed by a suitably-equipped garage.

3 Top dead centre (TDC) for number 1 piston - locating

1 Top dead centre (TDC) is the highest point in the cylinder that each piston reaches as the

3.2 When No 1 piston is at TDC, the timing mark on the camshaft and injection pump sprockets should be aligned with the pointers on the timing belt cover

crankshaft turns. Each piston reaches TDC at the end of the compression stroke and again at the end of the exhaust stroke; however, for the purpose of timing the engine, TDC refers to the position of No 1 piston at the end of its compression stroke. On all engines in this manual, No 1 piston (and cylinder) is at the flywheel end of the engine.

2 When No 1 piston is at TDC, the timing mark on the camshaft and injection pump sprockets should be aligned with the pointers on the outer timing belt cover (the sprocket mark can be viewed through the cut-outs in the timing belt cover, above the pointers) **(see illustration)**. Additionally, the timing mark on the flywheel should be aligned with the TDC (0°) mark on the transmission bellhousing. However, unless the engine is removed from the vehicle, it is almost impossible to see the flywheel and bellhousing marks.

3 To align the timing marks, the crankshaft must be turned. This should be done by using a spanner on the crankshaft pulley bolt. Access from above is limited but can just be managed from below.

4 Turn the crankshaft in the normal direction of rotation until the timing marks just appear in the viewing windows on the timing belt cover, then align the marks with the pointers. To lock the crankshaft at the TDC position, remove the brass plug from the crankcase, located just forward of the starter motor. Insert a dowel rod of 8.0 mm diameter through the hole to engage in the slot provided for this purpose in the crankshaft counterbalance weight **(see illustrations)**. It may be necessary to move the crankshaft very slightly back and forth to check for positive engagement of the dowel rod in the crankshaft slot. Make sure that the rod is not inserted into one of the balancing holes either side of the TDC slot. Check that the crankshaft will not turn when the rod is fully engaged. Slight movement one way or the other indicates that the rod is in a balance hole.

2B

3.4a To lock the crankshaft, unscrew the plug from the cylinder block ...

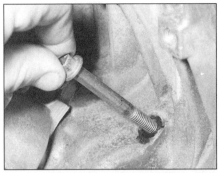

3.4b . . . and insert an 8.0 mm dowel rod to lock the crankshaft at TDC

4 Cylinder head cover - removal and refitting

Removal

1 Disconnect the battery negative lead.
2 Slacken the retaining clip (where fitted) and disconnect the breather hose from the rear of the cover.
3 Slacken and remove the cylinder head cover retaining bolts, noting the correct fitted positions of all brackets retained by the bolts, then lift off the cover, complete with gasket **(see illustration)**. Remove the cover from the engine compartment.
4 Remove the gasket from the cover and examine it for signs damage or deterioration, and renew if necessary.

Refitting

5 On reassembly, carefully clean the cylinder head mating surfaces and the cover gasket's groove and remove all traces of oil. Seat the gasket in its groove in the cover noting that the gasket is not symmetrical and can only be fitted one way. On later models the gasket is equipped with a locating lug which should be positioned at the rear of the cover, and on early models the gasket must be fitted with its graphite surface facing the cylinder head cover.
6 Ensure the gasket is correctly fitted then manoeuvre the cover into position on the cylinder head.

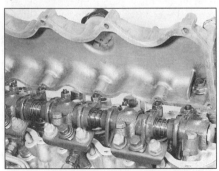

4.3 Position a new gasket on the cylinder head and refit the head cover

7 Refit the cover retaining bolts and tighten them securely, ensuring all the relevant brackets are correctly positioned.
8 Reconnect the breather hose to the cylinder head cover and reconnect the battery negative lead.

5 Crankshaft pulley - removal and refitting

Removal

1 As access to the crankshaft pulley is very limited when the engine is fitted to the vehicle, drain the cooling system (Chapter 1) then remove the radiator as described in Chapter 3.
2 Remove the power steering pump and/or alternator auxiliary drivebelt(s) (as applicable) as described in Chapter 1.
3 To prevent crankshaft rotation whilst the pulley retaining bolt is slackened, select top gear and have an assistant apply the brakes firmly. If the engine has been removed from the vehicle, lock the flywheel ring gear using a screwdriver engaged with the ring gear teeth, or a home-made locking device. **Do not** attempt to lock the crankshaft by inserting the locking pin through the cylinder block and into the crankshaft TDC slot.
4 Unscrew the retaining bolt and remove the pulley from the end of the crankshaft.

Refitting

5 Locate the pulley on the end of the crankshaft, aligning its locating holes with the sprocket roll pins, and refit the retaining bolt .
6 Lock the crankshaft by the method used on removal and tighten the pulley retaining bolt to the specified torque setting.
7 Refit the auxiliary drivebelts as described in Chapter 1.
8 Refit the radiator (Chapter 3) and refill the cooling system (Chapter 1).

6 Timing belt cover - removal and refitting

Removal

1 As access to the timing belt cover and its associated components is very limited when the engine is fitted to the vehicle, drain the cooling system (Chapter 1) then remove the radiator as described in Chapter 3.
2 Remove all the auxiliary drivebelts as described in Chapter 1. Note that on vehicles equipped with air conditioning and having their drivebelt situated behind the timing belt, this drivebelt can be left in position.
3 Undo the nuts and free the cable guide from the front of the timing belt cover.
4 Work around the cover and remove all the nuts and bolts along with their washers.
5 Carefully withdraw the cover from the engine compartment and recover the collars from the centre of the each cover rubber mounting.
6 With the cover removed, slide the three spacers **off** the cover mounting studs, noting the correct location of each spacer as it is removed **(see illustration)**.
7 Where necessary, unbolt and remove the rear timing belt cover from the cylinder head.
8 Examine the cover mounting rubbers for signs of damage or deterioration and renew as necessary.

Refitting

9 Refit the rear timing belt cover (where removed) to the cylinder head and securely tighten its retaining bolts.
10 Noting that all three spacers are a different length, refit each spacer to its respective cover mounting stud.
11 Ensure all the cover mounting rubbers are correctly fitted and fit the collars into position in the centre of each rubber.

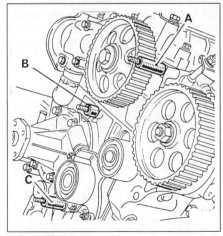

6.6 Timing belt cover spacer locations

A Long spacer
B Short spacer   C Medium spacer

12 Refit the timing belt cover to the engine, taking great care not to displace the mounting rubbers or collars. Refit the washers and cover retaining nuts and bolts, tightening them securely.

13 Refit the cable guide and securely tighten its retaining nuts.

14 Refit the auxiliary drivebelt(s) as described in Chapter 1.

15 Refit the radiator (Chapter 3) and refill the cooling system (Chapter 1).

---

7 Timing belt - removal, inspection and refitting

Note: *To prevent the camshaft and injection pump sprockets rotating whilst the timing belt is removed, Renault technicians use a special tool (Mot. 854) **(see illustration)**. The tool slots in between the two sprockets, engaging with their teeth and so locking them together. The use of this tool greatly reduces the risk of incorrectly setting the valve and/or injection pump timing when installing the new belt. Therefore, where possible, if access to this tool can be gained it is highly recommended that it be used. Alternatively a suitable home-made substitute can be fabricated to lock the sprockets together.*

Removal

1 Disconnect the battery negative lead.

2 Position No. 1 piston at TDC as described in Section 3, and lock the crankshaft in position with the locking pin.

3 Remove the crankshaft pulley as described in Section 5. To prevent the possibility of the locking pin being damaged, remove the pin temporarily as the pulley retaining bolt is slackened and refit it once the bolt is slack.

4 Remove the timing belt cover as described in Section 6.

5 Check that the camshaft, injection pump and crankshaft sprockets are correctly positioned **(see illustration)**. The camshaft sprocket timing mark should be aligned with the boss on the centre of the cylinder head cover and the injection pump sprocket mark should be aligned with the centre of the boss

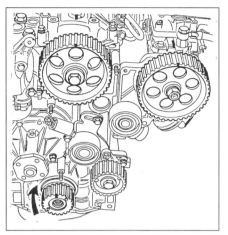

7.5a Sprocket timing mark locations

on the injection pump. If alignment marks do not already exist, use white paint or similar to mark the cylinder head cover and injection pump; the marks can then be used on refitting to ensure that the valve and pump timing is correctly set **(see illustration)**.

6 Insert the sprocket locking tool (where available) in-between the camshaft and injection pump sprockets.

7 If the timing belt is to be re-used and the original direction of rotation arrows are not visible, use white paint or similar to mark the direction of rotation on the belt.

8 Slacken both the tensioner pulley retaining nut and bolt and pivot the pulley fully away from the timing belt. Hold the tensioner in this position and securely tighten the retaining nut and bolt to keep it there.

9 Slip the belt off the sprockets and remove it from the engine. If the camshaft and injection pump sprockets were not locked in position, they must not be rotated whilst the belt is removed.

10 Examine the air conditioning compressor drivebelt for signs of damage or deterioration and renew if necessary. Due to the amount of work required to renew the belt, it is recommended that it should be renewed regardless of its apparent condition. Refer to Chapter 1 for further information.

Inspection

11 Check the timing belt carefully for any signs of uneven wear, splitting or oil contamination and renew it if there is the slightest doubt about its condition. If the engine is undergoing an overhaul and has covered more than or close to 72 000 miles (115 000 km) since the original belt was fitted, renew the belt as a matter of course. If signs of oil contamination are found, trace the source of the oil leak and rectify it, then wash down the engine timing belt area and all related components to remove all traces of oil. Whilst the belt is removed examine the tensioner and idler pulley bearings as described in Section 8.

Refitting

12 Prior to refitting the timing belt, check the clearance between the tensioner pulley backplate and the adjusting screw on the auxiliary shaft cover is 0.1 mm. This is best done using feeler blades, a 0.1 mm feeler blade should be a light, sliding fit between the two components. If not, slacken the locknut and adjust the screw as required **(see illustration)**. Once the clearance is correctly adjusted, hold the screw stationary and securely tighten its locknut.

13 On reassembly, thoroughly clean the timing belt sprockets and check that they are positioned so that the camshaft and injection pump sprockets are correctly aligned with the marks made or noted prior to removal. If the sprockets were locked in position they should not have moved.

14 Offer up the timing belt, observing any marks indicating the direction of rotation and, starting at the crankshaft sprocket and working in an anti-clockwise direction, align the lines on the belt with the timing marks on each sprocket and engage the belt with the auxiliary shaft, injection pump and camshaft sprockets **(see illustrations)**. Ensure that the belt front run and top run is taut ie, all slack is on the tensioner pulley side of the belt. Do not twist the belt sharply while refitting it, ensuring that the belt teeth are correctly seated centrally in the sprockets and that the timing marks remain in alignment. If a used belt is

2B

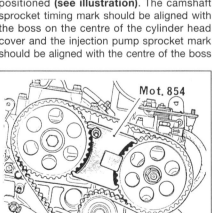

7.0 Special Renault tool for locking the injection pump and camshaft sprockets in position

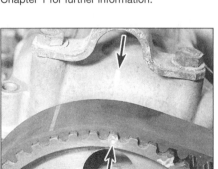

7.5b Make marks on the cylinder head and injection pump for the sprocket timing marks prior to removing the timing belt

7.12 Adjusting the tensioner pulley backplate clearance

7.14a On fitting align the lines on the timing belt with the timing marks on the crankshaft sprocket . . .

7.14b . . . camshaft sprocket . . .

7.14c . . . and injection pump sprocket

being refitted, ensure that the arrow mark made on removal points in the normal direction of rotation as before. Note that if the belt is correctly installed, there should be a total of twenty tooth troughs (on the timing belt) between the camshaft and injection pump sprocket timing marks.

15 Remove the sprocket locking tool (where fitted) and slacken the tensioner pulley retaining nut and bolt. Check that the tensioner pulley is forced against the timing belt under spring pressure then securely tighten the pulley retaining nut and bolt.

16 Temporarily refit the timing belt cover and check that the camshaft sprocket and injection pump timing marks are aligned with their respective pointers. If not, the belt will have to be removed and the refitting procedure repeated.

17 Refit the crankshaft pulley, tightening its retaining bolt loosely only at this stage, and remove the crankshaft locking pin. Rotate the crankshaft through two complete turns in a clockwise direction until both the sprocket timing marks are realigned with their pointers. **Do not** under any circumstances rotate the crankshaft anti-clockwise.

18 Remove the timing belt cover then slacken the tensioner retaining nut and bolt by half a turn and retighten them securely.

19 The belt tension should now ideally be checked using the Renault service tool Ele. 346. If the tool is available, use it to check that the belt deflection is 3 to 5 mm midway

7.20 Using a spring balance and ruler to check timing belt tension

between the camshaft and injection pump sprockets.

20 If the special tool is not available, an approximate check of the belt tension can be made using a spring balance and steel rule. At the mid-point between the camshaft and injection pump sprockets the belt deflection should be 3 to 5 mm under a force of 30 N **(see illustration)**. It must be stressed however that this is only an approximate check, the tension can only be accurately checked using the Renault tool.

21 If the belt tension is not correctly set, repeat the operations described in paragraphs 17 to 20 (as applicable) until the correct tension is achieved.

22 Once the belt is correctly tensioned refit the timing belt cover as described in Section 6.

23 Refit the plug to the cylinder block/ crankcase locking pin hole and tighten the crankshaft pulley retaining bolt to the specified torque setting.

24 Refit and tension the auxiliary drivebelt(s) as described in Chapter 1.

8 Timing belt tensioner and sprockets - removal, inspection and refitting

Note: *This Section describes as individual operations the removal and refitting of the components concerned - if more than one of them are to be removed at the same time, start by removing the timing belt as described in Section 7, then remove the actual component as described below, ignoring the preliminary dismantling steps.*

Removal

1 Disconnect the battery negative lead.

2 Position No. 1 piston at TDC as described in Section 3, and lock the crankshaft in position with the locking pin.

3 Remove the timing belt cover as described in Section 6, and proceed as described under the relevant sub-heading.

Camshaft sprocket

4 Carry out the operation described in paragraph 5 of Section 7.

5 Slacken both the tensioner pulley retaining nut and bolt and pivot the pulley fully away from the timing belt. Hold the tensioner in this position and securely tighten the retaining nut and bolt to keep it there.

6 Remove the belt from the camshaft sprocket taking care not to twist it too sharply; use the fingers only to handle the belt.

7 Slacken the camshaft sprocket retaining bolt whilst holding the sprocket stationary with a suitable peg spanner which engages with the sprocket holes. A suitable home-made tool can be fabricated from two lengths of steel strip (one long, the other short) and three nuts and bolts; one nut and bolt forming the pivot of a forked tool with the remaining two nuts and bolts at the tips of the "forks" to engage with the sprocket spokes.

8 Unscrew the retaining bolt and washer and remove the sprocket from the end of the camshaft, noting which way around it is fitted. If the Woodruff key is a loose fit in the camshaft end, remove it and store it with the sprocket for safe-keeping. Note that the camshaft must not be rotated whilst the sprocket is removed.

Crankshaft sprocket

9 Remove the crankshaft pulley as described in Section 5. To prevent the possibility of the locking pin being damaged, temporarily

TOOL TIP

Using a home-made tool to hold the camshaft sprocket stationary whilst the bolt is tightened (shown with cylinder head removed)

8.13a Slide off the crankshaft sprocket . . .

8.13b . . . then remove the Woodruff key

8.20 Using a puller to draw the sprocket off the injection pump shaft taper

remove the pin from the crankshaft as the bolt is slackened and refit it once the bolt is slack.

10 Carry out the operation described in paragraph 5 of Section 7. If the sprocket locking tool is available, insert it in-between the camshaft and injection pump sprockets to lock the sprockets together.

11 Slacken both the tensioner pulley retaining nut and bolt and pivot the pulley fully away from the timing belt. Hold the tensioner in this position and securely tighten the retaining nut and bolt to keep it there.

12 Work the belt clear of the crankshaft sprocket taking care not to twist it too sharply; use the fingers only to handle the belt.

13 Slide the sprocket off the end of the crankshaft. If the Woodruff key is a loose fit in the crankshaft end, remove it and store it with the sprocket for safe-keeping **(see illustrations)**.

14 On models not equipped with air conditioning, slide the spacer off the end of the crankshaft and store it with the sprocket.

15 On models with air conditioning, the air conditioning compressor drivebelt drive pulley is situated behind the crankshaft sprocket. Where necessary, remove the drivebelt as described in Chapter 1 and slide off the drive pulley.

Injection pump sprocket

16 Carry out the operation described in paragraph 5 of Section 7.

17 Slacken both the tensioner pulley retaining nut and bolt and pivot the pulley fully away from the timing belt. Hold the tensioner in this position and securely tighten the retaining nut and bolt to keep it there.

18 Remove the belt from the injection pump sprocket taking care not to twist it too sharply; use the fingers only to handle the belt.

19 Hold the sprocket stationary using the tool described in paragraph 7 and slacken the sprocket retaining nut. Unscrew the nut and position it so that it is flush with the end of the pump shaft; the nut will protect shaft threads during the following operation.

20 A suitable puller will then be needed to free the sprocket from its taper on the pump shaft. The puller should be inserted through the holes in the sprocket so that its legs bear against the back of the sprocket and not

positioned so that they bear against the sprocket teeth. Screw in the puller centre bolt until it contacts the pulley shaft and draw the sprocket off the pump shaft taper **(see illustration)**. **Do not** be tempted to strike the pump with a hammer in an attempt to free the sprocket as the pump internals will almost certainly be damaged.

21 Remove the puller then remove the sprocket retaining nut and washer and slide off the sprocket. If the Woodruff key is a loose fit in the pump shaft, remove it and store it with the sprocket for safe-keeping.

Auxiliary shaft sprocket

22 Carry out the operation described in paragraph 5 of Section 7. If the sprocket locking tool is available, insert it in-between the camshaft and injection pump sprockets to lock the sprockets together.

23 Slacken both the tensioner pulley retaining nut and bolt and pivot the pulley fully away from the timing belt. Hold the tensioner in this position and securely tighten the retaining nut and bolt to keep it there.

24 Remove the belt from the auxiliary shaft sprocket taking care not to twist it too sharply; use the fingers only to handle the belt.

25 In the absence of the special Renault sprocket holding tool, Mot. 855, a length of old timing belt will be required to prevent the auxiliary shaft from rotating as the bolt is slackened. Wrap the timing belt around the sprocket and clamp it firmly with a pair of grips. Another possible way of retaining the sprocket is to jam a large flat-bladed screwdriver in the sprocket teeth but this is not recommended due to the risk of damaging the sprocket.

26 Slacken and remove the retaining bolt and washer and slide the sprocket off the end of the shaft. If the Woodruff key is a loose fit in the shaft, remove it and store it with the sprocket for safe-keeping.

Tensioner assembly

27 Carry out the operation described in paragraph 5 of Section 7. If the sprocket locking tool is available, insert it in-between the camshaft and injection pump sprockets to lock the sprockets together.

28 Slacken both the tensioner pulley

retaining nut and bolt and pivot the pulley fully away from the timing belt. Hold the tensioner in this position and securely tighten the retaining nut and bolt to keep it there.

29 Position the belt clear of the tensioner assembly, taking care not to twist it too sharply; use the fingers only to handle the belt.

30 Slacken and remove the tensioner retaining nut and bolt along with their washers whilst firmly holding the tensioner pulley. With the nut and bolt removed slowly pivot the pulley assembly away from the spring, until all tension is relieved, then remove the tensioner pulley assembly and withdraw the plunger and spring from the coolant pump housing.

Tensioner idler pulley

Note: *The tensioner idler pulley is an integral part of the injection pump front mounting bracket and is not available separately.*

31 Remove the injection pump sprocket as described in paragraphs 16 to 21 of this Section.

32 Slacken and remove the nuts and washers securing the injection pump to the front mounting bracket studs.

33 Undo the bolts securing the front pump mounting bracket to the side of the cylinder block/crankcase and remove the bracket from the engine.

Inspection

34 Thoroughly clean the relevant sprocket(s) and renew any that show signs of wear, damage or cracks.

35 Clean the idler and tensioner pulleys but do not use any strong solvent which may enter the pulley bearings. Check that each pulley rotates freely on the backplate, with no sign of stiffness or of free play. Renew the assembly if there is any doubt about its condition or if there are any obvious signs of wear or damage. It is recommended that the tensioner spring is renewed regardless of its apparent condition, since its condition is critical.

Refitting

Camshaft sprocket

36 Refit the Woodruff key (where removed) to the slot in the camshaft end and slide on the

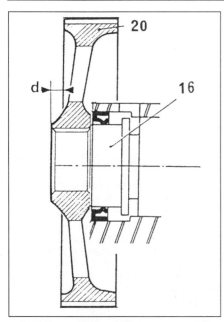

8.36 Ensure the camshaft sprocket (20) is fitted on the camshaft (16) so that the sprocket hub protrudes out in front of the timing belt run (d)

sprocket, ensuring it is fitted the correct way around **(see illustration)**. If the sprocket is installed incorrectly it will not be aligned centrally with the timing belt.

37 Refit the sprocket retaining bolt and washer and tighten it to the specified torque setting whilst preventing rotation using the method employed on removal.

38 Ensure the camshaft and injection pump sprocket timing marks are aligned with the marks made or noted prior to removal.

39 Ensuring that the belt front run and top run is taut ie, all slack is on the tensioner pulley side of the belt, engage the belt with injection pump and camshaft sprockets. Do not twist the belt sharply while refitting it and ensure that the belt teeth are correctly seated centrally in the sprockets and that the timing marks remain in alignment.

40 Slacken the tensioner pulley retaining nut and bolt. Check that the tensioner pulley is forced against the timing belt under spring pressure then securely tighten the pulley retaining nut and bolt.

41 Temporarily refit the timing belt cover and check that the camshaft sprocket and injection pump timing marks are aligned with their respective pointers. If not, the tensioner will have to be released and the belt relocated on the sprockets.

42 Remove the crankshaft locking pin and rotate the crankshaft through two complete turns in a clockwise direction until both the sprocket timing marks are realigned with their pointers. **Do not** under any circumstances rotate the crankshaft anti-clockwise.

43 Remove the timing belt cover then slacken the tensioner retaining nut and bolt by half a turn each then retighten them securely. Check

the timing belt tension as described in paragraphs 19 to 21 of Section 7.

44 Once the timing belt is correctly tensioned, refit the timing belt cover as described in Section 6.

45 Refit the plug to the cylinder block/crankcase timing hole and reconnect the battery.

Crankshaft sprocket

46 On models not equipped with air conditioning, slide the spacer onto the end of the crankshaft.

47 On models with air conditioning, where necessary, slide the drive pulley onto the crankshaft and refit the air conditioning compressor drivebelt as described in Chapter 1.

48 Refit the Woodruff key (where removed) to the slot in the crankshaft, and slide on the sprocket ensuring it is fitted the correct way around. On models equipped with air conditioning ensure that the sprocket roll pins engage correctly with the holes in the drive pulley.

49 Ensure that the camshaft and injection pump sprockets are correctly aligned with the marks made or noted on removal. If the locking tool has been used the sprockets will not have moved.

50 Ensuring that the belt front run and top run is taut ie, all slack is on the tensioner pulley side of the belt, engage the belt with crankshaft. Do not twist the belt sharply while refitting it and ensure that the belt teeth are correctly seated centrally in the sprockets and that the timing marks remain in alignment.

51 Adjust the timing belt tension as described in paragraphs 17 to 24 of Section 7.

Injection pump sprocket

52 Ensure the sprocket and pump shaft are clean and dry and (where necessary) refit the Woodruff key to the pump shaft.

53 Slide the sprocket onto the shaft and refit the washer and retaining nut.

54 Hold the sprocket stationary using the method employed on removal and tighten the sprocket retaining nut to the specified torque setting.

55 Carry out the operations described in paragraphs 38 to 45 of this Section.

Auxiliary shaft sprocket

56 Refit the Woodruff key to the auxiliary shaft slot and slide on the sprocket, ensuring it is fitted the correct way around **(see illustration)**. If the sprocket is installed incorrectly it will not be aligned centrally with the timing belt.

57 Refit the retaining bolt and washer and tighten it to the specified torque setting, using the method employed on removal to prevent rotation.

58 Ensure that the camshaft and injection pump sprockets are correctly aligned with the marks made or noted on removal. If the sprockets were locked in position they will not have moved.

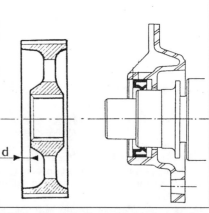

8.56 Auxiliary shaft sprocket is installed so that the side with the largest recess (d) faces away from the cylinder block

59 Ensuring that the belt front run and top run is taut ie, all slack is on the tensioner pulley side of the belt, engage the belt with auxiliary shaft sprocket. Do not twist the belt sharply while refitting it and ensure that the belt teeth are correctly seated centrally in the sprockets and that the timing marks remain in alignment.

60 Carry out the operations described in paragraphs 40 to 45 of this Section.

Tensioner assembly

61 Fit the spring to the inside of the plunger and refit the plunger assembly to the coolant pump housing.

62 Compress the plunger and manoeuvre the tensioner pulley assembly into position **(see illustration)**. Refit the tensioner retaining nut and bolt and check that the tensioner assembly pivots smoothly and is forced towards the timing belt by the tensioner spring.

63 Pivot the pulley fully away from the timing belt and securely tighten its retaining nut and bolt to keep it there.

64 Ensure that the camshaft and injection pump sprockets are correctly aligned with the marks made or noted on removal. If the sprockets were locked in position they will not have moved.

65 Locate the belt in front of the tensioner pulley ensuring that the belt front run and top run is taut and all slack is on the tensioner

8.62 Install the timing belt tensioner pulley and check that it is free to pivot smoothly

pulley side of the belt. Do not twist the belt sharply while refitting it and ensure that the belt teeth are correctly seated centrally in the sprockets and that the timing marks remain in alignment.

66 Carry out the operations described in paragraphs 40 to 45 of this Section.

Tensioner idler pulley

67 Manoeuvre the injection pump mounting bracket into position, engaging its studs with the front of the injection pump. Refit the bolts which secure the bracket to the cylinder block/crankcase and tighten them securely.

68 Refit the washers and nuts securing the bracket to the injection pump and tighten them securely.

69 Refit the injection pump sprocket as described in paragraphs 52 to 55 of this Section.

---

9 Camshaft and auxiliary shaft oil seals - renewal

Note: *If either the camshaft or auxiliary shaft oil seal is to be renewed with the timing belt still in place, check that the belt is free from oil contamination (renew the belt as a matter of course if signs of oil contamination are found; see Section 7), then cover the belt to protect it from contamination by oil while work is in progress and ensure that all traces of oil are removed from the area before the belt is refitted.*

Camshaft oil seal

1 Remove the camshaft sprocket as described in Section 8.

2 Make a note of the correct fitted depth of the seal then punch or drill two small holes opposite each other in the oil seal. Screw a self-tapping screw into each and pull on the screws with pliers to extract the seal.

3 Clean the seal housing and polish off any burrs or raised edges which may have caused the seal to fail in the first place.

4 Lubricate the lips of the new seal with clean engine oil and ease it into position on the end of the shaft. Press the seal into its housing until it is positioned at the same depth as the original was prior to removal. If necessary, a suitable tubular drift, such as a socket, which bears only on the hard outer edge of the seal can be used to tap the seal into position. Take great care not to damage the seal lips during fitting and ensure that the seal lips face inwards. Note that if the surface of the shaft was noted to be badly scored, press the new seal slightly further into its housing so that its lip is running on an unmarked area of the shaft.

5 Refit the camshaft sprocket as described in Section 8.

Auxiliary shaft oil seal

6 Remove the auxiliary shaft sprocket as described in Section 8. Secure the timing belt

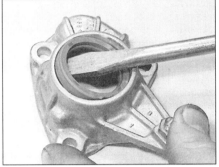

9.8 Lever out the auxiliary shaft oil seal with a suitable flat-bladed screwdriver

clear of the working area so that it is not contaminated with oil during the following procedure.

7 Undo the retaining bolts and slide the auxiliary shaft cover off the end of the shaft. Recover the gasket and discard it, a new one should be used on refitting.

8 Using a suitable flat-bladed screwdriver, lever the seal out of the cover whilst taking great care not to mark the cover **(see illustration)**.

9 Position the new seal in the cover and tap it into position using a suitable tubular drift, such as a socket, which bears only on the hard outer edge of the seal. Ensure that the seal lip is facing inwards.

10 Remove all traces of gasket from the cover and cylinder block/crankcase mating surfaces and position a new gasket on the cylinder block.

11 Slide the cover into position carefully easing the seal over the end of the auxiliary shaft.

12 To prevent the possibility of oil leakage smear the shafts of the cover retaining bolts with a suitable sealant. Renault recommend the use of a Loctite sealant (available from your Renault dealer); in the absence of this ensure a good quality sealant is used.

13 Ensure the gasket is correctly positioned then refit the cover retaining bolts and tighten them securely.

14 Refit the auxiliary shaft sprocket as described in Section 8.

---

10 Camshaft and rocker arms - removal, inspection and refitting

Removal

Rocker arm assembly

1 Position No. 1 piston at TDC as described in Section 3, and lock the crankshaft in position with the locking pin.

2 Remove the cylinder head cover as described in Section 4.

3 Working in a diagonal sequence, evenly and progressively slacken the rocker arm pedestal retaining bolts by half a turn at a time until all

10.4 Remove the rocker arm assembly noting the correct fitted locations of the locating dowels (arrowed)

valve spring pressure is relieved from the arms. The bolts can then be unscrewed and removed from the cylinder head.

4 Lift the rocker arm assembly away from the cylinder head noting the correct locations of the pedestal locating dowels **(see illustration)**. If the dowels are a loose fit, remove them and store them with the rocker shaft for safe-keeping.

5 To dismantle the rocker arm assembly, unscrew the bolt from the rear end of the rocker shaft whilst retaining the rocker pedestal to prevent it be sprung off the end of the shaft. Recover the oil filter from inside the shaft then slide off the various components, keeping all components in their correct fitted order. Make a note of each components correct fitted position as it is removed, to ensure it is positioned correctly on reassembly.

6 To separate the front pedestal and shaft, unscrew the grub screw from the top of the pedestal. If necessary, the camshaft thrust plate can also be unbolted from the front of the pedestal.

Camshaft

7 Remove the cylinder head as described in Section 12. Remove the rocker arm assembly as previously described.

8 Remove the camshaft sprocket as described in Section 8.

9 Make a note of the correct fitted depth of the seal then punch or drill two small holes opposite each other in the oil seal. Screw a self-tapping screw into each and pull on the screws with pliers to extract the seal.

10 Slide the camshaft out of the front of the cylinder head.

Inspection

Rocker arm assembly

11 Examine the rocker arm bearing surfaces which contact the camshaft lobes for wear ridges and scoring. Renew any rocker arms on which these conditions are apparent. If a rocker arm bearing surface is badly scored also examine the corresponding lobe on the camshaft for wear as it is likely that both will be worn. Renew worn components as necessary, the rocker arm assembly can be

2B

dismantled as in paragraphs 5 and 6. Renew the rocker shaft oil filter regardless of its apparent condition.

12 Inspect the ends of the adjusting screws for signs of wear or damage and renew as required.

13 If the rocker arm assembly has been dismantled, examine the rocker arm and shaft bearing surfaces for wear ridges and scoring. If there are obvious signs of wear, the relevant rocker arm(s) and/or shaft must be renewed. Also check that the rocker arm oil holes are clear by passing a piece of wire through each one.

Camshaft

14 Examine the camshaft bearing surfaces and cam lobes for signs of wear ridges and scoring. Renew the camshaft if any of these conditions are apparent. Examine the condition of the bearing surfaces both on the camshaft journals and in the cylinder head. If the head bearing surfaces are worn excessively, the cylinder head will need to be renewed.

15 Examine the camshaft thrust plate for signs of wear or scoring. If worn, the thrust plate must be renewed otherwise camshaft endfloat will be excessive. The thrust plate is secured to the front of the front rocker arm pedestal by two bolts.

Refitting

Camshaft

16 Ensure the cylinder head and camshaft bearing surfaces are clean then liberally oil the camshaft bearings and lobes and slide the camshaft back into position in the cylinder head.

17 Lubricate the lips of the new seal with clean engine oil and ease it into position on the end of the shaft. Press the seal into the cylinder head until it is positioned at the same depth as the original was prior to removal. If necessary, a suitable tubular drift, such as a socket, which bears only on the hard outer edge of the seal can be used to tap the seal into position. Take great care not to damage the seal lips during fitting and ensure that the seal lips face inwards.

18 Refit the camshaft sprocket as described in Section 8.

19 Refit the cylinder head as described in Section 12, then refit the rocker arm assembly as follows.

Rocker arm assembly

20 If the rocker arm assembly was dismantled, refit the rocker shaft to the front pedestal, aligning its locating hole with the pedestal threaded hole, and refit the grub screw tightening it securely. Apply a smear of clean engine oil to the shaft then slide on all removed components, ensuring each is correctly fitted in its original position. Note that the pedestals are not symmetrical and must be fitted the correct way around with the

protruding side of the pedestal facing the rear end of the rocker shaft.

21 Once all components are in position on the shaft, compress the rear pedestal. Install the new oil filter in the shaft bore, then refit the bolt and tighten it to the specified torque setting.

22 Ensure that the pedestal locating dowels are correctly positioned then lower the rocker arm assembly into position on the cylinder head, ensuring that the thrust plate engages correctly with the camshaft slot.

23 Refit the retaining bolts and, working in a diagonal sequence, evenly and progressively tighten them until all the pedestals are contacting the cylinder head. As the bolts are tightened ensure that the thrust plate remains correctly aligned with the groove in the camshaft. With all the pedestals in contact with the head, work around the retaining bolts and tighten them to the specified torque setting.

24 Check and, if necessary, adjust the valve clearances as described in Section 11. then refit the cylinder head cover as described in Section 4.

---

11 Valve clearances - checking and adjustment

1 The importance of having the valve clearances correctly adjusted cannot be overstressed as they vitally affect the performance of the engine. That being said the check should not be regarded as routine maintenance and should only be carried out

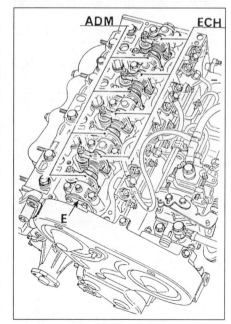

11.4 Valve locations

ADM = Inlet valves
ECH = Exhaust valves
E shows the front end of the camshaft

when the valve gear has become noisy, after engine overhaul, or when trying to trace the cause of power loss which may be attributed to the valve. The clearances are checked as follows noting that the engine must be cold (engine not having been started for at least two and a half hours) for the check to be accurate.

2 Access to the crankshaft pulley bolt (to turn the engine over) is extremely limited but it should just be possible to engage a socket and bar on the bolt from below. If this is not possible, then it will be necessary to remove the radiator (see Chapter 3) to gain the necessary working clearance.

3 Remove the cylinder head cover as described in Section 4.

4 It is important that the clearance of the relevant valve is checked and adjusted when the valve is fully closed and the rocker arm rests on the heel of the cam (directly opposite the peak). This can be ensured by carrying out the adjustments in the following sequence, noting that No 1 cylinder is at the transmission end of the engine.

Valve fully open	Adjust valve
No 1 cyl exhaust	*No 3 cyl inlet and No 4 cyl exhaust*
No 3 cyl exhaust	*No 4 cyl inlet and No 2 cyl exhaust*
No 4 cyl exhaust	*No 2 cyl inlet and No 1 cyl exhaust*
No 2 cyl exhaust	*No 1 cyl inlet and No 3 cyl exhaust*

The correct valve clearances are given in the *Specifications* at the start of this Chapter, the valve locations are as shown **(see illustration)**.

5 With the relevant valve fully open, check the clearances of the two valves specified. Clearances are checked by inserting a feeler blade of the correct thickness between the valve stem and the rocker arm adjusting screw, the feeler blade should be a light, sliding fit. If adjustment is necessary, slacken the adjusting screw locknut and turn the screw as necessary until the feeler blade is a light sliding fit **(see illustration)**. Once the correct clearance is obtained hold the adjusting screw and securely tighten the locknut. Recheck the valve clearance and adjust again if necessary.

11.5 Adjusting the valve clearances

6 Rotate the crankshaft until the next valve in the sequence is fully open and check the clearances of the next two specified valves.

7 Repeat the procedure until all eight valve clearances have been checked and, if necessary, adjusted then refit the cylinder head cover as described in Section 4.

12 Cylinder head - removal and refitting

Note: *Great care must be taken not to allow dirt to enter the fuel system during the following procedure.*

Removal

1 Disconnect the battery negative lead.

2 Position No. 1 piston at TDC as described in Section 3, and lock the crankshaft in position with the locking pin.

3 Remove the timing belt cover as described in Section 6, and carry out the operation described in paragraph 5 of Section 7.

4 Slacken both the tensioner pulley retaining nut and bolt and pivot the pulley fully away from the timing belt. Hold the tensioner in this position and securely tighten the retaining nut and bolt to keep it there. Disengage the belt from the camshaft sprocket taking care not to twist it too sharply; use the fingers only to handle the belt.

5 Remove the cylinder head cover as described in Section 4.

6 Remove the rocker shaft assembly as described in Section 10.

7 If not already done, drain the cooling system as described in Chapter 1.

8 Remove the inlet and exhaust manifolds and turbocharger as described in Chapter 4C.

9 On models where the thermostatic fast idle valve is mounted onto the injection pump, slacken the retaining clips and disconnect the coolant hoses from the valve.

10 Undo the retaining nuts and disconnect the wiring from each of the glow plugs. Also disconnect the wiring connector from the injection pump stop solenoid and the coolant temperature sender unit(s) which is/are screwed into the front of the cylinder head.

11 On models with clamp-type injectors, wipe clean the injectors then undo the union bolt securing the fuel return hose to the top of each injector and recover the sealing washer from each side of the hose union and, where necessary, the filter. With all four union bolts removed position the return hose clear of the cylinder head. Cover the hose and injector unions to prevent the ingress of dirt into the fuel system. Undo the union nuts and free the injector pipes from the four injectors noting there is not need to remove the injector pipes completely.

12 On models with screw-type injectors, wipe clean the pipe unions then slacken the union nut securing the injector pipes to the top of each injector and the four union nuts

securing the pipes to the rear of the injection pump; as each pump union nut is slackened, retain the adapter with a suitable open-ended spanner to prevent it being unscrewed from the pump. With all the union nuts undone remove the injector pipe assembly from the engine. Disconnect the fuel return pipe from rear injector then cover the pump and injector unions to prevent the ingress of dirt into the fuel system.

13 Where necessary, undo the retaining bolts and free the oil separator chamber from the rear of the cylinder head.

14 Slacken the retaining clips and disconnect all the relevant coolant hoses from thermostat housing and cylinder head.

15 Slacken and remove the bolt securing the rear injection pump mounting bracket to the side of the cylinder head.

16 Working in the reverse of the sequence shown, progressively slacken the cylinder head nuts and bolts by half a turn at a time until all nuts and bolts can be unscrewed by hand **(see illustration 12.42)**.

17 With the exception of the front right-hand bolt, remove each nut/bolt and washer in turn and store it in its correct fitted order by pushing it through a clearly-marked cardboard template.

18 With the front right-hand bolt (bolt No 16 in the tightening sequence) still in position, the joint between the cylinder head and gasket and the cylinder block/crankcase must now be broken without disturbing the wet liners; although these liners are better located and sealed than some wet liner engines, there is still a risk of coolant and foreign matter leaking into the sump if the cylinder head is lifted carelessly. If care is not taken and the liners are moved, there is also a possibility of the bottom seals being disturbed, causing leakage after refitting the head.

19 To break the joint, strike the side of the head firmly using a soft-faced mallet or hammer and block of wood. Movement of the head will be minimal due to the clearance between the head and its three locating studs but it should be sufficient to free the head from the gasket.

20 Once the gasket seal is broken, remove the right-hand front bolt and washer from the cylinder head and press it into the cardboard template.

21 The cylinder head can then be lifted out of the engine compartment; use assistance if possible as it is a heavy assembly. Remove the gasket from the top of the block, noting the position of the locating dowel. If the dowel is a loose fit, remove it and store it with the head for safe-keeping. Do not discard the gasket, it will be needed for identification purposes (see paragraphs 30 and 31).

22 Note **do not** attempt to rotate the crankshaft with the cylinder head removed, otherwise the wet liners may be displaced. Operations that require the rotation of the crankshaft (eg cleaning the piston crowns), should only be carried out once the cylinder

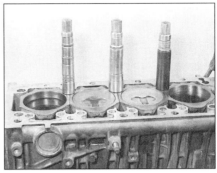

12.22 Cylinder liners clamped in position using sockets positioned over the cylinder head studs

liners are firmly clamped in position. In the absence of the special Renault liner clamping tool (Mot. 521-01), the liners can be clamped in position using large flat washers positioned underneath suitable-length bolts, or the original head bolts with suitable spacers fitted to their shanks **(see illustration)**.

23 If the cylinder head is to be dismantled for overhaul, remove the camshaft as described in Section 10, then refer to the relevant Sections of Part C of this Chapter.

Preparation for refitting

24 The mating faces of the cylinder head and cylinder block/crankcase must be perfectly clean before refitting the head. Use a hard plastic or wood scraper to remove all traces of gasket and carbon; also clean the piston crowns. Take particular care as the soft aluminium alloy is damaged easily. Also, make sure that the carbon is not allowed to enter the oil and water passages - this is particularly important for the lubrication system, as carbon could block the oil supply to any of the engine's components. Using adhesive tape and paper, seal the water, oil and bolt holes in the cylinder block/crankcase. To prevent carbon entering the gap between the pistons and bores, smear a little grease in the gap. After cleaning each piston, use a small brush to remove all traces of grease and carbon from the gap, then wipe away the remainder with a clean rag. Clean all the pistons in the same way.

25 Check the mating surfaces of the cylinder block/crankcase and the cylinder head for nicks, deep scratches and other damage. If slight, they may be removed carefully with a file, but if excessive, machining may be the only alternative to renewal.

26 If warpage is suspected of the cylinder head gasket surface, use a straight-edge to check it for distortion. Refer to Part C of this Chapter if necessary.

27 Check the condition of the cylinder head bolts and particularly their threads whenever they are removed. Wash the bolts and wipe dry, then check each for any sign of visible wear or damage, renewing any bolt if necessary. Although Renault do not actually specify that the bolts must be renewed, it is

2B

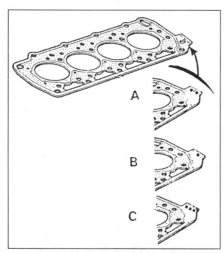

12.31 Cylinder head gasket thickness identification hole(s)

A 1.6 mm thick gasket
B 1.7 mm thick gasket
C 1.8 mm thick gasket

highly recommended that are renewed as a complete set whenever they are disturbed.

28 Prior to refitting the cylinder head, check the cylinder liner protrusion as described in Section 13 of Part C of this Chapter. Although the measuring procedure specifies that the liners should be fitted without seals, the seals have no effect on liner protrusion. If the liner protrusion exceeds the specified limits, seek the advice of a Renault dealer prior to refitting the head. If the liner protrusion is within the specified limits the new cylinder head gasket should be selected as follows.

29 When purchasing a new cylinder head gasket, it is vital that a gasket of the correct thickness is obtained. Three thicknesses are available; 1.6 mm, 1.7 mm and 1.8 mm.

30 On early models the gasket is identified as follows; the 1.6 mm gasket has "1.6" stamped on the gasket surface, the 1.7 mm gasket has no marking and the 1.8 mm gasket has "1.8" stamped on the gasket surface. It is unlikely, however, that this marking will still be visible on the original gasket.

31 On later models the gasket thickness is indicated by the hole(s) punched in the tab situated at the rear end of the gasket; this tab is visible even when the head is still fitted to the block **(see illustration)**. The 1.6 mm gasket has 2 holes punched in the tab, the 1.7 mm gasket has 1 hole punched in the tab and the 1.8 mm gasket three holes punched in the tab.

32 If the gasket thickness can be determined from its original markings, and no work which could affect the piston protrusion has been carried out, then a gasket of the same thickness as the original can be fitted. That being said, it is still advisable that the new gasket should be selected by direct measurement as described in the following paragraphs.

33 If the thickness of the original gasket is

unknown, or if work has been carried out which affects piston protrusion, then the correct gasket must be selected by using the following procedure. Note that all gaskets now supplied by Renault have the later type of identification marking.

34 Ensure the liners are clamped squarely and securely in position so that are correctly seated in the cylinder block then remove all traces of carbon from the piston crowns as described above.

35 Using a dial gauge, establish where TDC is, then measure the protrusion of each piston above the cylinder block gasket surface **(see illustration)**. Take two measurements from each piston, one on each side of the piston and take the average of the two as the correct piston protrusion. Note that the piston must not move during the measuring procedure, do not exert any force on the piston crown as this will cause the piston to tip in the bore; if the piston moves repeat both measurements. The correct gasket is selected using the **largest** piston protrusion measurement obtained; the required gasket thickness is as follows.

Piston protrusion	Gasket thickness required
Less than 0.96 mm	1.6 mm gasket
0.96 to 1.04 mm	1.7 mm gasket
More than 1.04 mm	1.8 mm gasket

36 Remove all traces of carbon from the valve heads and cylinder head combustion chamber surface. Using a dial gauge, measure the amount by which each valve head is recessed below the cylinder head combustion chamber surface. Note down these measurements and check that they are all within the specified limits given in the *Specifications* at the start of this Chapter. If not the cylinder head should be dismantled and overhauled as described in Part C of this Chapter. Make a special note of the valve with the smallest recess on the cylinder with the greatest piston protrusion (ie. the cylinder which was used to calculate the thickness of the head gasket required) as this valve is the one on which the piston-to-cylinder head clearance will be checked once the head has been refitted (see paragraphs 45 to 50).

12.35 Measuring piston protrusion

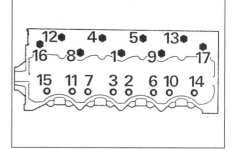

12.42 Cylinder head nut and bolt tightening sequence

Refitting

37 Wipe clean the mating surfaces of the cylinder head and cylinder block/crankcase. Check that the locating dowel is in position at the front right-hand corner of the cylinder block/crankcase surface. Where necessary, remove the cylinder liner clamps.

38 Position the new gasket on the cylinder block/crankcase surface ensuring that its identification tab is situated at the rear end of the gasket.

39 With the aid of an assistant lower the head into position, engaging it with the locating dowel.

40 Keeping all the cylinder head bolts in their correct fitted order, lightly oil under the head and on the threads of each bolt

41 Carefully enter each bolt into its original hole, screwing it in by hand only until finger-tight, then refit the three washers and nuts to the head studs.

42 Working in the sequence shown, tighten all the head nuts and bolts first to their stage 1 torque setting, then working again in the specified sequence, tighten them to the specified stage 2 torque setting **(see illustration)**.

43 Once they are tightened to the stage 2 specified torque setting, working again in the specified sequence, tighten the nuts and bolts to the specified stage 3 torque setting. Once the last bolt in the sequence is tightened, go around a second time and check that all the nuts and bolts are tightened to the specified stage 3 setting, retightening as necessary.

44 With the cylinder head in position, the piston-to-cylinder head clearance should now be checked. If no work affecting the clearance has been carried out and a cylinder head gasket of the same thickness as the original is being fitted, this operation is not strictly necessary. However, it is still recommended that the clearance is checked as a precaution. Proceed as described in paragraphs 45 to 50 to check the piston-to-cylinder head clearance. If it is not wished to check the clearance proceed as described in paragraph 51 onwards.

45 The piston-to-cylinder head clearance is checked on the cylinder with the largest piston protrusion, by measuring the clearance between the valve with the smallest recess and the piston crown when the piston is at TDC (see paragraphs 35 and 36).

46 Rotate the crankshaft so that the required piston is at TDC then remove the valve spring from the valve with the smallest recess. This is best achieved using a bar type valve spring compressor which is bolted to the cylinder head. Compress the valve spring and withdraw the collets then release the compressor and lift off the spring retainer and valve spring.

47 Drop the valve down so that it rests on the piston crown and set up a dial gauge on the tip of the valve stem. Rotate the crankshaft back and forth slightly whilst using the dial to establish when the piston is at TDC. With TDC established, zero the dial gauge then lift the valve whilst measuring the piston-to-valve clearance (ie. the amount of movement of the valve).

48 The piston-to-cylinder head clearance is then calculated by subtracting the valve head recess measurement from the piston-to-valve clearance. For example, if the piston-to-valve clearance was 1.57 mm and the valve recess measurement was 0.87 mm, the piston-to-cylinder head clearance would be 0.7 mm (1.57 mm - 0.87 mm = 0.7 mm).

49 The piston-to-cylinder head clearance must be at least 0.6 mm or greater. If this is not the case then a cylinder head gasket of the wrong thickness has been fitted. **Note:** *The engine **must not** be run if the clearance is less than 0.6 mm as serious engine damage is likely to occur. The cylinder head must be removed and a thicker gasket fitted.* If the thickest head gasket is already fitted then some other problem exists and the advice of your Renault dealer must be sought about the best course of action.

50 When the piston-to-cylinder head clearance is known to be correct, refit the valve spring and retainer to the valve. Compress the valve spring and refit the collets ensuring that they are correctly located in the recess on the valve stem. Remove the valve spring compressor and, using a hammer and interposed block of wood, tap the end of the valve stem to settle the components in position.

51 With the head correctly installed, refit the injection pump rear bracket retaining bolt and tighten it securely.

52 Connect all the relevant coolant hoses to the cylinder head and securely tighten their retaining clips.

53 Where necessary, refit the oil separator to the rear of the cylinder head tightening its retaining bolts securely.

54 On models with screw-type injectors, remove the plugs from the fuel unions and manoeuvre the injector pipe assembly back into position. Align the pipe ends with the injectors and injection pump unions and tighten the pipe union nuts to the specified torque setting. Reconnect the return pipe to the rear injector.

55 On models with clamp-type injectors, align the injector pipes with their unions on the injectors and tighten the pipe union nuts to the specified torque setting. Position a new sealing washer on both sides of each return pipe union and, where necessary, refit the filter to the return hose union. Refit both union bolts, tightening them to the specified torque setting.

56 Reconnect the wiring to the glow plugs and securely tighten the retaining nuts. Where necessary, reconnect the wiring connector to the coolant temperature sender unit.

57 Where removed, refit the thermostatic fast idle valve as described in Chapter 4C.

58 Refit the inlet and exhaust manifolds and turbocharger as described in Chapter 4C.

59 With No. 1 cylinder at TDC and the crankshaft locked in position with the locking pin, position the camshaft and injection pump sprockets so that their timing marks are aligned with marks made or noted on removal.

60 Refit the rocker shaft assembly as described in Section 10.

61 With the shaft in position, carry out the operations described in paragraphs 38 to 44 of Section 8.

62 With the timing belt correctly fitted and the cover installed, check and, if necessary, adjust the valve clearances as described in Section 11.

63 Refit the cylinder head cover as described in Section 4. Noting that the cover will have to be removed again once the engine has been run, refit the cover with the old gasket (where possible). The new gasket can then be installed later.

64 Refill the cooling system as described in Chapter 1.

65 Refit the plug to the cylinder block/crankcase timing hole and reconnect the battery.

66 Ensuring that the oil and coolant levels are correct, start-up the engine and warm it up to normal operating temperature. Allow it to run for 20 minutes then switch it off and leave it to cool for at least two and half hours.

67 Once the engine is cool, slacken and remove the bolt securing the rear injection pump bracket to the side of the cylinder head and remove the cylinder head cover as described in Section 4.

68 Working in the sequence shown, slacken the first nut/bolt (number 1) by half a turn then tighten it to the specified retightening torque setting (**see illustration 12.42**). Repeat this procedure on every cylinder head nut/bolt, working numerically through the tightening sequence.

69 Once all bolts have been slackened and retightened, go around in the specified sequence and check that all the nuts and bolts are tightened to the specified stage 3 setting, retightening as necessary.

70 Refit the injection pump rear mounting bracket bolt and tighten it securely.

71 Refit the cylinder head cover as described in Section 4 using the new gasket.

13 Sump - removal and refitting

Refer to Part A, Section 13, noting that on some engines it will be necessary to unbolt the engine movement limiter before raising the engine. The limiter is located either at the front of the engine attached to the front chassis member, or at the rear attached to the steering crossmember.

14 Oil pump - removal, inspection and refitting

Refer to Part A, Section 14, noting that on some engines it will be necessary to undo the union nuts and remove the pipe connecting the oil pump to the lubrication gallery before removing the pump. Tighten the union nuts securely when refitting.

15 Oil cooler components - removal and refitting

Removal

1 Disconnect the battery negative lead and proceed as described under the relevant sub-heading.

Oil cooler

2 Position a suitable container beneath the oil filter, then unscrew the filter using an oil filter removal tool, and drain the oil into the container. If the oil filter is damaged or disfigured during removal, it must be renewed and the engine should be filled with clean oil on refitting. Disconnect the oil hoses from the cooler as described in paragraph 5 (**see illustration**).

3 Release the hose clips and disconnect the coolant hoses from the oil cooler. To minimise coolant loss, clamp the coolant hoses using a suitable brake hose or G-clamp prior to disconnecting them.

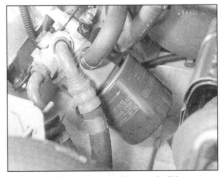

15.2 Oil cooler coolant and oil hose connections

4 Unscrew the oil cooler/oil filter mountings, and withdraw the cooler. Discard the oil cooler sealing ring, a new one must be used on refitting.

Oil hoses

5 To remove an oil cooler hose, position a suitable hose beneath the oil cooler then slacken the union nut securing the hose to the cooler mounting plate. Disconnect the hose and allow the oil to drain into the container then unscrew the hose from the adapter plate on the cylinder block/crankcase and remove it from the engine compartment. Recover the sealing ring from each hose union and discard them; new ones should be used on refitting.

6 If necessary, remove the second hose in the same way. If both hoses are to be removed or disconnected at the same time, make alignment marks between the hose unions and adapter plate/cooler mounting plate (as applicable) to remove the possibility of the hoses being wrongly reconnected on refitting.

Cylinder block/crankcase adapter plate

7 Remove both the oil hoses as described above.

8 There are two possible types of adapter plate fitted; the first is secured to the cylinder block by three bolts and the second by a large centre bolt.

9 To remove the first type, slacken and remove the three bolts and washers securing the plate to the side of the block then remove the plate and recover both its sealing rings. Discard both sealing rings; new ones should be used on refitting.

10 To remove the second type, unscrew the large centre bolt and washer then slide the adapter plate off its mounting stud. Recover the large sealing ring from the back of the adapter plate and discard it; a new one should be used on refitting.

Refitting

Oil cooler

11 Fit a new sealing ring to the recess in the top of the oil cooler and locate the cooler on the mounting plate. Ensure that the cooler coolant hose unions are facing towards the rear of the vehicle then refit the oil cooler/oil filter mounting bolt and tighten it securely.

12 Apply a smear of clean engine oil to the oil filter sealing ring and screw the filter securely onto the cooler, tightening it only by hand.

13 Reconnect the coolant hoses to the oil cooler, securing them in position with the retaining clips, and remove the clamp.

14 Lower the vehicle to the ground and top-up or refill the engine oil (as applicable).

15 Check the coolant level as described in *"Weekly checks"*, then start the engine and check the oil cooler assembly for leakage.

Oil hoses

16 Fit a new sealing ring to the hose union then reconnect the hose to the adapter, tightening it securely. If both hoses have been disconnected or removed use the marks made on removal to ensure that the hose is reconnected to the correct union.

17 Fit a new sealing ring to the cooler end of the hose then reconnect the hose to the cooler mounting plate and securely tighten its union nut. Again, if both hoses have been disconnected use the marks made on removal to ensure that the hose is connected to the correct union.

18 Where necessary fit the second hose in the same way.

19 Reconnect the battery then start up the engine and check the hose unions for signs of leakage.

Cylinder block/crankcase adapter plate

20 Where the first type of adapter plate is fitted, locate the new sealing rings in their recesses in the rear of the adapter plate. Manoeuvre the plate into position on the block, taking great care not displace either sealing ring, then refit the three retaining bolts and washers and tighten them securely.

21 Where the second type of adapter plate is fitted, locate the new sealing ring in the recess in the rear of the adapter plate. Locate the adapter plate on its retaining stud, ensuring that the sealing ring is not displaced, noting that the locating lug should be positioned at the top of the plate. With the plate correctly positioned, refit the centre bolt and washer and tighten it securely.

22 Refit the oil hoses as described above.

16 Crankshaft oil seals - renewal

Front (timing belt) oil seal

1 Remove the crankshaft sprocket and spacer/air conditioning drive pulley (as applicable) as described in Section 8. Secure the timing belt clear of the working area so that it cannot be contaminated with oil. Make a note of the correct fitted depth of the seal in its housing.

2 Punch or drill two small holes opposite each other in the seal. Screw a self-tapping screw into each and pull on the screws with pliers to extract the seal. Alternatively, the seal can be levered out of position using a suitable flat-bladed screwdriver taking great care not to damage the crankshaft shoulder or seal housing.

3 Clean the seal housing and polish off any burrs or raised edges which may have caused the seal to fail in the first place.

4 Lubricate the lips of the new seal with clean engine oil and carefully locate the seal on the end of crankshaft noting that its sealing lip must be facing inwards. Take care not to damage the seal lips during fitting.

5 Press the seal into its housing until it is positioned at the same depth as the original was prior to removal. If necessary, a suitable tubular drift, such as a socket, which bears only on the hard outer edge of the seal can be used to tap the seal into position. Take great care not to damage the seal lips during fitting and ensure that the seal lips face inwards. Note that if the surface of the crankshaft was noted to be badly scored, press the new seal slightly further into its housing so that its lip is running on an unmarked area of the crank.

6 Wash off any traces of oil, then refit the crankshaft sprocket and associated components as described in Section 8.

Rear (flywheel) oil seal

7 Remove the flywheel as described in Section 17. Make a note of the correct fitted depth of the seal in its housing.

8 Renew the seal as described above in paragraphs 2 to 5.

9 Wash off any traces of oil, then refit the flywheel as described in Section 17.

17 Flywheel - removal, inspection and refitting

Refer to Part A, Section 16.

18 Engine/transmission mountings - inspection and renewal

Refer to Part A, Section 17, noting that on some engines it will be necessary to unbolt the engine movement limiter before raising the engine. The limiter is located either at the front of the engine attached to the front chassis member, or at the rear attached to the steering crossmember.

Chapter 2 Part C:
Engine removal and overhaul procedures

Contents

Degrees of difficulty

Easy, suitable for novice with little experience	**Fairly easy,** suitable for beginner with some experience	**Fairly difficult,** suitable for competent DIY mechanic	**Difficult,** suitable for experienced DIY mechanic	**Very difficult,** suitable for expert DIY or professional

2C

Specifications

Cylinder head

Cylinder head height:	
Petrol engines	111.6 mm
Diesel engines	104.5 mm
Maximum acceptable gasket face distortion	0.05 mm
Swirl chamber protrusion (diesel engines only)	0.01 to 0.04 mm
Inlet valve seat angle:	
Petrol engines	120°
Diesel engines	90°
Exhaust valve seat angle	90°
Inlet valve seat width:	
Petrol engines	1.8 mm
Diesel engines	1.6 to 1.9 mm
Exhaust valve seat width:	
Petrol engines	1.6 mm
Diesel engines	1.6 to 1.9 mm

Inlet valves

Head diameter:	
Petrol engines	44.0 mm
Diesel engines	40.2 mm
Stem diameter	8.0 mm
Valve seat angle:	
Petrol engines	120°
Diesel engines	90°

Exhaust valves

Head diameter:	
Petrol engines	38.5 mm
Diesel engines	33.2 mm
Stem diameter	8.0 mm
Valve seat angle	90°

Valve springs

Free length	
Petrol engines	46.0 mm
Diesel engines	45.2 mm

Cylinder liners

Height (upper face to O-ring seal flange):
Petrol engines . . . . 93.065 to 93.095 mm
Diesel engines . . . . 93.035 to 93.065 mm
Bore diameter:
Petrol engines . . . . 88.0 mm
Diesel engines . . . . 86.0 mm
Base locating diameter . . . . 93.6 mm
Protrusion (without O-ring seal):
Petrol engines . . . . 0.08 to 0.15 mm
Diesel engines . . . . 0.5 to 0.12 mm
Maximum protrusion difference between any two adjacent liners . . . . . 0.04 mm

Piston rings

Ring thickness:
Petrol engines:
Top compression ring . . . . 1.75 mm
Second compression ring . . . . 2.0 mm
Oil control ring . . . . 4.0 mm
Diesel engines:
Top and second compression rings . . . . 2.5 mm
Oil control ring . . . . 4.0 mm

Gudgeon pins

Diameter:
Petrol engines . . . . 23.00 mm
Diesel engines . . . . 28.0 mm
Length . . . . 75.0 mm

Auxiliary shaft

Endfloat:
Petrol engines . . . . 0.17 to 0.22 mm
Diesel engines . . . . 0.5 to 0.15 mm

Crankshaft

Main bearing journal diameter:
Standard . . . . 62.88 mm
Reground . . . . 62.11 to 62.630 mm
Main bearing running clearance* . . . . 0.025 to 0.050 mm
Main bearing out-of-round* . . . . 0.006 mm max
Main bearing taper* . . . . 0.006 mm max
Connecting rod bearing journal diameter:
Petrol engines:
J6R and J7R:
Standard . . . . 52.296 mm
Reground . . . . 52.046 mm
J7T:
Standard . . . . 56.296 mm
Reground . . . . 56.046 mm
Diesel engines:
Standard . . . . 56.296 mm
Reground . . . . 56.046 mm
Connecting rod bearing running clearance* . . . . 0.023 to 0.067 mm
Connecting rod bearing out-of-round* . . . . 0.1 mm max
Connecting rod bearing taper* . . . . 0.01 mm max
Crankshaft endfloat:
Petrol engines:
J6R and J7R . . . . 0.07 to 0.25 mm
J7T . . . . 0.13 to 0.30 mm
Diesel engines . . . . 0.14 to 0.23 mm
*These are suggested figures, typical for this type of engine - no exact values are quoted by Renault

Torque wrench settings

Refer to Chapter 2A or 2B Specifications

1 General information

Included in this part of Chapter 2 are details of removing the engine/transmission from the vehicle and general overhaul procedures for the cylinder head, cylinder block/crankcase and all other engine internal components.

The information given ranges from advice concerning preparation for an overhaul and the purchase of replacement parts, to detailed step-by-step procedures covering removal, inspection, renovation and refitting of engine internal components.

After Section 4, all instructions are based on the assumption that the engine has been removed from the vehicle. For information concerning in-vehicle engine repair, as well as the removal and refitting of those external components necessary for full overhaul, refer to Part A or B of this Chapter (as applicable) and to Section 4. Ignore any preliminary dismantling operations described in Part A or B that are no longer relevant once the engine has been removed from the vehicle.

Apart from torque wrench settings, which are given at the beginning of Part A or B (as applicable), all specifications relating to engine overhaul are at the beginning of this Part of Chapter 2.

2 Engine overhaul - general information

It is not always easy to determine when, or if, an engine should be completely overhauled, as a number of factors must be considered.

High mileage is not necessarily an indication that an overhaul is needed, while low mileage does not preclude the need for an overhaul. Frequency of servicing is probably the most important consideration; an engine which has had regular and frequent oil and filter changes, as well as other required maintenance, should give many thousands of miles of reliable service. Conversely, a neglected engine may require an overhaul very early in its life.

Excessive oil consumption is an indication that piston rings, valve seals and/or valve guides are in need of attention. Make sure that oil leaks are not responsible before deciding that the rings and/or guides are worn. Perform a compression test, as described in Part A (petrol engine) or B (diesel engine) of this Chapter, to determine the likely cause of the problem.

Check the oil pressure with a gauge fitted in place of the oil pressure switch and compare it with that specified. If it is extremely low, the main and big-end bearings and/or the oil pump are probably worn out.

Loss of power, rough running, knocking or metallic engine noises, excessive valve gear noise and high fuel consumption may also point to the need for an overhaul, especially if they are all present at the same time. If a complete service does not remedy the situation, major mechanical work is the only solution.

An engine overhaul involves restoring all internal parts to the specification of a new engine. During an overhaul, the cylinder liners (where applicable), the pistons and the piston rings are renewed. New main and big-end bearings are generally fitted and if necessary, the crankshaft may be renewed or reground (as applicable) to restore the journals. The valves are also serviced as well, since they are usually in less than perfect condition at this point. While the engine is being overhauled, other cooling, fuel and engine electrical components, can be overhauled as well. The end result should be an as-new engine that will give many trouble-free miles.

Note: *Critical cooling system components such as the hoses, thermostat and coolant pump should be renewed when an engine is overhauled. The radiator should be checked carefully to ensure that it is not clogged or leaking. Also it is a good idea to renew the oil pump whenever the engine is overhauled.*

Before beginning the engine overhaul, read through the entire procedure to familiarise yourself with the scope and requirements of the job. Overhauling an engine is not difficult if you follow carefully all of the instructions, have the necessary tools and equipment and pay close attention to all specifications; however, it can be time consuming. Plan on the vehicle being off the road for a minimum of two weeks, especially if parts must be taken to an engineering works for repair or reconditioning. Check on the availability of parts and make sure that any necessary special tools and equipment are obtained in advance. Most work can be done with typical hand tools, although a number of precision measuring tools are required for inspecting parts to determine if they must be renewed. Often the engineering works will handle the inspection of parts and offer advice concerning reconditioning and renewal.

Note: *Always wait until the engine has been completely dismantled and all components, especially the cylinder block/crankcase, the cylinder bores and the crankshaft have been inspected before deciding what service and repair operations must be performed by an engineering works. Since the condition of these components will be the major factor to consider when determining whether to overhaul the original engine or buy a reconditioned unit, do not purchase parts or have overhaul work done on other components until they have been thoroughly inspected. As a general rule, time is the primary cost of an overhaul, so it does not pay to fit worn or substandard parts.*

As a final note, to ensure maximum life and minimum trouble from a reconditioned engine, everything must be assembled with care in a spotlessly clean environment.

3 Engine/transmission removal - methods and precautions

If you have decided that the engine must be removed for overhaul or major repair work, several preliminary steps should be taken.

Locating a suitable place to work is extremely important. Adequate work space, along with storage space for the vehicle, will be needed. If a workshop or garage is not available, at the very least a flat, level, clean work surface is required.

Cleaning the engine compartment and engine/transmission before beginning the removal procedure will help keep tools clean and organised.

An engine hoist or A-frame will also be necessary. Make sure the equipment is rated in excess of the weight of the engine or engine and transmission (as applicable). Safety is of primary importance, considering the potential hazards involved in lifting the engine or engine/transmission out of the vehicle.

If the unit is being removed by a novice, a helper should be available. Advice and aid from someone more experienced would also be helpful. There are many instances when one person cannot simultaneously perform all of the operations required when lifting the engine out of the vehicle.

Plan the operation ahead of time. Before starting work, arrange for the hire of or obtain all of the tools and equipment you will need. Some of the equipment necessary to perform engine/transmission removal and installation safely and with relative ease (in addition to an engine hoist) is as follows: a heavy duty trolley jack, complete sets of spanners and sockets, wooden blocks, and plenty of rags and cleaning solvent for mopping up spilled oil, coolant and fuel. If the hoist must be hired, make sure that you arrange for it in advance, and perform all of the operations possible without it beforehand. This will save you money and time.

Plan for the vehicle to be out of use for quite a while. An engineering works will be required to perform some of the work which the do-it-yourselfer cannot accomplish without special equipment. These places often have a busy schedule, so it would be a good idea to consult them before removing the engine in order to accurately estimate the amount of time required to rebuild or repair components that may need work.

Always be extremely careful when removing and refitting the engine/transmission. Serious injury can result from careless actions. Plan ahead, take your time and a job of this nature, although major, can be accomplished successfully.

2C

4 Engine (without transmission) - removal and refitting

Note: *The engine can be removed from the vehicle either on its own, or as a complete unit with the transmission. Removal of the engine on its own is described in this Section; removal of the unit with the transmission attached is described in Section 5.*

Removal

1 Disconnect the battery negative lead.

2 Remove the bonnet (see Chapter 11).

3 Drain the cooling system (see Chapter 1).

4 It is now necessary to gain as much access to the front of the engine as possible by removing the various detachable panels and components. The arrangement and attachment method varies according to model type and year, but includes:

a) The upper front crossmember over the radiator.
b) The radiator and electric cooling fans.
c) The front grille and support struts.
d) The front bumper.
e) The lower crossmember.

Refer to the appropriate Chapters of this manual for additional details of the above components.

5 If the engine is to be dismantled, drain the oil and remove the oil filter then clean and refit the drain plug, tightening it securely.

6 Refer to the appropriate Part of Chapter 4 and remove the air cleaner housing (petrol engines) or the inlet ducts connecting the air cleaner and intercooler to the turbocharger and inlet manifold (diesel engines).

7 Remove the power steering pump as described in Chapter 10.

8 On later models, refer to Chapter 3 and remove the soundproofing in the engine compartment then remove the heater fan motor assembly.

9 Refer to the relevant Part of Chapter 4 and disconnect the accelerator cable from the carburettor, pivot quadrant or injection pump. Free the outer cable from the support bracket on the engine and move the cable clear.

10 Undo the nuts/bolts and disconnect the earth leads from the engine.

11 On petrol engines, disconnect the fuel hoses from the carburettor or fuel injection equipment.

12 On diesel engines with clamp-type injectors, wipe clean the injector unions and the injection pump. Undo the union bolt securing the fuel return hose to the top of each injector and the injection pump and recover the sealing washers from each hose union. With all five union bolts removed position the return hose clear of the cylinder head. Screw the union bolts back into position for safe-keeping and cover the hose and injector unions to prevent the ingress of dirt into the fuel system.

13 On diesel engines with screw-type injectors, wipe clean the injection pump fuel unions. Slacken and remove the fuel return hose union bolt from the pump and recover the sealing washer from each side of the hose union. Disconnect the return pipe from the end injector and position the hose clear of the pump. Screw the union bolt back into position on the pump for safe-keeping and cover both the hose end and union bolt to prevent the ingress of dirt into the fuel system.

14 On all diesel engines, remove the injection pump feed hose union bolt and recover the sealing washers. Detach the hose from the pump and position the hose clear of the engine. Screw the union bolt back into position on the pump for safe-keeping and cover both the hose end and union bolt to prevent the ingress of dirt into the fuel system.

Note: *The injection pump feed and return hose union bolts are not interchangeable. Great care must be taken to ensure that the bolts are not swapped.*

15 On models fitted with an oil cooler, disconnect the oil feed and return hose unions from the adapter assembly on the side of the cylinder block.

16 Disconnect the coolant hoses from the engine, oil cooler and fuel filter heater housing as applicable. Also disconnect the hose connecting the expansion tank to the engine/oil cooler, from the tank so that the hose will be removed with the engine.

17 Disconnect the servo vacuum hose from the manifold or vacuum pump. Release the hose from any relevant retaining clips or ties and position it clear of the engine.

18 Disconnect the wiring connectors from the various engine sensors, switches, control units, starter motor and alternator. Note and label the wiring runs and connectors to avoid confusion on refitting.

19 On models equipped with air conditioning, unbolt the compressor and disengage it from the drivebelt. Position the compressor clear of the engine and support the weight of the compressor by tying it to the vehicle body to prevent any excess strain being placed on the compressor lines whilst the engine is removed. **Do not** disconnect the refrigerant lines from the compressor (see the warnings given in Chapter 3). The drivebelt can be left in position on the engine.

20 On diesel engines, undo the retaining bolts and remove the movement limiter from the front (early models) or rear (later models) of the engine.

21 Chock the rear wheels then jack up the front of the vehicle and support it on axle stands (see *"Jacking and vehicle support"*).

22 Remove the exhaust system front pipe as described in Chapter 4D.

23 Disconnect the clutch cable from the transmission as described in Chapter 6.

24 Remove the starter motor as described in Chapter 5A.

25 On petrol engines, remove the angular position/speed sensor from the bellhousing.

26 On engines with a single-piece steel sump, remove the flywheel cover plate from the bellhousing.

27 Attach suitable lifting chains to the brackets at each end of the cylinder head and take the weight of the engine on the hoist. On diesel engines, it is recommended that a third lifting bracket and chain should be attached to the exhaust manifold, to prevent the engine tilting as it is removed. Due to the lack of working clearance at the rear of the engine, it will be difficult to attach the rear chain without it fouling the upper body area. Therefore, it may be beneficial to support the engine under the sump on a trolley jack, roll the jack out with the engine initially, then reposition the rear chain when sufficient clearance exists.

28 Support the transmission from below, using a second trolley jack for preference. Pad the jack head with rags or wood.

29 Work around the clutch bellhousing and unscrew the other bolts securing the transmission to the engine, noting the correct location of the various brackets and clips.

30 From underneath the vehicle, undo the nuts securing the front engine mountings to the chassis brackets.

31 Make a final check that all components have been removed or disconnected that will prevent the removal of the engine from the vehicle.

32 With the aid of an assistant, move the engine forwards to disengage it from the locating dowels then move it squarely away from the transmission, ensuring that the clutch components are not damaged.

33 Once the engine is clear of the transmission primary shaft, reposition the rear chain if necessary, then raise the engine ensuring that nothing is trapped or damaged. Withdraw the unit from the front of the vehicle and lower it to the ground. If the locating dowels are a loose fit, remove them and store them with the engine for safe-keeping.

Refitting

34 Apply a smear of high-melting-point grease to the splines of the transmission primary shaft. Do not apply too much, otherwise there is a possibility of the grease contaminating the clutch friction plate. Ensure that the locating dowels are correctly positioned in the engine or transmission.

35 With the aid of an assistant, reconnect the hoist and lifting tackle to the engine lifting brackets, and lift the assembly into the engine compartment.

36 Ensuring that the engine is manoeuvred as necessary to clear surrounding components, as during removal, position the assembly in the engine compartment, manipulating the hoist and lifting tackle as necessary.

37 Align the engine with the transmission primary shaft, and carefully move the engine rearwards until the locating dowels are engaged. Ensure that the weight of the engine is not allowed to hang on the primary shaft as it is engaged with the clutch friction plate.

38 If all is well, lower the engine until the mountings engage with the chassis brackets. Refit the transmission bellhousing-to-engine bolts, ensuring that all the necessary brackets and clips are correctly positioned.

39 Remove the hoist and rock the engine to settle the disturbed mountings in position. Refit and tighten the mounting nuts.

40 The remainder of the refitting procedure is a reversal of the removal sequence, noting the following points.

 a) *Tighten all nuts and bolts to their specified torque setting (where given).*

 b) *Ensure all coolant hoses and wiring are correctly routed and securely reconnected.*

 c) *Adjust the clutch cable as described in Chapter 6.*

 d) *Reconnect the feed and return hoses to the injection pump using new sealing washers.*

 e) *Refit the power steering pump to the engine as described in Chapter 10.*

 f) *Where necessary, refit the air conditioning compressor to the engine and adjust the drivebelt as described in Chapter 1.*

 g) *Refill the cooling system as described in Chapter 1.*

 h) *Refill the engine with oil as described in Chapter 1.*

 i) *On completion, adjust the accelerator cable and, on diesel engines, bleed the fuel system as described in Chapter 4C, then start the engine and check for leaks.*

5 Engine (with transmission) - removal, separation and refitting

Note: *The engine can be removed from the vehicle either on its own, or as a complete unit with the transmission. Removal of the engine on its own is described in Section 4; removal of the unit with the transmission attached is described in this Section.*

Removal and separation

1 Proceed as in Section 4, paragraphs 1 to 23.

2 Remove both front roadwheels.

3 Remove the transmission undertray which is secured by screws and locating pegs.

4 Undo the two bolts each side securing the brake calipers to the hub carriers. Slide the calipers, complete with pads, off the discs and tie them up using string or wire from a suitable place under the wheel arch.

5 Using a parallel pin punch of suitable diameter, knock out the driveshaft roll pins at the transmission end of each driveshaft CV joint. Note that there are two roll pins fitted each side, one inside the other. Obtain new roll pins for reassembly.

6 Refer to Chapter 10 and detach the steering arm outer balljoints from the hub carriers. Also detach the upper suspension arm from each hub carrier by separating the upper balljoint.

7 Pivot the hub carriers outwards at the top

and simultaneously withdraw the driveshafts from the transmission. On later models, collect the insulating rubber washer from the differential side gear shafts.

8 Disconnect the speedometer cable from the transmission by gripping the retaining pin with a pair of pliers and pulling it outwards to release the cable.

9 Disconnect the reversing light leads at the in-line connector.

10 Disconnect the gearchange linkage at the transmission end as described in Chapter 7.

11 Support the transmission from below, using a trolley jack for preference. Pad the jack head with rags or wood.

12 Disconnect the transmission flexible mountings and brackets.

13 Attach suitable lifting chains to the brackets at each end of the cylinder head and take the weight of the engine on the hoist. On diesel engines, it is recommended that a third lifting bracket and chain should be attached to the exhaust manifold, to prevent the engine tilting as it is removed. Due to the lack of working clearance at the rear of the engine, it will be difficult to attach the rear chain without it fouling the upper body area. Therefore, it may be beneficial to roll out the transmission support jack with the engine/transmission initially, then reposition the rear chain when sufficient clearance exists.

14 Undo the nuts securing the front engine mountings to the chassis brackets.

15 Make a final check that all components have been removed or disconnected that will prevent the removal of the engine from the vehicle.

16 With the aid of an assistant, lift the engine/transmission until the engine mountings are clear of their brackets

17 Ensure nothing is trapped or damaged, carefully withdraw the assembly from the front of the vehicle and lower it to the ground.

18 To separate the engine and transmission first remove the starter motor, referring to Chapter 5A if necessary.

19 Unscrew the remaining bolts securing the transmission to the engine, noting the correct location of the various brackets and retaining clips.

20 Gently prise the transmission off its locating dowels and move the transmission squarely away from the engine, ensuring that the clutch components are not damaged.

Refitting

21 If the engine and transmission have been separated, perform the operations described below in paragraphs 22 to 26. If not, proceed as described from paragraph 27 onwards.

22 Apply a smear of high-melting-point grease to the splines of the transmission primary shaft. Do not apply too much, otherwise there is a possibility of the grease contaminating the clutch friction plate.

23 Ensure that the locating dowels are correctly positioned in the engine or transmission.

24 Carefully offer the transmission to the engine, until the locating dowels are engaged, ensuring that the weight of the transmission is not allowed to hang on the primary shaft as it is engaged with the clutch friction plate.

25 Refit the transmission housing-to-engine bolts, ensuring that all the necessary brackets and clips are correctly positioned.

26 Refit the starter motor and securely tighten its retaining bolts.

27 With the aid of an assistant, reconnect the hoist and lifting tackle to the engine lifting brackets, and lift the assembly into the engine compartment.

28 Ensure that the assembly is tilted as necessary to clear surrounding components, as during removal, and lower it into position in the engine compartment, manipulating the hoist and lifting tackle as necessary.

29 Align the front engine mountings with their respective holes in the chassis brackets, then lower the engine and engage the mountings.

30 Refit the rear mounting assemblies to the transmission and tighten their retaining bolts. Refit the engine mounting nuts and tighten these also.

31 Detach the hoist and lifting gear.

32 The remainder of the refitting procedure is a direct reversal of the removal sequence, noting the following points.

 a) *On later models, the driveshaft inner joints are fitted with an insulating rubber washer. Ensure that the washer is in position when assembling the joint to the differential stub shaft.*

 b) *Smear the driveshaft inner joint splines with molybdenum disulphide grease, then position the splines so that the roll pin holes will align when the joint is pushed fully home.*

 c) *Position the two new roll pins so that their slots are 90° apart and seal their ends with suitable hard setting sealant after installation.*

 d) *Clean the threads of the brake caliper mounting bolts and apply thread locking compound to them before refitting.*

 e) *Tighten all nuts and bolts to the specified torque where given (see also Chapters 9 and 10).*

 f) *Ensure all coolant hoses and wiring are correctly routed and securely reconnected.*

 g) *Adjust the clutch cable as described in Chapter 6.*

 h) *Reconnect the feed and return hoses to the injection pump using new sealing washers.*

 i) *Refit the power steering pump to the engine as described in Chapter 10.*

 j) *Where necessary, refit the air conditioning compressor to the engine and adjust the drivebelt as described in Chapter 1.*

 k) *Refill the cooling system as described in Chapter 1.*

 l) *Refill the engine with oil as described in Chapter 1.*

2C

m) Check and if necessary top-up the transmission oil as described in Chapter 1.

n) On completion, adjust the accelerator cable and, on diesel engines, bleed the fuel system as described in Chapter 4C, then start the engine and check for leaks.

6 Engine overhaul - dismantling sequence

1 It is much easier to dismantle and work on the engine if it is mounted on a portable engine stand. These stands can often be hired from a tool hire shop. Before the engine is mounted on a stand, the flywheel should be removed, so that the stand bolts can be tightened into the end of the cylinder block/ crankcase.

2 If a stand is not available, it is possible to dismantle the engine with it blocked up on a sturdy workbench, or on the floor. Be extra-careful not to tip or drop the engine when working without a stand.

3 If you are going to obtain a reconditioned engine, all the external components must be removed first, to be transferred to the replacement engine (just as they will if you are doing a complete engine overhaul yourself). These components include the following:

a) Fuel system components (Chapter 4, Part A, B or C).
b) All electrical switches and sensors.
c) Alternator (Chapter 5, Part A).
d) Power steering pump (Chapter 10).
e) Distributor - petrol engines (Chapter 5, Part B).
f) Vacuum pump - diesel engines (Chapter 9).
g) Ancillary component mounting brackets.
h) Coolant pump (Chapter 3).
i) Thermostat housing/outlet elbow (Chapter 3).
j) Inlet and exhaust manifolds (Chapter 4).
k) Oil filter (Chapter 1).
l) Flywheel (Part A or B of this Chapter).

Note: When removing the external components from the engine, pay close attention to details that may be helpful or important during refitting. Note the fitted position of gaskets, seals, spacers, pins, washers, bolts, and other small items.

4 If you are obtaining a "short" engine (which consists of the engine cylinder block/crankcase, crankshaft, pistons and connecting rods all assembled), then the cylinder head, sump, oil pump, and timing belt will have to be removed also.

5 If you are planning a complete overhaul, the engine can be dismantled, and the internal components removed, in the order given below, referring to Part A or B of this Chapter unless otherwise stated.

a) Timing belt, sprockets and tensioner.
b) Cylinder head.
c) Flywheel.
d) Sump.
e) Oil pump.
f) Auxiliary shaft (Section 10).
g) Piston/connecting rod assemblies (Section 11).
h) Crankshaft (Section 12).

6 Before beginning the dismantling and overhaul procedures, make sure that you have all of the correct tools necessary. Refer to *Tools and working facilities* for further information.

7 Cylinder head - dismantling

Note: New and reconditioned cylinder heads are available from the manufacturer and from engine overhaul specialists. Due to the fact that some specialist tools are required for the dismantling and inspection procedures, and new components may not be readily available, it may be more practical and economical for the home mechanic to purchase a reconditioned head rather than dismantle, inspect and recondition the original head.

1 Remove the cylinder head as described in Part A, Section 11 (petrol engines) or Part B, Section 12 (diesel engines). Remove the following components, if not already having done so.

a) Inlet and exhaust manifolds (Chapter 4, Part A, B or C).
b) Spark plugs - petrol engines (Chapter 1).
c) Fuel injectors and pipes - diesel engines (Chapter 4, Part C).

d) Glow plugs - diesel engines (Chapter 4, Part C).
e) Camshaft (Part A or B of this Chapter).

2 Using a valve spring compressor, compress each valve spring in turn until the split collets can be removed **(see illustration).** Release the compressor and lift off the spring retainer, spring and spring seat.

3 If, when the valve spring compressor is screwed down, the spring retainer refuses to free and expose the split collets, gently tap the top of the tool, directly over the retainer with a light hammer. This will free the retainer.

4 Withdraw the valve through the combustion chamber. Using a pair of pliers, carefully extract the valve stem seal from the top of the guide.

5 It is essential that each valve is stored together with its collets, retainer and spring, and that all valves are in their correct sequence unless they are so badly worn that they are to be renewed. If they are going to be kept and used again, place each valve assembly in a labelled polythene bag or similar small container **(see illustration).** Note that No 1 valve is nearest to the flywheel end of the engine.

8 Cylinder head and valves - cleaning and inspection

1 Thorough cleaning of the cylinder head and valve components, followed by a detailed inspection, will enable you to decide how much valve service work must be carried out during the engine overhaul. **Note:** *If the engine has been severely overheated, it is best to assume that the cylinder head is warped and to check carefully for signs of this.*

Cleaning

2 Scrape, or clean away with a suitable solvent, all traces of old gasket material and sealing compound from the cylinder head.

3 Remove the carbon from the combustion chambers and ports, then wash the cylinder head thoroughly with paraffin or a suitable solvent.

4 Scrape off any heavy carbon deposits that may have formed on the valves, then use a power-operated wire brush to remove deposits from the valve heads and stems.

5 If the head is extremely dirty, it should be steam cleaned.

6 If the head has been steam cleaned, clean all oil holes and oil galleries one more time on completion. Flush all internal passages with warm water until the water runs clear, dry the head thoroughly and wipe all machined surfaces with a light oil. If you have access to compressed air, use it to speed the drying process and to blow out all the oil holes and galleries.

 Warning: Be sure to wear eye protection when using compressed air!

7.2 Compressing a valve spring

7.5 Keep all valve components together in a labelled plastic bag

7 If the head is relatively clean, an adequate cleaning job can be achieved with hot soapy water and a stiff brush. Take plenty of time and do a thorough job. Regardless of the cleaning method used, be sure to clean all oil holes and galleries very thoroughly, dry the head completely and coat all machined surfaces with light oil.

8 The threaded holes in the cylinder head must be clean to ensure accurate torque readings when tightening fixings during reassembly. Run the correct size tap (which can be determined from the size of the relevant bolt which fits in the hole) into each of the holes to remove rust, corrosion, thread sealant or other contamination, and to restore damaged threads. If possible, use compressed air to clear the holes of debris produced by this operation. Do not forget to clean the threads of all bolts and nuts as well.

Inspection

Note: *Be sure to perform all the following inspection procedures before concluding that the services of a machine shop or engine overhaul specialist are required. Make a list of all items that require attention.*

Cylinder head

9 Inspect the head very carefully for cracks, evidence of coolant leakage and other damage. If cracks are found, a new cylinder head should be obtained.

10 Use a straight-edge and feeler blade to check that the cylinder head gasket surface is not distorted **(see illustration)**. Check the head surface both diagonally, and along its edge. On diesel engines, do not position the straight-edge over the swirl chambers, as these may be proud of the cylinder head face. If the specified distortion limit is exceeded the cylinder head should be renewed; machining of the gasket face is not recommended by the manufacturers.

11 Check that the overall height of the cylinder head is within the specified limits. The height measurement is taken from the camshaft/cylinder head cover to head gasket sealing faces. If the overall height is outside the specified limits, the cylinder head should be renewed.

12 On diesel engines, inspect the swirl chambers for burning or damage such as cracking **(see illustration)**. Small cracks in the chambers are acceptable; renewal of the chambers will only be required if chamber tracts are badly burned and disfigured or if they are no longer a tight fit in the cylinder head. If there is any doubt as to the swirl chamber condition, seek the advice of a Renault dealer or a suitable repairer who specialises in diesel engines. Swirl chamber renewal should be entrusted to a specialist.

13 Using a dial test indicator check that the swirl chamber protrusion is within the limits given in the *Specifications*. Zero the dial test indicator on the gasket surface of the cylinder head, then measure the protrusion of the swirl chamber **(see illustration)**. If the protrusion is not within the specified limits the advice of a Renault dealer or suitable repairer who specialises in diesel engines should be sought.

14 Examine the valve seats in the cylinder head. If the seats are badly pitted, cracked or burned, then they will need to be recut by an engine overhaul specialist. Note that renewal of the valve seats is not possible and if the damage is severe, the only course of action available is to renew the cylinder head.

15 If only slight pitting of the seats is evident, this can be removed by grinding the valve heads and seats together with coarse then fine grinding paste as described later in this Section.

16 Check for play (side-to-side movement) of the valves in the valve guides. Excessive play in the guide may be caused by wear in either component. Measure the valve stem with a micrometer, or try the fit of a new valve, if available, to establish whether it is the valve or the guide which is worn. If the valve guides are worn, they can be renewed, but this work is best carried out by a Renault dealer or an engine overhaul specialist.

17 Inspect the studs for the manifolds and rocker arm pedestals. Renew them if necessary by using a proprietary stud extractor, or lock two nuts together on the exposed threads. Studs which have come out by mistake should be cleaned up and refitted using thread locking fluid.

18 Inspect the camshaft bearing surfaces and associated components as described in Part A, Section 12, or Part B, Section 10 (as applicable).

Valves

19 Examine the head of each valve for pitting, burning, cracks and general wear, and check the valve stem for scoring and wear ridges. Rotate the valve and check for any obvious indication that it is bent. Look for pitting and excessive wear on the end of each valve stem. If the valve appears satisfactory at this stage, measure the valve stem diameter at several points using a micrometer **(see illustration)**. Any significant difference in the readings obtained indicates wear of the valve stem. Should any of these conditions be apparent, the valve(s) must be renewed.

20 If the valves are in satisfactory condition, they should be ground (lapped) onto their respective seats to ensure a smooth gas-tight seal.

21 Valve grinding is carried out as follows. Place the cylinder head upside down on a bench, with a block of wood at each end to give clearance for the valve stems.

22 Smear a trace of coarse carborundum paste on the seat face in the cylinder head, and press a suction grinding tool onto the relevant valve head. With a semi-rotary action, grind the valve head to its seat, lifting the valve occasionally to redistribute the grinding paste. When a dull, matt, even surface is produced on the faces of both the valve seat and the valve, wipe off the paste and repeat the process with fine carborundum paste. A light spring placed under the valve head will greatly ease this operation. When a smooth unbroken ring of light grey matt finish is produced on both the valve and seat faces, the grinding operation is complete. Carefully clean away every trace of grinding paste, taking great care to leave none in the ports or in the valve guides. Clean the valves and valve seats with a paraffin-soaked rag, then with a clean rag, and finally, if an air line is available, blow the valves, valve guides and cylinder head ports clean.

Valve springs

23 Examine the valve springs for signs of damage and discoloration. Stand each spring

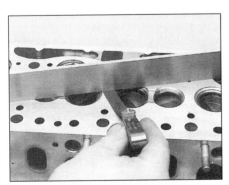

8.10 Checking cylinder head gasket surface distortion

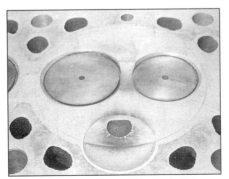

8.12 This swirl chamber is showing initial signs of cracking

8.13 Measuring swirl chamber protrusion

2C

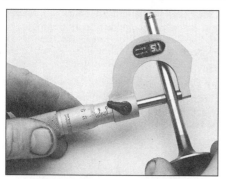

8.19 Measuring valve stem diameter

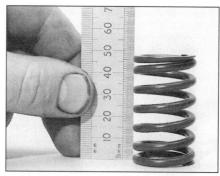

8.24 Measuring valve spring free length

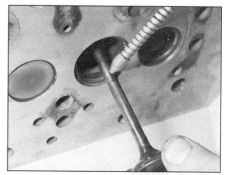

9.1 Lubricate the valve stems and insert the valves into their original locations

on a flat surface and check it for squareness. If any of the springs are damaged, distorted or have lost their tension, obtain a complete new set of springs.

24 The condition of each spring can be judged be measuring its free length **(see illustration)**. If the length of any spring is significantly different to that given in the *Specifications* at the start of this Chapter, then all the valve springs should be renewed as a complete set.

9 Cylinder head - reassembly

1 Lubricate the stems of the valves and insert them into their original locations. If new valves

9.2 Fit the valve guide oil seals; use a socket to press them onto the guides

are being fitted, insert them into the locations to which they have been ground **(see illustration)**.

2 Working on the first valve, dip the valve stem seal in fresh engine oil then carefully locate it over the valve and onto the guide. Take care not to damage the seal as it is passed over the valve stem. Use a suitable socket or metal tube to press the seal firmly onto the guide **(see illustration)**.

3 Refit the spring seat and locate the spring on the seat, followed by the spring retainer **(see illustrations)**.

4 Compress the valve spring and locate the split collets in the recess in the valve stem. Carefully release the compressor.

> **HAYNES HiNT** *Use a little dab of grease to hold the collets in position on the valve stem while the spring compressor is released.*

5 Repeat these procedures on the remaining valves.

6 With all the valves installed, place the cylinder head on blocks on the bench and, using a hammer and interposed block of wood, tap the end of each valve stem to settle the components.

7 Refit the camshaft and associated components then refit the cylinder head as described in the relevant Sections of Part A or Part B of this Chapter (as applicable).

10 Auxiliary shaft - removal and refitting

Removal

1 Remove the auxiliary shaft sprocket as described in Part A, Section 9, or Part B, Section 8, as applicable.

2 Undo the retaining bolts then slide the cover off the end of the auxiliary shaft and recover the gasket

3 If not already done, remove the distributor (if mounted on the cylinder block) and fuel pump (carburettor petrol engines) or braking system vacuum pump (diesel engines) as described in Chapters 5B, 4A or 9 respectively. On all other petrol engines, unbolt the blanking plate over the auxiliary shaft on the side of the cylinder block. Recover the blanking plate seal.

4 Carefully withdraw the oil pump drivegear, taking great care not to dislodge the oil pump driveshaft **(see illustration)**. **Note:** *Great care must be taken to ensure that the driveshaft is not dislodged from the oil pump. If the driveshaft is dislodged it will drop down into the bottom sump. If this happens, the sump will have to be removed in order to recover the driveshaft.*

5 Unscrew the retaining bolt and washer then slide out the auxiliary shaft thrust plate and withdraw the auxiliary shaft.

9.3a Refit the spring seat . . .

9.3b . . . followed by the valve spring . . .

9.3c . . . and spring retainer

10.4 Withdrawing the oil pump drivegear

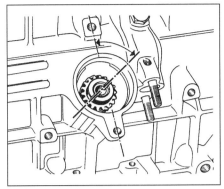

10.16 Correct fitted position of the oil pump drivegear slot, at 45° to the bolt hole centreline

11 Piston/connecting rod assembly - removal

Inspection

6 Examine the auxiliary shaft and oil pump driveshaft for pitting, scoring or wear ridges on the bearing journals, and for chipping or wear of the gear teeth. Renew as necessary. Check the auxiliary shaft bearings in the cylinder block for wear and, if worn, have these renewed by your Renault dealer or suitably-equipped engineering works. Wipe them clean if they are still serviceable.

7 Temporarily fit the thrust plate to its position on the auxiliary shaft, and use a feeler blade to check that the endfloat is as given in the *Specifications*. If it is greater than the upper tolerance, a new thrust plate should be obtained, but first check the thrust surfaces on the shaft to ascertain if wear has occurred here.

Refitting

8 Clean off all traces of the old gasket or sealant from the auxiliary shaft cover. Lever the old oil seal out of the cover and position a new seal in the cover and tap it into position using a suitable tubular drift, such as a socket, which bears only on the hard outer edge of the seal. Ensure that the seal lip is facing inwards.

9 Liberally lubricate the auxiliary shaft, and slide it into its bearings.

10 Slide the thrust plate in position and securely tighten its retaining bolts.

11 Place a new gasket in position on the cylinder block/crankcase.

12 Carefully ease the cover over the end of the shaft and slide it into position.

13 To prevent the possibility of oil leakage smear the shafts of the cover retaining bolts with a suitable sealant. Renault recommend the use of a Loctite sealant (available from your Renault dealer); in the absence of this ensure a good quality sealant is used.

14 Ensure the gasket is correctly positioned then refit the cover retaining bolts, tightening them securely.

15 Refit the auxiliary shaft sprocket as described in Part A, Section 9, or Part B, Section 8, as applicable.

16 On carburettor petrol engines having their ignition distributor driven from the auxiliary shaft, the installation position of the oil pump drivegear is critical. Temporarily refit the timing belt cover to the engine and turn the auxiliary shaft sprocket until the notch on the rim is aligned with the timing pointer in the cover. Hold the sprocket and auxiliary shaft in this position while fitting the drivegear. Engage the drivegear over the oil pump driveshaft and into mesh with the worm gear on the auxiliary shaft. When the drivegear is fully engaged, its slot must be at 45° to an imaginary centreline drawn through the two distributor retaining studs **(see illustration)**. It may take two or three attempts to achieve this. Once the drivegear is in place, and with the auxiliary shaft sprocket notch still aligned with the timing pointer, temporarily refit the distributor and check that the rotor arm is pointing towards the No. 1 cylinder HT lead segment in the cap.

17 On all other engines the installed position of the drivegear is not critical, but ensure that it is correctly engaged with the oil pump driveshaft and fully seated.

18 Refit the blanking plate using a new seal, or refit the distributor, fuel pump or vacuum pump according to engine, and with reference to the relevant Chapters of this manual.

11.2 Make identification marks on the connecting rod/bearing cap prior to removal

1 Remove the cylinder head, sump and oil pump as described in the relevant Sections of Part A or B of this Chapter (as applicable).

2 Using a hammer and centre punch, paint or similar, mark each connecting rod big-end bearing cap with its respective cylinder number on the flat, machined surface provided; if the engine has been dismantled before, note carefully any identifying marks made previously **(see illustration)**. Note that No 1 cylinder is at the flywheel end of the engine.

3 Turn the crankshaft to bring pistons 1 and 4 to BDC (bottom dead centre).

4 Unscrew the nuts or bolts from number 1 piston big-end bearing cap, then take off the cap and recover the bottom half bearing shell **(see illustration)**. If the bearing shells are to be re-used, tape the cap and the shell together. If the bearing cap locating dowels/pins (as applicable) are a loose fit, remove them and store them with the cap for safe-keeping.

5 Push the piston up the liner bore to disengage the connecting rod from the crankshaft. Recover the upper bearing shell, and tape it to the connecting rod for safe keeping. **Note:** *The piston/connecting rod assemblies are removed complete with the cylinder liners.*

6 Using a suitable piece of wood, such as the handle of a hammer, tap the liner upwards and out of position from the base of the cylinder block/crankcase.

7 Withdraw the liner/piston and connecting rod assembly from the top of the cylinder block/crankcase. Remove the sealing ring (where fitted) and O-ring from the base of liner and discard.

8 Refit the big-end cap to the connecting rod and loosely tighten its retaining bolts. This will help to keep the components in their correct order.

9 Repeat the procedure and remove No 4 liner/piston and connecting rod assembly in the same way.

11.4 Unscrew the bolts and remove the big-end bearing cap

2C

10 Turn the crankshaft through 180° to bring pistons 2 and 3 to BDC (bottom dead centre) and remove them in the same way.

11 If necessary, mark the relevant cylinder number on the liner and withdraw the piston/connecting rod assembly from the base of each liner.

12 Crankshaft - removal

1 Remove the crankshaft sprocket, flywheel and the oil pump as described in the relevant Sections of Part A or B of this Chapter (as applicable).

2 Remove the liner/piston and connecting rod assemblies as described in Section 11. If no work is to be done on the pistons and connecting rods, there is no need to remove the cylinder head and withdraw the liner assemblies from the cylinder block/crankcase. Instead unbolt the big-end bearing caps and push the pistons sufficiently up the bores so that the connecting rods are positioned clear of the crankshaft journals.

3 Before removing the crankshaft, check the crankshaft endfloat as described in Section 15.

4 The main bearing caps should be numbered 1 to 5 from the transmission (flywheel) end of the engine **(see illustration)**. If not, mark them accordingly using a centre punch. Also note the correct fitted depth of both the front and rear crankshaft oil seals in the bearing caps.

5 Slacken and remove the main bearing cap retaining bolts and lift off each bearing cap. Recover the lower bearing shells and tape them to their respective caps for safe-keeping. Remove the rubber sealing strips (where fitted) from the sides of number 1 and/or 5 main bearing caps and discard them (as applicable).

6 Lift out the crankshaft and discard the oil seals.

7 Recover the upper bearing shells from the cylinder block and tape them to their respective caps for safe keeping. Remove the thrustwasher halves from the side of No 2 main bearing and store them with the bearing caps.

12.4 Main bearing cap identification numbers are cast onto each cap

13 Cylinder block/crankcase - cleaning and inspection

Cleaning

1 Remove all external components and electrical switches/sensors from the block.

2 On diesel engines, undo the retaining bolts and washers and remove the piston oil jet nozzles from the inside the cylinder block. Note that the nozzles are different and are not interchangeable; note the correct fitted position of each nozzle as it is removed and recover the O-ring from the back of each nozzle. On some engines it will also be necessary to undo the union nuts and remove the lubrication gallery.

3 Scrape all traces of gasket from the cylinder block/crankcase, taking care not to damage the gasket/sealing surfaces.

4 Remove all oil gallery plugs. The plugs are usually very tight - they may have to be drilled out and the holes re-tapped. Use new plugs when the engine is reassembled.

5 If any of the castings are extremely dirty, all should be steam cleaned.

6 After the castings are returned, clean all oil holes and oil galleries one more time. Flush all internal passages with warm water until the water runs clear, then dry thoroughly and apply a light film of oil to all mating surfaces to prevent rusting. If you have access to compressed air, use it to speed up the drying process and to blow out all the oil holes and galleries.

 Warning: Be sure to wear eye protection when using compressed air!

7 If the castings are not very dirty, you can do an adequate cleaning job with hot (as hot as you can stand!), soapy water and a stiff brush. Take plenty of time and do a thorough job. Regardless of the cleaning method used, be sure to clean all oil holes and galleries very thoroughly and to dry all components well; protect all mating surfaces as described above to prevent rusting.

8 All threaded holes must be clean to ensure accurate torque readings during reassembly. To clean all threads, run the proper size tap into each of the holes to remove rust, corrosion, thread sealant or sludge and to restore damaged threads. If possible, use compressed air to clear the holes of debris produced by this operation.

HAYNES HiNT *A good alternative is to inject aerosol-applied water dispersant lubricant into each hole, using the long spout usually supplied. Make sure each hole is dried thoroughly afterwards.*

 Warning: Wear eye protection when cleaning out these holes in this way!

9 Apply suitable sealant to the new oil gallery plugs and insert them into the holes in the block. Tighten them securely.

10 On diesel engines, fit a new O-ring to rear of each piston oil jet nozzles. Install the nozzles in their original positions inside the cylinder block and refit the retaining bolts and washers, tightening then to the specified torque setting. Where applicable, refit the lubrication gallery.

11 If the engine is not going to be reassembled right away, cover it with a large plastic bag to keep it clean; protect the all mating surfaces as described above to prevent rusting.

Inspection

12 Check the each cylinder liner for scuffing and scoring. Check for signs of a wear ridge at the top of the cylinder indicating that the liner is excessively worn.

13 Since Renault do not state any specific wear limits for the cylinder liners or pistons, it is not possible to assess the amount of wear by direct measurement. If there is any doubt about the condition of the cylinder liner seek the advice of a Renault dealer or suitable engine reconditioning specialist.

14 If renewal is necessary, new liners complete with piston and piston rings can be purchased from a Renault dealer. Note that it is not possible to renew the liners individually, as they are supplied as a matched assembly complete with piston and rings.

15 With the sealing rings removed from each liner, install the liners in their original position in the cylinder block. Using a dial gauge or a straight-edge and feeler blade, check that the protrusion of each liner above the upper surface of the cylinder block is within the limits given in the *Specifications*, and that the maximum difference between any two liners is not exceeded **(see illustration)**. If this is not the case seek the advice of a Renault dealer before proceeding with the engine rebuild.

16 Note that if new liner assemblies are being installed the liners must be arranged so that the liner protrusions gradually decrease/increase from one end of the cylinder block to the other, ie. the largest protrusion is at one end with the smallest at the opposite end **(see illustration)**. Use the liner protrusion measurements to arrange the liners as required then number

13.15 Measuring liner protrusion

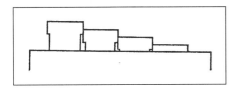

13.16 If new liners are being installed position them so that the protrusions step down from one end of the block to the other

each one with its respective cylinder number, remembering No.1 cylinder is at the flywheel end of the engine.

14 Piston/connecting rod assembly - inspection

1 Before the inspection process can begin, the piston/connecting rod assemblies must be cleaned, and the original piston rings removed from the pistons.

2 Carefully expand the old rings over the top of the pistons. The use of two or three old feeler blades will be helpful in preventing the rings dropping into empty grooves **(see illustration)**. Be careful not to scratch the piston with the ends of the ring. The rings are brittle, and will snap if they are spread too far. They are also very sharp - protect your hands and fingers. Note that the third ring may incorporate an expander. Always remove the rings from the top of the piston. Keep each set of rings with its piston if the old rings are to be re-used.

3 Scrape away all traces of carbon from the top of the piston. A hand-held wire brush (or a piece of fine emery cloth) can be used, once the majority of the deposits have been scraped away.

4 Remove the carbon from the ring grooves in the piston, using an old ring. Break the ring in half to do this (be careful not to cut your fingers - piston rings are sharp). Be careful to remove only the carbon deposits - do not remove any metal, and do not nick or scratch the sides of the ring grooves.

5 Once the deposits have been removed, clean the piston/connecting rod assembly

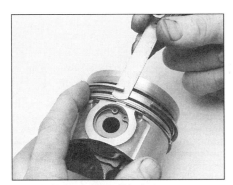

14.2 Using a feeler blade to remove a piston ring

with paraffin or a suitable solvent, and dry thoroughly. Make sure that the oil return holes in the ring grooves are clear.

6 If the pistons and cylinder liners are not damaged or worn excessively, and if the liners do not need to be renewed, the original pistons can be refitted. Normal piston wear shows up as even vertical wear on the piston thrust surfaces, and slight looseness of the top ring in its groove. New piston rings should always be used when the engine is reassembled.

7 Carefully inspect each piston for cracks around the skirt, around the gudgeon pin holes, and at the piston ring "lands" (between the ring grooves).

8 Look for scoring and scuffing on the piston skirt, holes in the piston crown, and burned areas at the edge of the crown. If the skirt is scored or scuffed, the engine may have been suffering from overheating, and/or abnormal combustion which caused excessively high operating temperatures. The cooling and lubrication systems should be checked thoroughly and also the fuel and ignition systems on petrol engines. Scorch marks on the sides of the pistons show that blow-by has occurred. A hole in the piston crown, or burned areas at the edge of the piston crown, indicates that abnormal combustion (pre-ignition, knocking, or detonation) has been occurring. If any of the above problems exist, the causes must be investigated and corrected, or the damage will occur again. The causes may include a worn carburettor, incorrect ignition/injection pump timing, or a faulty injector (as applicable).

9 Corrosion of the piston, in the form of pitting, indicates that coolant has been leaking into the combustion chamber and/or the crankcase. Again, the cause must be corrected, or the problem may persist in the rebuilt engine.

10 Note that it is not possible to renew the pistons separately; pistons are only supplied with piston rings and a liner, as a part of a matched assembly (see Section 13).

11 Examine each connecting rod carefully for signs of damage, such as cracks around the big-end and small-end bearings. Check that the rod is not bent or distorted. Damage is highly unlikely, unless the engine has been seized or badly overheated. Detailed checking of the connecting rod assembly can only be carried out by a Renault dealer or engine repair specialist with the necessary equipment.

12 On all engines, due to the tightening procedure for the connecting rod big-end cap retaining nuts/bolts, it is essential that the big-end cap nuts and/or bolts are renewed as a complete set prior to refitting.

13 On all petrol engines, the gudgeon pins are an interference fit in the connecting rod small-end bearing. Therefore, piston and/or connecting rod renewal should be entrusted to a Renault dealer or engine repair specialist, who will have the necessary tooling to remove and install the gudgeon pins.

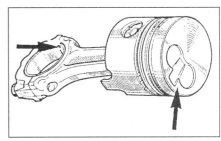

14.19 Position each piston so that its turbulence chamber is opposite the connecting rod big-end bearing shell cutouts

14 On diesel engines, the gudgeon pins are of the floating type, secured in position by two circlips. On these engines, the pistons and connecting rods can be separated as follows.

15 Using a small flat-bladed screwdriver, prise out the circlips, and push out the gudgeon pin. Hand pressure should be sufficient to remove the pin. Identify the piston and rod to ensure correct reassembly. Discard the circlips - new ones *must* be used on refitting.

16 Examine the gudgeon pin and connecting rod small-end bearing for signs of wear or damage. Wear can be cured by renewing both the pin and bush. Bush renewal, however, is a specialist job - press facilities are required, and the new bush must be reamed accurately.

17 The connecting rods themselves should not be in need of renewal, unless seizure or some other major mechanical failure has occurred. Check the alignment of the connecting rods visually, and if the rods are not straight, take them to an engine overhaul specialist for a more detailed check.

18 Examine all components, and obtain any new parts from your Renault dealer. If new pistons are purchased, they will be supplied complete with gudgeon pins and circlips. Circlips can also be purchased individually.

19 Position the piston so that its turbulence chamber is on the opposite side to the connecting rod big-end bearing shell cut-out **(see illustration)**. Apply a smear of clean engine oil to the gudgeon pin. Slide it into the piston and through the connecting rod small-end. Check that the piston pivots freely on the rod, then secure the gudgeon pin in position with two new circlips. Ensure that each circlip is correctly located in its groove in the piston.

15 Crankshaft - inspection

Checking crankshaft endfloat

1 If the crankshaft endfloat is to be checked, this must be done when the crankshaft is still installed in the cylinder block/crankcase, but is free to move (see Section 12).

2 Check the endfloat using a dial gauge in contact with the end of the crankshaft. Push

the crankshaft fully one way and then zero the gauge. Push the crankshaft fully the other way and check the endfloat. The result can be compared with the specified amount and will give an indication as to whether new thrustwashers are required. Note that thrustwashers are available in four different thicknesses.

3 If a dial gauge is not available, feeler blades can be used. First push the crankshaft fully towards the flywheel end of the engine, then use feeler blades to measure the gap between the web of number 2 crankpin and the thrustwasher.

Inspection

4 Clean the crankshaft using paraffin or a suitable solvent, and dry it, preferably with compressed air if available.

 Warning: Wear eye protection when using compressed air! Be sure to clean the oil holes with a pipe cleaner or similar probe, to ensure they are not obstructed.

5 Check the main and big-end bearing journals for uneven wear, scoring, pitting and cracking.

6 Big-end bearing wear is accompanied by distinct metallic knocking when the engine is running, particularly noticeable when the engine is pulling from low revs, and some loss of oil pressure.

7 Main bearing wear is accompanied by severe engine vibration and rumble - getting progressively worse as engine revs increase - and again by loss of oil pressure.

8 Check the bearing journal for roughness by running a finger lightly over the bearing surface. Any roughness (which will be accompanied by obvious bearing wear) indicates the that the crankshaft requires regrinding (where possible) or renewal.

9 If the crankshaft has been reground, check for burrs around the crankshaft oil holes (the holes are usually chamfered, so burrs should not be a problem unless regrinding has been carried out carelessly). Remove any burrs with a fine file or scraper, and thoroughly clean the oil holes as described previously.

10 Using a micrometer, measure the diameter of the main and big-end bearing journals and compare the results with the *Specifications* (see illustration). By measuring the diameter at a number of points around each journal's circumference, you will be able to determine whether or not the journal is out-of-round. Take the measurement at each end of the journal, near the webs, to determine if the journal is tapered. Compare the results obtained to those given in the *Specifications*. Note that Renault do not specify crankshaft taper or ovality (out-of-round) figures for these engines. The figures given in the *Specifications* are a guide figure which is typical for this type of engine. Before condemning the components concerned, seek the advice of your Renault dealer or suitable engine repair specialist. They will also be able to inform as to the best course of action and

15.10 Measuring the diameter of a crankshaft main bearing journal

whether it is possible to have the crankshaft journals reground or whether renewal will be necessary.

11 Check the oil seal contact surfaces at each end of the crankshaft for wear and damage. If the seal has worn an excessive groove in the surface of the crankshaft, consult an engine overhaul specialist who will be able to advise whether a repair is possible or whether a new crankshaft is necessary.

12 If the crankshaft has worn beyond the specified limits, it must be renewed. Note that Renault produce a set of oversize bearing shells for both the main bearings and big-end bearings so, if the crankshaft journals have not already been reground, it may be possible to have the crankshaft reconditioned and fit the oversize shells instead of renewing the crankshaft. Seek the advice of your Renault dealer or suitable engine specialist on the best course of action.

16 Main and big-end bearings - inspection

1 Even though the main and big-end bearings should be renewed during the engine overhaul, the old bearings should be retained for close examination, as they may reveal valuable information about the condition of the engine. The size of the bearing shells is indicated by numbers stamped on the rear of the shell; these numbers should be given to your Renault dealer when ordering new bearing shells.

2 Bearing failure occurs because of lack of lubrication, the presence of dirt or other foreign particles, overloading the engine and corrosion (see illustration). Regardless of the cause of bearing failure, it must be corrected before the engine is reassembled to prevent it from happening again.

3 When examining the bearing shells, remove them from the cylinder block/crankcase, the connecting rods and the connecting rod big-end bearing caps and lay them out on a clean surface in the same general position as their location in the engine. This will enable you to match any bearing problems with the corresponding crankshaft journal. **Do not**

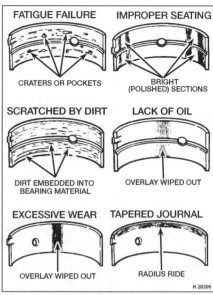

16.2 Typical bearing failures

touch any shell's bearing surface with your fingers while checking it, or the delicate surface may be scratched.

4 Dirt and other foreign particles get into the engine in a variety of ways. It may be left in the engine during assembly, or it may pass through filters or the crankcase ventilation system. It may get into the oil and from there into the bearings. Metal chips from machining operations and normal engine wear are often present. Abrasives are sometimes left in engine components after reconditioning, especially when parts are not thoroughly cleaned using the proper cleaning methods. Whatever the source, these foreign objects often end up embedded in the soft bearing material and are easily recognised. Large particles will not embed in the bearing and will score or gouge the bearing and journal. The best prevention for this cause of bearing failure is to clean all parts thoroughly and keep everything spotlessly clean during engine assembly. Frequent and regular engine oil and filter changes are also recommended.

5 Lack of lubrication (or lubrication breakdown) has a number of interrelated causes. Excessive heat (which thins the oil), overloading (which squeezes the oil from the bearing face) and oil leakage (from excessive bearing clearances, worn oil pump or high engine speeds) all contribute to lubrication breakdown. Blocked oil passages, which usually are the result of misaligned oil holes in a bearing shell, will also oil starve a bearing and destroy it. When lack of lubrication is the cause of bearing failure, the bearing material is wiped or extruded from the steel backing of the bearing. Temperatures may increase to the point where the steel backing turns blue from overheating.

6 Driving habits can have a definite effect on bearing life. Full throttle, low speed operation (labouring the engine) puts very high loads on

bearings, which tends to squeeze out the oil film. These loads cause the bearings to flex, which produces fine cracks in the bearing face (fatigue failure). Eventually the bearing material will loosen in pieces and tear away from the steel backing. Short-distance driving leads to corrosion of bearings because insufficient engine heat is produced to drive off the condensed water and corrosive gases. These products collect in the engine oil, forming acid and sludge. As the oil is carried to the engine bearings, the acid attacks and corrodes the bearing material.

7 Incorrect bearing installation during engine assembly will lead to bearing failure as well. Tight fitting bearings leave insufficient bearing running clearance and will result in oil starvation. Dirt or foreign particles trapped behind a bearing shell result in high spots on the bearing which lead to failure. **Do not** touch any shell's bearing surface with your fingers during reassembly; there is a risk of scratching the delicate surface or of depositing particles of dirt on it.

17 Engine overhaul - reassembly sequence

1 Before reassembly begins ensure that all new parts have been obtained and that all necessary tools are available. Read through the entire procedure to familiarise yourself with the work involved, and to ensure that all items necessary for reassembly of the engine are at hand. In addition to all normal tools and materials, a thread-locking compound will be needed. A tube of liquid sealant will also be required for the joint faces that are fitted without gaskets. It is advisable that the products recommended by Renault should be used; the relevant products are given in the text of each Section where they are required.
2 In order to save time and avoid problems, engine reassembly can be carried out in the following order.

a) Crankshaft (Section 19).
b) Piston/connecting rod assemblies (Section 20).
c) Oil pump (Part A or B of this Chapter).
d) Auxiliary shaft (Section 10).
e) Sump (Part A or B of this Chapter).
f) Flywheel (Part A or B of this Chapter).
g) Cylinder head (Part A or B of this Chapter).
h) Timing belt inner cover, tensioner and sprockets, and timing belt (Part A or B of this Chapter).
i) Engine external components.

3 At this stage, all engine components should be absolutely clean and dry, with all faults repaired and should be laid out (or in individual containers) on a completely clean work surface.

18 Piston rings - refitting

1 Install the new rings by fitting them over the top of the piston, starting with the oil control ring. On petrol engines, ensure that the second compression ring is fitted the correct way around, so that the mark, or the surface stamped "TOP" is uppermost.
2 On diesel engines, ensure that the second compression is fitted with its stepped surface at the bottom.
3 With the piston rings correctly installed, check that each ring is free to rotate easily in its groove. Position the ring end gaps so that are spaced at 120° intervals.

19 Crankshaft - refitting and main bearing running clearance check

Selection of bearing shells

1 On all engines covered in this manual, there are two different sizes of bearing shell available; the standard size shell for use with an original crankshaft and an oversize shell for use once the crankshaft has been reground.
2 The relevant set of bearing shells required can be obtained by measuring the diameter of the crankshaft main bearing journals (see Section 15). This will show if the crankshaft is original or whether its journals have been reground, identifying if either standard or oversize bearing shells are required.
3 If access to the necessary measuring equipment cannot be gained, the size of the bearing shells can be identified by the markings stamped on the rear of each shell. Details of these markings should be supplied to your Renault dealer who will then be able to identify the size of shell fitted.
4 Whether the original shells or new shells are being fitted, it is recommended that the running clearance is checked as follows prior to installation.

Main bearing running clearance check

5 Clean the backs of the bearing shells and the bearing locations in both the cylinder block/crankcase and the main bearing caps.
6 Press the bearing shells into their locations, ensuring that the tab on each shell engages in the notch in the cylinder block/crankcase or main bearing cap, and taking care not to touch any shell's bearing surface with your fingers.
7 If the original bearing shells are being used for the check ensure that they are refitted in their original locations. The clearance can be checked in either of two ways.
8 One method (which will be difficult to achieve without a range of internal micrometers or internal/external expanding

calipers) is to refit the main bearing caps with their retaining bolts correctly tightened, then measure the internal diameter of each assembled pair of bearing shells. If the diameter of each corresponding crankshaft journal is measured and then subtracted from the bearing internal diameter, the result will be the main bearing running clearance.
9 The second (and more accurate) method is to use Plastigage. This consists of a fine thread of perfectly round plastic which is compressed between the bearing shell and the journal. When the shell is removed, the plastic is deformed and can be measured with a special card gauge supplied with the kit. The running clearance is determined from this gauge. The procedure for using Plastigage is as follows.
10 With the main bearing upper shells in place, carefully lay the crankshaft in position. Do not use any lubricant; the crankshaft journals and bearing shells must be perfectly clean and dry.
11 Cut several lengths of the appropriate size Plastigage (they should be slightly shorter than the width of the main bearings) and place one length on each crankshaft journal axis **(see illustration)**.
12 With the main bearing lower shells in position, refit the main bearing caps, tightening their retaining bolts to the specified torque. Take care not to disturb the Plastigage and **do not** rotate the crankshaft at any time during this operation.
13 Remove the main bearing caps again taking great care not to disturb the Plastigage or rotate the crankshaft.
14 Compare the width of the crushed Plastigage on each journal to the scale printed on the Plastigage envelope to obtain the main bearing running clearance **(see illustration)**. Compare the clearance measured with that given in the *Specifications* at the start of this Chapter.
15 If the clearance is significantly different from that expected, the bearing shells may be the wrong size (or excessively worn if the original shells are being re-used). Before deciding that the crankshaft is worn, make sure that no dirt or oil was trapped between the bearing shells and the caps or block when the clearance was measured. If the Plastigage

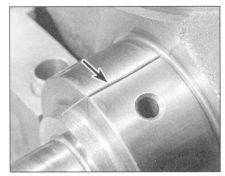

19.11 Plastigage in place on a main bearing journal

19.14 Measuring the width of the deformed Plastigage using the card gauge supplied

19.20 Ensure the crankshaft thrust washers are fitted with their oil grooves facing outwards

was wider at one end than at the other, the crankshaft journal may be tapered.

16 Note that Renault do not specify a running clearance for these engines. The figure given in the *Specifications* is a guide figure which is typical for this type of engine. Before condemning the components concerned, seek the advice of your Renault dealer or suitable engine repair specialist. They will also be able to inform as to the best course of action and whether it is possible to have the crankshaft journals reground or whether renewal will be necessary.

17 Where necessary, obtain the correct size of bearing shell and repeat the running clearance checking procedure as described above.

18 On completion, carefully scrape away all traces of the Plastigage material from the crankshaft and bearing shells using a fingernail or other object which is unlikely to score the bearing surfaces.

Final crankshaft refitting

19 Carefully lift the crankshaft out of the cylinder block once more.

20 Using a little grease, stick the thrustwashers to each side of the No 2 main bearing upper location; ensure that the oilway grooves on each thrustwasher face outwards (away from the cylinder block) **(see illustration)**.

21 Place the bearing shells in their locations as described above in paragraphs 5 to 7. If new shells are being fitted, ensure that all traces of the protective grease are cleaned off using paraffin. Wipe dry the shells and connecting rods with a lint-free cloth.

22 Liberally lubricate each bearing shell in the cylinder block/crankcase with clean engine oil then lower the crankshaft into position ensuring that the bearing shells and thrustwashers remain correctly seated.

23 Check the crankshaft endfloat as described in Section 12.

24 Fit bearing cap numbers 2 to 4. Ensure the caps are fitted in their correct locations and the correct way round (the bearing shell lug recesses in the block and caps must be on the same side). Insert the bearing cap bolts and tighten them to the specified torque setting.

25 There are two possible ways of sealing the end main bearing cap(s) (as applicable). The first is by fitting rubber sealing strips to the cap grooves, and the second is by filling the grooves with a special sealant kit available from your Renault dealer. The second method using the sealant is extremely messy and if carried out carelessly can lead to the oilways being blocked. It is therefore recommended that the sealing strips are used as follows.

26 Two different thicknesses of sealing strip are available and it is first necessary to decide which size is needed. The thinner (5.1 mm thick) sealing strip is unmarked whereas the thicker (5.4 mm thick) sealing strip has a colour marking on it.

27 To select the correct size of sealing strip, fit the main bearing end cap(s) in position and

19.27 Using a twist drill to measure main bearing cap groove to cylinder block clearance

19.28b ... and position the strip so that it protrudes above the cap mating surface by approximately 0.2 mm

lightly tighten the retaining bolts. Using a suitable twist drill, measure the gap between the inner edge of each main bearing cap seal groove and the cylinder block/crankcase **(see illustration)**. If this dimension is less than 5 mm then the thinner sealing strips will be required. If the dimension is greater than or equal to 5 mm then the thicker sealing strips will be required. Unbolt the bearing cap(s) and remove.

28 Fit the correct rubber sealing strips to each groove in the bearing cap ensuring that the groove in each strip is facing outwards. Position each sealing strip so that is protrudes approximately 0.2 mm above the upper (cylinder block/crankcase) mating surface of the bearing cap **(see illustrations)**.

29 To ease installation, obtain two thin metal strips of 0.25 mm thickness or less. These can then be used to prevent the strips moving as the cap is being fitted. Old feeler blades are ideal for this purpose, provided all burrs which may damage the sealing strips are first removed.

30 Apply a thin coating of sealant to the mating surface of the cylinder block/crankcase, taking great care not to block the oil return holes. Renault recommend the use of CAF 4/60 THIXO (available from your Renault dealer); in the absence of this ensure a good quality sealant is used.

31 Oil both sides of the metal strips, and hold them on the sealing strips. Ease the main bearing cap into position and insert the bolts loosely **(see illustration)**. Just before the cap

19.28a Fit the sealing strips to the bearing cap so that its groove is facing away from the cap ...

19.31 Slide the bearing cap assembly into position using the metal strips to ensure the sealing strips are not displaced

touches the cylinder block/mating surface, check that the sealing strips are still protruding from the cap. If not remove the cap and repeat the fitting procedure.

32 With the cap in position tighten the retaining bolts to the specified torque setting then carefully pull out the metal strips with a pair of pliers in a horizontal direction. Using a sharp knife, trim the lower end of each sealing strip so that the strips protrude above the sump mating surface by approximately 0.5 mm.

33 Repeat the procedure for the opposite bearing cap.

34 Refit/reconnect the piston connecting rod assemblies to the crankshaft as described in Section 20.

35 Refit the crankshaft oil seals, crankshaft sprocket, flywheel and the oil pump as described in the relevant Sections of Part A or B of this Chapter (as applicable).

---

20 Pistons/connecting rods - refitting and big-end bearing running clearance check

Selection of bearing shells

1 Refer to Section 19.

Big-end bearing running clearance check

2 Clean the backs of the bearing shells and the bearing locations in both the connecting rod and bearing cap.

3 Press the bearing shells into their locations, ensuring that the tab on each shell engages in the notch in the connecting rod and cap and taking care not to touch any shell's bearing surface with your fingers.

4 The upper shells, which are fitted to the connecting rods may have an oil hole in them, whereas the lower shells which are fitted to the bearing caps, are always plain. If the original bearing shells are being used for the check ensure that they are refitted in their original locations. The clearance can be checked in either of two ways.

5 One method is to refit the big-end bearing cap to the connecting rod, with bearing shells in place. With the cap retaining bolts tightened to the specified torque, use an internal micrometer or vernier caliper to measure the internal diameter of each assembled pair of bearing shells. If the diameter of each corresponding crankshaft journal is measured and then subtracted from the bearing internal diameter, the result will be the big-end bearing running clearance.

6 The second method is to use Plastigage as described in Section 19, paragraphs 9 to 18. Place a strand of Plastigage on each (cleaned) crankpin journal and refit the (clean) piston/connecting rod assemblies, shells and big-end bearing caps, tightening the bolts to the specified torque wrench settings. Take care not to disturb the Plastigage. Dismantle the assemblies without rotating the crankshaft

and use the scale printed on the Plastigage envelope to obtain the big-end bearing running clearance. On completion of the measurement, carefully scrape off all traces of Plastigage from the journal and shells using a fingernail or other object which will not score the components.

Final piston/connecting rod assembly refitting

7 Check the liner protrusions as described in Section 13. If the original liner/piston and connecting rod assemblies are being refitted then ensure that they are refitted in their original positions. If new liner/piston and connecting rod assemblies are being installed, position and number the assemblies as described in Section 13.

8 Ensure the bearing shells are correctly refitted as described above in paragraphs 2 to 4. If new shells are being fitted, ensure that all traces of the protective grease are cleaned off using paraffin. Wipe dry the shells and connecting rods with a lint-free cloth.

9 Lubricate the liner bores, the pistons and piston rings then lay out each piston/connecting rod assembly with its liner.

10 Starting with assembly number 1, make sure that the piston rings are still spaced as described in Section 18, then clamp them in position with a piston ring compressor **(see illustration)**.

11 Insert the piston/connecting rod assembly into the bottom of number 1 liner and tap into position. Once the piston rings have entered the liner, remove the ring compressor, then

slide the piston into position until the piston crown is flush with the top of the liner.

12 Fit a new O-ring to the liner seat and, on diesel engines, locate a new sealing ring against the lower ridge on the base of the liner **(see illustrations)**. Apply a smear of oil to the liner seal and O-ring to ease installation.

13 Ensure that the bearing shell is still correctly installed and carefully install the liner/piston and connecting rod assembly in the cylinder block. Note that the liner will only fit one way **(see illustration)**.

14 Ensure the piston/connecting rod assembly is correctly positioned; on petrol engines the arrow on the piston crown must point toward the flywheel end of the engine - on diesel engines, the turbulence chamber on the piston crown must be toward the auxiliary shaft (injection pump) side of the engine, and the oil spray hole in the connecting rod (where applicable) must face away from the auxiliary shaft.

15 Taking care not to mark the liner bores, liberally lubricate the crankpin and both bearing shells, then pull the piston/connecting rod assembly down the liner and onto the crankpin. Refit the big-end bearing cap, aligning the cap with its locating pins/dowels (which means that the bearing shell locating tabs abut each other), and tighten its retaining bolts to the specified torque setting.

16 Refit the remaining three liner/piston and connecting rod assemblies in the same way.

17 Once all assemblies are correctly installed, clamp the liner in position as

20.10 Fit a piston ring compressor to the piston, then insert the piston into the bottom of the relevant liner

20.12a Fit a new O-ring to the liner seating flange . . .

20.12b . . . and a new sealing ring to the base of the liner

20.13 Inserting a liner/piston and connecting rod assembly into the block

described in Section 11 of Part A, or Section 12 of Part B, as applicable.

18 Rotate the crankshaft, and check that it turns freely, with no binding or tight spots.

19 Refit the cylinder head and oil pump as described in the relevant Sections of Part A or B of this Chapter.

21 Engine - initial start-up after overhaul

1 With the engine refitted in the vehicle, double-check the engine oil and coolant levels. Make a final check that everything has been reconnected, and that there are no tools or rags left in the engine compartment.

Petrol engine models

2 Remove the spark plugs, then disconnect the ignition coil LT wiring connections. On fuel-injected models, disconnect the wiring connectors at each injector.

3 Turn the engine on the starter until the oil pressure warning light goes out. Refit the spark plugs, and reconnect the wiring.

Diesel engine models

4 Disconnect the wiring from the stop solenoid on the injection pump (Chapter 4B), then turn the engine on the starter motor until the oil pressure warning light goes out. Reconnect the wire to the stop solenoid.

5 Prime the fuel system as described in Chapter 4B.

6 Fully depress the accelerator pedal, turn the ignition key to position "M", and wait for the preheating warning light to go out.

All models

7 Start the engine, noting that this may take a little longer than usual, due to the fuel system components having been disturbed.

8 While the engine is idling, check for fuel, water and oil leaks. Don't be alarmed if there are some odd smells and smoke from parts getting hot and burning off oil deposits.

9 Assuming all is well, keep the engine idling until hot water is felt circulating through the top hose, then switch off the engine.

10 Check the injection pump timing (diesel engines), and the idle speed settings (as appropriate), then switch the engine off.

11 After a few minutes, recheck the oil and coolant levels as described in "*Weekly Checks*", and top-up as necessary.

12 On diesel engines, if the cylinder head has been removed it will be necessary to retighten the cylinder head bolts as described in Part B, Section 12.

13 On petrol engines, there is no need to re-tighten the cylinder head bolts once the engine has first run after reassembly.

14 If new pistons, rings or crankshaft bearings have been fitted, the engine must be treated as new, and run-in for the first 500 miles (800 km). *Do not* operate the engine at full-throttle, or allow it to labour at low engine speeds in any gear. It is recommended that the oil and filter be changed at the end of this period.

Chapter 3
Cooling, heating and air conditioning systems

Contents

Degrees of difficulty

| Easy, suitable for novice with little experience | Fairly easy, suitable for beginner with some experience | Fairly difficult, suitable for competent DIY mechanic | Difficult, suitable for experienced DIY mechanic | Very difficult, suitable for expert DIY or professional |

Specifications

General

System type	Pressurised, pump assisted thermosyphon system with electric cooling fan(s)

Thermostat

Opening commences	81°C
Fully open at	93°C
Valve stroke	7.5 mm

1 General information and precautions

The system is of pressurised semi-sealed type with the inclusion of an expansion tank to accept coolant displaced from the system when hot and to return it when the system cools.

Coolant is circulated by thermosyphon action and is assisted by means of the impeller in the belt-driven coolant pump.

A thermostat is fitted to control coolant flow through the radiator. When the engine is cold, the thermostat valve remains closed so that the coolant flow which occurs at normal operating temperatures through the radiator matrix is interrupted.

As the coolant warms up, the thermostat valve starts to open and allows the coolant flow through the radiator to resume.

The engine temperature will always be maintained at a constant level (according to the thermostat rating) whatever the ambient air temperature.

The coolant circulates around the engine block and cylinder head and absorbs heat as it flows, then travels out into the radiator to pass across the matrix. As the coolant flows across the radiator matrix, air flow created by the forward motion of the vehicle cools it, and it returns via the bottom tank of the radiator to the cylinder block. This is a continuous process, assisted by the coolant pump impeller.

On carburettor petrol engines hot coolant is used to control the operation of the automatic choke and to heat the carburettor base for improved atomisation of the air/fuel mixture. On diesel engines, cold coolant is directed to the engine oil cooler unit.

All models are fitted with an electric cooling fan which is actuated by the thermostat switch according to coolant temperature. Certain models are equipped with two cooling fans.

The vehicle interior heater operates by means of coolant from the engine cooling system. Coolant flow through the heater matrix is constant; temperature control being achieved by blending cool air from outside the vehicle with the warm air from the heater matrix, in the desired ratio.

Precautions

Warning: Do not attempt to remove the expansion tank filler cap or disturb any part of the cooling system while the engine is hot, as there is a high risk of scalding. If the expansion tank filler cap must be removed before the engine and radiator have fully cooled (even though this is not recommended) the pressure in the cooling system must first be relieved. Cover the cap with a thick layer of cloth, to avoid scalding, and slowly unscrew the filler cap until a hissing sound can be heard. When the hissing has stopped, indicating that the pressure has reduced, slowly unscrew the filler cap until it can be removed; if more hissing sounds are heard, wait until they have stopped before unscrewing the cap completely. At all times keep well away from the filler cap opening.

Warning: Do not allow antifreeze to come into contact with skin or painted surfaces of the vehicle. Rinse off spills immediately with plenty of water. Never leave antifreeze lying around in an open container or in a puddle in the driveway or on the garage floor. Children and pets are attracted by its sweet smell. Antifreeze can be fatal if ingested.

Warning: If the engine is hot, the electric cooling fan may start rotating even if the engine is not running, so be careful to keep hands, hair and loose clothing well clear when working in the engine compartment or around the front of the vehicle.

Warning: Refer to Section 11 for precautions to be observed when working on models equipped with air conditioning.

2 Cooling system hoses - disconnection and renewal

Note: *Refer to the warnings given in Section 1 of this Chapter before proceeding. Hoses should only be disconnected once the engine has cooled sufficiently to avoid scalding.*

1 If the checks described in Chapter 1 reveal a faulty hose, it must be renewed as follows.

2 First drain the cooling system (Chapter 1); if the antifreeze is not due for renewal, the drained coolant may be re-used, if it is collected in a clean container.

3 To disconnect any hose, use a pair of pliers to release the spring clamps (or a screwdriver to slacken screw-type clamps), then move them along the hose clear of the union. Carefully work the hose off its stubs. The hoses can be removed with relative ease when new - on an older vehicle, they may have stuck.

4 If a hose proves stubborn, try to release it by rotating it on its unions before attempting to work it off. Gently prise the end of the hose with a blunt instrument (such as a flat-bladed

screwdriver), but do not apply too much force, and take care not to damage the pipe stubs or hoses. Note in particular that the radiator hose unions are fragile; do not use excessive force when attempting to remove the hoses. If all else fails, cut the hose with a sharp knife, then slit it so that it can be peeled off in two pieces. While expensive, this is preferable to buying a new radiator. Check first, however, that a new hose is readily available.

5 When refitting a hose, first slide the clamps onto the hose, then engage the hose with its unions. Work the hose into position, then check that the hose is settled correctly and is properly routed. Slide each clip along the hose until it is behind the union flared end, before tightening it securely.

6 Refill the system with coolant (Chapter 1).

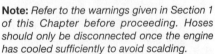

If the hose is stiff, use a little soapy water as a lubricant, or soften the hose by soaking it in hot water. Do not use oil or grease, which may attack the rubber.

7 Check carefully for leaks as soon as possible after disturbing any part of the cooling system.

3 Antifreeze - general information

Note: *Refer to the warnings given in Section 1 of this Chapter before proceeding.*

1 The cooling system should be filled with a water/ethylene glycol-based antifreeze solution, of a strength which will prevent freezing down to at least -23°C, or lower if the local climate requires it. Antifreeze also provides protection against corrosion, and increases the coolant boiling point.

2 The cooling system should be maintained according to the schedule described in Chapter 1. If antifreeze is used that is not to Renault's specification, old or contaminated coolant mixtures are likely to cause damage, and encourage the formation of corrosion and scale in the system. Use distilled water with the antifreeze, if available - if not, be sure to use only soft water. Clean rainwater is suitable.

3 Before adding antifreeze, check all hoses and hose connections, because antifreeze tends to leak through very small openings. Engines don't normally consume coolant, so if the level goes down, find the cause and correct it.

4 Mix the required quantity of antifreeze and water, as recommended on the antifreeze container, to give the desired level of protection. To prevent freezing down to -23°C, this will be approximately 35% antifreeze to 65% water. Fill the system as described in Chapter 1, and *"Weekly checks"* and save any surplus mixture for topping-up.

4 Thermostat - removal, testing and refitting

Removal

1 On petrol engines the thermostat is located either in a housing attached to the front right-hand side of the cylinder head, or inside the radiator top hose at the cylinder head end. On all diesel engines the thermostat is located in a housing attached to the front right-hand side of the cylinder head.

2 To remove the thermostat, first drain the cooling system as described in Chapter 1.

3 Where the thermostat is located in the top hose, slacken both the retaining clips and detach the hose at the cylinder head end. Extract the thermostat from the hose **(see illustration)**.

4 On all other versions, Slacken the clip securing the radiator top hose to the thermostat housing and disconnect the hose.

5 Undo the thermostat housing cover bolts and remove the cover. Remove the thermostat and recover the sealing ring or gasket.

Testing

6 Suspend the (closed) thermostat on a length of string in a container of cold water, with a thermometer beside it; ensure that neither touches the side or bottom of the container.

7 Heat the water, and check the temperature at which the thermostat begins to open, or is fully open. Compare this value with the figures given in the *Specifications*, then remove the thermostat and allow it to cool down; check that it closes fully.

8 If the thermostat does not open and close as described, if it sticks in either position, or if it does not open at the specified temperature, it must be renewed.

Refitting

9 Refitting is a reversal of removal, bearing in mind the following points.

a) *Where fitted, examine the sealing ring for signs of damage or deterioration or damage and, if necessary, renew.*

b) *Where a gasket is used to seal the cover, remove all traces of old gasket and fit a new one.*

4.3 Thermostat removal from the top hose

c) *Ensure that the thermostat is fitted the correct way round, with the spring towards the cylinder head.*

d) *On completion refill the cooling system as described in Chapter 1.*

5 Radiator - removal, inspection and refitting

Removal

1 Drain the cooling system (see Chapter 1).

2 Unclip and detach the top and bottom hoses from the radiator.

3 Remove the front grille panel, referring to Chapter 11 if necessary.

4 Undo the bolts and remove the crossmember or strengthening brace from above the radiator **(see illustration)**.

5 Disconnect the wiring harnesses and connectors from the cooling fan thermoswitch and the cooling fan(s), unbolt the radiator upper retaining brackets, then lift out the radiator together with the fan(s).

6 If required, the cooling fan(s) can be detached from the radiator as described in Section 6.

Inspection

7 If the radiator has been removed due to suspected blockage, reverse flush it as described in Chapter 1.

8 Clean dirt and debris from the radiator fins using a soft brush. Be careful, as the fins are easily damaged, and are sharp.

9 If necessary, a radiator specialist can perform a "flow test" on the radiator, to establish whether an internal blockage exists.

10 A leaking radiator must be referred to a specialist for permanent repair. Do not attempt to weld or solder a leaking radiator, as damage to the plastic components may result.

11 In an emergency, minor leaks from the radiator can be cured by using a radiator sealant in accordance with the manufacturers instructions with the radiator *in situ*.

12 If the radiator is to be sent for repair or renewed, remove all hoses, and the cooling fan switch.

13 Inspect the condition of the radiator mounting rubbers, and renew them if necessary.

Refitting

14 Refitting is a reversal of removal, but ensure that the bottom locating pegs are engaged in their bushes.

15 Refill the cooling system, as described in Chapter 1.

6 Radiator electric cooling fan - removal and refitting

Removal

The fan assembly and its mounting bracket may be clipped, bolted, screwed or riveted in position according to model and engine type. Once the radiator is removed (see Section 5) the fan assembly can be detached after removal of the relevant fastenings. Where the assembly is secured by rivets, these must be drilled out and the unit secured with new pop rivets on reassembly.

Refitting

Refitting is a reversal of removal.

7 Cooling system electrical switches and sensors - testing, removal and refitting

Cooling fan thermoswitch

Removal

1 Partially drain the cooling system (see Chapter 1) to below the level of the thermoswitch. The switch is located in the radiator side tank **(see illustration)**.

2 Disconnect the thermoswitch leads, unscrew it and remove it.

Testing

3 To test the switch, connect a battery and test light to its terminals. Heat the switch in hot water. The switch should close (test light comes on) at approximately the temperature

stamped on it, and open again (test light goes off) as it cools down. If not, renew it.

Refitting

4 Refit the thermoswitch, using sealant on the threads, and reconnect its leads.

5 Refill the cooling system (Chapter 1).

Coolant temperature sensor

Testing

6 If the temperature gauge indicates Hot at any time, consult the *"Fault finding"* section at the rear of this manual, to assist in tracing possible cooling system faults. Testing of the sensor should be entrusted to a Renault dealer, or by the substitution of a known good unit.

Removal

7 Partially drain the cooling system (see Chapter 1) to below the level of the sensor unit. The sensor is located in the thermostat housing on petrol engines and in the front left-hand side of the cylinder head on diesel engines **(see illustration)**.

8 Disconnect the lead from the sensor unit and unscrew it from its location.

Refitting

9 Screw in the new sensor unit, using a smear of sealant on the threads. Reconnect the lead.

10 Refill the cooling system (Chapter 1).

8 Coolant pump - removal and refitting

Note: *Coolant pump failure is indicated by water leaking from the gland at the front of the pump, or by rough and noisy operation. This is usually accompanied by excessive play of the pump spindle which can be checked by moving the pulley from side to side. Repair or overhaul of a faulty pump is not possible as internal parts are not available separately. In the event of failure a replacement pump must be obtained.*

Removal

1 Disconnect the battery negative lead then drain the cooling system (see Chapter 1).

3

5.4 Strengthening brace right-hand side attachment. Note earth wire location

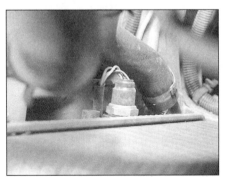

7.1 Radiator cooling fan thermoswitch location

7.7 Coolant temperature sensor location on petrol engine models

2 Remove the radiator as described in Section 5.

3 Refer to Chapter 1 and remove the auxiliary drivebelt(s) as necessary.

4 Unbolt and remove the coolant pump pulley.

5 Disconnect the hoses from the coolant pump.

6 Unscrew the coolant pump fixing bolts, tap the pump gently to break its gasket seal and remove the pump, at the same time compressing the timing belt tensioner plunger spring (where applicable).

Refitting

7 Remove all traces of old gasket from the pump, spacer plate and cylinder block mating surfaces.

8 On diesel engines, cut away the areas of the new gasket and manoeuvre the new gasket into position between the spacer plate and pump **(see illustration)**.

9 Fit the pump using a new gasket and securely tighten its retaining bolts. Note that the gasket must be fitted dry, without jointing compound. If a new pump is being fitted transfer the tensioner spring and plunger over to the pump (where applicable).

10 Refit the pulley, tightening its retaining bolts securely.

11 Refit the auxiliary drivebelt(s) as described in Chapter 1.

12 Refit the radiator as described in Section 5, and refill the cooling system, as described in Chapter 1.

9 Heating and ventilation system - general information

1 Depending on model type and options, the heater may be fitted alone or in conjunction with an air conditioning unit. The same housings and heater components are used in all cases. The air conditioning system is described in Section 12.

2 The heater is of the fresh air type. Air enters through a grille in front of the windscreen. On its way to the various vents a variable proportion of the air passes through the heater matrix, where it is warmed by engine coolant flowing through the matrix.

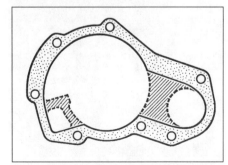

8.8 Coolant pump gasket areas to be cut away on diesel engines

3 Distribution of air to the vents, and through or around the matrix, is controlled by cable operated flaps or shutters.

4 A multi-speed electric blower is fitted to boost the airflow through the heater.

5 On early models the heater temperature and air distribution flaps are operated by sliding lever controls. On later models a redesigned heater unit is fitted which is controlled by rotary knobs.

10 Heater/ventilation system components (early models) - removal and refitting

Note: *The following operations are applicable to early models with sliding lever temperature/air distribution controls. For later models refer to Section 11.*

Heater blower motor

Removal

1 Remove the facia assembly as described in Chapter 11.

2 Disconnect the blower motor wiring.

3 Undo the two screws and lift out the air duct elbow.

4 Undo the remaining three screws, release the blower motor housing from the heater unit and withdraw the unit from the passenger compartment.

5 To remove the blower motor from the motor housing, release the seven clips and separate the two half housings.

6 Extract the retaining clip securing the fan to the blower motor shaft.

7 Disconnect the wiring at the blower motor shaft.

8 Undo the two motor retaining screws, free the fan from the motor shaft and remove the motor from the housing.

Refitting

9 Refitting is a reversal of removal.

Heater unit

Removal

10 Drain the cooling system as described in Chapter 1.

11 Remove the facia, referring to Chapter 11.

12 Disconnect the two heater hoses from the heater matrix pipe stubs.

13 Identify the location of the two control cables to aid refitting. Disconnect the control cables from the flap levers by releasing the retaining clip and sliding the inner cable ends off the lever pegs.

14 Disconnect the blower motor wiring.

15 Undo the two screws and lift out the air duct elbow.

16 Undo the remaining three screws, and remove the blower motor housing from the heater unit.

17 Undo the remaining securing screws and withdraw the heater unit from the passenger compartment.

Refitting

18 Refitting is a reversal of removal but reconnect and adjust the control cables as follows.

19 Move the temperature control lever to the "cold" position and ensure that the hot air/cold air flap in the heater unit is closed. Engage the control inner cable end with the flap lever then secure the outer cable with the retaining clip. Adjustment is made by slightly repositioning the outer cable in its clip as necessary.

20 Move the air distribution control lever to its lowest "face only" position and ensure that the two distribution flaps in the heater unit are closed. Connect and adjust the cable as described in the previous paragraph.

21 On completion of refitting, refill the cooling system as described in Chapter 1.

Heater matrix

Removal

22 Remove the heater unit as described previously.

23 Release the four lugs at the side of the heater unit and carefully slide out the matrix.

Refitting

24 Refitting is a reversal of removal.

Heater/ventilation control unit

Removal

25 Remove the facia as described in Chapter 11. With the facia removed the control unit can be accessed for removal.

Refitting

26 Refitting is a reversal of removal but adjust the control cables as refitting progresses, as described in paragraphs 19 and 20 above.

11 Heater/ventilation system components (later models) - removal and refitting

Note: *The following operations are applicable to later models with rotary temperature/air distribution controls. For early models refer to Section 10.*

Heater blower motor

Removal

1 Disconnect the battery negative lead.

2 From within the engine compartment, unscrew the five nuts and remove the soundproofing panel from around the blower motor assembly.

3 Disconnect the blower motor wiring and resistor connections.

4 Unscrew the cable clamp and disconnect the recirculating flap control cable from the side of the blower motor assembly.

5 Undo the four nuts at the side, and single bolt at the front, and withdraw the blower motor assembly from the engine compartment.

6 Undo the seven bolts securing the two half casings together and lift off the top half.

7 Release the motor retaining strap, disconnect the two wiring connectors and lift the blower motor out of the lower casing.

Refitting

8 Refitting is a reversal of removal but adjust the recirculating flap control cable as described in paragraph 33 before refitting the soundproofing panel.

Heater unit

Removal

9 Drain the cooling system as described in Chapter 1.

10 Remove the facia as described in Chapter 11.

11 Disconnect the two heater hoses from the heater matrix pipe stubs in the engine compartment.

12 Slacken the two nuts and remove the pipe stub support plate from the engine compartment bulkhead.

13 Unscrew the five nuts and remove the soundproofing panel from around the blower motor assembly.

14 Unscrew the cable clamp and disconnect the recirculating flap control cable from the side of the blower motor assembly.

15 From inside the passenger compartment, undo the two bolts and remove the clamps securing the heater unit to the facia crossmember.

16 Undo the four bolts securing the steering column and pedal box assembly upper mountings to the facia crossmember. Undo the two bolts each side and lift out the crossmember.

17 Withdraw the two ventilation ducts.

18 Undo the four nuts securing the heater unit to the bulkhead.

19 Disconnect the blower motor wiring from the heater unit then pull the heater unit off the bulkhead studs. Release any remaining ducts, control cable clips and wiring connectors as the unit is withdrawn, then remove the heater unit from the passenger compartment.

Refitting

20 Refitting is a reversal of removal but adjust the recirculating flap control cable as described in paragraph 33, before refitting the soundproofing panel.

21 On completion of refitting, refill the cooling system as described in Chapter 1.

Heater matrix

Removal

22 Drain the cooling system as described in Chapter 1.

23 Remove the facia as described in Chapter 11.

24 Unscrew the nut securing the matrix pipe stub mounting plate to the side of the matrix and separate the two pipes.

25 Undo the four screws and slide the matrix out of the side of the heater unit.

Refitting

26 Refitting is a reversal of removal, but renew the pipe stub O-rings if they show any sign of deterioration.

27 On completion of refitting, refill the cooling system as described in Chapter 1.

Heater/ventilation control unit

Removal

28 Remove the facia as described in Chapter 11. When the facia has been removed sufficiently for access to the control panel, unclip the panel by pushing on its front face.

29 From within the engine compartment, unscrew the five nuts and remove the soundproofing panel from around the blower motor assembly.

30 Unscrew the cable clamp and disconnect the recirculating flap control cable from the side of the blower motor assembly.

31 Disconnect the hot air/cold air mixer flap cable from the heater unit and remove the control unit and cables from the passenger compartment.

Refitting

32 Refitting is a reversal of removal but adjust the recirculating flap control cable as follows before refitting the soundproofing panel.

33 Turn the knob on the control unit to the recirculation setting. From within the engine compartment, move the recirculation flap lever on the side of the blower motor assembly downward, toward the control cable clamp, as far as it will go. With the lever in this position, secure the outer cable in the clamp, and tighten the clamp screw. Check for full movement of the lever as the knob on the control unit is turned through its full range of travel.

12 Air conditioning system -
general information and
precautions

General information

An air conditioning system is available on certain models. It enables the temperature of incoming air to be lowered, and also dehumidifies the air, which makes for rapid demisting and increased comfort.

The cooling side of the system works in the same way as a domestic refrigerator. Refrigerant gas is drawn into a belt-driven compressor, and passes into a condenser mounted on the front of the radiator, where it loses heat and becomes liquid. The liquid passes through an expansion valve to an evaporator, where it changes from liquid under high pressure to gas under low pressure. This change is accompanied by a drop in temperature, which cools the evaporator. The refrigerant returns to the compressor, and the cycle begins again.

Air blown through the evaporator passes to the air distribution unit, where it is mixed with hot air blown through the heater matrix to achieve the desired temperature in the passenger compartment.

The heating side of the system works in the same way as on models without air conditioning (see Section 9).

Precautions

When an air conditioning system is fitted, it is necessary to observe special precautions whenever dealing with any part of the system, or its associated components. If for any reason the system must be disconnected, entrust this task to your Renault dealer or a refrigeration engineer.

⚠ *Warning: The refrigeration circuit may contain a liquid refrigerant (Freon), and it is therefore dangerous to disconnect any part of the system without specialised knowledge and equipment. The refrigerant is potentially dangerous, and should only be handled by qualified persons. If it is splashed onto the skin, it can cause frostbite. It is not itself poisonous, but in the presence of a naked flame (including a cigarette) it forms a poisonous gas. Uncontrolled discharging of the refrigerant is dangerous, and potentially damaging to the environment.*

Do not operate the air conditioning system if it is known to be short of refrigerant, as this may damage the compressor.

13 Air conditioning system components - removal and refitting

⚠ *Warning: Do not attempt to open the refrigerant circuit. Refer to the precautions given in Section 12.*

The only operation which can be carried out without discharging the refrigerant is the renewal of the compressor drivebelt, although this in itself is a complex operation. Refer to Chapter 1 for further details. All other operations must be entrusted to a Renault dealer or an air conditioning specialist.

If necessary, the compressor can be unbolted and moved aside, without disconnecting its flexible hoses, after releasing the drivebelt.

3

Notes

Chapter 4 Part A:
Fuel system - carburettor petrol models

Contents

Degrees of difficulty

Easy, suitable for novice with little experience	**Fairly easy,** suitable for beginner with some experience	**Fairly difficult,** suitable for competent DIY mechanic	**Difficult,** suitable for experienced DIY mechanic	**Very difficult,** suitable for expert DIY or professional

Specifications

General

System type .... Centrally-mounted fuel tank, mechanical fuel pump, Weber DARA carburettor

Carburettor

General

Type:
  Pre-1988 models .... Weber 32 DARA 40
  1988 models onward .... Weber 28/36 DARA 0
Choke type .... Automatic
Idle speed:
  Pre-1988 models .... 800 ± 50 rpm
  1988 models onward .... 700 ± 50 rpm
Idle mixture CO content .... 1.5 ± 0.5%

Calibration	Primary	Secondary
Weber 32 DARA 40:		
Venturi	26	26
Main jet	132	140
Idling jet	55	45
Air compensating jet	155	140
Emulsifier	F58	F6
Diffuser	3.5	4
Accelerator pump	60	-
Needle valve	2.25	-
Weber 28/36 DARA 0:		
Venturi	22	29
Main jet	112	155
Idling jet	42	42
Air compensating jet	200	100
Emulsifier	F99	F56
Diffuser	3.5	4
Accelerator pump	50	-
Needle valve	225	-

4A

Overhaul data

Weber 32 DARA 40:
Float setting	7.0 mm
Float stroke	15.0 mm
Initial throttle opening (see text)	1.30 mm
Vacuum part-open setting:	
Compensator compressed	5.5 mm
Compensator released	10.0 mm
Deflooding device	5.5 mm

Weber 28/36 DARA 0:
Float setting	7.0 mm
Float stroke	15.0 mm
Initial throttle opening (see text)	0.80 mm
Vacuum part-open setting:	
Compensator compressed	3.0 mm
Compensator released	7.5 mm
Deflooding device	5.5 mm

Recommended fuel .... 98 RON leaded (refer to dealer for latest recommendations)

---

1 General information and precautions

The fuel system consists of a centrally-mounted fuel tank, mechanical fuel pump and a Weber carburettor. The fuel pump is operated by an eccentric on the auxiliary shaft and is mounted on the left-hand side of the cylinder block. The air cleaner contains a disposable paper filter element and incorporates a flap valve air temperature control system; this allows cold and warm air to be mixed and enter the air cleaner in the correct proportions.

The Weber DARA carburettor is a twin barrel, fixed jet, downdraught unit utilising an automatic choke for cold starting. Further details of the carburettor will be found in Section 8.

 Warning: Many of the procedures in this Chapter require the removal of fuel lines and connections, which may result in some fuel spillage. Before carrying out any operation on the fuel system, refer to the precautions given in "Safety first!" at the beginning of this manual, and follow them implicitly. Petrol is a highly dangerous and volatile liquid, and the precautions necessary when handling it cannot be overstressed.

2 Air cleaner assembly - removal and refitting

Removal

1 Remove the air cleaner element (see Chapter 1).
2 Disconnect the hot and cold air inlet ducting from the housing, together with any vacuum or vent hoses.

3 Release the securing bolt(s) or strap and lift the housing from the engine compartment.
4 The operation of the air temperature control system can be checked by immersing the housing in water up to the level of the thermostatic element in the cold air inlet. With the water at a temperature of up to 26° C the flap valve should shut off the cold air inlet after approximately five minutes. With the water temperature at 36° C or higher the flap valve should shut off the hot air inlet after approximately five minutes. If the system does not operate as described renewal will be necessary; adjustment or repair is not possible.

Refitting

5 Refit by reversing the removal operations.

3 Fuel pump - removal and refitting

Note: *Refer to the warning note in Section 1 before proceeding.*

Removal

1 Disconnect the battery negative lead.
2 Clean around the hose unions on the pump, then slacken the hose clamps and disconnect the hoses. Be prepared for fuel spillage. Suitably plug the hoses after disconnection.
3 Unbolt the fuel pump from the block and remove it. Recover the gasket and any spacers.
4 On some models, the pump cover may be removed for cleaning of the filter screen if wished. Further dismantling should not be attempted unless a repair kit can be obtained.

Refitting

5 Refit by reversing the removal operations, using a new gasket.
6 Run the engine and check for leakage.

4 Fuel gauge sender unit - removal and refitting

Note: *Refer to the warning note in Section 1 before proceeding.*

Removal

1 Remove the fuel tank as described in Section 5.
2 Noting the alignment marks on the tank and sender unit, unscrew the large locking ring. If necessary, use a "soft" tool such as a strap wrench to release the locking ring.
3 Carefully lift the sender unit from the top of the tank taking care not to bend the float. Recover the rubber sealing ring between the sender unit and tank flange.

Refitting

4 Refitting is a reversal of removal, bearing in mind the following points:
a) Renew the sealing ring if the original shows any signs of deterioration.
b) Apply a bead of mastic sealant to the sealing ring before fitting the assembly to the fuel tank.
c) Align the marks on the tank and sender unit then tighten the locking ring securely.

5 Fuel tank - removal and refitting

Note: *Refer to the warning note in Section 1 before proceeding.*

Removal

1 A drain plug is not provided on the fuel tank and it is therefore preferable to carry out the removal operation when the tank is nearly empty. Before proceeding, disconnect the battery negative lead, and then syphon or hand pump the remaining fuel from the tank.

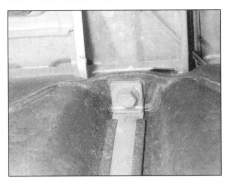

5.5a Fuel tank retaining strap and bolt

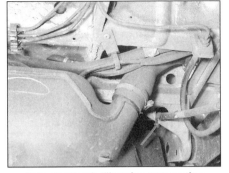

5.5b Fuel tank filler pipe connection

6.2 Removing the accelerator cable from the support bracket

2 Chock the front wheels then jack up the rear of the vehicle and support it on axle stands (see *"Jacking and vehicle support"*).

3 Where fitted, remove the protection panel from the front face of the tank.

4 Take the weight of the tank on a suitable jack, with a block of wood interposed to prevent damage.

5 Undo the tank retaining strap bolts and detach the fuel filler pipe connector hose **(see illustrations)**. An assistant may be required at this point to help in steadying the tank as it is lowered.

6 Carefully lower the tank until sufficient clearance exists then disconnect the wiring connector at the fuel gauge sender unit. Identify the fuel and vent hose connections at the tank to aid refitting and disconnect them.

7 Carefully lower the fuel tank and withdraw it from under the vehicle.

8 If the tank is contaminated with sediment or water, remove the fuel gauge sender unit as described in Section 4, and swill out the tank with clean fuel. If the tank is damaged, or leaks, it should be repaired by a specialist or renewed.

Refitting

9 Refitting is a reversal of removal but take care not to trap any hoses between the tank and vehicle underbody. Ensure all hoses are correctly connected in their original locations and retained with clips or straps where necessary.

6 Accelerator cable - removal, refitting and adjustment

Removal

1 Working in the engine compartment, open the throttle by hand and release the inner cable from its attachment on the carburettor.

2 Withdraw the outer cable adjuster from the support bracket and remove the spring clip **(see illustration)**

3 Work back along the length of the outer cable and free it from any necessary retaining clips or brackets whilst noting its correct routing.

4 Working from inside the vehicle, release the cable end fitting by slipping it out of the elongated slot on the pedal clevis. Tie a length of string to the end of the cable.

5 Withdraw the cable through the bulkhead into the engine compartment. When the end of the cable appears, untie the string and leave it in position, it can then be used to draw the cable back into position on refitting.

Refitting and adjustment

6 Refitting is a reversal of removal using the piece of string to draw the cable through the bulkhead. Ensure that the cable is routed as noted before removal, and retained by all the necessary retaining clips and brackets. On completion, check the cable adjustment as follows.

7 With the spring clip removed, gently pull the outer cable out of its grommet, ensuring that the accelerator lever remains fully against its stop, until all free play is removed from the inner cable.

8 With the cable held in this position refit the spring clip to the last exposed outer cable groove in front of the rubber grommet, ie. so that when the clip is refitted and the outer cable is released there is only a small amount of freeplay in the inner cable.

9 Have an assistant depress the accelerator pedal and check that the carburettor throttle linkage opens fully and returns smoothly to its stop.

7 Accelerator pedal - removal and refitting

Removal

1 Working inside the vehicle, release the accelerator cable end fitting from the pedal.

2 Undo the bolt securing the pedal assembly to the bulkhead and remove the assembly.

Refitting

3 Refitting is a reversal of removal applying a smear of grease to the pedal pivot. On completion adjust the accelerator cable as described in Section 6.

8 Carburettor - general information

The carburettor is of dual barrel, downdraught type with a coolant-heated automatic choke and throttle valve plate block.

The carburettor incorporates a constant CO idling circuit controlled by a mixture screw and a volume (idle speed) screw which operates on a supplementary circuit.

An accelerator pump, power and full throttle enrichment devices are also fitted, together with a secondary barrel lock-out system which uses a diaphragm to prevent the secondary throttle valve from opening when the diaphragm is subject to vacuum.

An anti-diesel (run-on) valve shuts off the idle circuit as soon as the ignition is switched off, and on certain models another solenoid valve is used to close the constant CO idling supplementary circuit.

4A

9 Carburettor - idle speed and mixture adjustment

Note: *An accurate tachometer exhaust gas analyser will be needed for this operation.*

1 Before checking the idle speed and mixture setting, always check the following first referring to the appropriate Sections and Chapters of this manual as necessary:

a) *Check that the spark plugs are in good condition and correctly gapped.*

b) *Check that the accelerator cable is correctly adjusted.*

c) *Check that the crankcase breather hoses are secure, with no leaks or kinks.*

d) *Check that the air cleaner filter element is clean.*

e) *Check that the exhaust system is in good condition.*

f) *If the engine is running very roughly, check the compression pressures and valve clearances.*

2 Take the vehicle on a journey of sufficient length to warm it up to normal operating

temperature. On return, connect a tachometer to the engine in accordance with the maker's instructions. Start the engine and wait for the radiator electric cooling fan to operate. When the fan stops, clear any excess fuel from the inlet manifold by racing the engine two or three times to between 2000 and 3000 rpm, then allow it to idle again.

3 The idle speed (volume) screw is located on the carburettor base on the side nearest to the cylinder head **(see illustration)**. Turn the volume screw until the tachometer indicates the specified idle speed.

4 The idle mixture (exhaust gas CO level) is set at the factory and should require no further adjustment. If, due to a change in engine characteristics (carbon build-up, engine wear) or after a major carburettor overhaul, the mixture setting is lost, it can be reset. Note however that an exhaust gas analyser (CO meter) will be required to check the mixture and to set it with the necessary standard of accuracy. If an analyser is not available, the vehicle must be taken to a Renault dealer for the work to be carried out.

5 If an exhaust gas analyser is available, follow its maker's instructions to check the exhaust gas CO level. If adjustment is required, prise free the tamperproof cap (with the aid of a thin-bladed screwdriver), to gain access to the mixture screw.

6 Turn the mixture adjustment screw clockwise in very small amounts to weaken the mixture or anti-clockwise to richen it until the CO reading is as given in the *Specifications*.

7 If necessary, re-adjust the idling speed then check the CO reading again. Repeat as necessary until both the idling speed and CO reading are correct.

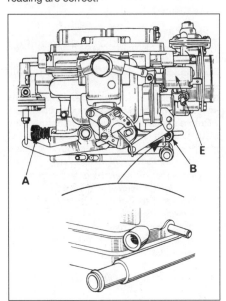

9.3 Carburettor adjustment screws

A Idle speed (volume) screw
B Idle mixture screw
E Fuel cut-off solenoid

8 When the adjustments are complete, switch off the engine, disconnect the test equipment and fit a new tamperproof cap over the mixture screw.

10 Carburettor - removal and refitting

Note: *Refer to the warning note in Section 1 before proceeding.*

Removal

1 Disconnect the ventilation hose then undo the three nuts and lift the inlet elbow off the top of the carburettor.

2 With the engine completely cold, remove the expansion tank filler cap to release the pressure in the cooling system.

3 Disconnect the coolant hoses from the automatic choke housing and the carburettor throttle block. If the hoses are tied up as high as possible, coolant loss will be minimal and the need to drain the cooling system avoided.

4 Disconnect the fuel hoses, the throttle link rod and the wiring connector(s) from the solenoid valve(s).

5 Unscrew the carburettor mounting nuts and lift the unit from the inlet manifold.

Refitting

6 Refitting is a reversal of removal, always use a new flange gasket.

7 Bleed the choke housing and top-up the cooling system as described in "*Weekly checks*".

11 Carburettor - fault diagnosis and overhaul

Fault diagnosis

1 If a carburettor fault is suspected, always check first that the spark plugs are in good condition and correctly gapped, that the accelerator cable is correctly adjusted, and that the air cleaner filter element is clean; refer to the relevant Sections of this Chapter and Chapter 1. If the engine is running very roughly, first check the valve clearances then check the compression pressures as described in Chapter 2A.

2 If careful checking of all the above produces no improvement, the carburettor must be removed for cleaning and overhaul.

3 Prior to overhaul, check the availability of component parts before starting work; note that most sealing washers, screws and gaskets are available in kits, as are some of the major sub-assemblies. In most cases it will be sufficient to dismantle the carburettor and to clean the jets and passages.

Overhaul

Note: *Refer to the warning note in Section 1 before proceeding. The operations described here should be regarded as the limit of possible overhaul. It may be more satisfactory to renew a well worn carburettor.*

4 The operations described in paragraphs 6 to 11 can be carried out without the need to remove the carburettor from the engine.

5 The adjustments described in this Section are vital to the success of the overhaul.

6 Disconnect the ventilation hose then undo the three nuts and lift the inlet elbow off the top of the carburettor. Disconnect the fuel hose from the carburettor top cover.

7 Unscrew the plug just above the fuel inlet nozzle, remove and clean the filter gauze. Refit the gauze and the plug.

8 Extract the screws and take off the top cover. This will be as far as most overhaul work will need to go, as the jets can be removed and blown through with air from a tyre pump - never probe them with wire or their calibration will be ruined **(see illustration)**. In extreme cases of clogging a nylon bristle may be used to clear a jet.

9 Mop out dirt and sediment from the fuel bowl.

10 The tightness of the fuel inlet needle valve may be checked, but this will mean driving out the float pivot pin to locate a ring spanner on the valve. Fuel seeping out through the needle valve seating washer will cause too high a fuel level and consequent flooding.

11 Check the float setting as follows. With a new cover gasket in position, hold the cover vertically with the float hanging down so that the float closes the needle valve but without forcing the ball inside the needle valve. The

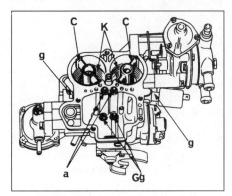

11.8 Location of carburettor jets

a Air compensating jet
C Diffuser
g Idling jet
Gg Main jet
K Venturi

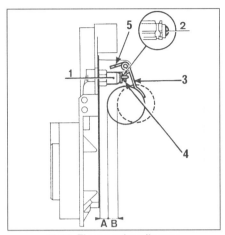

11.11 Float setting diagram

1 Fuel inlet needle valve
2 Needle valve ball
3 Float arm
4 Valve operating tab
5 Float stop
A Float setting dimension
A + B = float stroke

nearest point of the float to the surface of the cover gasket should be 7.0 mm **(see illustration)**. If necessary bend the float arm. Now gently lift the float with the finger. Dimension A + B (float stroke) should be 15.0 mm. If necessary, bend the stop tab.

12 If the carburettor is to be completely dismantled, remove the unit, as described in Section 10, and clean away external dirt.

13 Remove the top cover and jets as previously described. A carburettor overhaul kit should now be obtained which will contain all the necessary gaskets, diaphragms and seals which will require renewal.

14 Remove the diaphragm units, invert the carburettor and extract the throttle valve block screws. Do not attempt to dismantle the throttle flap plates or spindles.

15 Remove the choke housing cover and housing if necessary. Clean, inspect and renew any worn items.

16 As reassembly progresses, carry out the following adjustments.

Initial throttle opening

17 To adjust the initial throttle opening, fully close the choke flaps with the fingers and set the adjusting screw on the specified cam step **(see illustration)**. On the 32 DARA 40 carburettor the adjusting screw should be positioned on the "very cold" step of the cam. On the 28/36 DARA carburettor, the screw should be positioned on the "medium cold" step of the cam.

18 Using a twist drill or similar gauge, check that the gap between the primary throttle flap and barrel is as given in the *Specifications*. If not, turn the screw as necessary.

Automatic choke (vacuum part-open) setting

19 To adjust the automatic choke (vacuum part-open setting) remove the cover and bi-

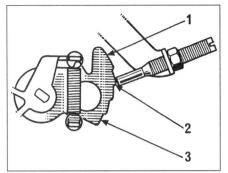

11.17 Cam step positions for initial throttle opening setting

1 Very cold   2 Medium cold   3 Warm

metallic spring then manually close the choke flaps **(see illustration)**. Fully raise the vacuum capsule pushrod and turn the choke operating lever against it. Using a twist drill check that the gap between the choke flap and barrel is as given in the *Specifications*. If not, turn the adjustment screw inside the top of the vacuum capsule as necessary. Refit the bi-metallic spring and cover, making sure that the spring engages the lever correctly and the assembly marks on the cover and body are in alignment.

Deflooding mechanism - adjustment

20 To adjust the deflooding mechanism, fully close the choke flaps manually then fully open the throttle lever **(see illustration)**. Using a twist drill check that the gap between the choke flaps and barrel is as given in the *Specifications*. If not, turn the adjusting screw as necessary. After making an adjustment check the initial throttle opening, as described in paragraphs 17 and 18.

21 To adjust the float level proceed as described in paragraph 11.

Defuming valve

22 Some carburettors are fitted with a defuming valve which vents the float chamber to atmosphere when idling.

23 To adjust, hold the choke flap open and depress the defuming valve lever **(see illustration)**. Using a twist drill, measure the

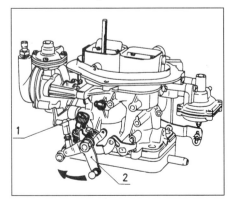

11.20 Deflooding mechanism

1 Adjusting screw   2 Throttle lever

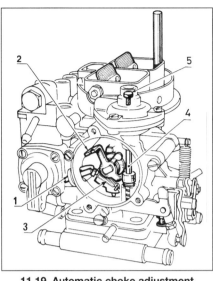

11.19 Automatic choke adjustment

1 Initial throttle opening screw
2 Operating lever
3 Cam
4 Pushrod
5 Adjusting screw

throttle flap opening. If it is not as specified (see *Specifications*) turn the adjusting nut.

24 With the checks and adjustments completed, the remainder of reassembly is a reversal of the dismantling procedure. Adjust the idle speed and mixture settings (see Section 9) after refitting the carburettor.

12 Inlet manifold - removal and refitting

4A

Removal

1 Disconnect the battery negative lead.

2 Remove the carburettor (see Section 9), or disconnect all services from it but leave it attached to the manifold.

3 Disconnect the vacuum hoses from the manifold, making identifying marks if required. Clamp and disconnect coolant hoses also.

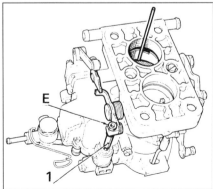

11.23 Defuming valve adjustment

E Nut   1 Valve lever

4 Unbolt and remove the manifold. Recover the gasket.

Refitting

5 Refit by reversing the removal operations, using a new gasket.
6 Refit the carburettor (if removed), then top-up the cooling system as described in "*Weekly checks*". Run the engine and check the idle speed and mixture on completion.

13 Exhaust manifold - removal and refitting

Removal

1 Remove the hot air trunking (when so equipped).

2 Disconnect the exhaust downpipe from the manifold.
3 Undo the nuts and remove the manifold from the cylinder head **(see illustration)**. Recover the gaskets.

Refitting

4 When refitting, use new gaskets and apply anti-seize compound to the stud threads. Fit the manifold to the head and tighten the nuts evenly.
5 Reconnect the exhaust downpipe and the hot air trunking.
6 Run the engine and check for leaks.

13.3 Exhaust manifold nut locations

Chapter 4 Part B:
Fuel system - fuel-injected petrol models

Contents

4B

Degrees of difficulty

| **Easy,** suitable for novice with little experience | | **Fairly easy,** suitable for beginner with some experience | | **Fairly difficult,** suitable for competent DIY mechanic | | **Difficult,** suitable for experienced DIY mechanic | | **Very difficult,** suitable for expert DIY or professional | |

Specifications

General
System type . . . . Centrally mounted fuel tank, electric roller cell fuel pump, Renix, computer controlled multi-point fuel injection system

Fuel system data
Idle speed (nominal)* . . . . 800 ± 25 rpm
Idle mixture CO content** . . . . 1.5 ± 0.5%

*Non-adjustable - controlled by fuel/ignition system ECU
**Adjustable on certain non-catalyst equipped engines only. Controlled by fuel/ignition system ECU on all other models

Recommended fuel
Minimum octane rating:
    Engines without catalytic converter* . . . . 95 RON leaded or unleaded
    Engines with catalytic converter . . . . 91 RON unleaded (leaded fuel must **not** be used)

*Refer to dealer for latest recommendations

2.2 Disconnect the wiring connector from the inlet air temperature sensor

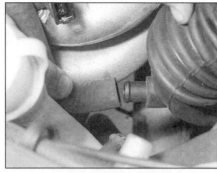

2.3a Detach the breather hose from the base of the inlet ducting . . .

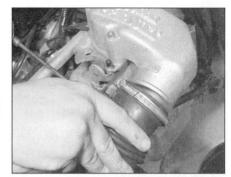

2.3b . . . then slacken the clip and withdraw the ducting from the throttle casing cover

1 General information and precautions

The fuel system consists of a centrally-mounted fuel tank, electric fuel pump, fuel filter and Renix multi-point fuel injection system. The fuel pump supplies fuel to the fuel rail, which acts as a reservoir for the four fuel injectors which inject fuel into the inlet tracts. The fuel filter incorporated in the feed line from the pump to the fuel rail ensures that the fuel supplied to the injectors is clean. Further details of the fuel injection system will be found in Section 9.

> ⚠ **Warning:** *Many of the procedures in this Chapter require the removal of fuel lines and connections, which may result in some fuel spillage. Before carrying out any operation on the fuel system, refer to the precautions given in "Safety first!" at the beginning of this manual, and follow them implicitly. Petrol is a highly dangerous and volatile liquid, and the precautions necessary when handling it cannot be overstressed.*

2 Air cleaner assembly - removal and refitting

Removal

1 Remove the air cleaner element (see Chapter 1).
2 Disconnect the wiring connector from the inlet air temperature sensor on the side of the inlet ducting **(see illustration)**.
3 Detach the breather hose from the base of the inlet ducting then slacken the clip and withdraw the ducting from the throttle casing cover **(see illustrations)**.
4 Release the air cleaner housing from its location, lift it up and remove it from the engine compartment **(see illustration)**.

Refitting

5 Refit by reversing the removal operations.

3 Fuel pump - removal and refitting

Note: *Refer to the warning note in Section 1 before proceeding.*

Removal

1 The fuel pump is located just forward of the fuel tank underneath the vehicle on the right-hand side.
2 Disconnect the battery negative lead.
3 Jack up the front and rear of the vehicle and support it on axle stands (see "Jacking and vehicle support"). Alternatively raise the vehicle on ramps.
4 Remove the protective cover over the pump (where fitted) then disconnect the electrical leads, noting the colours of the wires and the corresponding terminals **(see illustration)**.
5 Using brake hose clamps or similar tools, clamp the flexible fuel inlet and outlet hoses adjacent to the pump. Disconnect the fuel hoses from the pump being prepared for fuel spillage. Plug or cap the open unions.
6 Unbolt the pump mounting strap and remove the pump.

Refitting

7 Refitting is a reversal of removal. On completion, run the engine and check for leakage.

4 Fuel gauge sender unit - removal and refitting

Refer to Chapter 4A, Section 4.

5 Fuel tank - removal and refitting

Refer to Chapter 4A, Section 5.

6 Accelerator cable - removal, refitting and adjustment

Removal

1 Working in the engine compartment, detach the throttle return spring, open the throttle by hand and release the inner cable end from its attachment on the pivot quadrant **(see illustration)**.
2 Pull the outer cable adjuster out from the support bracket rubber grommet, then remove the spring clip.
3 Work back along the length of the outer cable and free it from any necessary retaining clips or brackets whilst noting its correct routing.

2.4 Release the air cleaner housing then lift it up and remove it from the engine compartment

3.4 Fuel pump location showing connections and mounting strap

6.1 Disconnecting the accelerator cable from the pivot quadrant

4 Working from inside the vehicle, release the cable end fitting by slipping it out of the elongated slot on the pedal clevis. Tie a length of string to the end of the cable.

5 Withdraw the cable through the bulkhead into the engine compartment. When the end of the cable appears, untie the string and leave it in position, it can then be used to draw the cable back into position on refitting.

Refitting and adjustment

6 Refitting is a reversal of removal using the piece of string to draw the cable through the bulkhead. Ensure that the cable is routed as noted before removal, and retained by all the necessary retaining clips and brackets. On completion, check the cable adjustment as follows.

7 With the spring clip removed, gently pull the outer cable out of its grommet, ensuring that the accelerator lever remains fully against its stop, until all free play is removed from the inner cable.

8 With the cable held in this position refit the spring clip to the last exposed outer cable groove in front of the rubber grommet, ie, so that when the clip is refitted and the outer cable is released there is only a small amount of freeplay in the inner cable.

9 Have an assistant depress the accelerator pedal and check that the throttle linkage opens fully and returns smoothly to its stop.

7 Accelerator pedal - removal and refitting

Refer to Chapter 4A, Section 7.

8 Fuel injection system - general information

The Renix fuel injection system is a microprocessor-controlled engine manage-ment system, designed to meet stringent emission control legislation whilst still providing excellent engine performance and fuel economy. This is achieved by continuously monitoring the engine using various sensors, whose data is input to the system's electronic control unit (ECU). Based on this information, the ECU program and memory then determine the exact amount of fuel necessary, which is injected directly into the inlet manifold, for all actual and anticipated driving conditions.

The Renix ECU also controls the ignition system to provide a total engine management package. In addition, it also controls various aspects of the emissions control systems described in Part D of this Chapter.

The main components of the system and their individual operation is as follows.

Electronic control unit: The fuel/ignition ECU is a microprocessor, which controls the entire operation of the system. Contained in the unit's memory is a program which controls the fuel supply to the injectors, and their opening duration as well as a basic set of ignition advance values. The program enters sub-routines to alter these parameters, according to inputs from the other components of the system. In addition to this, the engine idle speed is also controlled by the ECU, which uses an idle speed regulating valve to open or close an air passage as required. In the event of a fault in the system due to loss of a signal from one of the sensors, the ECU reverts to an emergency ("limp-home") program. This will allow the car to be driven, although engine operation and performance will be limited.

Fuel injectors: Each fuel injector consists of a solenoid-operated needle valve, which opens under commands from the ECU. Fuel from the fuel rail is then delivered through the injector nozzle into the inlet manifold.

Coolant temperature sensor: This resistive device is mounted on the thermostat housing, where its element is in direct contact with the engine coolant. Changes in coolant temperature are detected by the ECU as a change in sensor resistance. Signals from the coolant temperature sensor are also used to regulate the ignition advance setting.

Intake air temperature sensor: This resistive device is located in the air inlet ducting, where its element is in direct contact with the air entering the engine. Changes in air temperature are detected by the ECU as a change in sensor resistance. From the signals received from the inlet air temperature sensor and manifold absolute pressure sensor, the ECU can calculate the volume of air inducted into the engine.

Angular position/speed sensor: This sensor is mounted in the transmission bellhousing just above the engine flywheel. As the crankshaft rotates, a series of teeth in the flywheel periphery pass the inductive head of the sensor, which transmits a pulse to the ECU every time a tooth passes it. As there are two missing teeth 180° apart, the ECU recognises the absence of a pulse from the sensor at these points, and uses them to establish the TDC and BDC position for Nos 1 and 4 pistons. The time interval between pulses, and the location of the missing pulses, allow the ECU to accurately determine crankshaft speed and position.

Manifold absolute pressure sensor: The pressure sensor is connected to the inlet manifold via a hose and uses a piezo-electrical crystal to convert manifold pressure to an electrical signal. From the signals received from the manifold absolute pressure sensor and inlet air temperature sensor, the ECU can calculate the volume of air inducted into the engine.

No load/full load switch: The no load/full load switch is attached to the throttle shaft in the throttle casing. The unit sends signals to ECU that the throttle is either closed or fully open.

Idle speed regulating valve: The idle speed regulating valve contains a small electric motor that open or shuts a bypass air passage inside the valve. The valve operates in response to signals from the ECU and maintains the engine idle speed at a constant value irrespective of any additional load from the various accessories.

Idle speed mixture potentiometer: Certain engines without catalytic converters are provided with an idle speed mixture potentiometer to allow manual adjustment of the air/fuel mixture. On catalyst equipped engines the air/fuel mixture ratio is constantly regulated by the ECU in conjunction with the oxygen sensor in the exhaust system.

Fuel pump: An electric roller type pump located under the vehicle supplies fuel to the fuel rail on the inlet manifold via an in-line fuel filter.

Fuel pressure regulator: The regulator is a vacuum-operated mechanical device, which ensures that the pressure differential between fuel in the fuel rail and fuel in the inlet manifold is maintained at a constant value. As manifold depression increases, the regulated fuel pressure is reduced in direct proportion. When fuel pressure in the fuel rail exceeds the regulator setting, the regulator opens to allow fuel to return via the return line to the tank.

9 Fuel injection system - testing and adjustment

Testing

1 If a fault appears in the fuel injection system, first ensure that all the system wiring connectors are securely connected and free of corrosion. Ensure that the fault is not due to poor maintenance; ie, check that the air cleaner filter element is clean, the spark plugs are in good condition and correctly gapped, the cylinder compression pressures are correct, and that the engine breather hoses are clear and undamaged, referring to Chapters 1, 2 and 4D for further information.

2 If these checks fail to reveal the cause of the problem, the vehicle should be taken to a

4B

suitably-equipped Renault dealer for testing. A wiring block connector is incorporated in the engine management circuit, into which a special electronic diagnostic tester can be plugged. The tester will locate the fault quickly and simply, alleviating the need to test all the system components individually, which is a time-consuming operation that carries a risk of damaging the ECU.

Adjustment

3 The only adjustment possible, is that of the idle mixture CO content on certain 2.0 litre models without catalytic converters.
4 Due to the need for special diagnostic equipment to accurately adjust the CO content it is recommended that the vehicle is taken to a suitably equipped Renault dealer for this work to be carried out.

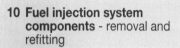

10 Fuel injection system components - removal and refitting

Fuel Injectors

Note: *Refer to the warning note in Section 1 before proceeding.*
1 Disconnect the battery negative lead.
2 Disconnect the throttle link rod from the linkage ball studs.
3 Disconnect the wiring plug from each injector **(see illustration)**. Free the wiring harness from the fuel rail, cutting cable-ties where necessary.
4 Disconnect the fuel supply and return hoses, being prepared for fuel spillage. Suitably plug the disconnected hoses.
5 Remove the bolts which secure the fuel rail to the inlet manifold. Pull the rail upwards to release the injectors from the manifold and remove the rail complete with injectors.
6 Individual injectors may now be removed from the rail by removing the securing clips and pulling them out.
7 Refit by reversing the removal operations. Check that the injector O-rings are in good condition and renew them if necessary; smear them with petroleum jelly or silicone grease as an assembly lubricant.

Fuel pressure regulator

Note: *Refer to the warning note in Section 1 before proceeding.*
8 Disconnect the battery negative lead.
9 The regulator is located under the inlet manifold just in front of the throttle casing.
10 Disconnect the vacuum and fuel hoses from the regulator, being prepared for fuel spillage. Suitably plug the disconnected fuel hoses.
11 Undo the retaining screws and remove the regulator with its bracket.
12 Refit by reversing the removal operations.

Idle speed regulating valve

13 The valve is located at the front of the

10.3 Disconnecting the fuel injector wiring plugs

engine, either attached to the body panel or the inlet manifold.
14 Disconnect the wiring connector from the valve. **(see illustration)**
15 Slacken the hose clips and carefully pull the air hoses off the valve stubs.
16 Undo the retaining clamp bolts, remove the clamp and withdraw the valve.
17 Refit by reversing the removal operations, using new hoses and clips if necessary. Ensure that the valve is fitted the correct way round. An arrow on the base of the unit indicates the direction of air flow.

Throttle casing

18 Disconnect the throttle link rod from the linkage ball studs **(see illustration)**.
19 Disconnect the no load/full load switch wiring plug.
20 Disconnect the crankcase ventilation hose and the air inlet ducting from the throttle casing cover.
21 Undo the three screws and lift off the cover.
22 Undo the bolts and remove the throttle casing from the inlet manifold.
23 Clean the mating surfaces and refit using the reversal of removal. New sealing gaskets must always be fitted during reassembly and the crankcase ventilation hose should be inspected to ensure that its orifice is clear.

No load/full load switch

24 Remove the throttle casing as described previously.

10.18 Disconnecting the throttle link rod from the ball studs

10.14 Disconnecting the idle speed regulating valve wiring connector

25 Undo the two screws and remove the switch from the casing.
26 When refitting, align the flat on the switch to coincide with flat on the throttle butterfly spindle and then move it in the direction of the arrow until the light throttle "click" is heard.
27 Hold the switch in this position and tighten the two screws lightly.
28 Using an ohmmeter and feeler blades, accurately adjust the switch position as follows.
29 With the throttle completely closed use the ohmmeter to measure the resistance across the switch terminals. The resistance across terminals A and B should be zero and the resistance across terminals B and C should be infinite. Reposition the switch by slackening the two screws and turning the switch in whichever direction is necessary until the correct values are obtained. Tighten the screws and verify the adjustment by checking the resistances at the partial and full load positions as follows.
30 Insert a feeler blade greater than 0.3 mm thick, between the throttle lever and the stop screw on the other side of the throttle casing **(see illustration)**. The resistance across terminals A and B and terminals B and C should now both be infinite.
31 Finally, open the throttle fully until it is possible to insert a drill bit or similar, of diameter greater than 22.0 mm, between the throttle butterfly and the casing wall. In this position, the resistance between terminals A and B should be infinite and between terminals B and C it should be zero.

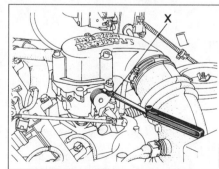

10.30 Feeler blade (X) inserted between throttle lever and stop screw for no load/full load switch adjustment

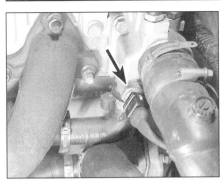

10.37 Coolant temperature sensor location (arrowed)

Intake air temperature sensor

32 Disconnect the wiring connector at the temperature sensor.

33 Slacken the retaining clips and remove the air inlet ducting from the air cleaner housing and throttle casing cover.

34 Pull the sensor from its location in the ducting.

35 Refit by reversing the removal operations.

Coolant temperature sensor

36 With the engine cold, unscrew the cooling system expansion tank cap to relieve any pressure in the system.

37 Disconnect the wiring connector from the sensor which is located in the side of the thermostat housing **(see illustration)**.

38 Unscrew the sensor and quickly plug the hole to prevent coolant loss.

39 Smear the sensor threads with sealant then screw in the sensor and tighten securely. Refit the wiring connector and top-up the cooling system as necessary (Chapter 1).

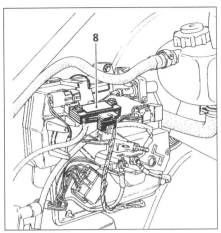

10.40 Manifold absolute pressure sensor location (8) in fuel/ignition ECU case

Manifold absolute pressure sensor

40 The location of this sensor varies according to model and year. It is usually located either underneath the ignition system power module on the left-hand side of the engine compartment bulkhead, or inside the fuel/ignition ECU case on the right-hand side of the engine compartment **(see illustration)**. If it is not in either of these locations, trace the vacuum hose from its source on the inlet manifold adjacent to the throttle casing, to its termination, which will be the manifold absolute pressure sensor.

41 Once located, disconnect the vacuum hose by prising it off with a screwdriver (do not pull it off or the pipe stub or the sensor may be damaged. Disconnect the wiring

connector and withdraw the sensor from its mounting lugs.

42 Refitting is a reversal of removal.

Angular position/speed sensor

43 Refer to Chapter 5B, Section 5.

Fuel/ignition electronic control unit (ECU)

44 Refer to Chapter 5B, Section 5.

11 Inlet manifold - removal and refitting

Removal

1 Disconnect the battery negative lead.

2 Remove the fuel injectors, throttle casing, fuel pressure regulator, and idle speed regulating valve as described in Section 10.

3 Disconnect the remaining hoses and wires from the manifold. Note the connection point of each to avoid confusion when refitting.

4 Unbolt and remove the manifold. Recover the gasket.

Refitting

5 Refitting is a reversal of removal. Ensure that the mating surfaces are clean and use a new gasket. Refit the remainder of the components as described in Section 10.

12 Exhaust manifold - removal and refitting

Refer to Chapter 4A, Section 13.

Notes

Chapter 4 Part C:
Fuel system - diesel models

Contents

Degrees of difficulty

Easy, suitable for novice with little experience	**Fairly easy,** suitable for beginner with some experience	**Fairly difficult,** suitable for competent DIY mechanic	**Difficult,** suitable for experienced DIY mechanic	**Very difficult,** suitable for expert DIY or professional

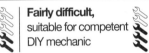

Specifications

General

System type . . . . Centrally-mounted fuel tank, distributor fuel injection pump with integral transfer pump, indirect injection. Turbocharger and intercooler on all models

Firing order . . . . 1-3-4-2 (No 1 at flywheel end)

Adjustment data

Idle speed . . . . 750 ± 50 rpm
Fast idle speed (see text):
    Early type pump . . . . Not adjustable (factory set)
    Later type pump . . . . 1000 ± 50 rpm
Maximum speed . . . . 4700 to 4800 rpm

Injection pump

Type . . . . Bosch VE4/9F2200
Direction of rotation . . . . Clockwise, viewed from sprocket end
Static timing:
    Engine position . . . . No 1 piston at TDC
    Pump timing measurement . . . . 0.70 ± 0.02 mm
Dynamic timing (at idle speed) . . . . 13.5° ± 1°

Injectors

Type . . . . Bosch
Opening pressure . . . . 125 to 138 bars

Turbocharger

Type . . . . Garrett T2
Boost pressure (approximate) . . . . 0.6 to 0.7 bar at 2500 rpm

4C

Torque wrench settings

	Nm
Clamp-type injectors:	
Clamp retaining nuts	17
Return hose union bolts	10
Screw-type injectors	70
Injector pipe union nuts	25
Injection pump:	
Feed and return hose union bolts	25
Mounting nuts and bolts	25
Stop solenoid	20

1 General information and precautions

General information

The fuel system consists of a centrally-mounted fuel tank, a fuel filter with integral water separator, a fuel injection pump, injectors and associated components. On certain models (fitted with the Lucas/CAV filter arrangement), as the fuel passes through the filter, the fuel is heated by coolant flowing through the filter bowl. A turbocharger and intercooler are fitted to all models.

Fuel is drawn from the fuel tank to the fuel injection pump by a vane-type transfer pump incorporated in the fuel injection pump. Before reaching the pump the fuel passes through a fuel filter where foreign matter and water are removed. Excess fuel lubricates the moving components of the pump and is then returned to the tank.

The fuel injection pump is driven at half crankshaft speed by the timing belt. The high pressure required to inject the fuel into the compressed air in the swirl chambers is achieved by a cam plate acting on a single piston. The fuel passes through a central rotor with a single outlet drilling which aligns with ports leading to the injector pipes.

Fuel metering is controlled by a centrifugal governor which reacts to accelerator pedal position and engine speed. The governor is linked to a metering valve which increases or decreases the amount of fuel delivered at each pumping stroke. A separate device also increases fuel delivery with increasing turbocharger boost pressure.

Basic injection timing is determined when the pump is fitted. When the engine is running it is varied automatically to suit the prevailing engine speed by a mechanism which turns the cam plate.

A solenoid valve in the pump is used to advance the injection timing briefly after a cold start. The system operates by increasing the pump transfer pressure via a restrictor valve.

The four fuel injectors produce a homogeneous spray of fuel into the swirl chambers located in the cylinder head. The injectors are calibrated to open and close at critical pressures to provide efficient and even combustion. Each injector needle is lubricated by fuel which accumulates in the spring chamber and is channelled to the injection pump return hose by leak-off pipes.

Cold starting is assisted by preheater or "glow" plugs fitted to each swirl chamber (see Chapter 5C for further details). In addition, a thermostatic sensor in the cooling system operates a fast idle lever on the injection pump, via a cable, to increase the idling speed when the engine is cold.

A stop solenoid cuts the fuel supply to the injection pump rotor when the ignition is switched off. On some pumps there is also a hand-operated stop lever for use in an emergency.

Provided that the specified maintenance is carried out, the fuel injection equipment will give long and trouble-free service. The injection pump itself may well outlast the engine. The main potential cause of damage to the injection pump and injectors is dirt or water in the fuel.

Servicing of the injection pump and injectors is very limited for the home mechanic, and any dismantling or adjustment other than that described in this Chapter must be entrusted to a Renault dealer or fuel injection specialist.

Precautions

⚠️ **Warning: It is necessary to take certain precautions when working on the fuel system components, particularly the fuel injectors. Before carrying out any operations on the fuel system, refer to the precautions given in "Safety first!" at the beginning of this manual, and to any additional warning notes at the start of the relevant Sections.**

2 Air cleaner assembly - removal and refitting

Removal

1 Remove the air cleaner element (see Chapter 1).

2 Disconnect the air inlet and outlet ducting from the housing.

3 Release the securing strap nut or bolt until the strap can be disengaged then lift the housing from the engine compartment **(see illustration)**. Take care not to lose the securing strap tension spring.

Refitting

4 Refit by reversing the removal operations.

3 Fuel gauge sender unit - removal, testing and refitting

Refer to Chapter 4A, Section 4.

4 Fuel tank - removal and refitting

Refer to Chapter 4A, Section 5.

5 Accelerator cable - removal, refitting and adjustment

Removal

1 Working in the engine compartment, operate the accelerator lever on the fuel injection pump, and release the cable inner from the lever. Alternatively, on models with a press-fit balljoint cable end fitting, pull the cable end from the lever.

2 Withdraw the outer cable adjuster from the support bracket and remove the spring clip **(see illustration)**.

2.3 Air cleaner housing retaining bolt

5.2 Withdraw the accelerator cable adjuster (arrowed) from the support bracket

7.3a Priming the fuel system; note bleed screw (arrowed) - Lucas/CAV filter

7.3b Fuel system bleed screw (arrowed) on the Bosch filter

3 Work back along the length of the outer cable and free it from any necessary retaining clips or brackets whilst noting its correct routing.

4 Working from inside the vehicle, release the cable end fitting by slipping it out of the elongated slot on the pedal clevis. Tie a length of string to the end of the cable.

5 Withdraw the cable through the bulkhead into the engine compartment. When the end of the cable appears, untie the string and leave it in position, it can then be used to draw the cable back into position on refitting.

Refitting and adjustment

6 Refitting is a reversal of removal using the piece of string to draw the cable through the bulkhead. Ensure the cable is routed as noted before removal, and retained by all necessary retaining clips and brackets. On completion, check the cable adjustment as follows.

7 With the spring clip removed, gently pull the outer cable out of its grommet, ensuring that the accelerator lever remains fully against its stop, until all free play is removed from the inner cable.

8 With the cable held in this position refit the spring clip to the last exposed outer cable groove in front of the rubber grommet, ie. so that when the clip is refitted and the outer cable is released there is only a small amount of freeplay in the inner cable.

9 Have an assistant depress the accelerator pedal. Check that the pump accelerator lever opens fully and returns smoothly to its stop.

6 Accelerator pedal - removal and refitting

Refer to Chapter 4A, Section 7.

7 Fuel system - priming and bleeding

Note: *Refer to the precautions given in Section 1 before proceeding.*

1 After disconnecting part of the fuel supply system or running out of fuel, it is necessary to prime the system and bleed off any air which may have entered the system components.

2 All models are fitted with a hand-operated priming pump, operated by a plunger located on the top of the fuel filter head. The fuel filter itself is located on the left-hand side of the engine compartment.

3 To prime the system, loosen the bleed screw, located either on the filter outlet union bolt (Lucas/CAV filter arrangement) or the top of the fuel filter head (Bosch filter arrangement) **(see illustrations)**. If no bleed screw is fitted, loosen the outlet union itself (note that on certain models, a bleed screw is also provided on the fuel inlet union at the injection pump).

4 Pump the priming plunger until fuel free from air bubbles emerges from the outlet union or bleed screw (as applicable). Note that on certain Bosch filters it will be necessary to unscrew the priming plunger knob before pumping. Retighten the bleed screw or outlet union.

5 Switch on the ignition (to activate the stop solenoid) and continue pumping the priming plunger until firm resistance is felt, then pump a few more times.

6 If a large amount of air has entered the pump, place a wad of rag around the fuel return union on the pump (to absorb spilt fuel), then slacken the union. Operate the priming plunger (with the ignition switched on to activate the stop solenoid), or crank the engine on the starter motor in 10 second bursts, until fuel free from air bubbles emerges from the fuel union. Tighten the union and mop up split fuel.

⚠ **Warning: Be prepared to stop the engine if it should fire, to avoid excessive fuel spray and spillage.**

7 If air has entered the injector pipes, place wads of rag around the injector pipe unions at the injectors (to absorb spilt fuel), then slacken the unions. Crank the engine on the starter motor with the accelerator pedal fully depressed, until fuel emerges from the unions, then stop cranking the engine and retighten the unions. Mop up spilt fuel.

8 Start the engine in the normal way (preheating circuit activated before starting) noting that additional cranking may be necessary to finally bleed the system before the engine starts.

8 Idle speed and anti-stall speed - checking and adjustment

Note: *The following procedure varies according to the type of fast idle thermostatic valve fitted. Two different types of valve may be encountered; one type is screwed into the cylinder head and the other type is mounted on a bracket attached to the rear of the injection pump. Identify the type fitted, then proceed as described below under the relevant sub-headings.*

General

1 The usual type of tachometer (rev counter), which works from ignition system pulses, cannot be used on diesel engines. A diagnostic socket is provided for the use of Renault test equipment, but this will not normally be available to the home mechanic. If it is not felt that adjusting the idle speed "by ear" is satisfactory, one of the following alternatives may be used.

a) *Purchase or hire of an appropriate tachometer.*
b) *Delegation of the job to a Renault dealer or other specialist.*
c) *Timing light (strobe) operated by a petrol engine running at the desired speed. If the timing light is pointed at a mark on the camshaft or injection pump sprocket, the mark will appear stationary when the two engines are running at the same speed (or multiples of that speed). The sprocket will be rotating at half the crankshaft speed but this will not affect the adjustment. (In practice it was found impossible to use this method on the crankshaft pulley due to the acute viewing angle.)*

2 Before making adjustments warm up the engine to normal operating temperature. Make sure that the accelerator cable is correctly adjusted (see Section 5).

4C

Idle speed checking and adjustment

3 With the accelerator lever resting against the idle stop, check that the engine idles at the specified speed. If necessary adjust as follows.

Pump mounted fast idle valve

4 Loosen the locknut on the idle speed adjustment screw. Turn the screw as required and retighten the locknut **(see illustration)**.

Cylinder head mounted fast idle valve

5 Loosen the locknut and unscrew the anti-stall speed adjustment screw until it is clear of the pump accelerator lever.
6 Loosen the locknut and turn the idle speed adjustment screw as required, then retighten the locknut **(see illustration)**.
7 Make the anti-stall speed adjustment as described later in this Section.
8 Stop the engine and disconnect the tachometer, where applicable.

Anti-stall speed checking and adjustment

Pump mounted fast idle valve

9 On these pumps it is not possible to adjust the anti-stall speed setting.

Cylinder head mounted fast idle valve

10 Make sure that the engine is at normal operating temperature, and idling at the specified speed, as described previously.
11 Insert a 1.0 mm shim or feeler blade between the pump accelerator lever and the anti-stall speed adjustment screw. The idle speed should rise by approximately 10 to 20 rpm.
12 If adjustment is necessary, loosen the locknut and turn the anti-stall speed adjustment screw as required. Retighten the locknut.
13 Remove the shim and move the pump accelerator lever to increase the engine speed

to approximately 3000 rpm, then quickly release the lever and check that the engine returns to the specified idle speed. Recheck the anti-stall speed setting and readjust, if necessary.
14 With the anti-stall speed correctly set, move the fast idle lever fully towards the flywheel end of the engine and check that the engine speed increases to the specified fast idle speed. If necessary loosen the locknut and turn the fast idle adjusting screw as required, then retighten the locknut.
15 Where applicable, disconnect the tachometer on completion.

9 Maximum speed - checking and adjustment

Caution: The maximum speed adjustment screw is sealed by the manufacturers at the factory using paint or a locking wire and a lead seal and should not be disturbed.

1 Run the engine to normal operating temperature.
2 Have an assistant fully depress the accelerator pedal and check that the maximum engine speed is as given in the *Specifications*. Do not keep the engine at maximum speed for more than two or three seconds.
3 If adjustment is necessary the vehicle should taken to Renault dealer or suitable diesel specialist. Adjustment should not be attempted by the home mechanic.

10 Fast idle thermostatic valve and cable - removal, refitting, testing and adjustment

Note: *Two different types of thermostatic valve may be encountered; one type is screwed into the cylinder head and the other type is mounted on a bracket attached to the rear of the injection pump. Identify the type fitted, then proceed as described below under the relevant sub-headings.*

Removal

Cylinder head mounted valve

1 Disconnect the battery negative lead.
2 Partially drain the cooling system as described in Chapter 1.
3 Loosen the clamp screw or nut (as applicable) and slide the fast idle cable end fitting off from the injection pump end of the inner cable.
4 Free the fast idle cable from the bracket on the fuel injection pump. Remove the cable fitting (where fitted) from the pump lever and store it with the valve for safe-keeping.
5 Using a suitable open-ended spanner, unscrew the thermostatic valve from the cylinder head, and remove the valve and cable assembly. Recover the sealing ring.

Injection pump mounted valve

6 Disconnect the battery negative lead.
7 Using a hose clamp or similar, clamp both the fast idle valve coolant hoses to minimise coolant loss during the subsequent operation.

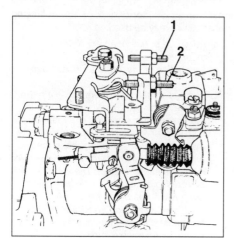

**8.4 Adjustment points -
pump mounted fast idle valve**

1 Idle speed adjustment screw
2 Maximum speed adjustment screw

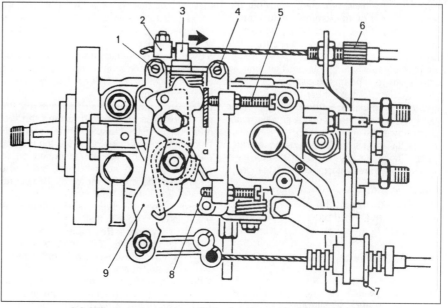

8.6 Adjustment points - cylinder head mounted fast idle valve

1 Fast idle adjustment screw
2 Cable end clamp
3 Fast idle lever
4 Idle speed adjustment screw
5 Anti-stall adjustment screw
6 Fast idle cable adjustment screw
7 Accelerator cable spring clip
8 Maximum speed adjustment screw
9 Accelerator lever
a Shim for anti-stall speed adjustment

8 Slacken the retaining clips and disconnect both coolant hoses from the valve whilst being prepared for some coolant spillage. Wash off any spilt coolant immediately with cold water and dry the surrounding area before proceeding further.

9 Loosen the clamp screw and nut and slide the fast idle cable end fitting arrangement off from the end of the cable.

10 Slacken and remove the bolts securing the fast idle valve mounting bracket to the rear of the injection pump. Remove the bracket and valve assembly from the pump, freeing the cable from the fast idle lever. Remove the cable fitting (where fitted) from the pump lever and store it with the valve for safe-keeping. If necessary, the valve assembly can be dismantled as follows.

11 Slacken the two bolts securing the two halves of the valve housing together. As the bolts near the ends of their threads, compress the two halves of the valve together to relieve spring pressure on the bolts. With the bolts removed, carefully separate the valve, gradually relieving spring pressure, removing both halves from the bracket.

12 Remove the rubber gaiter and cable guide from the front half of the valve housing then withdraw the cable and springs. The cable rubber boot and guide are available separately.

13 Using a suitable peg spanner, unscrew the thermostatic capsule ring nut from the rear half of the valve. Lift out the capsule and recover the sealing ring. Both the capsule and sealing ring are available separately.

Refitting

Cylinder head mounted valve

14 Fit a new sealing ring to the valve and screw the valve into position in the cylinder head, tightening it securely.

15 Refit the cable fitting to the pump fast idle lever and insert the cable through the pump bracket and pass the inner cable through the fitting. Slide the end fitting onto the inner and lightly tighten its clamp screw or nut (as applicable).

16 Refill the cooling system (see Chapter 1).

17 Adjust the cable as described under the appropriate sub-heading below.

Injection pump mounted valve

18 If the valve has been dismantled proceed as follows, if not proceed straight to paragraph 22.

19 Fit a new sealing ring to the thermostatic capsule and fit the capsule to the rear half of the valve. Refit the ring nut and tighten it securely.

20 Fit the springs to the cable and insert the cable through the front half of the valve. Locate the cable guide in the rubber gaiter then slide the gaiter into position ensuring it is correctly seated in the groove on the front of the valve.

21 Position the valve halves on either side of the mounting bracket. With the aid of an assistant, compress the two halves and refit the retaining bolts, tightening them securely.

22 Refit the cable fitting to the pump lever and manoeuvre the fast idle valve and bracket assembly into position, passing the cable through its fitting.

23 Refit the injection pump rear mounting bracket and securely tighten both the fast idle valve and mounting bracket retaining nuts and bolts.

24 Connect the coolant hoses to the fast idle valve and securely tighten their retaining clips. Remove the hose clamps and top-up the cooling system as described in Chapter 1.

25 Slide the cable end fitting arrangement onto the cable and lightly tighten its clamp screw and nut.

26 Adjust the cable as described under the appropriate sub-heading below.

Testing and adjustment

Cylinder head mounted valve

27 Warm the engine up to normal operating temperature and adjust the idle speed, anti-stall speed and fast idle speed as described in Section 8.

28 Pull the inner cable tight to remove any slack, then measure the clearance between the cable end fitting and the lever. There should be a gap of approximately 6.0 mm. If not, slacken the clamp screw or nut (as applicable), move the end fitting to the correct position and securely retighten the screw or nut.

29 Switch off the engine and allow it to cool. As the engine cools the fast idle valve cable should retract and eventually pull the lever back towards the rear of the pump.

Injection pump mounted valve

30 Loosen the injection pump fast idle lever stop retaining screw and move the stop away from the lever.

31 With the cable end fitting positioned clear of the fast idle lever, move the lever towards the rear of the pump until the position is reached where resistance is felt; this is the point where the lever is starting to act on the fast idle mechanism in the pump. Hold the fast idle lever in this position and set the lever stop so that there is a gap of 0.5 mm between the stop and the lever **(see illustration)**. With the stop correctly positioned securely tighten its retaining screw.

32 With the engine cold, accurately measure the temperature of the fast idle valve thermostatic capsule located in the rear half of the valve. Referring to the following table, obtain the relevant dimensions "A" and "B" **(see illustration 10.33)** which correspond to the temperature of capsule.

Capsule temp.	A (mm)	B (mm)
Less than 18° C	6.5	4.5
22°C	5.9	3.5
25°C	5.5	2.7
30°C	4.75	1.5
35°C	4.0	0.2
40°C	3.25	0

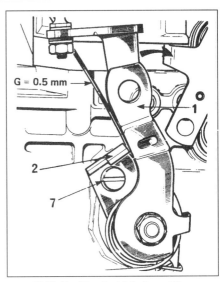

10.31 Position fast idle lever (1) as described in text and adjust gap "G" by slackening screw (7) and repositioning lever stop (2) - pump mounted fast idle valve

33 Insert shims equal in thickness to dimension "A" in between the pump fast idle lever and its stop **(see illustration)**. Remove all slack from the cable then slide the end fitting along the cable until it abuts the fast idle lever and securely tighten its clamp screw and nut. Withdraw the shims and check the clearance between the fast idle lever and stop is equal to dimension "A". If not repeat the adjustment procedure.

34 With dimension "A" correctly set, slacken the fast idle lever balljoint nut and slide the balljoint away from the accelerator lever.

35 Insert shims equal in thickness to dimension "B" in between the idle speed

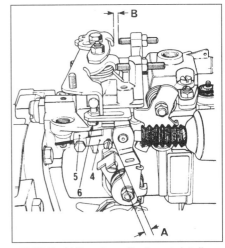

10.33 Fast idle valve adjustment details - pump mounted fast idle valve

4 Cable end fitting front section
5 Cable end fitting rear section
6 Balljoint
A Fast idle lever-to-stop clearance
B Idle screw-to-accelerator lever clearance

4C

adjusting screw and the accelerator lever. Slide the balljoint along its slot until it abuts the accelerator lever and securely tighten its retaining nut. Withdraw the shims and check the clearance between the accelerator lever and the idle speed adjusting screw is equal to dimension "B". If not repeat the adjustment procedure.

36 Start the engine and warm it up to its normal operating temperature. As the engine warms up the cable end fitting should slowly extend until the fast idle lever returns to its stop and the cable end fitting is clear of the lever. At the same time the accelerator lever should be back against the idle speed adjusting screw.

11 Stop solenoid - description, removal and refitting

Description

1 The stop solenoid is located on the rear end of the top of the fuel injection pump. Its purpose is to cut the fuel supply when the ignition is switched off. If an open circuit occurs in the solenoid or supply wiring it will be impossible to start the engine, as the fuel will not reach the injectors. The same applies if the solenoid plunger jams in the "stop" position. If the solenoid jams in the "run" position, the engine will not stop when the ignition is switched off.

2 If the solenoid has failed and the engine will not run, a temporary repair may be made by removing the solenoid as described in the following paragraphs. Refit the solenoid body without the plunger and spring. Tape up the wire so that it cannot touch earth. The engine can now be started as usual, but it will be necessary to use the manual stop lever on the fuel injection pump (or to stall the engine in gear) to stop it.

Removal

Caution : Be careful not to allow dirt into the injection pump during this procedure. A new sealing washer or O-ring must be used on refitting.

3 Disconnect the battery negative lead.
4 Withdraw the rubber boot (where applicable), then unscrew the terminal nut and disconnect the wire from the top of the solenoid.
5 Carefully clean around the solenoid, then unscrew and withdraw the solenoid, and recover the sealing washer or O-ring (as applicable). Recover the solenoid plunger and spring if they remain in the pump. Operate the hand priming pump as the solenoid is removed to flush away any dirt.

Refitting

6 Refitting is a reversal of removal, using a new sealing washer or O-ring.

12 Fuel injection pump - removal and refitting

Caution: Refer to the precautions given in Section 1 of this Chapter before proceeding. Be careful not to allow dirt into the pump or injector pipes during this procedure. New sealing rings should be used on the fuel pipe banjo unions when refitting.

Removal

1 Disconnect the battery negative lead.
2 Referring to Chapter 2B, Section 3, rotate the crankshaft until No.1 cylinder is positioned on TDC at the end of its compression stroke.
3 Remove the timing belt cover as described in Chapter 2B.
4 Check the sprocket timing marks are positioned as described in Chapter 2B, Section 7, paragraph 5.
5 Rotate the crankshaft backwards slightly so that the injection pump sprocket timing mark moves back by three teeth, ie. so that the tooth three in front of the timing mark is aligned with the pointer in the timing cover window.
6 Remove the injection pump sprocket as described in Chapter 2B Section 8. Note that the crankshaft and camshaft must not be rotated whilst the sprocket is removed.
7 Cover the alternator with a clean cloth or plastic bag to prevent the possibility of fuel being spilt onto it during the following operations.
8 On models where the fast idle thermostatic valve is screwed into the cylinder head, loosen the clamp screw or nut (as applicable) and slide the end fitting off the end of the fast idle inner cable. Where necessary, remove the cable fitting from the pump lever and store it with the valve for safe-keeping.
9 On models where the fast idle thermostatic valve is mounted on the injection pump, using a hose clamp or similar, clamp both the fast idle valve coolant hoses to minimise coolant loss. Slacken the retaining clips and disconnect both coolant hoses from the valve whilst being prepared for some coolant spillage. Wash off any spilt coolant immediately with cold water and dry the surrounding area before proceeding further.
10 On all models, unclip the accelerator cable end fitting from the lever balljoint and free the cable from the injection pump bracket.
11 Wipe clean the fuel feed and return unions on the injection pump.
12 Slacken and remove the fuel feed hose union bolt from the pump and recover the sealing washer from each side of the hose union. Position the hose clear of the pump and screw the union bolt back into position on the pump for safe-keeping. Cover both the hose end and union bolt to prevent the ingress of dirt into the fuel system.

12.16 Mark the injection pump in relation to the mounting bracket (arrowed)

13 Detach the fuel return hose from the pump as described in the previous paragraph. **Note:** *The injection pump feed and return hose union bolts are not interchangeable. Great care must be taken to ensure that the bolts are not swapped.*
14 Wipe clean the pipe unions then slacken the union nut securing the injector pipes to each injector, and the four union nuts securing the pipes to the rear of the injection pump; as each pump union nut is slackened, retain the adapter with a suitable open-ended spanner to prevent it being unscrewed from the pump. With all the union nuts undone remove the injector pipes from the engine.
15 Undo the retaining nut and disconnect the wiring from the injection pump stop solenoid. Where necessary, trace the wiring back from the pump microswitch(es) and disconnect it at the connector(s) (as applicable). Free all wiring from any relevant retaining clips.
16 Using a scriber or suitable marker pen, make alignment marks between the injection pump front flange and the front mounting bracket **(see illustration)**. These marks can then be used to ensure that the pump is correctly positioned on refitting.
17 Undo the retaining nuts/bolts securing the injection pump rear mounting bracket to the cylinder head.
18 Slacken and remove the three nuts securing the pump to its front mounting bracket and manoeuvre the pump away from the bracket and out of the engine compartment **(see illustration)**. Do not rotate the crankshaft or camshaft whilst the pump is removed.

12.18 Removing the injection pump from the engine

Refitting

19 If a new pump is being installed transfer the alignment mark from the original pump onto the mounting flange of the new pump.

20 Manoeuvre the pump into position and refit its three front retaining nuts. Align the marks made prior to removal then securely tighten the retaining nuts.

21 Refit the rear bracket to the injection pump and securely tighten its retaining nuts/bolts.

22 Refit the injection pump sprocket as described in Chapter 2B, Section 8. When aligning the camshaft and injection pump sprocket marks with their TDC marks, note that it will also be necessary to rotate the crankshaft slightly and insert the locking pin (see Section 3 of Chapter 2B) to position the crankshaft at TDC.

23 With the timing belt correctly fitted, set up the injection pump timing (see Section 14).

24 Reconnect all the relevant wiring to the pump.

25 Reconnect the fuel feed and return hose unions to the pump. Position a new sealing washer on each side of both unions and tighten the union bolts to the specified torque setting.

26 Refit the injector pipes and tighten their union nuts to the specified torque setting.

27 On models where the fast idle valve is mounted onto the injection pump, reconnect the coolant hoses to the fast idle valve and securely tighten their retaining clips. Remove the hose clamps and top-up the cooling system as described in Chapter 1.

28 Mop up any spilt fuel/coolant then remove the cover from the alternator.

29 Reconnect the accelerator cable and adjust as described in Section 5.

30 Reconnect the fast idle valve cable and adjust as described in Section 10.

31 Reconnect the battery negative lead.

32 Bleed the fuel system as described in Section 7.

33 On completion, start the engine and adjust the idle speed and anti-stall speed as described in Section 8.

13 Injection timing - checking methods and adjustment

1 Checking the injection timing is not a routine operation. It is only necessary after the injection pump has been disturbed.

2 Dynamic timing equipment does exist, but it is unlikely to be available to the home mechanic. The equipment works by converting pressure pulses in an injector pipe into electrical signals. If such equipment is available, use it in accordance with its maker's instructions.

3 Static timing as described in this Chapter gives good results if carried out carefully. A dial test indicator will be needed, with probes

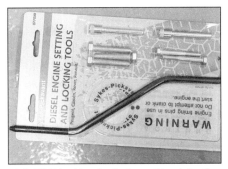

13.3 TDC locking tools for setting injection timing on Renault diesel engines

and adapters appropriate for the Bosch injection pump **(see illustration)**. Read through the procedures before starting work, to find out what is involved.

14 Injection timing - checking and adjustment

Caution: Some of the injection pump settings and access plugs may be sealed by the manufacturers at the factory using paint or locking wire and lead seals. Do not disturb the seals if the vehicle is still within the warranty period, otherwise the warranty will be invalidated. Also do not attempt the timing procedure unless accurate instrumentation is available. Refer to the precautions given in Section 1 of this Chapter before proceeding.

1 If the injection timing is being checked with the pump in position on the engine, rather than as part of the pump refitting procedure, disconnect the battery negative lead and cover the alternator with a clean cloth or plastic bag to prevent the possibility of fuel being spilt onto it. Remove the injector pipes as described in paragraph 14 of Section 12.

2 If not already having done so, slacken the clamp screw and/or nut (as applicable) and slide the fast idle cable end fitting arrangement along the cable so that its no longer in contact with the pump fast idle lever (ie, so the fast idle lever returns to its stop).

3 Referring to Section 3 of Chapter 2B, rotate the crankshaft until No.1 cylinder is positioned on TDC at the end of its compression stroke, then turn the crankshaft backwards (anti-clockwise) approximately a quarter-turn.

4 Unscrew the access screw, situated in the centre of the four injector pipe unions, from the rear of the injection pump. As the screw is removed, position a suitable container beneath the pump to catch any escaping fuel. Mop up any split fuel with a clean cloth.

5 Screw the adapter into the rear of the pump and mount the dial gauge in the adapter. If access to the special adapter cannot be gained (Part of Renault tool kit Mot. 856), they can be purchased from most good motor factors. Position the dial gauge so that its

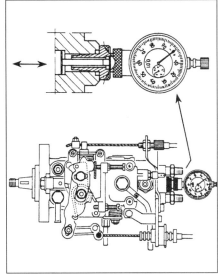

14.5 Checking the injection timing

plunger is at the mid-point of its travel and securely tighten the adapter locknut **(see illustration)**.

6 Slowly rotate the crankshaft back and forth whilst observing the dial gauge, to determine when the injection pump piston is at the bottom of its travel (BDC). When the piston is correctly positioned, zero the dial gauge.

7 Rotate the crankshaft slowly in the correct direction of rotation to bring No.1 piston to TDC. Referring to Section 3 of Chapter 2B, unscrew the plug from the cylinder block/crankcase and lock the crankshaft in position by inserting a suitable locking pin.

8 The reading obtained on the dial gauge should be equal to the specified pump timing measurement given in the *Specifications* at the start of this Chapter. If adjustment is necessary, slacken the front and rear pump mounting nuts and bolts and slowly rotate the pump body until the point is found where the specified reading is obtained. When the pump is correctly positioned, tighten both its front and rear mounting nuts and bolts securely.

9 Rotate the crankshaft through one and three quarter rotations in the normal direction of rotation. Find the injection pump piston BDC position as described in paragraph 6 and zero the dial gauge.

10 Rotate the crankshaft slowly in the correct direction of rotation until the crankshaft locking tool can be re-inserted (bringing the engine back to TDC). Recheck the timing measurement.

11 If adjustment is necessary, slacken the pump mounting nuts and bolts and repeat the operations in paragraphs 8 to 10.

12 When the pump timing is correct, unscrew the adapter and remove the dial gauge.

13 Refit the screw and sealing washer to the pump and tighten it securely.

14 If the procedure is being carried out as part of the pump refitting sequence, proceed as described in Section 12.

4C

15 If the procedure is being carried out with the pump fitted to the engine, refit the injector pipes tightening their union nuts to the specified torque setting. Reconnect the battery then bleed the fuel system as described in Section 7. Start the engine and adjust the idle speed and anti-stall speeds (see Section 8).

15 Fuel injectors - testing, removal and refitting

Warning: Exercise extreme caution when working on the fuel injectors. Never expose the hands or any part of the body to injector spray, as the high working pressure can cause the fuel to penetrate the skin, with possibly fatal results. You are strongly advised to have any work which involves testing the injectors under pressure carried out by a dealer or fuel injection specialist. Refer to the precautions given in Section 1 of this Chapter before proceeding.

Testing

1 Injectors do deteriorate with prolonged use and it is reasonable to expect them to need reconditioning or renewal after 60 000 miles (100 000 km) or so. Accurate testing, overhaul and calibration of the injectors must be left to a specialist. A defective injector which is causing knocking or smoking can be located without dismantling as follows.

2 Run the engine at a fast idle. Slacken each injector union in turn, placing rag around the union to catch spilt fuel and being careful not to expose the skin to any spray. When the union on the defective injector is slackened, the knocking or smoking will stop.

Removal

Note: *Take great care not to allow dirt into the injectors or fuel pipes during this procedure. Do not drop the injectors or allow the needles at their tips to become damaged. The injectors are precision-made to fine limits and must not be handled roughly. In particular, do not mount them in a bench vice.*

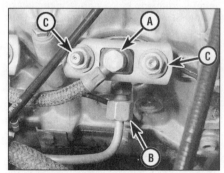

15.4 View of a typical clamp-type injector

A *Return hose union bolt*
B *Injector pipe union nut*
C *Retaining nuts*

Clamp-type injector

3 Disconnect the battery negative lead and cover the alternator with a clean cloth or plastic bag to prevent the possibility of fuel being spilt onto it.

4 Wipe clean the injector then unscrew the union bolt and disconnect the return hose from the top of the injector **(see illustration)**. Recover the sealing washer positioned on each side of the hose union and cover the hose and injector union to prevent the entry of dirt into the system.

5 Slacken the union nut and free the injector pipe from the side of the injector. Cover the hose and injector union to prevent the entry of dirt into the system.

6 Slacken and remove the two retaining nuts and washers and lift off the injector retaining clamp.

7 Lift out the injector and recover the sealing and flame shield washers. Also remove the injector sleeve if it is a loose fit in the head.

Screw-type injector

8 Disconnect the battery negative lead and cover the alternator with a clean cloth or plastic bag to prevent the possibility of fuel being spilt onto it.

9 Carefully clean around the injectors and pipe union nuts and disconnect the return pipe from the injector.

10 Wipe clean the pipe unions then slacken the union nut securing the injector pipes to each injector and the four union nuts securing the pipes to the rear of the injection pump; as each pump union nut is slackened, retain the adapter with a suitable open-ended spanner to prevent it being unscrewed from the pump. With all the union nuts undone remove the injector pipes from the engine. Cover the injector and pipe unions to prevent the entry of dirt into the system.

11 Unscrew the injector, using a deep socket or box spanner, and remove it from the cylinder head.

12 Recover the sealing and flame shield washers. Also remove the injector sleeve if it is a loose fit in the cylinder head.

Refitting

Clamp-type injector

13 Obtain a new sealing washer and flame shield washer. Where removed, also renew the injector sleeve if it is damaged.

14 Where necessary, refit the injector sleeve to the cylinder head.

15 Fit the new flame shield washer to the sleeve, noting that it should be fitted with its convex side downwards (facing the cylinder head).

16 Fit the new sealing washer to the top of the sleeve.

17 Slide the injector into position ensuring that it enters the sleeve squarely.

18 Reconnect the injector pipe and tighten its union nut by hand only at this stage.

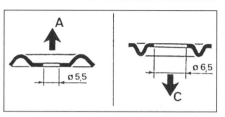

15.24 Early (A) and later (C) flame shield washers

19 Install the injector clamp and refit the washers and retaining nuts. Tighten the retaining nuts evenly and progressively to the specified torque setting.

20 Position a new sealing washer on each side of the return hose union and refit the union bolt to the top of the injector. Tighten both the union bolt and the injector pipe union nut to their specified torque settings.

21 Start the engine. If difficulty is experienced, bleed the fuel system as described in Section 7.

Screw-type injector

22 Obtain a new sealing washer and flame shield washer. Where removed, also renew the injector sleeve if it is damaged.

23 Where necessary, refit the injector sleeve to the cylinder head.

24 Fit the new flame shield washer to the sleeve. Note that two types of flame shield washers have been fitted to the engines covered by this manual. The earlier type of washer has a hole diameter of 5.5 mm, and should be fitted with the convex side upwards (facing the fuel injector). The later type of washer has a hole diameter of 6.5 mm, and should be fitted with the convex side downwards (facing the cylinder head) **(see illustration)**. It is likely that the new washers supplied by a Renault parts centre will be of the later type. Ensure that the washers are fitted correctly, according to type.

25 Fit the new sealing washer to the top of the sleeve.

26 Screw the injector into position and tighten it to the specified torque.

27 Refit the injector pipes and tighten the union nuts to the specified torque setting. Position any clips attached to the pipes as noted before removal.

28 Reconnect the return pipe securely to the injector.

29 Start the engine. If difficulty is experienced, bleed the fuel system as described in Section 7.

16 Manifolds - removal and refitting

Removal

1 Although the manifolds are separate, they are retained by the same nuts, since the stud holes are split between the manifold flanges.

2 Note the location of any wiring or hose brackets/clips attached to the manifolds, and remove them. Where necessary also unbolt the dipstick tube from the manifold.

3 Release the retaining clip, and disconnect the inlet duct from the inlet manifold.

4 Remove the turbocharger as described in Section 18. Undo the two nuts and remove the heatshield from the inlet manifold.

5 Disconnect the relevant breather/vacuum hoses from the inlet manifold, noting their correct fitted locations.

6 Progressively unscrew the nuts/bolts (as applicable) securing the inlet and exhaust manifolds. Where necessary, free the crankcase ventilation pipes from the manifold studs and position them clear of the manifolds.

7 Withdraw the inlet and exhaust manifolds from the cylinder head and recover the manifold gasket.

Refitting

8 Refitting is a reversal of removal, bearing in mind the following points.

  a) *Ensure that the cylinder head and manifold mating surfaces are clean and use a new gasket.*

  b) *Refit the turbocharger as described in Section 18.*

  c) *Ensure that any wiring or hose brackets/clips are positioned as noted before removal.*

17 Turbocharger - description and precautions

Description

1 A turbocharger is fitted to all Espace diesel models. It increases engine efficiency by raising the pressure in the inlet manifold above atmospheric pressure. Instead of the air simply being sucked into the cylinders, it is forced in. Additional fuel is supplied by the injection pump in proportion to the increased air inlet.

2 Energy for the operation of the turbocharger comes from the exhaust gas. The gas flows through a specially-shaped housing (the turbine housing) and in so doing, spins the turbine wheel. The turbine wheel is attached to a shaft, at the end of which is another vaned wheel known as the compressor wheel. The compressor wheel spins in its own housing, and compresses the inlet air on the way to the inlet manifold.

3 Between the turbocharger and the inlet manifold, the compressed air passes through an intercooler. This is an air-to-air heat exchanger, mounted on the right-hand side of the engine compartment, and supplied with cooling air ducted through the front spoiler. The purpose of the intercooler is to remove from the inducted air some of the heat gained in being compressed. Because cooler air is

denser, removal of this heat further increases engine efficiency.

4 Boost pressure (the pressure in the inlet manifold) is limited by a wastegate, which diverts the exhaust gas away from the turbine wheel in response to a pressure-sensitive actuator.

5 The turbo shaft is pressure-lubricated by an oil feed pipe from the main oil gallery. The shaft "floats" on a cushion of oil. A drain pipe returns the oil to the sump.

Precautions

6 The turbocharger operates at extremely high speeds and temperatures. Certain precautions must be observed, to avoid premature failure of the turbo, or injury to the operator.

7 Do not operate the turbo with any of its parts exposed, or with any of its hoses removed. Foreign objects falling onto the rotating vanes could cause excessive damage, and (if ejected) personal injury.

8 Do not race the engine immediately after start-up, especially if it is cold. Give the oil a few seconds to circulate.

9 Always allow the engine to return to idle speed before switching it off - do not blip the throttle and switch off, as this will leave the turbo spinning without lubrication.

10 Allow the engine to idle for several minutes before switching off after a high-speed run.

11 Observe the recommended intervals for oil and filter changing, and use a reputable oil of the specified quality. Neglect of oil changing, or use of inferior oil, can cause carbon formation on the turbo shaft, leading to subsequent failure.

18 Turbocharger - removal and refitting

Removal

1 Disconnect the battery negative lead.

2 Undo the retaining nuts and remove the heatshield from the turbocharger.

3 Slacken the retaining clips and disconnect both inlet ducts from the turbocharger **(see illustration)**.

18.3 Intlet duct attachments at the turbocharger

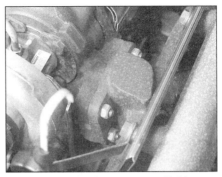

18.7 Turbocharger to manifold attachments

4 Undo the retaining bolt securing the support bracket to the turbocharger.

5 Undo the two nuts and free the exhaust system front pipe from the base of the turbocharger.

6 Whilst being prepared from some oil spillage, slacken the union nut and disconnect the oil supply pipe from the top of the top of the turbocharger. Slacken the retaining clip and detach the oil return hose from the base of the turbocharger. Plug the hose and pipe ends to minimise oil loss and prevent the entry of dirt into the system.

7 Slacken and remove the four nuts retaining nuts and remove the turbocharger from the exhaust manifold **(see illustration)**. Discard the four self-locking retaining nuts; new ones must be used on refitting.

Refitting

8 Ensure that the manifold and turbocharger mating surfaces are clean and dry and manoeuvre the turbocharger into position.

9 Fit the new turbocharger retaining nuts and tighten them securely.

10 Reconnect the exhaust system front pipe, ensuring its mating surface is clean, and securely tighten its retaining nuts.

11 Refit the support bracket retaining bolt and tighten it securely.

12 Reconnect the oil return hose and securely tighten its retaining clip.

13 Using a suitable oil can, inject some clean engine oil into the turbocharger oil feed hose union. Once the unit is full of oil, reconnect the feed hose and securely tighten its union nut.

14 Reconnect the inlet ducts and securely tighten the retaining clips.

15 Refit the turbocharger heatshield.

16 Disconnect the wiring from the injection pump stop solenoid and reconnect the battery.

17 Crank the engine on the starter motor until the instrument panel oil pressure warning lamp goes out (this may take several seconds).

18 Reconnect the wiring to the stop solenoid, then start the engine using the normal procedure. Run the engine at idle speed, and check the turbocharger oil unions for leakage. Rectify any problems without delay.

4C

19 Turbocharger - examination and renovation

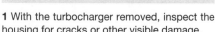

1 With the turbocharger removed, inspect the housing for cracks or other visible damage.

2 Spin the turbine or the compressor wheel to verify that the shaft is intact and to feel for excessive shake or roughness. Some play is normal since in use the shaft is "floating" on a film of oil. Check that the wheel vanes are undamaged.

3 The wastegate actuator is a separate unit, and can be renewed independently of the turbocharger. Consult a Renault dealer or other specialist if it is thought that testing or renewal is necessary.

4 If the exhaust or inlet passages are oil-contaminated, the turbo shaft oil seals have probably failed. (On the inlet side, this will also have contaminated the intercooler, which if necessary should be flushed with a suitable solvent.)

5 Check the oil feed and return pipes for contamination or blockage and clean if necessary.

6 No DIY repair of the turbocharger is possible. A new unit may be available on an exchange basis.

20 Intercooler - removal and refitting

Removal

1 The intercooler is located in the right-hand front corner of the engine compartment.

2 Release the retaining clips and disconnect both inlet hoses from the intercooler.

3 From under the front of the vehicle, undo the two bolts and lift the intercooler out of the engine compartment.

Refitting

4 Refitting is a reversal of removal.

21 Boost pressure fuel delivery corrector - general information

This device is mounted on the top of the injection pump and is connected to the inlet manifold by a vacuum pipe. Its purpose is to adjust the injection pump fuel metering in relation to the turbocharger boost pressure. Effectively, the quantity of fuel injected is increased as the boost pressure increases.

An adjustment screw is provided, but this is sealed at factory, and no attempt should be made to carry out adjustments without the use of specialist test equipment.

If a fault with the device is suspected, consult a Renault dealer or a suitably qualified specialist.

Chapter 4 Part D:
Emission control and exhaust systems

Contents

Degrees of difficulty

Easy, suitable for novice with little experience	**Fairly easy,** suitable for beginner with some experience	**Fairly difficult,** suitable for competent DIY mechanic ⚒	**Difficult,** suitable for experienced DIY mechanic ⚒	**Very difficult,** suitable for expert DIY or professional ⚒

1 General information

All diesel engine models are also designed to meet the strict emission requirements and are also equipped with a crankcase emission control system. In addition to this, certain models may also be fitted with a catalytic converter to reduce exhaust emissions.

The emission control systems function as follows.

Petrol models

Crankcase emission control

To reduce the emission of unburned hydrocarbons from the crankcase into the atmosphere, the engine is sealed and the blow-by gases and oil vapour are drawn from inside the crankcase, through an oil separator, into the inlet tract to be burned by the engine during normal combustion.

Under conditions of high manifold depression (idling, deceleration) the gases will be sucked positively out of the crankcase. Under conditions of low manifold depression (acceleration, full-throttle running) the gases are forced out of the crankcase by the (relatively) higher crankcase pressure; if the engine is worn, the raised crankcase pressure (due to increased blow-by) will cause some of the flow to return under all manifold conditions.

Exhaust emission control

To minimise the amount of pollutants which escape into the atmosphere, some models are fitted with a catalytic converter in the exhaust system. On all models where a catalytic converter is fitted, the system is of the closed-loop type, in which an oxygen sensor in the exhaust system provides the fuel injection/ignition system ECU with constant feedback, enabling the ECU to adjust the mixture to provide the best possible conditions for the converter to operate.

The oxygen sensor has a heating element built-in that is controlled by the ECU to quickly bring the sensor's tip to an efficient operating temperature. The sensor's tip is sensitive to oxygen and sends the ECU a varying voltage depending on the amount of oxygen in the exhaust gases; if the inlet air/fuel mixture is too rich, the exhaust gases are low in oxygen so the sensor sends a low-voltage signal, the voltage rising as the mixture weakens and the amount of oxygen rises in the exhaust gases. Peak conversion efficiency of all major pollutants occurs if the inlet air/fuel mixture is maintained at the chemically-correct ratio for the complete combustion of petrol of 14.7 parts (by weight) of air to 1 part of fuel (the "stoichiometric" ratio). The sensor output voltage alters in a large step at this point, the ECU using the signal change as a reference point and correcting the inlet air/fuel mixture accordingly by altering the fuel injector pulse width.

Evaporative emission control

To minimise the escape into the atmosphere of unburned hydrocarbons, an evaporative emission control system is fitted to models equipped with a catalytic converter. The fuel tank filler cap is sealed and a charcoal canister is mounted under the vehicle on the left-hand side to collect the petrol vapours generated in the tank when the vehicle is parked. It stores them until they can be cleared from the canister (under the control of the fuel injection/ignition system ECU) via the purge valve into the inlet tract to be burned by the engine during normal combustion.

To ensure that the engine runs correctly when it is cold and/or idling and to protect the catalytic converter from the effects of an over-rich mixture, the purge control valve is not opened by the ECU until the engine has warmed up, and the engine is under load; the valve solenoid is then modulated on and off to allow the stored vapour to pass into the inlet tract.

Diesel models

Crankcase emission control

Refer to paragraphs 4 and 5.

Exhaust emission control

To minimise the level of exhaust pollutants released into the atmosphere, a catalytic converter is fitted in the exhaust system of some models.

The catalytic converter consists of a canister containing a fine mesh impregnated with a catalyst material, over which the hot exhaust gases pass. The catalyst speeds up the oxidation of harmful carbon monoxide, unburnt hydrocarbons and soot, effectively reducing the quantity of harmful products released into the atmosphere via the exhaust gases.

Exhaust system

The exhaust system is fully described in Section 4.

2 Emission control systems - testing and component renewal

Petrol models

Crankcase emission control

1 The components of this system require no attention other than to check that the hose(s) are clear and undamaged at regular intervals **(see illustration)**.

Evaporative emission control system

Testing

2 If the system is thought to be faulty, disconnect the hoses from the charcoal

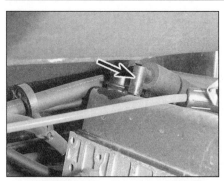

2.1 Emission control hose and adapter (arrowed) on camshaft cover

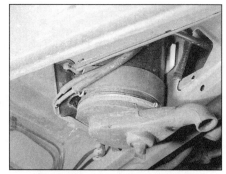

2.3 Charcoal canister location under left-hand side of vehicle

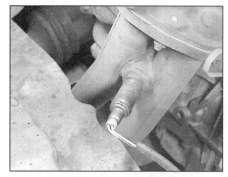

2.14 Oxygen sensor location in exhaust front pipe

canister and purge control valve and check that they are clear by blowing through them. If the purge control valve or charcoal canister are thought to be faulty, they must be renewed.

Charcoal canister - renewal

3 The charcoal canister is located under the vehicle on the left-hand side beneath the front seat **(see illustration)**. For access, raise and support the vehicle on axle stands (see *"Jacking and vehicle support"*).

4 Identify the location of the two hoses then disconnect them from the top of the canister.

5 Unbolt the securing strap and remove the canister from its location.

6 Refitting is a reverse of the removal procedure ensuring that the hoses are correctly reconnected.

Purge valve - renewal

7 The purge valve is attached to the ignition power module located on the engine compartment bulkhead on the left-hand side.

8 To renew the purge valve, disconnect the battery negative lead then disconnect the wiring connector from the valve.

9 Disconnect the hoses from either end of the valve then release the valve from its retaining clip and remove it from the engine compartment, noting which way around it is fitted.

10 Refitting is a reversal of removal ensuring that the valve is fitted the correct way around and the hoses are securely connected.

Exhaust emission control

Testing

11 The performance of the catalytic converter can be checked only by measuring the exhaust gases using a good-quality, carefully-calibrated exhaust gas analyser as described in Chapter 1.

12 If the CO level at the tailpipe is too high, the vehicle should be taken to a Renault dealer so that the complete fuel injection and ignition systems, including the oxygen sensor, can be thoroughly checked using the special diagnostic equipment. Once these have been checked and are known to be free from faults, the fault must be in the catalytic converter, which must be renewed as described in Section 4.

Catalytic converter - renewal

13 Refer to Section 4.

Oxygen sensor - renewal

Note: *The oxygen sensor is delicate and will not work if it is dropped or knocked, if its power supply is disrupted, or if any cleaning materials are used on it.*

14 Trace the wiring back from the oxygen sensor, which is screwed into the top of the exhaust front pipe, just below the manifold flange **(see illustration)**. Disconnect the wiring connector and free the wiring from any relevant retaining clips or ties.

15 Unscrew the sensor from the exhaust system front pipe and remove it along with its sealing washer.

16 Refitting is a reverse of the removal procedure using a new sealing washer. Prior to installing the sensor apply a smear of high temperature grease to the sensor threads. Ensure that the sensor is securely tightened and that the wiring is correctly routed and in no danger of contacting either the exhaust system or engine.

Diesel models

Crankcase emission control

17 The components of this system require no attention other than to check that the hose(s) are clear and undamaged at regular intervals.

Exhaust emission control

Testing

18 The performance of the catalytic converter (where fitted) can be checked only by measuring the exhaust gases using a good-quality, carefully-calibrated exhaust gas analyser as described in Chapter 1.

19 If the catalytic converter is thought to be faulty, before assuming the catalytic converter is faulty, it is worth checking the problem is not due to a faulty injector(s). Refer to your Renault dealer for further information.

Catalytic converter - renewal

20 Refer to Section 4.

3 Catalytic converter - general information and precautions

The catalytic converter is a reliable and simple device which needs no maintenance in itself, but there are some facts of which an owner should be aware if the converter is to function properly for its full service life.

Petrol models

a) *DO NOT use leaded petrol in a car equipped with a catalytic converter - the lead will coat the precious metals, reducing their converting efficiency and will eventually destroy the converter.*

b) *Always keep the ignition and fuel systems well-maintained in accordance with the manufacturer's schedule.*

c) *If the engine develops a misfire, do not drive the car at all (or at least as little as possible) until the fault is cured.*

d) *DO NOT push- or tow-start the car - this will soak the catalytic converter in unburned fuel, causing it to overheat when the engine does start.*

e) *DO NOT switch off the ignition at high engine speeds.*

f) *DO NOT use fuel or engine oil additives - these may contain substances harmful to the catalytic converter.*

g) *DO NOT continue to use the car if the engine burns oil to the extent of leaving a visible trail of blue smoke.*

h) *Remember that the catalytic converter operates at very high temperatures. DO NOT, therefore, park the car in dry undergrowth, over long grass or piles of dead leaves after a long run.*

i) *Remember that the catalytic converter is FRAGILE - do not strike it with tools during servicing work.*

j) *In some cases a sulphurous smell (like that of rotten eggs) may be noticed from the exhaust. This is common to many catalytic converter-equipped cars and once the car has covered a few thousand miles the problem should disappear.*

k) The catalytic converter, used on a well-maintained and well-driven car, should last for between 50 000 and 100 000 miles - if the converter is no longer effective it must be renewed.

Diesel models

Refer to the information given in parts *f, g, h* and *i* of the petrol models information given above.

4 Exhaust system - general information, removal and refitting

General information

1 A multiple section exhaust system is fitted, the number of sections being dependent on engine type and model year. The sections are joined either by a flanged joint, or by a collared sleeve and clamp type joint. The joint at the lower end of the downpipe is secured by nuts and bolts with a centre, thermo-fusing sealing ring. The joint is of the spring-loaded ball type, to allow for movement in the exhaust system.
2 Where fitted, the catalytic converter is located on the front section of the exhaust.
3 The system is suspended throughout its entire length by rubber mountings.

Removal

4 Each exhaust section can be removed individually. Due to the location of the rear suspension components it is not possible to remove the complete system without disconnecting the rear tailpipe first.
5 To remove part of the system, first jack up the front or rear of the vehicle and support it on axle stands (see *"Jacking and vehicle support")*. Alternatively, position the vehicle over an inspection pit or on car ramps.

Front pipe

6 On models fitted with a catalytic converter, either remove the oxygen sensor as described in Section 2, or disconnect its wiring connector.
7 Undo the nuts securing the front pipe to the exhaust manifold or turbocharger.
8 Undo the nuts and bolts securing the front pipe spring loaded joint to the first intermediate pipe. Recover the springs and on later models the spacers **(see illustration)**. Separate the joint and recover the sealing ring.
9 Undo the front mounting attachment and withdraw the front pipe from underneath the vehicle. Where fitted, remove the heat shield.

Intermediate pipes and silencers

10 Slacken the clamp ring bolt(s) and disengage the clamp(s) from the collard sleeve joint(s).
11 Undo the nuts and bolts securing the front pipe spring loaded joint to the first intermediate pipe. Recover the springs and on later models the spacers. Separate the joint and recover the sealing ring.
12 Twist the system to separate the collard joint(s) If tight, apply penetrating oil and leave it to soak. If the joint is still reluctant to separate, carefully apply local heat to the joint after taking the appropriate safety precautions. As a last resort, cut through the pipe using a hacksaw.
13 Unhook the first or second intermediate pipe and silencer from its mountings and remove from underneath the vehicle. Where fitted, remove the heat shield.

Tailpipe and silencer

14 Slacken the clamp ring bolts and disengage the clamps from the collard sleeve joints.
15 Twist the system to separate the collard joint. If tight, apply penetrating oil and leave it to soak. If the joint is still reluctant to separate, carefully apply local heat to the joint after taking the appropriate safety precautions. As a last resort, cut through the pipe using a hacksaw.

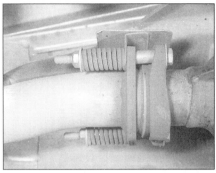

4.8 Front pipe spring-loaded joint

16 Unhook the tailpipe and silencer from its mountings and remove it from the vehicle.

Refitting

17 Each section is refitted by reversing the removal sequence, noting the following points:

a) Ensure that all traces of corrosion have been removed from the flanges and collard sleeves.
b) Inspect the rubber mountings for signs of damage or deterioration, and renew as necessary.
c) A new seal must always be used on the spring loaded front pipe joint. On early models, tighten the nuts until the springs are coil bound. On later models with spacer sleeves over the retaining bolts, tighten the nuts until they contact the spacer sleeves.
d) When fitting the clamp rings to the collard sleeves, ensure that the clamp is positioned over the split ends of the pipe, and that the clamp ring opening is at 90° to the pipe splits.
e) Prior to tightening the exhaust system fasteners, ensure that all rubber mountings are correctly located, and that there is adequate clearance between the exhaust system and vehicle.

4D

Chapter 5 Part A:
Starting and charging systems

Contents

Degrees of difficulty

Easy, suitable for novice with little experience	**Fairly easy,** suitable for beginner with some experience	**Fairly difficult,** suitable for competent DIY mechanic 	**Difficult,** suitable for experienced DIY mechanic	**Very difficult,** suitable for expert DIY or professional

Specifications

System type . . . . 12-volt, negative earth

Battery
Type . . . . Low maintenance or "maintenance-free" sealed for life
Charge condition:
   Poor . . . . 12.5 volts
   Normal . . . . 12.6 volts
   Good . . . . 12.7 volts

Alternator
Type . . . . Ducellier, Valeo or Paris-Rhône

Starter motor
Type . . . . Valeo, Mitsubishi or Paris-Rhône

---

1 General information and precautions

General information

The engine electrical system consists mainly of the charging and starting systems. Because of their engine-related functions, these components are covered separately from the body electrical devices such as the lights, instruments, etc (which are covered in Chapter 12). On petrol models refer to Part B for information on the ignition system, and on diesel models refer to Part C for information on the preheating system.

The electrical system is of the 12-volt negative earth type.

The battery is of the low maintenance or "maintenance-free" (sealed for life) type and is charged by the alternator, which is belt-driven from the crankshaft pulley.

The starter motor is of the pre-engaged type incorporating an integral solenoid. On starting, the solenoid moves the drive pinion into engagement with the flywheel ring gear before the starter motor is energised. Once the engine has started, a one-way clutch prevents the motor armature being driven by the engine until the pinion disengages from the flywheel.

Precautions

Further details of the various systems are given in the relevant Sections of this Chapter. While some repair procedures are given, the usual course of action is to renew the component concerned. The owner whose interest extends beyond mere component renewal should obtain a copy of the *"Automobile Electrical & Electronic Systems Manual"*, available from the publishers of this manual.

It is necessary to take extra care when working on the electrical system to avoid damage to semi-conductor devices (diodes and transistors), and to avoid the risk of personal injury. In addition to the precautions given in *"Safety first!"* at the beginning of this manual, observe the following when working on the system:

Always remove rings, watches, etc before working on the electrical system. Even with the battery disconnected, capacitive discharge could occur if a component's live terminal is earthed through a metal object. This could cause a shock or nasty burn.

Do not reverse the battery connections. Components such as the alternator, electronic control units, or any other components having semi-conductor circuitry could be irreparably damaged.

If the engine is being started using jump leads and a slave battery, connect the batteries positive-to-positive and negative-to-negative (see "Booster battery (jump) starting"). This also applies when connecting a battery charger.

Never disconnect the battery terminals, the alternator, any electrical wiring or any test instruments when the engine is running.

Do not allow the engine to turn the alternator when the alternator is not connected.

Never "test" for alternator output by "flashing" the output lead to earth.

Never use an ohmmeter of the type incorporating a hand-cranked generator for circuit or continuity testing.

Always ensure that the battery negative lead is disconnected when working on the electrical system.

Before using electric-arc welding equipment on the car, disconnect the battery, alternator and components such as the fuel injection/ignition electronic control unit to protect them from the risk of damage.

Some of the radio/cassette units fitted as standard or optional equipment may be equipped with a built-in security code to deter thieves. If the power source to the unit is cut, the anti-theft system will activate. Even if the power source is immediately reconnected, the radio/cassette unit will not function until the correct security code has been entered. Therefore, if you do not know the correct security code for the radio/cassette unit do not disconnect the negative terminal of the battery or remove the radio/cassette unit from the vehicle. Refer to "Radio/cassette unit anti-theft system precaution" in the Reference section of this manual for further information.

2 Electrical fault finding -
general information

Refer to Chapter 12.

3 Battery - testing and charging

Standard and low maintenance battery - testing

1 If the vehicle covers a small annual mileage, it is worthwhile checking the specific gravity of the electrolyte every three months to determine the state of charge of the battery. Use a hydrometer to make the check and compare the results with the following table. The temperatures quoted are ambient (air) temperatures. Note that the specific gravity readings assume an electrolyte temperature of 15°C; for every 10°C below 15°C subtract 0.007. For every 10°C above 15°C add 0.007.

	Above 25°C	Below 25°C
Fully-charged	1.210 to 1.230	1.270 to 1.290
70% charged	1.170 to 1.190	1.230 to 1.250
Discharged	1.050 to 1.070	1.110 to 1.130

2 If the battery condition is suspect, first check the specific gravity of electrolyte in each cell. A variation of 0.040 or more between any cells indicates loss of electrolyte or deterioration of the internal plates.

3 If the specific gravity variation is 0.040 or more, the battery should be renewed. If the cell variation is satisfactory but the battery is discharged, it should be charged as described later in this Section.

Maintenance-free battery - testing

4 In cases where a "sealed for life" maintenance-free battery is fitted, topping-up and testing of the electrolyte in each cell is not possible. The condition of the battery can therefore only be tested using a battery condition indicator or a voltmeter.

5 If testing the battery using a voltmeter, connect the voltmeter across the battery and compare the result with those given in the *Specifications* under "charge condition". The test is only accurate if the battery has not been subjected to any kind of charge for the previous six hours. If this is not the case, switch on the headlights for 30 seconds, then wait four to five minutes before testing the battery after switching off the headlights. All other electrical circuits must be switched off, so check that the doors and tailgate are fully shut when making the test.

6 If the voltage reading is less than 12.2 volts, then the battery is discharged, whilst a reading of 12.2 to 12.4 volts indicates a partially discharged condition.

7 If the battery is to be charged, remove it from the vehicle (Section 4) and charge it as described later in this Section.

Standard and low maintenance battery - charging

Note: *The following is intended as a guide only. Always refer to the manufacturer's recommendations (often printed on a label attached to the battery) before charging a battery.*

8 Charge the battery at a rate of 3.5 to 4 amps and continue to charge the battery at this rate until no further rise in specific gravity is noted over a four hour period.

9 Alternatively, a trickle charger charging at the rate of 1.5 amps can safely be used overnight.

10 Specially rapid "boost" charges which are claimed to restore the power of the battery in 1 to 2 hours are not recommended, as they can cause serious damage to the battery plates through overheating.

11 While charging the battery, note that the temperature of the electrolyte should never exceed 37.8°C (100°F).

Maintenance-free battery - charging

Note: *The following is intended as a guide only. Always refer to the manufacturer's recommendations (often printed on a label attached to the battery) before charging a battery.*

12 This battery type takes considerably longer to fully recharge than the standard type, the time taken being dependent on the extent of discharge, but it can take anything up to three days.

13 A constant voltage type charger is required, to be set to 13.9 to 14.9 volts with a charger current below 25 amps. Using this method, the battery should be usable within about three hours, giving a voltage reading of 12.5 volts, but this is for a partially discharged battery and, as mentioned, full charging can take considerably longer.

14 If the battery is to be charged from a fully discharged state (condition reading less than 12.2 volts), have it recharged by your Renault dealer or local automotive electrician, as the charge rate is higher and constant supervision during charging is necessary.

4 Battery - removal and refitting

Note: *If a Renault radio/cassette unit is fitted, refer to "Radio/cassette unit anti-theft system - precaution "in the Reference section of this manual.*

Removal

1 The battery is located on the right-hand side of the engine compartment on petrol models and on the left-hand side on diesel models..

2 Slacken the thumb screw and disconnect the clamp from the battery negative (earth) terminal.

3 Remove the insulation cover (where fitted) and disconnect the positive terminal lead(s) in the same way.

4 Unscrew the bolt and remove the battery retaining clamp bolt **(see illustration)**. Lift the battery out of the engine compartment.

Refitting

5 Refitting is a reversal of removal, but smear petroleum jelly on the terminals when reconnecting the leads, and always reconnect the positive lead first, and the negative lead last.

4.4 Battery clamp bolt (arrowed)

5 Charging system - testing

Note: *Refer to the warnings given in "Safety first!" and in Section 1 of this Chapter before starting work.*

1 If the ignition warning light fails to illuminate when the ignition is switched on, first check the alternator wiring connections for security. If satisfactory, check that the warning light bulb has not blown, and that the bulbholder is secure in its location in the instrument panel. If the light still fails to illuminate, check the continuity of the warning light feed wire from the alternator to the bulbholder. If all is satisfactory, the alternator is at fault and should be renewed or taken to an auto-electrician for testing and repair.

2 If the ignition warning light illuminates when the engine is running, stop the engine and check that the drivebelt is correctly tensioned (see Chapter 1) and that the alternator connections are secure. If all is so far satisfactory, have the alternator checked by an auto-electrician for testing and repair.

3 If the alternator output is suspect even though the warning light functions correctly, the regulated voltage may be checked as follows.

4 Connect a voltmeter across the battery terminals and start the engine.

5 Increase the engine speed until the voltmeter reading remains steady; the reading should be between 13.5 and 14.8 volts.

6 Switch on as many electrical accessories (eg, the headlights, heated rear window and heater blower) as possible, and check that the alternator maintains the regulated voltage between 13.5 and 14.8 volts.

7 If the regulated voltage is not as stated, the fault may be due to worn brushes, weak brush springs, a faulty voltage regulator, a faulty diode, a severed phase winding or worn or damaged slip rings. The alternator should be renewed or taken to an auto-electrician for testing and repair.

6 Alternator drivebelt - removal, refitting and tensioning

Refer to the procedure given for the auxiliary drivebelt in Chapter 1.

7 Alternator - removal and refitting

Removal

1 Disconnect the battery negative lead.

2 Slacken the auxiliary drivebelt as described in Chapter 1 and disengage it from the alternator pulley.

3 Disconnect the wiring multiplugs and the leads from the terminal studs at the rear of the alternator.

4 Unscrew and remove the mounting and adjuster link bolts and lift the alternator from its mounting bracket . On some models, it may be necessary to remove the air cleaner to gain access to the alternator mountings (depending on type).

Refitting

5 Refitting is a reversal of removal. Tension the auxiliary drivebelt as described in Chapter 1, and ensure that the alternator mountings are securely tightened.

8 Alternator - testing and overhaul

If the alternator is thought to be suspect, it should be removed from the vehicle and taken to an auto-electrician for testing. Most auto-electricians will be able to supply and fit brushes at a reasonable cost. However, check on the cost of repairs before proceeding as it may prove more economical to obtain a new or exchange alternator.

9 Starting system - testing

Note: *Refer to the precautions in "Safety first!" and Section 1 of this Chapter before starting.*

1 If the starter motor fails to operate when the ignition key is turned to the correct position, the following may be to blame.

a) *The battery is faulty.*

b) *The electrical connections between the switch, solenoid, battery and starter motor are somewhere failing to pass the necessary current from the battery through the starter to earth.*

c) *The solenoid is faulty.*

d) *The starter motor is mechanically or electrically defective.*

2 To check the battery, switch on the headlights. If they dim after a few seconds, this indicates that the battery is discharged - recharge (see Section 3) or renew the battery. If the headlights glow brightly, operate the ignition switch and observe the lights. If they dim, then this indicates that current is reaching the starter motor, therefore the fault must lie in the starter motor. If the lights continue to glow brightly (and no clicking sound can be heard from the starter motor solenoid), this indicates that there is a fault in the circuit or solenoid - see following paragraphs. If the starter motor turns slowly when operated, but the battery is in good condition, then this indicates that either the starter motor is faulty, or there is considerable resistance somewhere in the circuit.

3 If a fault in the circuit is suspected, disconnect the battery leads (including the earth connection to the body), the starter/solenoid wiring and the engine/transmission earth strap. Thoroughly clean the connections, and reconnect the leads and wiring, then use a voltmeter or test lamp to check that full battery voltage is available at the battery positive lead connection to the solenoid, and that the earth is sound. Smear petroleum jelly around the battery terminals to prevent corrosion - corroded connections are amongst the most frequent causes of electrical system faults.

4 If the battery and all connections are in good condition, check the circuit by disconnecting the wire from the solenoid blade terminal. Connect a voltmeter or test lamp between the wire end and a good earth (such as the battery negative terminal), and check that the wire is live when the ignition switch is turned to the "start" position. If it is, then the circuit is sound - if not, check the circuit wiring as described in Chapter 12.

5 The solenoid contacts can be checked by connecting a voltmeter or test lamp between the battery positive feed connection on the starter side of the solenoid, and earth. When the ignition switch is turned to the "start" position, there should be a reading or lighted bulb, as applicable. If not, the solenoid is faulty and should be renewed.

6 If the circuit and solenoid are proved sound, the fault must lie in the starter motor. In this event, it may be possible to have the starter motor overhauled by a specialist, but check on the cost of spares before proceeding, as it may prove more economical to obtain a new or exchange motor.

10 Starter motor - removal and refitting

Removal

1 Disconnect the battery negative lead.

2 So that access to the motor can be gained both from above and below, chock the rear wheels then jack up the front of the vehicle

5A

and support it on axle stands (see *"Jacking and vehicle support"*). Where applicable, to improve access to the motor remove the air cleaner unit as described in the relevant Part of Chapter 4.

3 Disconnect the wiring from the starter motor solenoid.

4 On petrol models, undo the two nuts and bolts securing the rear of the starter motor to the support bracket. Unbolt the support bracket from the engine noting the location of the earth lead.

5 Undo the three bolts securing the starter motor to the clutch bellhousing and manoeuvre the unit from its location.

Refitting

6 Refitting is a reversal of removal.

11 Starter motor - testing and overhaul

If the starter motor is thought to be suspect, it should be removed from the vehicle and taken to an auto-electrician for testing. Most auto-electricians will be able to supply and fit brushes at a reasonable cost. However, check on the cost of repairs before proceeding as it may prove more economical to obtain a new or exchange motor.

12 Ignition switch - removal and refitting

Refer to Chapter 12, Section 4.

13 Oil pressure warning light switch - removal and refitting

Removal

1 The switch is located on the right-hand side of the cylinder block on petrol engines and on the oil cooler/filter housing on diesel engines **(see illustration)**.

2 Remove the protective sleeve from the wiring plug (where applicable), then disconnect the wiring from the switch.

3 Unscrew the switch from the cylinder block, and recover the sealing washer. Be prepared for oil spillage, and if the switch is to be left removed from the engine for any length of time, plug the hole in the cylinder block.

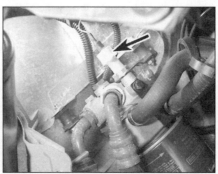

13.1 Oil pressure warning light switch (arrowed) on diesel engines

Refitting

4 Examine the sealing washer for signs of damage or deterioration and if necessary renew.

5 Refit the switch, complete with washer, and tighten it securely. Reconnect the wiring connector.

6 If necessary, top-up the engine oil as described in Chapter 1.

14 Oil level sensor - removal and refitting

The sensor is located on the left-hand side of the cylinder block **(see illustration)**.

The removal and refitting procedure is as described for the oil pressure switch in Section 13. Access is most easily obtained from underneath the vehicle.

14.1 Oil level sensor wiring plug connection

Chapter 5 Part B:
Ignition system - petrol models

Contents

Degrees of difficulty

Easy, suitable for novice with little experience	**Fairly easy,** suitable for beginner with some experience	**Fairly difficult,** suitable for competent DIY mechanic 	**Difficult,** suitable for experienced DIY mechanic	**Very difficult,** suitable for expert DIY or professional

Specifications

General

System type	Breakerless, computer-controlled, electronic ignition system
Firing order	1-3-4-2 (No 1 cylinder at flywheel end)

Ignition coil

Resistances:

Primary windings	0.4 to 0.8 ohms
Secondary windings	2.0 to 12.0 K ohms

Spark plugs . . . . See Chapter 1 *Specifications*

---

1 General information

Carburettor models

The electronic ignition system operates on an advanced principle whereby the main functions of the distributor are replaced by a computer module.

The system consists of three main components, namely the computer module which incorporates an ignition coil and a vacuum advance unit, the distributor, which directs the HT voltage received from the coil to the appropriate spark plug, and an angular position/speed sensor which determines the position and speed of the crankshaft by sensing special teeth on the flywheel periphery.

The computer module receives information on crankshaft position relative to TDC and BDC and also engine speed from the angular position/speed sensor, and receives information on engine load from the vacuum advance unit. From these constantly changing variables, the computer calculates the precise instant at which HT voltage should be supplied and triggers the coil accordingly. The voltage then passes from the coil to the appropriate spark plug, via the distributor in the conventional way. The functions of the centrifugal and vacuum advance mechanisms, as well as the contact breaker points normally associated with a distributor, are all catered for by the computer module, so that the sole purpose of the distributor is to direct the HT voltage from the coil to the appropriate spark plug.

Fuel injected models

On fuel-injected models, the ignition system is integrated with the fuel injection system to form a combined engine management system under the control of one electronic control unit (ECU).

The main components of the ignition side of the system are the fuel/ignition ECU, the ignition power module, the ignition coil, the distributor and the angular position/speed sensor.

The ECU receives information on crankshaft position and engine speed from the angular position/speed sensor which functions in the same way as described for carburettor models. Information on engine load is provided by a vacuum advance unit on non-catalyst equipped engines, or from a manifold absolute pressure sensor on engines fitted with a catalytic converter.

From this constantly-changing data, the fuel/ignition ECU selects a particular ignition advance setting from a basic map of ignition characteristics stored in its memory. The basic setting can be modified according to additional information sent to the ECU from a knock sensor. This sensor is screwed into the cylinder head and prevents the engine "pinking" under load. The sensor is sensitive to vibration and detects the knocking which occurs when the engine starts to "pink" (pre-ignite). When "pinking" is detected, the sensor sends a signal to the ECU which in turn retards the ignition advance until the "pinking" ceases. Additional sensors monitoring coolant temperature, inlet air temperature and throttle position are used by the ECU to further advance or retard the ignition to suit all engine operating conditions.

With the firing point established, the ECU sends a control signal to the ignition power module, which is an electronic switch controlling the current to the ignition coil primary windings. On receipt of the signal from the ECU, the power module interrupts the primary current to the ignition coil which induces a high-tension voltage in the coil secondary windings. This HT voltage is passed to the distributor and then on to the spark plugs via the distributor rotor arm and HT leads in the conventional manner. The cycle is then repeated many times a second for each cylinder in turn.

5B

2 Ignition system - testing

⚠️ **Warning: Voltages produced by an electronic ignition system are considerably higher than those produced by conventional ignition systems. Extreme care must be taken when working on the system if the ignition is switched on. Persons with surgically-implanted cardiac pacemaker devices should keep clear of the ignition circuits, components and test equipment.**

Carburettor models

Note: *Refer to the warnings given in Section 1 of Part A of this Chapter before starting work. Always switch off the ignition before disconnecting or connecting any component or test equipment.*

General

1 The components of the electronic ignition system are normally very reliable; most faults are far more likely to be due to loose or dirty connections, or to "tracking" of HT voltage due to dirt, dampness or damaged insulation, than to the failure of any of the system's components. **Always** check all wiring thoroughly before condemning an electrical component, and work methodically to eliminate all other possibilities before deciding that a particular component is faulty.

2 The old practice of checking for a spark by holding the live end of an HT lead a short distance away from the engine is **not** recommended; not only is there a high risk of a powerful electric shock, but the ignition coil or computer module may be damaged. Similarly, **never** try to "diagnose" misfires by pulling off one HT lead at a time.

Engine will not start

3 If the engine either will not turn over at all, or only turns very slowly, check the battery and starter motor. Connect a voltmeter across the battery terminals (meter positive probe to battery positive terminal), disconnect the ignition coil HT lead from the distributor cap and earth it, then note the voltage reading obtained while turning the engine over on the starter for (no more than) ten seconds. If the reading obtained is less than around 9.5 volts, first check the battery, starter motor and charging system as described in Part A of this Chapter.

4 If the engine turns over at normal speed but will not start, check the HT circuit by connecting a timing light (following its manufacturer's instructions) and turning the engine over on the starter motor; if the light flashes, voltage is reaching the spark plugs, so these should be checked first. If the light does not flash, check the HT leads themselves, followed by the distributor cap, carbon brush and rotor arm, using the information given in Chapter 1.

5 If there is a spark, check the fuel system for faults, referring to Chapter 4, Part A for further information.

6 If there is still no spark, check the voltage at the ignition coil "+" terminal; it should be the same as the battery voltage (ie, at least 11.7 volts). If the voltage at the coil is more than 1 volt less than that at the battery, check the condition of all the circuit wiring, referring to the wiring diagrams at the end of this manual.

7 If the feed to the coil is sound, check the condition of the coil, if possible, by substitution with a known good unit or by checking the primary and secondary resistances. If the fault persists the problem lies elsewhere; if the fault is now cleared, a new coil is the obvious cure. However, check carefully the condition of the LT connections themselves before doing so, to ensure that the fault is not due to dirty or poorly-fastened connectors.

8 If the coil is in good condition, the fault is probably within the computer module itself or the angular position/speed sensor. Testing of these components should be entrusted to a Renault dealer.

Engine misfires

9 An irregular misfire suggests either a loose connection or intermittent fault on the primary circuit, or an HT fault on the coil side of the rotor arm.

10 With the ignition switched off, check carefully through the system, ensuring that all connections are clean and securely fastened. If the equipment is available, check the LT circuit as described above.

11 Check that the ignition coil, the distributor cap and the HT leads are clean and dry. Check the leads themselves and the spark plugs (by substitution if necessary), then check the distributor cap, carbon brush and rotor arm as described in Chapter 1.

12 Regular misfiring is almost certainly due to a fault in the distributor cap, HT leads or spark plugs. Use a timing light (paragraph 4 above) to check whether HT voltage is present at all leads.

13 If HT voltage is not present on any particular lead, the fault will be in that lead, or in the distributor cap. If HT is present on all leads, the fault will be in the spark plugs; check and renew them if there is any doubt about their condition.

14 If no HT is present, check the ignition coil; its secondary windings may be breaking down under load.

Fuel injected models

15 If a fault appears in the engine management (fuel injection/ignition) system, first ensure that the fault is not due to a poor electrical connection or poor maintenance; ie, check that the air cleaner filter element is clean, the spark plugs are in good condition and correctly gapped, that the engine breather hoses are clear and undamaged, referring to Chapter 1 for further information. Also check

that the accelerator cable is correctly adjusted as described in the relevant part of Chapter 4. If the engine is running very roughly, check the compression pressures and the valve clearances as described in Chapter 2A.

16 If these checks fail to reveal the cause of the problem the vehicle should be taken to a suitably equipped Renault dealer for testing. A wiring block connector is incorporated in the engine management circuit into which a special electronic diagnostic tester can be plugged. The tester will locate the fault quickly and simply, alleviating the need to test all the system components individually which is a time consuming operation that carries a high risk of damaging the ECU.

17 The only ignition system checks which can be carried out by the home mechanic are those described in Chapter 1, relating to the spark plugs, and the ignition coil test described in this Chapter. If necessary, the system wiring and wiring connectors can be checked as described in Chapter 12, ensuring that the ECU wiring connector(s) have first been disconnected.

3 Distributor - removal and refitting

Removal

1 According to engine and model year, the distributor will be located on the front left-hand side of the cylinder block and driven by the engine auxiliary shaft, or at the rear of the cylinder head driven from the end of the camshaft.

2 To remove the distributor cap, undo the retaining screws and withdraw it together with the HT leads **(see illustration)**.

3 The rotor arm and shield can now be pulled free and removed **(see illustration)**.

4 To remove the cylinder block mounted distributor, undo the retaining nuts and lift the unit from its location.

5 To remove the cylinder head mounted distributor, undo the three retaining screws to remove the rotor housing if required **(see illustration)**. If necessary renew the O-ring seal.

3.2 Cylinder head mounted distributor cap

3.3 Distributor rotor arm and shield

6 Wipe clean the cap and leads and carry out a careful inspection as described in Chapter 1. If the camshaft oil seal requires renewal, refer to Chapter 2A.

Refitting

7 Refitting is a reversal of removal.

4 Ignition coil - removal, testing and refitting

Removal

Carburettor models

1 The ignition coil is attached to the computer module located on the engine compartment bulkhead on the left-hand side.
2 Disconnect the HT lead and LT wires from

4.4 Disconnecting the HT lead from the coil

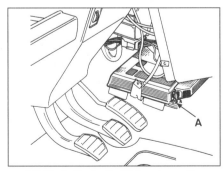

5.7 Undo the bolts (A) to release the fuel/ignition ECU from its location under the facia on early models

3.5 Rotor housing screws (arrowed)

the coil, then undo the two screws and withdraw the coil from the computer module.

Fuel injected models

3 The ignition coil is attached to the ignition power module located on the engine compartment bulkhead on the left-hand side.
4 Disconnect the HT lead from the coil by releasing the retaining clip legs and pulling off the lead **(see illustration)**.
5 Undo the two screws and withdraw the coil from the power module **(see illustration)**.

Testing

6 Testing of the coil consists of using a multimeter set to its resistance function, to check the primary (LT "+ " to "-" terminals) and secondary (LT "-" to HT lead terminal) windings for continuity. Compare the results with those in the *Specifications* at the start of this Chapter. The resistance of the coil windings will vary

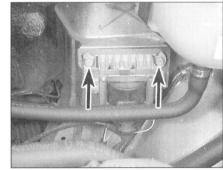

4.5 Undo the two screws (arrowed) to remove the coil from the power module

5.8a Undo the ECU case outer cover retaining nut . . .

slightly according to the coil temperature, the results in the *Specifications* are approximate values for when the coil is at 20°C.
7 Check that there is no continuity between the HT lead terminal and the coil body.
8 If the coil is thought to be faulty, have your findings confirmed by a Renault dealer before renewing the coil.

Refitting

9 Refitting is a reversal of removal ensuring that the wiring connectors are securely reconnected.

5 Ignition system control units and sensors - removal and refitting

Removal

Computer module (carburettor models)

1 The computer module is on the left-hand side of the engine compartment bulkhead.
2 Disconnect the battery negative lead.
3 Disconnect the vacuum hose and the wiring connectors, noting their respective locations. Undo the retaining nuts or bolts and remove the unit. If required the coil can be removed as described in Section 4. Do not attempt to remove the vacuum unit.

Fuel/ignition ECU (fuel-injected models)

4 The ECU is located under the facia centre section in the passenger compartment on early models, and in the engine compartment on the right-hand side on later models.
5 Disconnect the battery negative lead.
6 To remove the early unit, remove the facia centre section left-hand side panel, referring to Chapter 11 if necessary.
7 Undo the two bolts, disconnect the wiring connector, and slide the ECU from its location **(see illustration)**.
8 On later models, undo the retaining nut and remove the ECU outer cover. Release the centre spring clip and the two plastic clips and open the unit case **(see illustrations)**. On some versions it may also be necessary to unscrew an additional bolt at the bottom.

5.8b . . . release the spring clip and open the unit case to access the ECU

5B

9 Lift out the ECU and disconnect the wiring connector.

Power module (fuel-injected models)

10 The power module is removed in the same way as the computer module described above except that on later models there is no vacuum unit.

Knock sensor (fuel-injected models)

11 The knock sensor is located on the left-hand side of the cylinder head between cylinders 2 and 3. Access is gained by reaching underneath the inlet manifold.

12 Remove the air cleaner assembly and the air inlet ducting as described in Chapter 4, Part B.

13 Disconnect the wiring at the connector then unscrew the sensor from the cylinder head.

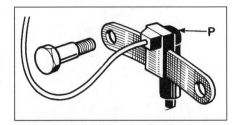

5.14 Angular position/speed sensor (P) and shouldered bolt

Angular position/speed sensor (all models)

14 The sensor is located on the transmission bellhousing and is secured by special shouldered bolts **(see illustration)**. Its position is pre-set in production to provide the required clearance. No adjustment of this clearance is necessary or possible.

15 To remove the sensor, proceed as follows.

16 Disconnect the battery negative lead.

17 Disconnect the smaller of the two wiring connectors from the front of the computer module (carburettor models), from the bottom of the power module or, where applicable, from the wiring connector near the sensor (fuel-injected models).

18 Undo and remove the two bolts securing the sensor to the top of the bellhousing and lift off the sensor. Note that the two retaining bolts are of the shouldered type and must not be replaced with ordinary bolts. When handling the sensor, take care not to damage it.

Refitting

19 In all cases, refitting is a reversal of removal ensuring that the wiring connectors are securely reconnected.

Chapter 5 Part C:
Preheating system (diesel models)

Contents

Degrees of difficulty

Easy, suitable for novice with little experience	**Fairly easy,** suitable for beginner with some experience	**Fairly difficult,** suitable for competent DIY mechanic	**Difficult,** suitable for experienced DIY mechanic	**Very difficult,** suitable for expert DIY or professional

Specifications

Torque wrench setting	Nm
Glow plugs	25

---

1 Preheating system - description and testing

Description

1 Each swirl chamber has a heater plug (commonly called a glow plug) screwed into it. The plugs are electrically operated before, during, and a short time after start-up when the engine is cold. Electrical feed to the glow plugs is controlled by the preheating control unit.

2 The glow plugs also provide a "post-heating" function, whereby the glow plugs remain switched on for a period after the engine has started. Once the starter has been activated, the glow plugs are supplied with full current for 10 seconds then, once the engine has started, the plugs are supplied with half the "preheating" current, alternately, in pairs, for up to 3 minutes. The exact "post-heating" time is controlled by the preheating control unit, and is dependant on the prevailing engine operating conditions. The supply to the plugs will be interrupted by:

   a) *Opening of the "no-load" switch. The supply is cut off 3 seconds after the switch opens (ie 3 seconds after the accelerator pedal is depressed). The current supply is restored as soon as the switch closes.*

   b) *A coolant temperature of more than 60°C*

3 A warning light in the instrument panel tells the driver that preheating is taking place. When the light goes out, the engine is ready to be started. The voltage supply to the glow plugs continues for several seconds after the light goes out. If no attempt is made to start, the timer then cuts off the supply in order to avoid draining the battery and overheating of the glow plugs.

Testing

4 If the system malfunctions, testing is ultimately by substitution of known good units, but some preliminary checks may be made as follows.

5 Connect a voltmeter or 12 volt test lamp between the glow plug supply cable and earth (engine or vehicle metal). Make sure that the live connection is kept clear of the engine and bodywork.

6 Have an assistant switch on the ignition and check that voltage is applied to the glow plugs. Note the time for which the warning light is lit and the total time for which voltage is applied before the system cuts out. Switch off the ignition.

7 At an under-bonnet temperature of 20°C typical times noted should be 5 or 6 seconds for warning light operation, followed by a further 4 to 5 seconds supply after the light goes out (provided the starter motor is not operated). Warning light time will increase with lower temperatures and decrease with higher temperatures.

8 If there is no supply at all, the relay or associated wiring is at fault.

9 To locate a defective glow plug, disconnect the main supply cable and the interconnecting wire or strap from the top of the glow plugs. Be careful not to drop the nuts and washers.

10 Use a continuity tester, or a 12 volt test lamp connected to the battery positive terminal, to check for continuity between each glow plug terminal and earth. The resistance of a glow plug in good condition is very low (less than 1 ohm), so if the test lamp does not light or the continuity tester shows a high resistance the glow plug is certainly defective.

11 If an ammeter is available, the current draw of each glow plug can be checked. After an initial surge of around 15 to 20 amps, each plug should draw around 10 amps. Any plug which draws much more or less than this is probably defective.

12 As a final check the glow plugs can be removed and inspected as described in Section 2.

2 Glow plugs - removal, inspection and refitting

Removal

Caution: If the preheating system has just been energised, or if the engine has been running, the glow plugs will be very hot.

5C

2.4 Removing a glow plug from the cylinder head

3.1 Preheating system control unit

1 Disconnect the battery negative lead.

2 Unscrew the nuts from the glow plug terminals, and recover the washers. Note that the main supply cable is connected to one of the glow plugs. Remove the interconnecting wire from the top of the glow plugs.

3 Where applicable, carefully move any obstructing pipes or wires to one side to enable access to the glow plugs.

4 Unscrew the glow plugs and remove them from the cylinder head **(see illustration)**.

Inspection

5 Inspect the glow plugs for physical damage. Burnt or eroded glow plug tips can be caused by a bad injector spray pattern. Have the injectors checked if damage is found.

6 If the glow plugs are in good physical condition, check them electrically using a 12 volt test lamp or continuity tester as described in the previous Section.

7 The glow plugs can be energised by applying 12 volts to them to verify that they heat up evenly and in the required time. Observe the following precautions.

a) Support the glow plug by clamping it carefully in a vice or self-locking pliers. Remember it will become red-hot.

b) Make sure that the power supply or test lead incorporates a fuse or overload trip to protect against damage from a short-circuit.

c) After testing, allow the glow plug to cool for several minutes before attempting to handle it.

8 A glow plug in good condition will start to glow red at the tip after drawing current for 5 seconds or so. Any plug which takes much longer to start glowing, or which starts glowing in the middle instead of at the tip, is defective.

Refitting

9 Refitting is a reversal of removal. Apply a smear of copper-based anti-seize compound to the plug threads and tighten the glow plugs to the specified torque. Do not overtighten, as this can damage the glow plug element.

3 Preheating system control unit - removal and refitting

Removal

1 The unit is located on the left-hand side of the engine compartment where it is mounted behind the battery **(see illustration)**.

2 Disconnect the battery negative lead, then disconnect the wiring from the base of the unit, noting the connector locations.

3 Unscrew the securing nut, and withdraw the unit from the vehicle.

Refitting

4 Refitting is a reversal of removal, ensuring the wiring connectors are correctly connected.

4 No-load switch - testing, adjustment, removal and refitting

Testing and adjustment

1 Ensure the idle speed and anti-stall settings are correctly adjusted (see Chapter 4C).

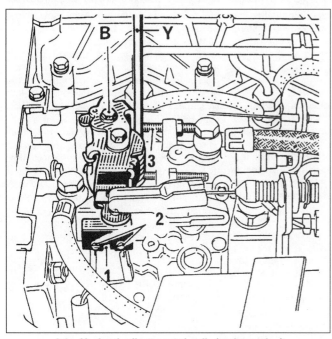

4.4a No-load adjustment details (early version)

1 No-load switch
2 No-load switch securing screws
3 Anti-stall adjustment screw
B Accelerator lever
Y Feeler blades

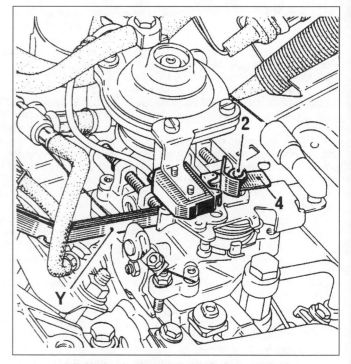

4.4b No-load adjustment details (later version)

2 Retaining nut   *4 Operating cam*   *Y Feeler blades*

2 To test and adjust the switch, first disconnect the switch wiring connector.

3 Connect a continuity tester or an ohmmeter across the wiring connector terminals.

4 Insert feeler blades of different thicknesses between the injection pump accelerator lever and the anti-stall adjustment screw, and note the readings on the continuity tester or ohmmeter, as applicable **(see illustrations)**. The readings obtained should be as follows:

Spacer thickness	Test reading
Up to 10.2 mm	Continuity/zero resistance
More than 11.5 mm	No continuity/infinite resistance

5 To adjust the switch, either slacken the switch retaining screws and repositioning the switch, or slacken the retaining nut and repositioning the operating cam (as applicable).

6 If the switch is permanently open or closed, renew it.

Removal

7 Disconnect the switch wiring connector, then remove the two securing screws, and withdraw the switch from its bracket on the injection pump.

Refitting

8 Refitting is a reversal of removal, but where applicable, before tightening the screws adjust the switch as described previously.

5 Post-heating cut-off switch - testing, removal and refitting

Testing

1 Remove the switch as described in the following sub-section.

2 Connect a continuity tester or an ohmmeter across the switch terminals. There should be continuity/zero resistance between the terminals.

3 Now suspend the switch in a container of water (using wire or string), along with a thermometer.

4 Gently heat the water, keeping note of the rise in temperature.

5 Periodically remove the switch from the water, ensure that the terminals are dry, and again check for continuity/resistance. The results obtained should be as shown in the following table.

Water temp. below 55°C ± 2°C	Continuity/zero resistance
Water temp. above 65°C ± 2°C	No continuity/infinite resistance

6 If the results obtained are not as specified, the switch is proved faulty and should be renewed.

Removal

7 The switch is screwed into the coolant hose at the left-hand rear corner of the engine.

8 Drain the cooling system as described in Chapter 1. Alternatively have the new switch or a suitable bung to hand.

9 Disconnect the switch wiring plug, then unscrew and remove the switch. Recover the sealing ring, where applicable.

Refitting

10 Refitting is a reversal of removal, using a new sealing ring, where applicable.

11 On completion, check the coolant level, and top-up or refill and bleed the cooling system, as necessary, as described in Chapter 1.

5C

Chapter 6
Clutch

Contents

Degrees of difficulty

Easy, suitable for novice with little experience		**Fairly easy,** suitable for beginner with some experience		**Fairly difficult,** suitable for competent DIY mechanic		**Difficult,** suitable for experienced DIY mechanic		**Very difficult,** suitable for expert DIY or professional	

Specifications

General

Type	Single dry plate with diaphragm spring, cable-operated
Adjustment:	
Pre-1990 models	Self-adjusting
1990 models onward	Manual adjustment
Clutch cable free play (1990 models onward)	3.0 to 4.0 mm

Friction plate

Diameter	215.0 mm

Torque wrench settings

	Nm
Clutch cover bolts	25

1 General information

The clutch unit consists of a friction plate, a cover assembly which contains a pressure plate and diaphragm spring, a release bearing and the release mechanism; all of these components are contained within the bellhousing, sandwiched between the engine and the transmission **(see illustration)**. The release mechanism is mechanical, being operated by a cable.

The friction plate is fitted between the engine flywheel and the clutch pressure plate, and is allowed to slide on the transmission primary shaft splines.

The cover assembly is doweled and bolted to the engine flywheel. When the engine is running, drive is transmitted from the crankshaft, via the flywheel, to the friction plate (these components being clamped securely together by the pressure plate) and from the friction plate to the transmission primary shaft.

When the clutch pedal is depressed, the pedal movement is transmitted to the release fork via the clutch cable. The fork moves the release bearing to press against the fingers at the centre of the pressure plate diaphragm spring. Spring pressure on the pressure plate is relieved, and the flywheel and pressure plate spin without moving the friction plate. As the pedal is released, spring pressure is restored and the drive is gradually taken up.

On early models, the clutch cable is automatically adjusted by a mechanism on the pedal. On later models, the cable must be adjusted manually at periodic intervals.

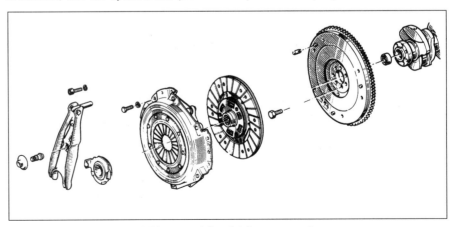

1.1 Layout of the clutch components

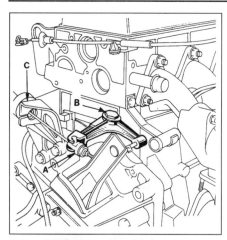

**2.2 Clutch cable attachments
at the transmission**

A *Inner cable attachment at bellcrank*
B *Bellcrank pivot bolt*
C *Outer cable attachment at transmission
bracket*

2 Clutch cable - removal and refitting

Models with self-adjusting clutch cable

Removal

1 Disconnect the battery negative lead.
2 Detach the inner cable end from the bellcrank and disengage the outer cable from the bracket on the transmission bellhousing **(see illustration)**.

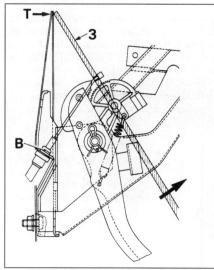

**2.10 Using the home-made lever to refit
the self-adjusting clutch cable**

B *Outer cable pad*
T *Lever fulcrum*
3 *Home-made lever*

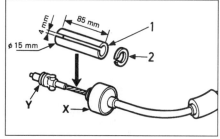

**2.6a Home-made spacer sleeve for
self-adjusting clutch cable refitting**

1 *Spacer sleeve*
2 *Split washer*
X *Outer cable pad*
Y *Inner cable end
fitting*

3 From inside the vehicle, undo the four screws and remove the parcel shelf below the steering column.
4 Undo the two screws at the top and two screws at the side securing the trim panel under the steering column. Remove the bonnet release handle assembly (later models) and lift out the trim panel.
5 Depress the clutch pedal, hold the inner cable, then release the pedal. Extract the inner cable end fitting from the pedal adjuster quadrant. Release the outer cable end fitting from the bulkhead by pushing it out with a screwdriver. Withdraw the cable through the bulkhead and remove it from the engine side.

Refitting

6 Before refitting, it will be necessary to make up two special tools. If the special tools are not used, it will be impossible to correctly locate the outer cable end fitting in the bulkhead due to the limited space available. The tools consist of a metal spacer sleeve which fits over the end of the cable at the transmission end, a split washer, and a length of steel bar to act as a lever to pull the cable into position. The tools should be made up to the dimensions shown **(see illustrations)**.
7 Place the spacer sleeve over the inner cable between the inner cable end fitting and the outer cable pad. Insert the split washer between the spacer sleeve and the outer cable pad to protect the pad.

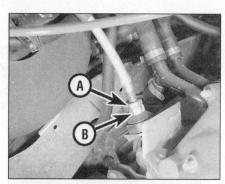

**2.16 Manually-adjusted clutch cable
locknut (A) and adjusting nut (B)**

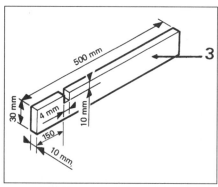

**2.6b Home-made lever (3) for
self-adjusting clutch cable refitting**

8 Feed the cable through the hole in the bulkhead from the engine compartment side.
9 From inside the vehicle, fit the inner cable end fitting into the slot in the home-made lever and rest the top of the lever against the bulkhead.
10 Guide the outer cable end fitting into the hole in the bulkhead then pull on the lever to draw the end fitting fully into place. Use a mirror and light to check that the end fitting is correctly in position **(see illustration)**.
11 Remove the lever, spacer and split washer.
12 Connect the cable end fitting to the self-adjusting quadrant at the pedal.
13 Working in the engine compartment, connect the inner cable end to the release fork and engage the outer cable with the bracket on the bellhousing. Check that the clutch operation is satisfactory.
14 Refit the trim panels below the steering column using a reversal of removal.

Models with manually-adjusted clutch cable

Removal

15 Disconnect the battery negative lead.
16 From within the engine compartment, slacken the locknut and adjusting nut on the outer cable as much as possible **(see illustration)**. Detach the cable end from the release fork and disengage the outer cable from the bracket on the transmission bellhousing.
17 From inside the vehicle, undo the five screws securing the steering column lower shroud. Where fitted, slacken the radio remote control unit mounting bolt on the steering column, then withdraw the shroud. Disconnect the switch wiring as the shroud is removed.
18 Unhook the inner cable from the clutch pedal and pull the cable assembly into the engine compartment. As the cable is released from the bulkhead, note the arrangement of the rubber gaiter and the washer as an aid to refitting.

Refitting

19 Refitting is a reversal of removal. Fit the large end of the rubber gaiter through the

bulkhead, then fit the washer over the gaiter on the engine compartment side of the bulkhead.

20 With the cable refitted, check the adjustment as follows.

21 Have an assistant hold the clutch pedal fully upwards.

22 From within the engine compartment, pull the outer cable away from the bracket on the transmission until resistance is felt. Adjust the cable, by means of the adjusting nut, until there is a clearance of 3.0 to 4.0 mm between the transmission bracket and the outer cable pad. Tighten the locknut against the adjusting nut when the correct clearance is obtained.

3 Clutch unit - removal, inspection and refitting

 Warning: Dust created by clutch wear and deposited on the clutch components may contain asbestos which is a health hazard. DO NOT blow it out with compressed air or inhale any of it. DO NOT use petrol or petroleum-based solvents to clean off the dust. Brake system cleaner or methylated spirit should be used to flush the dust into a suitable receptacle. After the clutch components are wiped clean with rags, dispose of the contaminated rags and cleaner in a sealed, marked container.

Removal

1 Access to the clutch may be gained in one of two ways. Either the engine, or engine/transmission, can be removed, as described in Chapter 2B, and the transmission separated from the engine, or the engine may be left in the vehicle and the transmission removed independently as described in Chapter 7.

2 Having separated the transmission from the engine, undo and remove the clutch cover bolts, working in a diagonal sequence and slackening the bolts only a few turns at a time.

3 Ease the clutch cover off its locating dowels and be prepared to catch the friction plate which will drop out as the cover is removed. Note which way round the plate is fitted.

4 It is important that no oil or grease is allowed to come into contact with the friction material or the pressure plate and flywheel faces during inspection and refitting.

Inspection

5 With the clutch assembly removed, clean off all traces of asbestos dust using a dry cloth. This is best done outside or in a well ventilated area; asbestos dust is harmful, and must not be inhaled

6 Examine the linings of the friction plate for wear and loose rivets, and the rim for distortion, cracks, broken torsion springs and worn splines. The surface of the friction linings

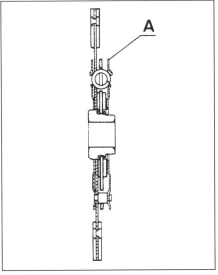

3.10 Fit the clutch plate with the larger offset (A) facing away from the flywheel

may be highly glazed, but, as long as the friction material pattern can be clearly seen, this is satisfactory. If there is any sign of oil contamination, indicated by a continuous or patchy, shiny black discolouration, the plate must be renewed and the source of the contamination traced and rectified. This will be either a leaking crankshaft oil seal or transmission primary shaft oil seal - or both. The friction plate must also be renewed if the lining thickness has worn down to, or just above, the level of the rivet heads.

7 Check the machined faces of the flywheel and pressure plate. If either is grooved, or heavily scored, renewal is necessary. The pressure plate must also be renewed if any cracks are apparent, or if the diaphragm spring is damaged or its pressure suspect.

8 With the transmission removed, check the condition of the release bearing, as described in Section 4.

Refitting

9 It is advisable to refit the clutch assembly with clean hands and to wipe down the pressure plate and flywheel faces with a clean dry rag before assembly begins.

10 Place the friction plate against the flywheel with the larger offset of the plate facing away from the flywheel **(see illustration)**.

11 Place the clutch cover over the dowels, refit the bolts and tighten them finger tight so that the friction plate is gripped, but can still be moved.

12 The plate must now be centralised so that, when the engine and transmission are mated, the splines of the transmission primary shaft will pass through the splines in the centre of the friction plate hub.

13 Centralisation can be carried out quite easily by inserting a round bar or long screwdriver through the hole in the centre of the friction plate so that the end of the bar rests in the hole in the end of the crankshaft.

3.17 Tighten the cover bolts in a diagonal sequence to the specified torque

14 Using this as a fulcrum, moving the bar sideways or up and down will move the clutch friction plate in whichever direction is necessary to achieve centralisation.

15 Centralisation is easily judged by removing the bar and viewing the friction plate hub in relation to the hole in the centre of the crankshaft. When the hole appears exactly in the centre of the friction plate hub, all is correct.

16 An alternative and more accurate method of centralisation is to use a commercially available clutch aligning tool obtainable from most accessory shops.

17 Once the clutch is centralised, progressively tighten the cover bolts in a diagonal sequence to the torque setting given in the *Specifications* **(see illustration)**.

18 Lightly smear the splines of the transmission primary shaft and the release bearing-to-diaphragm spring contact area with molybdenum disulphide grease.

19 The engine or transmission can now be refitted by referring to the appropriate Chapters of this manual.

4 Clutch release bearing - removal, inspection and refitting

Removal

1 To gain access to the release bearing it is necessary to separate the engine and transmission either by removing the engine or transmission individually, or by removing both units as an assembly and separating them after removal. Depending on the method chosen, the appropriate procedures will be found in Chapter 2B or Chapter 7 (as applicable).

2 With the transmission removed from the engine, tilt the release fork and slide the bearing assembly off the transmission primary shaft guide tube.

Inspection

3 Check the bearing for smoothness of operation and renew it if there is any roughness or harshness as the bearing is spun. It is a good idea to renew the bearing as a matter of course during clutch overhaul, regardless of its apparent condition.

6

Refitting

4 Refitting the release bearing is a reversal of removal, but lubricate the release fork pivot ball stud or fork arms, and the release bearing-to-diaphragm spring contact areas sparingly with molybdenum disulphide grease.
5 Ensure the flange on the release bearing carrier locates behind the release fork arm.

5 Clutch release fork - removal and refitting

Removal

1 Remove the clutch release bearing as described in Section 4.

2 On early models the fork is removed by simply disengaging the rubber cover and then pulling the fork upwards to release it from its ball pivot stud.
3 On later models the release fork is removed from the pivot shaft by driving out the retaining roll pins. As these roll pins are not very accessible, it is recommended that Renault special tools B. Vi. 606 and Car. 41 are used for this operation.

Refitting

4 On early models, refit the fork using a reversal of removal. Lubricate the ball pivot stud with molybdenum disulphide grease and ensure that the release fork spring retainer locates behind the flat shoulder of the ball pivot stud **(see illustration)**.

5 On later models, lubricate the fork pivot shaft with a liberal amount of grease and fit it with its seal rubber. Locate the fork with the plastic spacers and ensure that it is correctly orientated before fitting the new roll pins. Double roll pins are used and they must be fitted with their slots at right angles to the fork pivot shaft, and opposite one another **(see illustration)**.
6 On all models, refit the release bearing on completion.

6 Clutch pedal - removal and refitting

Removal

1 The clutch and brake pedals share a common mounting and pivot shaft. Remove the clutch pedal as follows.
2 Disconnect the clutch cable from the pedal as described in Section 2. Note that there is no need to remove the cable from the bulkhead.
3 Withdraw the pedal shaft retaining clip on the clutch pedal end of the shaft, then carefully withdraw the shaft just enough to allow the clutch pedal to be removed. If the shaft is withdrawn too far, the brake pedal will become detached as well, so take care.

Refitting

4 Refitting is a reversal of removal. Lubricate the pedal shaft and check for satisfactory operation of the clutch before refitting the trim panels.

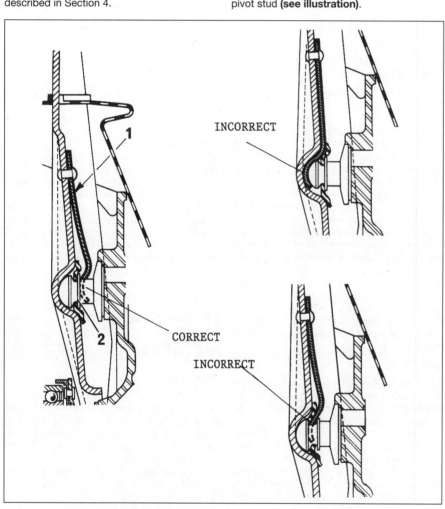

INCORRECT

CORRECT

INCORRECT

5.4 Place the clutch release fork sprint (1) behind the ball pivot stud (2)

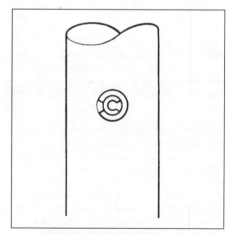

5.5 Release fork retaining roll pin orientation

Chapter 7
Transmission

Contents

Degrees of difficulty

| **Easy,** suitable for novice with little experience | | **Fairly easy,** suitable for beginner with some experience | | **Fairly difficult,** suitable for competent DIY mechanic | | **Difficult,** suitable for experienced DIY mechanic | | **Very difficult,** suitable for expert DIY or professional | |

Specifications

General

Type . . . . Five forward speeds (all synchromesh) and reverse.

Designation NG3

Gear ratios (typical)

1st 4.09:1

2nd 2.17:1

3rd 1.40:1

4th 0.97:1

5th 0.78:1

Reverse 3.54:1

Final drive ratio . . . . 3.22:1, 3.44:1, 3.55:1 or 3.77:1 according to model and year

---

1 General information

The transmission is located behind the engine in a similar manner to rear-wheel-drive vehicles but power is transmitted to the front roadwheels through driveshafts. The driveshafts are splined to the side gears of the differential/final drive which is integrated into the transmission casing.

Five forward gears are provided with one reverse gear. Baulk ring synchromesh gear engagement is used on all the forward gears.

Gearshift is by means of a floor mounted lever, connected by a remote control linkage to the transmission selector mechanism.

The transmission casing is of four section type; the clutch bellhousing, the rear cover (which houses the selector finger and 5th gear), and the two main casing sections which are split longitudinally.

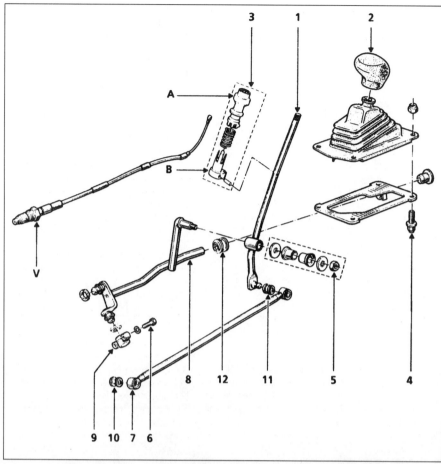

2.3 Reverse gear interlock cable union nut (arrowed)

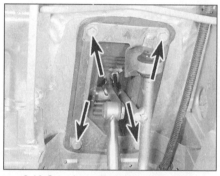

2.10 Gear lever base retaining bolts (arrowed)

2.1 Exploded view of the later type gearchange linkage components

1 Gear lever	7 Link rod	12 Control rod pivot
2 Gear lever knob	8 Control rod	mounting
3 Interlock assembly	9 Balljoint coupling	A Interlock lifting ring
4 Mounting bolt	10 Bush	B Locking cable stop
5 Control rod pivot nut	11 Bush	V Interlock cable union nut
6 Balljoint coupling bolts		

2 Gearchange linkage - removal and refitting

Removal

1 The system consists of two remote control rods and, on later models, a cable to release a locking finger when the ring on the gear lever is lifted during selection of reverse gear. This is part of an interlock device to prevent engagement of reverse gear when shifting from 3rd to 2nd **(see illustration).**

2 Chock the rear wheels then jack up the front of the vehicle and support it on axle stands (see *"Jacking and vehicle support"*).

3 On later models, unscrew the reverse gear interlock cable union nut from the rear of the transmission **(see illustration).**

4 Prise free the link rod balljoint at the transmission end using suitable pliers used as a lever.

5 On early models, unscrew the nut securing the control rod to the forked lever on the transmission. Slide the rod rearwards to disengage the lower pivot. On later models, undo the retaining bolts and disconnect the control rod framed balljoint coupling at the transmission end.

6 Release the link rod ball socket at the gear lever end and remove the link rod.

7 Working inside the car, lift up the gear lever gaiter or, where fitted, remove the centre console (Chapter 11).

8 The locking cable can be released after unclipping its stop and removing the cable sleeve from the interlock assembly on the gear lever.

9 Remove the gear lever knob from the lever then, on later models, extract the retaining pin and withdraw the interlock assembly from the gear lever.

10 Undo the four bolts (and nuts on later models) and remove the lever and base from underneath the vehicle **(see illustration).**

11 Unscrew the pivot nut and withdraw the control rod from the gear lever.

12 With the assembly removed, examine all the rubber bushes and renew as necessary.

Refitting

13 Refitting is a reversal of removal, but smear the threads of the locking cable union with gasket cement before screwing it into the transmission casing. The balljoint connections can be reassembled by pressing them together using suitable grips.

3 Reversing light switch - removal and refitting

Removal

1 Chock the rear wheels then jack up the front of the vehicle and support it on axle stands (see *"Jacking and vehicle support"*).

2 Drain the transmission oil as described in Chapter 1.

3 Disconnect the wiring from the switch which is located on the right-hand side of the transmission casing

4 Unscrew the switch from the transmission and remove the washer.

Refitting

5 Clean the switch location in the transmission and the switch threads.

6 Insert the switch together with a new washer, and tighten it securely.

7 Reconnect the wiring.

8 Refill the transmission with the correct quantity and grade of oil, with reference to Chapter 1.

9 Lower the vehicle to the ground.

4 Transmission oil seals - general information

Due to the design and construction of the NG3 transmission, renewal of the differential side gear oil seals and input shaft oil seal require considerable transmission dismantling. Renewal of the side gear oil seals also necessitates readjustment of the differential bearing preload for which special gauges and tooling are required.

In the event of leakage from the transmission oil seals, it is recommended that the work be carried out by a Renault dealer.

5 Transmission - removal and refitting

Removal

1 The transmission may be removed on its own as described in this Section, or together with the engine as described in Chapter 2C.

2 Remove the transmission undertray which is secured by screws and locating pegs.

3 Disconnect the battery negative lead.

4 On early models with a self-adjusting clutch cable, detach the inner cable end from the release fork and disengage the outer cable from the support bracket on the transmission bellhousing. Undo the pivot bolt and remove the cable bellcrank from the top of the bellhousing. Also undo the two bolts and remove the outer cable support bracket.

5 On later models with a manually adjusted clutch cable, slacken the locknut and adjusting nut on the outer cable as much as possible. Detach the cable end from the release fork and disengage the outer cable from the bracket on the transmission bellhousing.

6 Chock the rear wheels then jack up the front of the vehicle and support it on axle stands (see *"Jacking and vehicle support"*). Remove both front roadwheels.

7 Disconnect the exhaust downpipe at the manifold and at the intermediate section flange joint. Undo the mounting and remove the downpipe.

8 Undo the two bolts each side securing the brake calipers to the hub carriers. Slide the calipers, complete with pads, off the discs and tie them up using string or wire from a suitable place under the wheel arch.

9 Using a parallel pin punch of suitable diameter, knock out the driveshaft roll pins at the transmission end of each driveshaft CV joint. Note that there are two roll pins fitted each side, one inside the other. Obtain new roll pins for reassembly.

10 Refer to Chapter 10 and detach the steering arm outer balljoints from the hub carriers. Also detach the upper suspension arm from each hub carrier by separating the upper balljoint.

11 Pivot the hub carriers outwards at the top and simultaneously withdraw the driveshafts from the transmission. On later models, collect the insulating rubber washer from the differential side gear shafts.

12 Disconnect the speedometer cable from the transmission by gripping the retaining pin with a pair of pliers and pulling it outwards to release the cable **(see illustration)**.

13 Disconnect the reversing light leads at the in-line connector.

14 Disconnect the gearchange linkage at the transmission end as described in Section 2.

15 On petrol engine models, undo the two bolts securing the engine angular position/speed sensor to the top of the bellhousing. Note that the two bolts are of special shouldered type and must not be replaced by ordinary bolts. Move the sensor to one side taking care to protect its end.

16 Remove the flywheel cover plate from the bellhousing.

17 Undo the bolts securing the starter motor to the bellhousing.

18 Support the engine using a jack or hoist and place a second jack, preferably of trolley type, under the transmission.

19 Undo the bolts which connect the transmission to the engine, noting the location of the earth strap **(see illustration)**.

20 Disconnect the transmission flexible mountings and brackets **(see illustration)**.

21 Withdraw the transmission rearwards off the locating dowels and remove it from under the vehicle.

Refitting

22 Refitting is a reversal of removal, but observe the following points:

a) On later models, the driveshaft inner joints are fitted with an insulating rubber washer. Ensure that the washer is in position when assembling the joint to the differential stub shaft.

b) Smear the driveshaft inner joint splines with molybdenum disulphide grease, then position the splines so that the roll pin holes will align when the joint is pushed fully home.

c) Position the two new roll pins so that their slots are 90° apart and seal their ends with suitable hard setting sealant after installation.

d) Clean the threads of the brake caliper mounting bolts and apply thread locking compound to them before refitting.

e) Tighten all nuts and bolts to the specified torque where given (see Chapters 9 and 10).

f) On later models, adjust the clutch cable as described in Chapter 6.

g) Check and if necessary top-up the transmission oil as described in Chapter 1.

6 Transmission overhaul - general information

Overhauling a manual transmission is a difficult job for the do-it-yourselfer. It involves the dismantling and reassembly of many small parts. Numerous clearances must be precisely measured and, if necessary, changed with selected spacers and circlips. As a result, if transmission problems arise, while the unit can be removed and refitted by a competent do-it-yourselfer, overhaul should be left to a transmission specialist. Rebuilt

7

5.12 Speedometer cable retaining pin (arrowed)

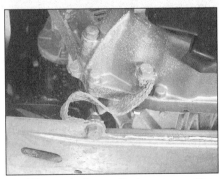

5.19 Transmission earth strap connection

5.20 Transmission right-hand mounting

transmissions may be available - check with your dealer parts department, motor factors, or transmission specialists. At any rate, the time and money involved in an overhaul is almost sure to exceed the cost of a rebuilt unit.

Nevertheless, it's not impossible for an inexperienced mechanic to rebuild a transmission, providing the special tools are available, and the job is done in a deliberate step-by-step manner so nothing is overlooked.

The tools necessary for an overhaul include: internal and external circlip pliers, a bearing puller, a slide hammer, a set of pin punches, a dial test indicator, and possibly a hydraulic press. In addition, a large, sturdy workbench and a vice or transmission stand will be required.

During dismantling of the transmission, make careful notes of how each part comes off, where it fits in relation to other parts, and what holds it in place.

Before taking the transmission apart for repair, it will help if you have some idea what area of the transmission is malfunctioning. Certain problems can be closely tied to specific areas in the transmission, which can make component examination and replacement easier. Refer to the *"Fault finding"* section at the rear of this manual for information regarding possible sources of trouble.

Chapter 8
Driveshafts

Contents

Degrees of difficulty

Easy, suitable for novice with little experience	**Fairly easy,** suitable for beginner with some experience	**Fairly difficult,** suitable for competent DIY mechanic	**Difficult,** suitable for experienced DIY mechanic	**Very difficult,** suitable for expert DIY or professional 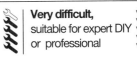

Specifications

General

Driveshaft type	Equal length solid steel shafts, splined to inner and outer constant velocity joints
Inner constant velocity joint	GI82 or RC490 tripod type
Outer constant velocity joint	Lobro 6-ball, ball-and-cage type

Torque wrench settings
	Nm
Driveshaft nut*	250
Wheel bolts	90

*Use a new nut

1 General information

Drive is transmitted from the differential to the front wheels by means of two, equal-length driveshafts incorporating constant velocity (CV) joints at their inner and outer ends.

A ball-and-cage type CV joint is fitted to the outer end of each driveshaft. The joint has an outer member, which is splined at its outer end to accept the wheel hub and is threaded so that it can be fastened to the hub by a large nut. The joint contains six balls within a cage, which engage with the inner member. The complete assembly is protected by a flexible gaiter secured to the driveshaft and joint outer member.

At the inner end, the driveshaft is splined to engage with a tripod type CV joint, containing needle roller bearings and cups. The tripod joint is free to slide within the yoke of the joint outer member, which is splined and retained by a double roll pin to the differential sun wheel stub shaft. As on the outer joints, a flexible gaiter secured to the driveshaft and outer member protects the complete assembly.

Due to the design and construction of the driveshaft components, repair operations are limited. Renewal of the gaiters at both ends of the driveshaft can be carried out on all models, together with renewal of the outer CV joints. Wear or damage to the inner CV joints or the driveshafts themselves, can only be rectified by fitting complete new driveshaft assemblies.

2 Driveshafts - removal and refitting

Removal

1 Chock the rear wheels then jack up the front of the vehicle and support it on axle stands (see *"Jacking and vehicle support"*). Remove the appropriate front roadwheel.
2 Refit at least two roadwheel bolts to the front hub flange, and tighten them securely. Have an assistant firmly depress the brake pedal to prevent the front hub from rotating. Using a socket and a long extension bar, slacken and remove the driveshaft retaining nut and washer. This nut is extremely tight. Alternatively, a tool can be fabricated from two lengths of steel strip (one long, one short)

and a nut an bolt; the nut and bolt form the pivot of a forked tool. Bolt the tool to the hub flange using two wheel bolts, and hold the tool to prevent the hub from rotating as the driveshaft retaining nut is undone **(see Tool Tip)**. Discard the driveshaft nut; a new one should be used on refitting.
3 Undo the two bolts securing the brake caliper to the hub carrier. Slide the caliper, complete with pads, off the disc and tie it up using string or wire from a suitable place under the wheel arch.

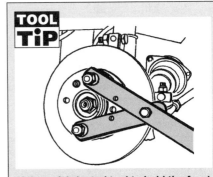

Using a fabricated tool to hold the front hub stationary whilst the driveshaft nut is slackened

8

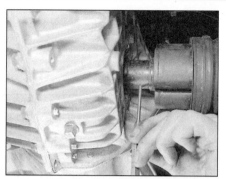

2.4 Removing the driveshaft roll pins at the transmission end

2.6 Withdrawing the driveshaft inner joint from the transmission

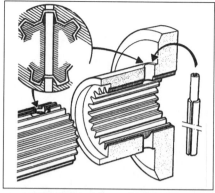

2.8 Driveshaft inner joint roll pin arrangement

4 Use a parallel pin punch of suitable diameter to knock out the driveshaft roll pins at the transmission end **(see illustration)**. Note that there are two roll pins fitted, one inside the other. Obtain new roll pins for reassembly.

5 Refer to Chapter 10 and detach the steering arm outer balljoint from the hub carrier. Also detach the upper suspension arm from the hub carrier by separating the upper balljoint.

6 Pivot the hub carrier outwards at the top and simultaneously withdraw the driveshaft from the transmission **(see illustration)**.

7 Withdraw the outer end of the driveshaft from the hub flange and remove the assembly from the vehicle. If the shaft is a tight fit in the hub, tap it out using a plastic mallet or use a suitable puller.

Refitting

8 Refitting is a reversal of removal, but observe the following points.

a) *New driveshafts are supplied with cardboard protectors over the gaiters. These protectors should be left in position until the driveshaft is correctly installed then removed by hand. Do not use sharp-ended tools to remove the protectors, as there is a risk of damaging the gaiter.*

b) *On later models, the driveshaft inner joint is fitted with an insulating rubber washer. Ensure that the washer is in position when assembling the joint to the differential stub shaft.*

c) *Smear the inner joint splines with molybdenum disulphide grease, then position the splines so that the roll pin holes will align when the joint is pushed fully home.*

d) *Position the two new roll pins so that their slots are 90° apart and seal their ends with suitable hard setting sealant after installation (see illustration).*

e) *Ensure that the driveshaft outer joint and hub flange splines are clean and dry, then apply a coat of locking fluid to the joint splines.*

f) *Clean the threads of the brake caliper mounting bolts and apply thread locking compound to them before refitting.*

g) *Tighten all nuts and bolts to the specified torque (see also Chapters 9 and 10).*

h) *Apply the footbrake two or three times to position the brake pads against the disc.*

3 Outer constant velocity joint gaiter - renewal

1 Remove the driveshaft as described in Section 2.

2 Release the gaiter outer retaining spring and inner collar, then slide the gaiter down the shaft to expose the outer constant velocity joint.

3 Scoop out as much grease as possible from the joint then, using circlip pliers, expand the joint internal circlip **(see illustration)**. At the same time, tap the exposed face of the ball hub with a mallet to separate the joint from the driveshaft. Slide off the gaiter and rubber collar.

4 With the constant velocity joint removed from the driveshaft, clean the joint using paraffin, or a suitable solvent, and dry it thoroughly. Carry out a visual inspection of the joint **(see illustration)**.

5 Move the inner splined driving member from side to side, to expose each ball in turn at the top of its track. Examine the balls for cracks, flat spots or signs of surface pitting.

6 Inspect the ball tracks on the inner and outer members. If the tracks have widened, the balls will no longer be a tight fit. At the same time, check the ball cage windows for wear or cracking between the windows. Obtain a new outer joint if any wear is apparent.

7 If the joint is in satisfactory condition, obtain a repair kit from your Renault dealer consisting of a new gaiter, rubber collar, retaining spring, and the correct type and quantity of grease.

8 Tape over the splines on the end of the driveshaft, then slide the rubber collar and gaiter onto the shaft. Locate the inner end of the gaiter on the driveshaft, and secure it in position with the rubber collar.

9 Remove the tape, then slide the constant velocity joint coupling onto the driveshaft until the internal circlip locates in the driveshaft groove.

10 Check that the circlip holds the joint securely on the driveshaft, then pack the joint with the grease supplied. Work the grease well into the ball tracks, and fill the gaiter with any excess.

11 Locate the outer lip of the gaiter in the groove on the joint outer member. With the coupling aligned with the driveshaft, lift the lip of the gaiter to equalise the air pressure. Secure the gaiter in position with the large retaining spring, using two lengths of hollow

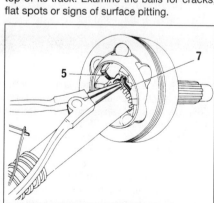

3.3 Expand the circlip (7) and tap the ball hub (5) to remove the driveshaft joint

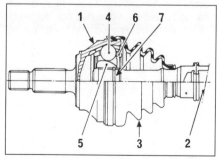

3.4 Sectional view of the outer constant velocity joint

1 Ball hub	4 Balls	6 Ball cage
2 Driveshaft	5 Driving	7 Circlip
3 Gaiter	member	

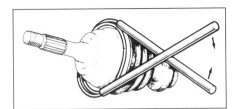

3.11 Using hollow metal tubes to fit the gaiter spring clip

metal tubing to ease the spring into position **(see illustration)**.

12 Check that the constant velocity joint moves freely in all directions, then refit the driveshaft to the vehicle as described in Section 2.

4 Inner constant velocity joint gaiter - renewal

1 Remove the driveshaft as described in Section 2.

2 On these models, two different types of inner constant velocity joint are used - type GI82 and type RC490. The joints can be identified by the shape of their outer members. The GI82 joint has a smooth, circular outer member; the RC490 joint has a recessed outer member which appears clover-shaped when viewed end-on. Identify the type of joint fitted, then proceed as described under the relevant sub-heading.

GI82-type joint

3 Release the large retaining clip and the inner retaining collar, then slide the gaiter down the shaft to expose the joint **(see illustration)**.

4 Using pliers, carefully bend up the anti-separation plate tangs at their corners **(see illustration)**. Slide the outer member off the tripod joint. Be prepared to hold the rollers in place, otherwise they may fall off the tripod ends as the outer member is withdrawn. If necessary, secure the rollers in place using

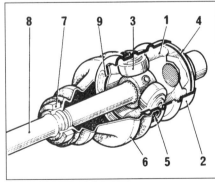

4.3 Sectional view of the GI 82 inner constant velocity joint

1 Outer member	5 Retaining clip
2 Casing	6 Gaiter
3 Tripod joint	7 Retaining ring
4 Seal	8 Driveshaft

tape after removal of the outer member. The rollers are matched to the tripod joint stems, and it is important that they are not interchanged.

5 Using circlip pliers, extract the circlip securing the tripod joint to the driveshaft **(see illustration)**. Note that on some models, the joint may be staked in position; if so, relieve the staking using a file. Mark the position of the tripod in relation to the driveshaft, using a dab of paint or a punch.

6 The tripod joint can now be removed **(see illustration)**. If it is tight, draw the joint off the driveshaft end using a puller. Ensure that the legs of the puller are located behind the joint inner member and do not contact the joint rollers. Alternatively, support the inner member of the tripod joint, and press the shaft out using a hydraulic press, again ensuring that no load is applied to the joint rollers.

7 With the tripod joint removed, slide the gaiter and inner retaining collar off the end of the driveshaft.

8 Wipe clean the joint components, taking care not to remove the alignment marks made on dismantling. **Do not** use paraffin or other solvents to clean this type of joint.

9 Examine the tripod joint, rollers and outer member for any signs of scoring or wear. Check that the rollers move smoothly on the tripod stems. If wear is evident, it will be necessary to obtain a complete new driveshaft assembly as the inner tripod joint is not available as a separate item. If the inner joint is in a satisfactory condition, obtain a

4.4 Bend up the anti-separation plate tabs with pliers

4.6 Remove the tripod joint from the driveshaft

new gaiter, retaining spring/collar and a quantity of the special lubricating grease. These parts are available in the form of a repair kit from your Renault dealer.

10 Tape over the splines on the end of the driveshaft, then carefully slide the inner retaining collar and gaiter onto the shaft.

11 Remove the tape, then, aligning the marks made on dismantling, engage the tripod joint with the driveshaft splines. Use a hammer and soft metal drift to tap the joint onto the shaft, taking great care not to damage the driveshaft splines or joint rollers. Alternatively, support the driveshaft, and press the joint into position using a hydraulic press and suitable tubular spacer which bears only on the joint inner member.

12 Secure the tripod joint in position with the circlip, ensuring that it is correctly located in the driveshaft groove. Where no circlip is fitted, secure the joint in position by staking the end of the driveshaft in three places, at intervals of 120°, using a hammer and punch.

13 Evenly distribute the grease contained in the repair kit around the tripod joint and inside the outer member. Pack the gaiter with the remainder of the grease.

14 Slide the outer member into position over the tripod joint.

15 Using a piece of 2.5 mm thick steel or similar material, make up a support plate to the dimensions shown **(see illustration)**.

16 Position the support plate under each anti-separation plate tang in the outer member in turn, and tap the tang down onto the support

4.5 Extract the tripod retaining circlip

8

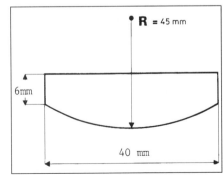

4.15 Support plate used to retain shape of anti-separation plate tangs

R = 45 mm
6mm
40 mm

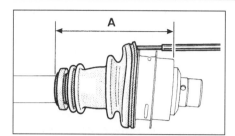

4.19 Expel any trapped air by lifting the gaiter with a rod, then check distance A

A = 161 to 163 mm

plate. Remove the plate when all the tangs have been returned to their original shape.

17 Slide the gaiter up the driveshaft. Locate the gaiter in the grooves on the driveshaft and outer member.

18 Slide the inner retaining collar into place over the inner end of the gaiter.

19 Using a blunt rod, carefully lift the outer lip of the gaiter to equalise the air pressure. With the rod in position, compress the joint until the dimension from the inner end of the gaiter to the flat end face of the outer member is as shown **(see illustration)**. Hold the outer member in this position and withdraw the rod.

20 Fit the retaining clip to the outer end of the gaiter. Remove any slack in the clip by carefully compressing the raised section. In the absence of the special tool, a pair of pincers may be used.

21 Check that the constant velocity joint moves freely in all directions, then refit the driveshaft as described in Section 2.

RC490-type joint

Note: *Three versions of this type of joint may be encountered. On the first version the gaiter is secured to the joint outer member by a retaining clip which is clearly visible. On the second and third versions, a large metal cover or heat shield is fitted over the gaiter and joint outer member, in place of the retaining clip. If working on the first version, ignore the references to the metal joint cover in the following procedure.*

22 Using a pair of grips, bend up the metal joint cover at the points where it has been staked into the outer member recesses **(see illustration)**.

23 Using a pair of snips, cut the gaiter inner retaining clip, or slide off the retaining collar as applicable. Cut the gaiter outer retaining clip if working on the first version.

24 Using a soft metal drift, tap the metal joint cover off the outer member **(see illustration)**. Slide the outer member off the end of the tripod joint. Be prepared to hold the rollers in place, otherwise they may fall off the tripod ends as the outer member is withdrawn. If necessary, secure the rollers in place using tape after removal of the outer member. The rollers are matched to the tripod joint stems, and it is important that they are not interchanged.

25 Remove the tripod joint and gaiter assembly, and examine the joint components for wear, using the information given in paragraphs 6 to 9 of this Section. Make alignment marks between the spider and the shaft for use when refitting. Obtain a repair kit consisting of a gaiter, retaining clip, metal insert and joint cover (where applicable), and the correct type and amount of grease.

26 Fit the metal insert into the inside of the gaiter, then locate the gaiter assembly inside the metal joint cover.

27 Tape over the driveshaft splines, and slide the gaiter and joint cover assembly onto the driveshaft.

28 Refit the tripod joint as described in paragraphs 11 and 12.

29 Evenly distribute the grease contained in the repair kit around the tripod joint and inside the outer member. Pack the gaiter with the remainder of the grease.

30 Slide the outer member into position over the tripod joint.

31 Slide the metal joint cover onto the outer member until it is flush with the outer member guide panel. Secure the joint cover in position by staking it into the recesses in the outer member, using a hammer and a round-ended punch.

32 Using a blunt rod, carefully lift the inner lip of the gaiter to equalise the air pressure. With the rod in position, compress the joint until the dimension from the inner end of the gaiter to the flat end face of the outer member is as shown **(see illustration)**. Hold the outer member in this position and withdraw the rod.

33 Fit the small retaining clip or collar to the inner end of the gaiter. Also fit the large clip if working on the first version. Where applicable, remove any slack in the gaiter retaining clip(s) by carefully compressing the raised section of the clip. In the absence of the special tool, a pair of pincers may be used.

34 Check that the constant velocity joint moves freely in all directions, then refit the driveshaft as described in Section 2.

5 Driveshaft overhaul - general information

1 If any of the checks described in Chapter 1 reveal wear in a driveshaft joint, first remove the roadwheel trim and check that the driveshaft retaining nut is still correctly tightened; if in doubt, use a torque wrench to check it. Refit the centre cap or trim, and repeat the check on the other driveshaft.

2 Road test the vehicle, and listen for a metallic clicking from the front as the vehicle is driven slowly in a circle with the steering on full-lock. If a clicking noise is heard, this indicates wear in the outer constant velocity joint.

3 If vibration, consistent with road speed, is felt through the vehicle when accelerating, there is a possibility of wear in the inner constant velocity joints.

4 Constant velocity joints can be dismantled and inspected for wear as described in Sections 3 and 4.

5 Wear in the outer constant velocity joint can be rectified by renewing the joint (see Section 3); wear in any of the other components, apart from the gaiters, will necessitate complete driveshaft renewal.

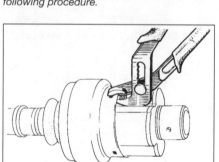

4.22 Bend up the metal cover on the RC 490 joint

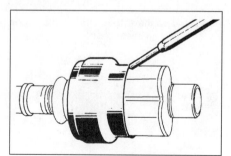

4.24 Tap the metal cover off the joint outer member

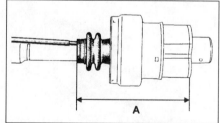

4.32 Expel any trapped air by lifting the gaiter with a rod, then check distance A

A = 155 to 157 mm

Chapter 9
Braking system

Contents

Degrees of difficulty

Easy, suitable for novice with little experience	**Fairly easy,** suitable for beginner with some experience	**Fairly difficult,** suitable for competent DIY mechanic 🔧	**Difficult,** suitable for experienced DIY mechanic 🔧	**Very difficult,** suitable for expert DIY or professional 🔧

Specifications

Front brakes

Type	Disc, with single piston sliding calipers
Brake pad minimum thickness (friction material and backing plate) . . .	6.0 mm
Disc diameter	238 or 259 mm
Disc thickness:	
238 mm disc:	
New	20.0 mm
Wear limit	18.0 mm
259 mm disc:	
New	21.0 mm
Wear limit	19.0 mm
Maximum disc run out	0.07 mm

Rear drum brakes

Type	Self-adjusting drum with leading and trailing shoes
Brake shoe minimum thickness (friction material and shoe)	2.5 mm
Drum diameter	228.6 mm
Maximum allowable drum diameter after refacing	229.6 mm

Rear disc brakes

Type	Disc, with single piston sliding calipers
Brake pad minimum thickness (friction material and backing plate) . . .	6.0 mm
Disc diameter	253 mm
Disc thickness:	
New	12.0 mm
Wear limit	11.0 mm
Maximum disc run out	0.07 mm

9

Torque wrench settings

	Nm
Front brake caliper mounting bolts (Bendix type)	100
Front brake caliper carrier bracket bolts (Girling type)	100
Front brake caliper guide pin bolts (Girling type)	35
Front brake disc retaining bolts	15
Rear hub nut:	
Drum brake models	160
Disc brake models	200
Rear brake caliper carrier bracket bolts	58
Rear brake disc retaining bolts	10
Master cylinder mounting nuts	13
Servo unit to mounting bracket	20
Hydraulic pipe and hose unions	13
Bleed screws	7
ABS wheel sensor bolts	8

1 General information

The braking system is of the servo-assisted, dual-circuit hydraulic type, incorporating disc brakes at the front on all models. Models without an anti-lock braking system (ABS) use drum brakes at the rear, whereas models with ABS are equipped with rear disc brakes. A diagonally-split dual circuit hydraulic system is employed, in which each circuit operates one front and one diagonally opposite rear brake from a tandem master cylinder. Under normal conditions, both circuits operate in unison; however, in the event of hydraulic failure in one circuit, full braking force will still be available at two wheels. A load conscious brake compensator is incorporated in the hydraulic system. This valve regulates the hydraulic pressure applied to each rear brake, and reduces the possibility of the rear wheels locking under heavy braking.

A cable-operated handbrake provides an independent means of rear brake application.

An anti-lock braking system (ABS) is available on later models and features many of the components in common with the conventional braking system. Further details on the ABS can be found later in this Chapter. **Note:** *When servicing any part of the system, work carefully and methodically; also observe scrupulous cleanliness when overhauling any part of the hydraulic system. Always renew components (in axle sets, where applicable) if in doubt about their condition, and use only genuine Renault replacement parts, or at least those of known good quality. Note the warnings given in "Safety first" and at relevant points in this Chapter concerning the dangers of asbestos dust and hydraulic fluid.*

2 Hydraulic system - bleeding

⚠ *Warning: Hydraulic fluid is poisonous; wash off immediately and thoroughly in the case of skin contact, and seek immediate medical advice if any fluid is swallowed or gets into the eyes. Certain types of hydraulic fluid are inflammable, and may ignite when allowed into contact with hot components; when servicing any hydraulic system, it is safest to assume that the fluid IS inflammable, and to take precautions against the risk of fire as though it is petrol that is being handled. Hydraulic fluid is also an effective paint stripper, and will attack plastics; if any is spilt, it should be washed off immediately, using copious quantities of clean water. Finally, it is hygroscopic (it absorbs moisture from the air). The more moisture is absorbed by the fluid, the lower its boiling point becomes, leading to a dangerous loss of braking under hard use. Old fluid may be contaminated and unfit for further use. When topping-up or renewing the fluid, always use the recommended type, and ensure that it comes from a freshly-opened sealed container.*

General

1 The correct functioning of the brake hydraulic system is only possible after removing all air from the components and circuit; this is achieved by bleeding the system.

2 During the bleeding procedure, add only clean, fresh hydraulic fluid of the specified type; never re-use fluid that has already been bled from the system. Ensure that sufficient fluid is available before starting work.

3 If there is any possibility of incorrect fluid being used in the system, the brake lines and components must be completely flushed with uncontaminated fluid and new seals fitted to the components.

4 If brake fluid has been lost from the master cylinder due to a leak in the system, ensure that the cause is traced and rectified before proceeding further.

5 Park the vehicle on level ground, switch off the ignition and select first gear. Chock the wheels and release the handbrake.

6 Check that all pipes and hoses are secure, unions tight, and bleed screws closed. Remove the dust caps and clean any dirt from around the bleed screws.

7 Unscrew the master cylinder reservoir cap, and top-up the reservoir to the "MAX" level line. Refit the cap loosely, and remember to maintain the fluid level at least above the "MIN" level line throughout the procedure, otherwise there is a risk of further air entering the system.

8 There are a number of one-man, do-it-yourself, brake bleeding kits currently available from motor accessory shops. It is recommended that one of these kits is used wherever possible, as they greatly simplify the bleeding operation, and also reduce the risk of expelled air and fluid being drawn back into the system. If such a kit is not available, the basic (two-man) method must be used, which is described in detail below.

9 If a kit is to be used, prepare the vehicle as described previously, and follow the kit manufacturer's instructions, as the procedure may vary slightly according to the type being used; generally, they are as outlined below in the relevant sub-section.

10 Whichever method is used, the correct sequence must be followed to ensure the removal of all air from the system.

Bleeding sequence

11 If the hydraulic system has only been partially disconnected and suitable precautions were taken to minimise fluid loss, it should only be necessary to bleed that part of the system (ie the primary or secondary circuit).

12 If the complete system is to be bled, then it should be done in the following sequence:

 a) Right-hand rear brake.
 b) Left-hand front brake.
 c) Left-hand rear brake.
 d) Right-hand front brake.

Bleeding - basic (two-man) method

13 Collect a clean glass jar and a suitable length of plastic or rubber tubing, which is a tight fit over the bleed screw, and a ring spanner to fit the screws. The help of an assistant will also be required.

14 If not already done, remove the dust cap from the bleed screw of the first wheel to be

2.14a Front brake bleed screw (arrowed)

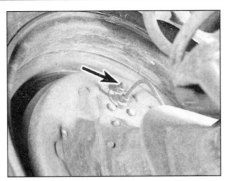

2.14b Rear disc brake bleed screw (arrowed)

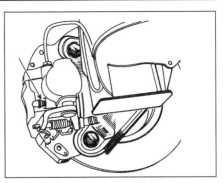

2.14c Rear disc brake bleed screw (arrowed)

bled and fit the bleed tube to the screw **(see illustrations)**.

15 Immerse the other end of the bleed tube in the jar, which should contain enough fluid to cover the end of the tube.

16 Ensure that the master cylinder reservoir fluid level is maintained at least above the "MIN" level line throughout the procedure.

17 Open the bleed screw approximately half a turn, and have your assistant depress the brake pedal with a smooth steady stroke down to the floor, and then hold it there. When the flow of fluid through the tube stops, tighten the bleed screw and have your assistant release the pedal slowly.

18 Repeat this operation (paragraph 18) until clean brake fluid, free from air bubbles, can be seen flowing from the end of the tube.

19 When no more air bubbles appear, tighten the bleed screw, remove the bleed tube and refit the dust cap. Repeat these procedures on the remaining calipers in sequence until all air is removed from the system and the brake pedal feels firm again.

Bleeding - using a one-way valve kit

20 As their name implies, these kits consist of a length of tubing with a one-way valve fitted, to prevent expelled air and fluid being drawn back into the system; some kits incorporate a translucent container, which can be positioned so that the air bubbles can be more easily seen flowing from the end of the tube.

21 The kit is connected to the bleed screw, which is then opened. The user returns to the driver's seat, depresses the brake pedal with a smooth steady stroke, and slowly releases it; this is repeated until the expelled fluid is clear of air bubbles.

22 Note that these kits simplify work so much that it is easy to forget the master cylinder fluid level; ensure that this is maintained at least above the "MIN" level line at all times.

Bleeding - using a pressure-bleeding kit

23 These kits are usually operated by the reserve of pressurised air contained in the spare tyre. However, note that it will probably

be necessary to reduce the pressure to a lower level than normal; refer to the instructions supplied with the kit.

24 By connecting a pressurised, fluid-filled container to the master cylinder reservoir, bleeding is then carried out by simply opening each bleed screw in turn (in the specified sequence) and allowing the fluid to run out, rather like turning on a tap, until no air bubbles can be seen in the expelled fluid.

25 This method has the advantage that the large reservoir of fluid provides an additional safeguard against air being drawn into the system during bleeding.

26 Pressure bleeding is particularly effective when bleeding "difficult" systems, or when bleeding the complete system at the time of routine fluid renewal. It is also the method recommended by Renault if the hydraulic system has been drained either wholly or partially.

All methods

27 When bleeding is completed, check and top-up the fluid level in the master cylinder reservoir.

28 Check the feel of the brake pedal. If it feels at all spongy, air must still be present in the system, and further bleeding is indicated. Failure to bleed satisfactorily after a reasonable repetition of the bleeding operations may be due to worn master cylinder seals.

29 Discard brake fluid which has been bled from the system; it will not be fit for re-use.

3 Hydraulic pipes and hoses - inspection and renewal

Note: *Before starting work, refer to the note at the beginning of Section 2 concerning the dangers of hydraulic fluid.*

Inspection

1 Raise and securely support the vehicle at the front and rear so that the pipes and hoses under the wheel arches and on the suspension assemblies can be inspected. (see *"Jacking and vehicle support"*).

2 Inspect the rigid pipes for security in their mountings. The pipes must be free from rust or impact damage.

3 Inspect the flexible hoses for cracks, splits and bulges. Bend the hoses between finger and thumb to show up small cracks. Renew any hoses whose condition is at all dubious. It is worth considering the renewal of the hoses on a precautionary basis at the time of fluid renewal.

Renewal

4 If any section of pipe or hose is to be removed, first unscrew the master cylinder reservoir filler cap and place a piece of polythene over the filler neck. Secure the polythene with an elastic band ensuring that an airtight seal is obtained. This will minimise brake fluid loss when the pipe or hose is removed.

5 Brake pipe removal is usually quite straightforward. The union nuts at each end are undone, the pipe and union pulled out and the centre section of the pipe removed from the body clips. Where the union nuts are exposed to the full force of the weather they can sometimes be quite tight. As only an open-ended spanner can be used, burring of the flats on the nuts is not uncommon when attempting to undo them. For this reason a self-locking wrench or special brake union split ring spanner should be used.

6 To remove a flexible hose, wipe the unions and brackets free of dirt and undo the union nut from the brake pipe end **(see illustration)**.

3.6 Front flexible hose and brake pipe connection

9

7 Next extract the hose retaining clip, or unscrew the nut, and lift the end of the hose out of its bracket. If a front hose is being removed, it can now be unscrewed from the brake caliper.

8 Brake pipes can be obtained individually, or in sets, from most accessory shops or garages with the end flares and union nuts in place. The pipe is then bent to shape, using the old pipe as a guide, and is ready for fitting to the vehicle.

9 Refitting the pipes and hoses is a reverse of the removal procedure. Make sure that the hoses are not kinked when in position and also make sure that the brake pipes are securely supported in their clips. After refitting, remove the polythene from the reservoir and bleed the brake hydraulic system, as described in Section 2.

4 Front brake pads - renewal

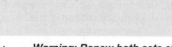

⚠ *Warning: Renew both sets of front brake pads at the same time - never renew the pads on only one wheel as uneven braking may result. Note that the dust created by wear of the pads may contain asbestos, which is a health hazard. Never blow it out with compressed air, and do not inhale any of it. An approved filtering mask should be worn when working on the brakes. DO NOT use petrol or petroleum-based solvents to clean brake parts; use brake cleaner or methylated spirit only. DO NOT allow any brake fluid, oil or grease to contact the brake pads or disc. Also refer to the warning in Section 2 concerning the dangers of hydraulic fluid.*

1 Chock the rear wheels then jack up the front of the vehicle and support it on axle stands (see "Jacking and vehicle support"). Remove the front roadwheels.

Bendix calipers

2 Disconnect the brake pad wear sensor wire at the connector.

3 Push the piston into its bore by pulling the caliper outwards.

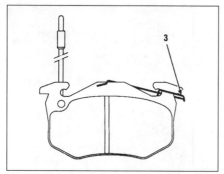

4.10 Anti-rattle spring (3) correctly fitted to inner brake pad (Bendix caliper)

4 Extract the small spring clip and then withdraw the pad retaining key **(see illustration)**.

5 Using pliers if necessary, withdraw the pads from the caliper, and remove the anti-rattle spring from each pad **(see illustration)**. If the pads are to be re-used, suitably identify them so that they can be refitted in their original positions.

6 Measure the thickness of the pad friction linings. If any one pad lining has worn down to the specified minimum, or if any are fouled with oil or grease, all four pads must be renewed. Do not interchange pads in an attempt to even out wear.

7 Brush the dust and dirt from the caliper, piston, disc, and pads.

⚠ *Warning: Take great care not to inhale the dust as it is injurious to health.*

8 Rotate the disc by hand, and scrape away any rust and scale. Carefully inspect the entire surface of the disc, and if there are any signs of cracks, deep scoring or severe abrasions, the disc must be renewed.

9 Inspect the caliper for fluid leaks around the piston, signs of corrosion, or other damage. Check that the caliper is free to slide on the guide sleeves and that the rubber dust excluders around the piston and guide sleeves are undamaged. Renew any suspect parts as necessary, with reference to Section 8.

10 To refit the pads, move the caliper sideways as far as possible towards the centre of the car. Fit the anti-rattle spring to the

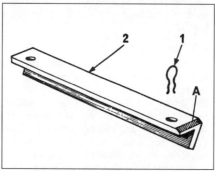

4.4 Spring clip (1), retaining key (2) and entry chamfer (A) to assist refitting (Bendix caliper)

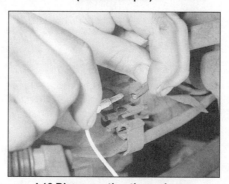

4.16 Disconnecting the pad wear sensor wire (Girling caliper)

innermost pad making sure that this pad is the one with the wear warning sensor wire, then locate the pad in position, with the backing plate against the piston **(see illustration)**.

11 Move the caliper outwards, then fit the anti-rattle spring to the outer pad and locate the pad in the caliper.

12 Slide the retaining key into place and refit the small spring clip at the inner end. It may be necessary to file an entry chamfer on the edge of the retaining key to enable it to be fitted without difficulty **(see illustration 4.4)**.

13 Reconnect the pad wear sensor wire, then refit the roadwheel and repeat the renewal procedure on the other front brake.

14 On completion, depress the brake pedal two or three times to bring the pads into contact with the disc. Lower the vehicle to the ground.

15 If necessary, top-up the master cylinder reservoir to the correct level as described in "Weekly checks".

Girling calipers

16 Disconnect the pad wear sensor wire at the connector on the upper suspension arm **(see illustration)**.

17 Push in the caliper piston by sliding the caliper body towards the outside of the vehicle by hand.

18 Unscrew the caliper upper and lower guide pin bolts using a ring spanner and an open-ended spanner to counterhold the guide pins **(see illustration)**. Discard the bolts, new ones should be used on refitting.

4.5 Removing the brake pads (Bendix caliper)

4.18 Removing the caliper lower guide pin bolt (Girling caliper)

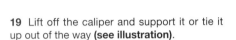

4.19 Lifting off the caliper from the carrier bracket (Girling caliper)

4.20 Removing the brake pads (Girling caliper)

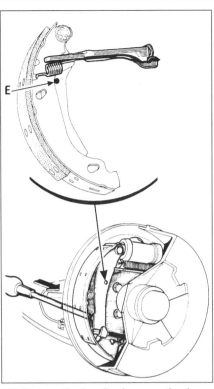

5.3 Push on the handbrake operating lever to free stud (E)

19 Lift off the caliper and support it or tie it up out of the way **(see illustration)**.

20 Lift out the two brake pads from the caliper carrier bracket **(see illustration)**. If the pads are to be re-used, suitably identify them so that they can be refitted in their original positions.

21 Inspect the brake pads and disc as described in paragraphs 6 to 9.

22 If new pads are to be fitted, it will be necessary to push the caliper piston back into its bore to accommodate the new, thicker pads. To do this push the piston into its bore, as far as it will go, using a G-clamp or suitable pieces of wood as levers. As the piston is retracted, the fluid level in the master cylinder reservoir will rise. Be prepared for spillage by placing rags around the reservoir.

23 Fit the brake pads to the carrier bracket; the inboard one has the sensor wire.

24 Locate the caliper over the pads and fit the new guide pin bolts. The bolts should be supplied with their threads already pre-coated with locking fluid, if not apply thread locking fluid to the threads of each bolt.

25 Tighten the bottom guide pin bolt first, followed by the upper one, to the specified torque.

26 Renew the pads on the remaining front brake in a similar way.

27 Apply the footbrake several times to position the pads against the discs.

28 Ensure that the pad wear sensor wire is correctly routed and located.

29 Fit the roadwheels and lower the vehicle to the ground.

30 If necessary, top-up the master cylinder reservoir to the correct level as described in "Weekly checks".

5 Rear brake drum - removal, inspection and refitting

Removal

1 Chock the front wheels then jack up the rear of the vehicle and support it on axle stands (see "Jacking and vehicle support"). Remove the rear roadwheel.

2 With the handbrake fully applied, unscrew and remove the two brake drum retaining screws, release the handbrake and withdraw the drum. If it is tight, try gently tapping it with a plastic or copper-faced hammer.

3 If the drum is still tight, slacken the adjuster nut on the handbrake primary rod right off. Remove the blanking plug on the rear face of the brake backplate. Insert a screwdriver through the hole in the backplate, and through the corresponding hole in the brake shoe, until it contacts the brake shoe handbrake lever. Push the lever to free its stud from the brake shoe, then move the lever rearwards. **(see illustration)**. It should now be possible to withdraw the brake drum.

Inspection

4 With the brake drum removed, brush or wipe the dust from the drum, brake shoes, wheel cylinder and backplate.

 Warning: Take great care not to inhale the dust as it is injurious to health.

5 Clean the brake drum thoroughly, then examine the internal surface for signs of scoring, wear ridges or cracks. If any deterioration of the surface finish is evident, the drums may be machined to renovate them. If machining is to be carried out, both drums must be done at the same time and to the same internal diameter. The maximum permissible internal diameter is shown on the outer face of the drum. If the drums are excessively worn, renewal will be necessary.

Refitting

6 Ensure that the brake shoe handbrake lever is repositioned with its stud is against the edge of the brake shoe web.

7 Locate the drum over the brake shoes and secure with the two screws.

8 Depress the brake pedal several times to operate the brake shoe self-adjusting mechanism.

9 If it was necessary to slacken the adjuster nut on the handbrake primary rod to allow drum removal, adjust the handbrake as described in Section 17.

10 Refit the roadwheel and lower the vehicle to the ground.

6 Rear brake shoes - inspection and renewal

 Warning: Renew both sets of rear brake shoes at the same time - never renew the shoes on only one wheel as uneven braking may result. Note that the dust created by wear of the shoes may contain asbestos, which is a health hazard. Never blow it out with compressed air, and don't inhale any of it. An approved filtering mask should be worn when working on the brakes. DO NOT use petrol or petroleum-based solvents to clean brake parts; use brake cleaner or methylated spirit only. DO NOT allow any brake fluid, oil or grease to contact the brake shoes or drum. Also refer to the warning at the start of Section 2 concerning the dangers of hydraulic fluid.

Inspection

1 Remove the brake drum as described in Section 5.

2 Working carefully, and taking the necessary precautions, brush away all traces of dust from the brake drum, backplate and shoes.

3 Measure the thickness of the friction material of each brake shoe at several points; if either shoe is worn at any point to the specified minimum thickness or less, all four shoes must be renewed as a set. The shoes

9

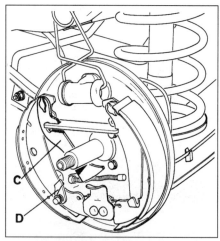

6.10 Push down on the quadrant (D) and move lever (C) toward the stub axle (Bendix brake shoes)

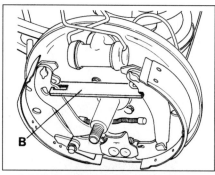

6.11 Pull away the shoes and detach link (B) (Bendix brake shoes)

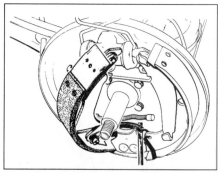

6.13 Disconnect the lower shoe return spring (Bendix brake shoes)

should also be renewed if any are fouled with oil or grease; there is no satisfactory way of degreasing friction material once contaminated.

4 If any of the brake shoes are worn unevenly or fouled with oil or grease, trace and rectify the cause before reassembly.

5 To renew the brake shoes, proceed as described under the relevant sub-heading.

Renewal

Bendix brake shoes

6 Tap off the hub dust cap, unscrew the hub nut and withdraw the hub and bearing assembly from the stub axle.

7 Prise free and remove the upper brake shoe return spring.

8 Disconnect the handbrake cable from the trailing shoe.

9 Remove the two shoe hold-down springs. Do this by inserting a screwdriver into the centre of the spring and rotating it.

10 Push down on the serrated quadrant and move the automatic adjuster lever as far as it will go towards the stub axle **(see illustration)**.

11 Pull both brake shoes away from the backplate and detach the connecting link from the automatic adjuster lever on the leading shoe **(see illustration)**.

12 Rotate the serrated quadrant and move the automatic adjuster lever back to its original position.

13 Twist the leading shoe at right angles to the backplate and disconnect the lower shoe return spring **(see illustration)**.

14 Remove both shoes. While the shoes are removed, do not touch the brake pedal or the wheel cylinder pistons will be ejected. It is advisable to secure them in position using an elastic band or a suitable spring type clip.

15 Transfer the handbrake lever and automatic adjuster lever to the new brake shoes. The levers are both retained by spring clips.

16 Disengage the tension spring and transfer the connecting link to the new trailing shoe.

17 Apply a smear of high melting-point grease to the shoe contact areas on the brake backplate, to the shoe lower anchor block recesses and to the end faces of the wheel cylinder pistons.

18 Refitting is a reversal of removal. Take care not to get grease or oil onto the brake linings or the drum friction surface. Set the automatic adjuster lever fully towards the stub axle. Before refitting the hub and the brake drum, check the initial brake shoe position as follows.

19 Position the handbrake lever so that the peg at the rear is contacting the trailing shoe web.

20 Check that a gap of approximately 1.0 mm exists between the brake shoe web and the inner contact face of the connecting link **(see illustration)**. If this is not the case, renew the link tension spring and the shoe upper and lower return springs.

21 Refit the rear hub, tighten the hub nut to the specified torque and refit the dust cap.

22 Ensure that the brake shoe handbrake lever is repositioned with its stud is against the edge of the brake shoe web.

23 Locate the drum over the brake shoes and secure with the two screws.

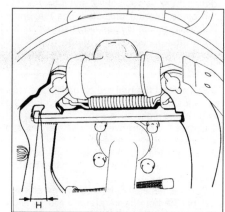

6.20 Correct setting of brake shoe to connecting link (Bendix brake shoes)

H = 1.0 mm

24 Repeat the operations on the other rear brake assembly.

25 Depress the brake pedal several times to operate the brake shoe self-adjusting mechanism.

26 If it was necessary to slacken the adjuster nut on the handbrake primary rod to allow drum removal, adjust the handbrake as described in Section 17.

27 Refit the roadwheels and lower the vehicle to the ground.

Girling brake shoes

28 Prise free and remove the upper and lower brake shoe return springs.

29 Disconnect the handbrake cable from the trailing shoe **(see illustration)**.

30 Disconnect the tension spring and remove the adjuster lever.

31 Grip one of the shoe hold-down caps with a pair of pliers, depress the cap and turn it through 90° so that it will pass over the T-shaped head of the hold-down pin. Remove the cap, spring and pin. Remove the hold-down assembly from the other brake shoe in a similar manner **(see illustration)**.

32 Detach and withdraw the leading brake shoe and thrust link.

33 Remove the trailing brake shoe.

34 While the shoes are removed, do not touch the brake pedal or the wheel cylinder pistons will be ejected. It is advisable to secure them in position using an elastic band or a suitable spring type clip.

6.29 Disconnect the handbrake cable (arrowed) from the trailing shoe (Girling brake shoes)

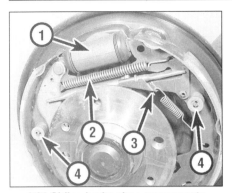

6.31 Girling brake shoe components

1 Wheel cylinder
2 Upper return spring
3 Tension spring and adjusting lever
4 Shoe hold-down assembly

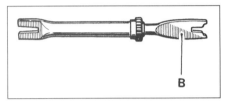

6.35 Adjuster screw unit identification (Girling brake shoes)

Left-hand side - silver end piece (B)
Right-hand side - gold end piece (B)

35 Clean the backplate and inspect the brake assembly components. Keep the sub-assemblies separate, as the right and left-hand assemblies are different and must not be interchanged. The toothed adjuster screw units are colour-coded for identification (see illustration). Clean the threads of the toothed adjusters and lightly grease them.

36 Apply a smear of high melting-point grease to the shoe contact areas on the brake backplate, to the shoe lower anchor block recesses and to the end faces of the wheel cylinder pistons.

37 Refitting is a reversal of removal. Take care not to get grease or oil onto the brake linings or the drum friction surface. Ensure that all connections are correctly and securely made.

38 Prior to refitting the drum, adjust the diameter of the brake shoes to between

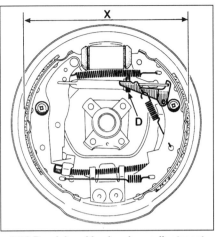

6.38 Provisional brake shoe adjustment (Girling brake shoes)

D Toothed adjuster
X = 227.9 to 228.5 mm

227.9 and 228.5 mm by turning the toothed adjuster as required (see illustration). This should just allow the brake drum to just pass over the shoes.

39 Locate the drum over the brake shoes and secure with the two screws.

40 Repeat the operations on the other rear brake assembly.

41 Depress the brake pedal several times to operate the brake shoe self-adjusting mechanism.

42 If it was necessary to slacken the adjuster nut on the handbrake primary rod to allow drum removal, adjust the handbrake as described in Section 17.

43 Refit the roadwheels and lower the vehicle to the ground.

7 Rear brake pads - renewal

⚠️ *Warning: Renew both sets of rear brake pads at the same time - never renew the pads on only one wheel as uneven braking may result. Note that the dust created by wear of the pads may contain*

asbestos, which is a health hazard. Never blow it out with compressed air, and don't inhale any of it. An approved filtering mask should be worn when working on the brakes. DO NOT use petrol or petroleum-based solvents to clean brake parts; use brake cleaner or methylated spirit only. DO NOT allow any brake fluid, oil or grease to contact the brake pads or disc. Also refer to the warning at the start of Section 2 concerning the dangers of hydraulic fluid.

1 Chock the front wheels then jack up the rear of the vehicle and support it on axle stands (see "Jacking and vehicle support"). Remove the rear roadwheels.

2 Fully release the handbrake then disconnect the cable from the caliper lever. If there is any difficulty in releasing the cable end fitting, slacken the adjuster on the handbrake primary rod right off.

3 Extract the two lockpins and then tap out the two sliding keys (see illustrations).

4 Lift the caliper from the disc and carrier bracket and tie it up out of the way.

5 Remove the brake pads and springs from the carrier bracket. If the pads are to be re-used, suitably identify them so that they can be refitted in their original positions.

6 Measure the thickness of the pad friction linings. If any one pad lining has worn down to the specified minimum, or if any are fouled with oil or grease, all four pads must be renewed. Do not interchange pads in an attempt to even out wear.

7 Brush the dust and dirt from the caliper, piston, disc, and pads, but **do not** inhale it, as it is injurious to health.

8 If new pads are to be fitted, the caliper piston must be fully retracted into its bore. Do this by turning the piston with the square section shaft of a screwdriver until the piston continues to turn but will not go in any further. As the piston is retracted, the fluid level in the master cylinder reservoir will rise. Be prepared for spillage by placing rags around the reservoir. Finally set the piston so that the line on the piston face is nearest to the bleed screw (see illustration).

7.3a Extract the lockpins . . .

7.3b . . . and remove the sliding keys

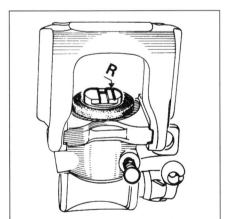

7.8 Rear brake caliper piston orientation

Line R to be nearest bleed screw

9

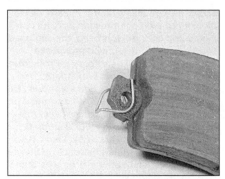

7.9a Locate the pad springs . . .

7.9b . . . and fit the pads

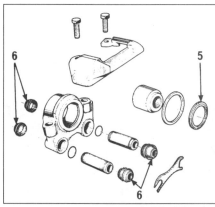

**8.10 Front brake caliper components
(Bendix shown, Girling similar)**

5 Piston dust excluders
6 Guide sleeve seals and caps

9 Locate the springs onto the pads and fit the pads **(see illustrations)**.

10 Fit the caliper by engaging one end of the caliper between the spring clip and the keyway on the bracket, compress the springs and engage the opposite end.

11 Insert the first key, then insert a screwdriver in the second key slot and use it as a lever until the slot will accept the key.

12 Fit new key lockpins.

13 Renew the pads on the remaining rear brake in a similar way.

14 Apply the footbrake several times to position the pads against the discs.

15 Reconnect the handbrake cable and adjust it if necessary as described in Section 17.

16 Fit the roadwheels and lower the vehicle to the ground.

17 If necessary, top-up the master cylinder reservoir to the correct level as described in *"Weekly checks"*.

8 Front brake caliper - removal, overhaul and refitting

Note: *Before starting work, refer to the warning at the beginning of Section 2 concerning the dangers of hydraulic fluid, and to the warning at the beginning of Section 4 concerning the dangers of asbestos dust.*

Removal

1 Chock the rear wheels then jack up the front of the vehicle and support it on axle stands (see *"Jacking and vehicle support"*). Remove the roadwheel.

2 To minimise fluid loss, unscrew the master cylinder reservoir filler cap and place a piece of polythene over the filler neck. Secure the polythene with an elastic band ensuring that an airtight seal is obtained. Alternatively, use a brake hose clamp, a G-clamp, or a similar tool with protected jaws, to clamp the flexible hose.

Bendix caliper

3 Remove the brake pads as described in Section 4.

4 Clean the area around the union, then loosen the brake hose union nut.

5 Slacken the two bolts securing the caliper assembly to the hub carrier, and remove them along with the mounting plate, noting which way around the plate is fitted. Lift the caliper assembly away from the brake disc, and unscrew it from the end of the brake hose.

Girling caliper

6 Clean the area around the union, then loosen the brake hose union nut.

7 Remove the brake pads as described in Section 4.

8 Unscrew the caliper from the brake hose.

9 If it is wished to remove the carrier bracket, undo the two bolts which secure it to the hub carrier.

Overhaul

10 Clean away external dirt from the caliper and remove the dust excluder and the retaining ring **(see illustration)**.

11 Eject the piston from the cylinder by applying air pressure to the fluid inlet hole. Only low air pressure is required such as is generated by a foot-operated tyre pump. Remove the piston seal ring from its groove in the caliper bore **(see illustration)**.

12 Inspect the surfaces of the piston and cylinder. If there is evidence of scoring or corrosion, renew the caliper cylinder assembly complete.

13 If the components are in good condition, remove the seal and wash them in clean hydraulic fluid or methylated spirit - nothing else.

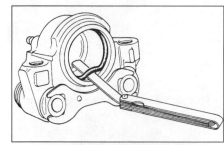

8.11 Removing the piston seal from the caliper bore

14 Obtain a repair kit which will contain all the necessary renewable items. Fit the new seal, using the fingers to manipulate it into its groove.

15 Dip the piston in clean hydraulic fluid and insert the piston into the cylinder.

16 Fit the dust excluder and retaining ring.

Refitting

Bendix caliper

17 Screw the caliper fully onto the flexible hose union nut. Position the caliper over the brake disc, then refit the two caliper mounting bolts and the mounting plate. Note that the mounting plate must be fitted so that its bend curves towards the caliper body. This is necessary to prevent the plate contacting the driveshaft gaiter when the steering is on full-lock. With the plate correctly positioned, tighten the caliper bolts to the specified torque.

18 Tighten the brake hose union, then refit the brake pads as described in Section 4.

19 Remove the brake hose clamp or polythene, where fitted, and bleed the hydraulic system as described in Section 2.

20 Apply the footbrake two or three times to settle the pads then refit the roadwheel and lower the vehicle.

Girling caliper

21 If removed, refit the carrier bracket applying thread locking compound to the retaining bolts. Tighten the bolts to the specified torque.

22 Refit the brake pads as described in Section 4, but screw the caliper onto the flexible hose before refitting it to the carrier bracket.

23 Tighten the flexible hose union ensuring that the hose is not kinked.

24 Remove the brake hose clamp or polythene, where fitted, and bleed the hydraulic system as described in Section 2.

25 Apply the footbrake two or three times to settle the pads then refit the roadwheel and lower the vehicle.

9 Rear brake caliper - removal, overhaul and refitting

Note: *Before starting work, refer to the warning at the beginning of Section 2 concerning the dangers of hydraulic fluid, and to the warning at the beginning of Section 7 concerning the dangers of asbestos dust.*

Removal

1 Chock the front wheels then jack up the rear of the vehicle and support it on axle stands (see *"Jacking and vehicle support"*). Remove the roadwheel.

2 Disconnect the handbrake cable from the lever on the caliper (see Section 7).

3 Release the flexible brake hose from the caliper by unscrewing it by no more than a quarter of a turn.

4 Remove the caliper from the disc as described in Section 7.

5 Unscrew the caliper from the hose and cap the end of the hose or use a brake hose clamp to prevent loss of fluid.

Overhaul

6 Clean away external dirt from the caliper and grip it in the jaws of a vice fitted with jaw protectors.

7 Remove the dust excluder from around the piston and then unscrew the piston, using the square section shaft of a screwdriver **(see illustration)**. Once the piston turns freely but does not come out any further, apply low air pressure to the fluid inlet hole and eject the piston. Only low air pressure is required such as is generated by a foot-operated tyre pump.

8 Inspect the surfaces of the piston and cylinder bore. If there is evidence of scoring or corrosion, renew the caliper cylinder.

9 To remove the cylinder a wedge will have to be made in accordance with the dimensions shown **(see illustration)**.

10 Drive the wedge in to slightly separate the support bracket arms and so slide out the cylinder which can be done once the spring-loaded locating pin has been depressed **(see illustrations)**.

11 If the piston and cylinder are in good condition, then the cylinder will not have to be removed from the support bracket but overhauled in the following way.

12 Remove and discard the piston seal and wash the components in methylated spirit.

13 Obtain a repair kit which will contain all the necessary renewable items. Fit the new seal using the fingers to manipulate it into its groove.

14 Dip the piston in clean hydraulic fluid and insert the piston into the cylinder.

15 Using the square section shaft of a screwdriver, turn the piston until it turns but will not go in any further. Set the piston so that the line on the piston face is nearest to the bleed screw.

16 Fit the new dust excluder.

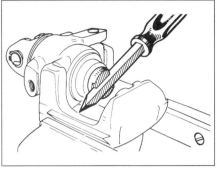

9.7 Unscrewing the rear caliper piston

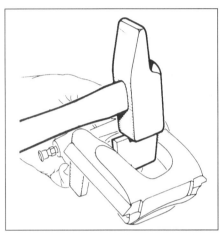

9.10a Driving in the wedge to spread the support bracket arm

17 If the handbrake operating mechanism is worn or faulty, dismantle it in the following way before renewing the piston seal.

18 Grip the caliper in a vice fitted with jaw protectors.

19 Remove the dust excluder, the piston, dust cover, and the circlip **(see illustration)**.

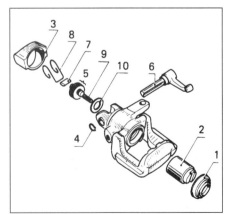

9.19 Exploded view of the rear caliper

1 *Dust excluder*	6 *Shaft*
2 *Piston*	7 *Plunger cam*
3 *Rear dust cover*	8 *Spring*
4 *Circlip*	9 *Adjusting screw*
5 *Spring washers*	10 *Washer*

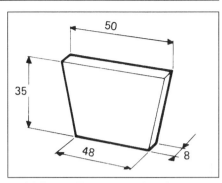

9.9 Rear caliper support bracket arm wedge dimensions

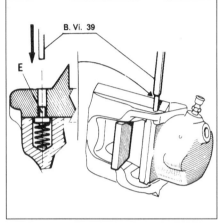

9.10b Depress the spring-loaded pin (E) - Renault tool shown

20 Compress the spring washers and pull out the shaft.

21 Remove the plunger cam, spring, adjusting screw, plain washer and spring washer.

22 Drive out the sleeve using a drift, and remove the sealing ring.

23 Clean all components and renew any that are worn.

24 Reassembly is a reversal of removal but observe the following points.

25 Drive in the sleeve until it is flush with the adjacent surface **(see illustration)**.

26 Make sure that the spring washers are fitted convex face to convex face.

27 Align the piston as previously described.

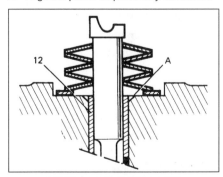

9.25 Rear caliper sleeve (12) fitted flush with face (A)

9

Refitting

28 Refit the caliper after screwing it onto the hydraulic hose. Tighten the hose union then refit the brake pads.

29 Reconnect the handbrake cable.

30 Bleed the hydraulic system (Section 2).

31 Apply the footbrake several times and adjust the handbrake cable (Section 17).

32 Fit the roadwheel and lower the vehicle.

---

10 Brake disc - inspection, removal and refitting

Note: *Before starting work, refer to the warning at the beginning of Section 4 concerning the dangers of asbestos dust.*

Inspection

1 Whenever the brake pads are being checked for wear, inspect the disc for deep grooving, scoring or cracks. Light scoring is normal.

2 Rust will normally build up on the edge of a disc and this should be removed by holding a sharp tool against the disc whilst it is rotated.

3 If there has been a history of brake judder, check the disc run-out using a dial test indicator with its probe positioned near the outer edge of the disc. If the run-out exceeds the figures given in the *Specifications*, the disc must be renewed.

> **HAYNES HINT** *If a dial test indicator is not available, check the run-out by positioning a fixed pointer near the outer edge, in contact with the disc face. Rotate the disc and measure the maximum displacement of the pointer with feeler blades.*

4 Disc thickness variation in excess of 0.015 mm can also cause judder. Check this using a micrometer.

5 If the disc is grooved, cracked or distorted it must also be renewed. Refinishing of a disc must not be carried out as this can cause the caliper piston to overextend when the brakes are applied. If a new disc is being fitted, new brake pads must also be fitted to both sides of the vehicle.

Front disc renewal

Bendix brake caliper

6 Remove the brake caliper as described in Section 8.

7 Unscrew the two disc retaining screws and remove the disc.

8 Clean any protective coating from the new disc and locate it on the hub.

9 Refit and tighten the disc retaining screws.

10 Refit the brake caliper as described in Section 8.

Girling brake caliper

11 Chock the rear wheels then jack up the front of the vehicle and support it on axle stands (see *"Jacking and vehicle support"*). Remove the roadwheel.

12 Disconnect the brake pad wear sensor wire at the wiring connector.

13 Remove the two caliper carrier bracket bolts.

14 Lift the caliper, complete with brake pads, off the disc and tie it up out of the way.

15 Unscrew the two disc retaining screws and remove the disc.

16 Clean any protective coating from the new disc and locate it on the hub.

17 Refit and tighten the disc retaining screws.

18 Clean the threads of the caliper carrier bracket bolts and apply thread locking fluid to them. Locate the caliper and pads over the disc, screw in the bolts and tighten them to the specified torque. Reconnect the pad wear sensor wiring.

19 Apply the brake pedal several times to position the pads up against the disc, fit the roadwheel and lower the vehicle.

Rear disc renewal

20 Refer to Section 7 and remove the brake pads.

21 Remove the two caliper carrier bracket bolts and lift off the carrier bracket.

22 Unscrew the two disc retaining screws and remove the disc.

23 Clean any protective coating from the new disc and locate it on the hub.

24 Refit and tighten the disc retaining screws.

25 Clean the threads of the caliper bracket bolts and apply thread locking fluid to them. Locate the carrier bracket over the disc, screw in the bolts and tighten them to the specified torque.

26 Refit the brake pads (see Section 7).

---

11 Rear wheel cylinder - removal and refitting

Note: *Before starting work, refer to the warning at the beginning of Section 2 concerning the dangers of hydraulic fluid, and to the warning at the beginning of Section 6 concerning the dangers of asbestos dust.*

Removal

1 Remove the brake drum, as described in Section 5.

2 Prise apart the upper ends of the brake shoes so that they are separated from the wheel cylinder pistons. It may be necessary to remove the upper brake shoe return spring to facilitate this.

3 Clean the area around the hydraulic pipe union at the wheel cylinder connection on the inboard side of the backplate, then loosen off the union nut using a brake pipe spanner.

4 Undo the two wheel cylinder mounting bolts and withdraw the cylinder. As the cylinder is withdrawn from the backplate, take care not to spill hydraulic fluid onto the brake linings or paintwork. Plug the hydraulic pipe to prevent spillage and the ingress of dirt.

5 A wheel cylinder which is seized or worn internally must be renewed as a unit; repair kits are not available.

Refitting

6 Refitting is a reversal of removal, bearing in mind the following points:

a) *Ensure that the hydraulic pipe connection at the wheel cylinder is clean. Do not fully tighten the nut until after the mounting bolts have been fitted.*

b) *Retract the brake shoe automatic adjuster to allow the shoes to contact the wheel cylinder pistons before fitting the brake drum.*

c) *Bleed the brake hydraulic system as described in Section 2 on completion.*

---

12 Master cylinder - removal and refitting

Note: *Before starting work, refer to the warning at the beginning of Section 2 concerning the dangers of hydraulic fluid.*

Removal

1 Syphon as much fluid as possible from the master cylinder reservoir.

> **HAYNES HINT** *An ideal way to remove fluid from the reservoir is to use a clean syringe or an old poultry baster.*

2 Disconnect the leads from the low fluid level switch and pull the reservoir upwards out of the sealing grommets. Where a remote reservoir is fitted, disconnect the fluid hoses from the master cylinder inlet ports.

3 Note the locations of the hydraulic pipes and then disconnect them from the master cylinder by unscrewing the unions. Catch any fluid which may drain out by placing rags beneath the master cylinder.

4 Unbolt the master cylinder from the front face of the servo unit and remove it **(see illustration)**.

12.4 Master cylinder brake pipe attachments and mounting nuts

5 A faulty master cylinder cannot be overhauled, only renewed, due to the fact that the internal roll pins cannot be extracted.

Refitting

6 Ensure that a new O-ring seal is fitted between the joint faces of the master cylinder and the servo unit.
7 Bolt the master cylinder into position and connect the fluid pipes.
8 Push the reservoir firmly into its grommets or reconnect the reservoir fluid hoses.
9 Fill the reservoir with clean hydraulic fluid and bleed the complete hydraulic system (Section 2).

13 Brake compensator -
removal and refitting

Note: *Before starting work, refer to the warning at the beginning of Section 2 concerning the dangers of hydraulic fluid.*

General

1 Checking and accurate adjustment of the brake compensator is not within the scope of the home mechanic as specialised equipment is required. The following procedure describes removal and refitting of the unit to enable other work on the vehicle to be carried out, or to enable the unit to be renewed if it is known to be faulty.
2 It will be necessary to have the vehicle standing on its wheels, either over an inspection pit or raised on a suitable hoist.
3 To carry out an initial adjustment after fitting, the vehicle must be standing on its wheels, with five seats fitted and the fuel tank full.

Removal

4 Chock the front wheels then jack up the rear of the vehicle and support it on axle stands (see *"Jacking and vehicle support"*).
5 The compensator unit is located on the underside of the vehicle, just to the right of centre, forward of the rear axle **(see illustration)**.
6 Clean the hydraulic pipe connections to the compensator, making an accurate note of their respective locations. Undo the hydraulic pipe unions and disconnect the pipes. Plug them to prevent the ingress of dirt and leakage.
7 Unscrew the adjusting nut from the end of the compensator threaded rod **(see illustration)**.
8 Undo the two bolts and remove the compensator.

Refitting

9 Locate the compensator in position and secure with the two bolts.
10 With the vehicle prepared as described in paragraph 2, screw the adjusting nut onto the threaded rod and turn the rod until the compensator spring height is 65 mm ± 0.5 mm.

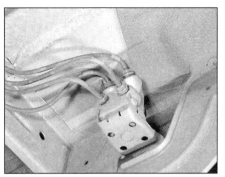

13.5 Brake compensator location on vehicle underside

Note: *This is an initial adjustment only to enable the vehicle to be driven to a Renault dealer for accurate setting.*
11 Reconnect the hydraulic pipes into their correct positions in the compensator.
12 Bleed the hydraulic system as described in Section 2.
13 On completion, have the compensator checked by a Renault dealer immediately.

14 Vacuum servo air filter -
renewal

1 Remove the servo unit as described in Section 16.
2 Using a scriber or similar tool, pick out the filter and cut it to remove it.
3 Cut the new filter as shown and push it neatly into position **(see illustration)**. Refit the dust excluding boot.
4 Refit the servo unit.

15 Vacuum servo non-return valve - renewal

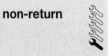

1 Disconnect the vacuum hose from the non-return valve on the front face of the servo unit.
2 Pull and twist the non-return valve elbow from its grommet.

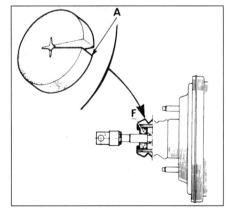

14.3 Vacuum servo unit air filter

A Cut   F Filter location

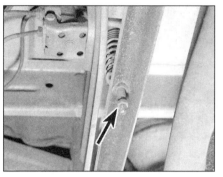

13.7 Brake compensator threaded rod and adjusting nut (arrowed)

3 Refitting is a reversal of removal but use a new grommet. A smear of rubber grease on the elbow spigot will ease its entry into the grommet. Do not force the elbow when fitting as it is possible to push the grommet into the interior of the servo.

16 Vacuum servo unit -
removal and refitting

Note: *Numerous changes have been made to the servo unit, the brake pedal assembly and the various connecting linkages during the course of production. If the settings of the brake pedal thrust rod or servo push rod are disturbed, or if a new servo unit is to be fitted, seek the advice of a Renault dealer as to the correct fitted dimensions of these components and adjust accordingly before refitting.*

Removal

1 Disconnect the battery negative lead
2 To gain access to the servo mounting bracket bolts it is necessary to remove a considerable amount of interior trim from the area around and beneath the steering column. The exact nature of the items that need to be removed varies according to model, type and year. Refer to Chapter 11 and remove all items necessary for access.
3 Refer to Chapter 6 and disconnect the clutch cable from the pedal.
4 Extract the spring clip and clevis pin and disconnect the brake thrust rod from the brake pedal. Release the rubber gaiter from the thrust rod.
5 Extract the spring clip and remove the brake and clutch pedal shaft.
6 Remove the master cylinder as described in Section 12.
7 Disconnect the vacuum hose from the non-return valve on the front face of the servo unit.
8 On carburettor engines, remove the hot air inlet duct and the carburettor cover.
9 On diesel engines, unbolt the fuel filter assembly, without disconnecting the fuel hoses, and move it to one side.
10 Remove any other components as necessary to allow clearance for the servo unit to be withdrawn into the engine compartment.

9

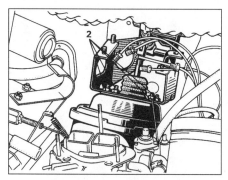

16.12 Servo to mounting bracket retaining nuts (2)

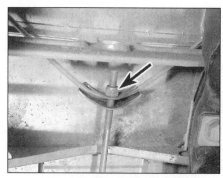

17.4 Handbrake cable primary rod adjusting nut (arrowed)

11 From inside the vehicle, undo the four nuts securing the servo unit mounting bracket to the bulkhead.

12 Push the mounting bracket assembly into the engine compartment. From within the engine compartment, extract the clip and clevis pin securing the servo push rod to the thrust lever. Undo the four nuts securing the servo to the mounting bracket and manoeuvre the unit out from the engine compartment **(see illustration)**.

Refitting

13 Before refitting the servo check and if necessary adjust the length of the thrust rod. On early units also check and if necessary adjust the length of the servo push rod and master cylinder push rod. Refer to a Renault dealer for the correct dimensions according to model type and year.

14 Refit the servo unit using a reversal of removal. Refit the master cylinder as described in Section 12 and reconnect the clutch cable as described in Chapter 6.

17 Handbrake - adjustment

General

1 The handbrake will normally be kept in adjustment by the action of the drum brake automatic adjuster or the self-adjusting action of the rear disc calipers.

2 The handbrake should only be adjusted when new brake linings, new handbrake cables, or a new handbrake lever has been fitted.

3 Chock the front wheels then jack up the rear of the vehicle and support it on axle stands (see *"Jacking and vehicle support"*).

4 Fully release the handbrake, then, working under the vehicle, slacken the primary rod adjusting nut (and locknut if fitted) so that the cable is completely slack **(see illustration)**.

Drum brake models

5 Remove both rear wheels, then the brake drum on each side (see Section 5).

6 Where Bendix brakes are fitted, push down on the serrated quadrant and move the automatic adjuster lever to slacken the adjustment by 3 to 4 notches. On Girling brakes, move the knurled automatic brake adjuster in each direction to ensure that it is operational, then loosen it off by 5 to 6 notches. On all brakes, check that the cables slide freely and that the handbrake actuating lever is in contact with the brake shoes.

7 Progressively tension the cable at the primary rod adjuster so that the actuating lever of each rear brake shoe starts to move at the 1st to 2nd notch position of the handbrake control lever travel. Retighten the primary rod locknut.

8 Fully release the handbrake, and refit the brake drums.

9 Depress the brake pedal several times to settle the shoes. Apply the handbrake lever and check that it locks the rear wheels.

10 Refit the wheels and lower the vehicle.

Disc brake models

11 Remove both rear wheels, then check that the handbrake actuating levers move without binding and move them as far as possible to the rear.

12 Progressively increase the tension of the cable from the primary rod adjustment point. Adjust so that the cable end piece is just in contact with the actuator lever but does not actually move it.

13 Now readjust the setting so that the actuating levers begin to move between the 1st and 2nd notch of the control lever travel, remaining lifted at the 2nd notch position. Retighten the primary rod locknut.

14 Check the handbrake for satisfactory operation as described in paragraph 9, then refit the wheels and lower the vehicle.

18 Handbrake lever - removal and refitting

Removal

1 Chock the front wheels then jack up the rear of the vehicle and support it on axle stands (see *"Jacking and vehicle support"*).

2 Fully release the handbrake then, working under the vehicle, unscrew the primary rod locknut and adjusting nut and slide the cable and compensator off the primary rod.

3 Where fitted, remove the centre console (Chapter 11) or the cover over the handbrake lever.

4 Disconnect the handbrake switch wire, undo the handbrake lever retaining bolts, then withdraw the lever.

Refitting

5 Refit in the reverse order of removal. Adjust the handbrake as described in Section 17 to give the correct lever travel.

19 Handbrake cable - removal and refitting

Removal

1 Chock the front wheels then jack up the rear of the vehicle and support it on axle stands (see *"Jacking and vehicle support"*).

2 Fully release the handbrake then, working under the vehicle, unscrew the primary rod locknut and adjusting nut and slide the cable and compensator off the primary rod.

3 On models with drum brakes, remove the drums and disconnect the cable from the shoe levers.

4 On models with rear disc brakes, disconnect the cable from the caliper levers.

5 Disconnect the cable from the body clips and remove it from under the vehicle.

Refitting

6 Refit the cable by reversing the removal operations. Apply grease to the compensator groove. Adjust as described in Section 17.

20 Brake pedal - removal and refitting

Removal

1 Remove the steering column cowls and/or lower facia trim panels as applicable according to type and year (refer to the relevant Sections in Chapter 11).

2 Extract the spring clip and clevis pin and disconnect the brake thrust rod from the brake pedal.

3 Disconnect the return and tension springs and remove the spring clip from the end of the pedal cross-shaft.

4 Push the cross-shaft out of the pedal bracket until the pedal can be removed.

Refitting

5 Refitting is reversal of removal.

21 Vacuum pump - testing and overhaul

Testing

1 The operation of the braking system vacuum pump can be checked using a vacuum gauge.
2 Disconnect the vacuum pipe from the pump and connect the gauge to the pump union using a suitable length of hose.
3 Run the engine at a minimum speed of 2000 rpm then measure the vacuum created by the pump. As a guide, a minimum of approximately 770 mbars should be recorded. If the vacuum registered is significantly less than this it is likely that the pump is faulty. However, seek the advice of a Renault dealer before condemning the pump.

Overhaul

4 If the pump is found to be faulty it must be renewed. The pump is a sealed unit and it is not possible to overhaul it.

22 Vacuum pump - removal and refitting

Removal

1 Disconnect the battery negative lead.
2 To improve access to the pump, firmly apply the handbrake then jack up the front of the vehicle and support it on axle stands (see "Jacking and vehicle support").
3 Slacken the retaining clip and disconnect the vacuum hose from the top of the pump which is situated on the left-hand side of the cylinder block.
4 Undo the two retaining bolts and carefully lift the pump away from the engine **(see illustration)**. Remove the O-ring from the pump sealing groove and discard it; a new one should be used on refitting.
5 If necessary, carefully withdraw the oil pump/vacuum pump drivegear, taking great care not to dislodge the oil pump driveshaft.
Note: *Great care must be taken to ensure that the driveshaft is not dislodged from the oil pump. If the driveshaft is dislodged it will drop down into the bottom sump. If this happens, the sump will have to be removed in order to recover the driveshaft.*

Refitting

6 Where necessary, ensure that the driveshaft is correctly engaged with the oil pump then refit the oil pump/vacuum pump drivegear, engaging it with driveshaft.
7 Fit a new O-ring to the vacuum pump groove and apply a smear of engine oil to it to aid installation.
8 Slide the vacuum pump into place, aligning its drive dog with the slot in the drivegear.
9 Refit the pump retaining bolts and tighten them securely.
10 Reconnect the vacuum hose to the pump.
11 Lower the vehicle to the ground then reconnect the battery. Check the operation of the braking system before taking the vehicle on the road.

23 Anti-lock braking system (ABS) - general information

1 When fitted, the anti-lock braking system monitors the rotational speed of the wheels under braking. Sudden deceleration of one wheel, indicating that lock-up is occurring, causes the hydraulic pressure to that wheel's brake to be reduced or interrupted momentarily. Monitoring and correction take place several times per second, giving rise to a "pulsing" effect at the brake pedal when correction is taking place. The system gives even inexperienced drivers a good chance of retaining control when braking hard on slippery surfaces.
2 The main components of the system are the sensors, the control unit and the hydraulic modulator.
3 One sensor is fitted to each wheel, picking up speed information from a pulse wheel carried on the front driveshafts or rear hubs.
4 Information from the sensors is fed to the control unit which is located in the engine compartment. The control unit operates solenoid valves in the hydraulic modulator, also located in the engine compartment, to restrict if necessary the hydraulic fluid supply to the brake calipers. The control unit also illuminates a warning light in the event of system malfunction.
5 The hydraulic modulator contains a pump as well as solenoid valves. It is a semi-active device, increasing the effort applied at the brake pedal. If the modulator fails, adequate braking effort will still be available from the master cylinder and servo, though the anti-lock function will be lost.
6 To avoid damage to the ABS control unit, do not subject it to voltage surges in excess of 16V, nor to temperatures in excess of 80°C.

24 Anti-lock Braking System (ABS) components - removal and refitting

Removal

Front wheel sensor

1 Apply the handbrake, chock the rear wheels then jack up the front of the vehicle and support it on axle stands (see "Jacking and vehicle support"). Remove the relevant roadwheel.
2 Disconnect the wheel sensor wiring connector under the wheel arch and release the wiring from any cable clips.
3 Remove the Allen screw which secures the sensor to the hub carrier **(see illustration)**. Withdraw the sensor and its wiring.

Front disc pulse wheel

4 The front pulse wheel is a press fit on the driveshaft outer constant velocity joint and special tools are required for removal. This work should be entrusted to a Renault dealer.

Rear wheel sensor

5 Chock the front wheels then jack up the rear of the vehicle and support it on axle stands (see "Jacking and vehicle support").
6 Disconnect the wheel sensor wiring connector from the underside of the vehicle and release the wiring from any cable clips.
7 Remove the Allen screw which secures the sensor to the rear hub carrier **(see illustration)**. Withdraw the sensor and its wiring.

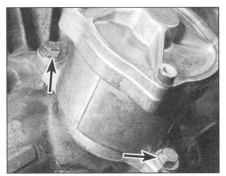

22.4 Vacuum pump retaining bolts (arrowed)

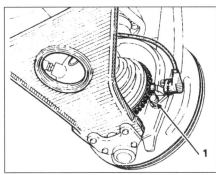

24.3 ABS front wheel sensor retaining screw (1)

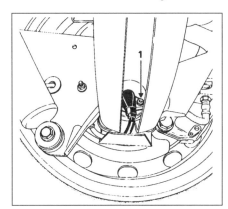

24.7 ABS rear wheel sensor retaining screw (1)

9

Control unit

8 The control unit is located in the right-hand rear corner of the engine compartment.

9 Disconnect the battery negative lead.

10 Undo the screws or bolts and lift off the control unit plastic cover **(see illustration)**.

11 Undo the two control unit retaining bolts, withdraw the unit and disconnect the wiring plug.

Hydraulic modulator

Note: *Before starting work, refer to the warning at the beginning of Section 2 concerning the dangers of hydraulic fluid.*

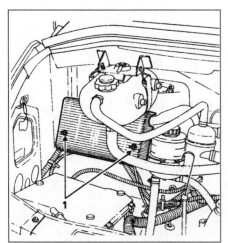

24.10 Undo the two screws (1) and remove the ABS control unit cover

12 Disconnect the battery negative lead.

13 Undo the screw and lift off the plastic cover over the hydraulic modulator. Unscrew the cable clamp and disconnect the modulator wiring multiplug.

14 Remove the master cylinder reservoir filler cap, and place a piece of polythene over the filler neck. Seal the polythene with an elastic band, ensuring that an airtight seal is obtained. This will minimise brake fluid loss during subsequent operations. Place rags beneath the modulator as an added precaution against fluid spillage.

15 The modulator body is stamped with a

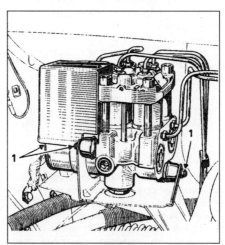

24.17 ABS hydraulic modulator mountings (1)

two-letter code adjacent to each modulator port , with a corresponding paint mark on each brake pipe as follows:

Modulator port	Brake pipe identification
VR = Right-hand front	Green pipe, no mark
VL = Left-hand front	Green pipe, yellow mark
HR = Right-hand rear	Green pipe, red mark
HL = Left-hand rear	Green pipe, white mark

16 Unscrew each brake pipe union at the modulator, withdraw the pipe, and immediately plug the pipe end and orifice.

17 Slacken the modulator mounting nuts and remove the unit from its location **(see illustration)**. Do not attempt to dismantle the modulator, as it is a sealed unit, and no repairs are possible.

Refitting

18 In all cases, refit by reversing the removal operations but noting the following points:

a) *When refitting the wheel sensors, apply a little grease (Renault part No. 77 01 422 308, or equivalent) to the body of the sensor.*

b) *Ensure the hydraulic modulator brake pipes are connected to their correct ports.*

c) *Bleed the complete hydraulic system after refitting the hydraulic modulator.*

Chapter 10
Suspension and steering

Contents

Degrees of difficulty

Easy, suitable for novice with little experience 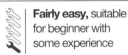	Fairly easy, suitable for beginner with some experience	Fairly difficult, suitable for competent DIY mechanic	Difficult, suitable for experienced DIY mechanic	Very difficult, suitable for expert DIY or professional

Specifications

Steering
Steering fluid type . . . . See end of "Weekly checks"

Front wheel alignment and steering angles
Castor:
   Early models . . . . 3°25' ± 20'
   Later models . . . . 4°24' ± 20'
Toe setting (measured at wheel rims) . . . . 4.0 ± 2.0 mm toe-out

Roadwheels
Type . . . . Pressed steel or aluminium alloy (depending on model)
Size . . . . 5.5J x 13, 5.5J x 14, 6J x 14
Run-out . . . . 1.2 mm

Torque wrench settings

Nm

Front suspension

	Nm
Driveshaft nut*	250
Upper arm balljoint to hub carrier	65
Lower arm balljoint to hub carrier	65
Bearing assembly to hub carrier	15
Shock absorber lower mounting locknut	40
Shock absorber/anti-roll bar link to upper arm	80
Upper arm inner pivot nuts	95
Lower arm inner pivot nuts (single pivot pin mounting)	90
Lower arm inner pivot (with separate rear mounting):	
Front mounting pivot bolt	135
Rear mounting bolts	45
Anti-roll bar saddle clamp nuts	20
Shock absorber upper mounting nuts	25
Shock absorber piston rod nut	20

10

Rear suspension

Stub axle hub nut:*
    Drum brake models 160
    Disc brake models 200
Bearing carrier to rear axle (disc brake models) 20
Shock absorber upper mounting 50
Shock absorber lower mounting 25
Transverse rod mounting bolts 50
Rear axle trailing arm mountings 20

Steering

Steering gear mounting bolts 40
Steering column mounting bolts 25
Steering wheel nut 90
Track rod end balljoint nut 40

Roadwheels

Wheel bolts 90
*Use new nuts

---

1 General information

The front suspension is of independent, double wishbone type with strut units, incorporating coil springs and telescopic shock absorbers, acting on the upper wishbone. The upper wishbones (suspension arms) are positively located by radius rods which are adjustable to alter the castor angle. An anti-roll bar is fitted to all models.

The rear suspension is of semi-independent type, featuring a "clover-shaped" axle located by twin longitudinal trailing arms and a transverse rod. Coil springs and inclined telescopic shock absorbers are attached to each side of the axle unit.

Steering is by power-assisted rack and pinion on all models. Power assistance is derived from a hydraulic pump, belt-driven from the crankshaft pulley.

2 Front hub bearings - checking and renewal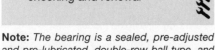

Note: *The bearing is a sealed, pre-adjusted and pre-lubricated, double-row ball type, and is intended to last the car's service life without maintenance or attention. Do not attempt to*

2.6 Forcing the hub flange from the bearing assembly (unit removed for clarity)

remove the bearing unless absolutely necessary, as it will be damaged during removal. Never overtighten the driveshaft nut in an attempt to "adjust" the bearing.

A press will be required to dismantle and rebuild the assembly; if one is not available, a large bench vice and suitable spacers (such as large sockets) is an adequate substitute. The bearing's inner races are an interference fit on the wheel hub flange; if the inner bearing inner race remains on the hub flange when the flange is removed, a suitable knife-edged bearing puller will be required to remove it.

Checking

1 Chock the rear wheels then jack up the front of the vehicle and support it on axle stands (see *"Jacking and vehicle support"*). Remove the appropriate roadwheel.

2 Wear in the front hub bearings can be checked by measuring the amount of side play present. To do this, a dial gauge should be fixed so that its probe is in contact with the disc face of the hub. The play should be between 0 and 0.05 mm. If it is greater than this, the bearings are worn excessively, and should be renewed.

Renewal

3 Refit at least two roadwheel bolts to the front hub, and tighten them securely. Have an assistant firmly depress the brake pedal to prevent the front hub from rotating. Using a

2.10 Driving the bearing assembly onto the hub flange

socket and a long extension bar, slacken and remove the driveshaft retaining nut and washer. This nut is extremely tight. Alternatively, a tool can be fabricated from two lengths of steel strip (one long, one short) and a nut an bolt; the nut and bolt form the pivot of a forked tool. Bolt the tool to the hub using two wheel bolts, and hold the tool to prevent the hub from rotating as the driveshaft retaining nut is undone (see Chapter 8, Section 2). Discard the driveshaft nut; a new one should be used on refitting.

4 Undo the two bolts securing the brake caliper to the hub carrier. Slide the caliper, complete with pads, off the disc and tie it up using string or wire from a suitable place under the wheel arch.

5 Unscrew the two disc retaining screws and remove the brake disc.

6 Using two roadwheel bolts and two steel packing pieces, screw the bolts into two diagonally opposite wheel bolt holes in the hub flange until they contact the packing pieces which should be positioned behind the flange **(see illustration)**. Screw in the bolts gradually and evenly to force the hub flange from the bearing assembly.

7 Using a suitable Torx bit, unscrew the six bolts and withdraw the bearing assembly from the hub carrier.

8 The outer bearing inner race will probably have stayed on the hub flange when the flange was removed from the bearing. Use a knife-edged bearing puller which will engage behind the race, to remove it from the hub flange or, alternatively, have it removed by a dealer or local garage.

9 Prior to reassembly, check (if possible) that the new bearing is packed with grease. Apply a light film of oil to the bearing inner races and to the hub flange shaft.

10 Position the hub flange face down on the bench and locate the new bearing assembly over the end of the hub flange. Ensure that the bearing is the right way round with its outer face facing the hub flange. Press or drive the bearing onto the hub flange, using a tubular spacer which bears only on the inner race, until it is fully seated **(see illustration)**. Check that the hub flange rotates freely. Wipe off any excess oil or grease.

11 Ensure that the driveshaft joint and hub flange splines are clean and dry, then apply a coat of locking fluid to the driveshaft joint splines.

12 Position the assembled bearing and hub flange over the driveshaft joint splines and into position in the hub carrier. Tap the assembly into place using a soft-faced mallet if necessary. Working through the wheel bolt holes in the hub flange, fit the six bearing retaining bolts and tighten them securely.

13 Slide on the washer and fit the new driveshaft nut, tightening it by hand only at this stage.

14 Refit the brake disc and securely tighten its retaining screws. Refit the brake caliper assembly and tighten the retaining bolts to the specified torque (see Chapter 9).

15 Insert and tighten two wheel bolts. Tighten the driveshaft nut to the specified torque, using the method employed during removal to prevent the hub from rotating.

16 Check that the hub rotates freely, then refit the roadwheel and lower the vehicle to the ground. Tighten the roadwheel bolts to the specified torque.

3 Front hub carrier - removal and refitting

Removal

1 Carry out the operations described in Section 2, paragraphs 2 to 5.

2 On models with ABS, disconnect or remove the wheel sensor.

3 Undo the retaining nuts then disconnect the suspension upper arm balljoint and the steering track rod end balljoint from the hub carrier using a balljoint separator tool.

4 Unscrew the suspension lower arm balljoint nut until it makes contact with the driveshaft outer joint. Continue unscrewing it so that it acts as an extractor to release the balljoint tapered shank from of the eye of the hub carrier **(see illustration)**. Note that a new nut will be required for reassembly.

5 Lever downward on the suspension lower arm and lift the hub carrier off the balljoint shank.

6 Tap the end of the driveshaft outer joint using a soft-faced mallet to release it from the hub flange. Withdraw the hub carrier from the suspension upper arm balljoint and remove it from the vehicle.

7 If required, the hub flange and bearing assembly can be removed by unscrewing the six retaining bolts using a Torx key inserted through the wheel bolt holes. Gently tap the bearing and hub flange assembly out of the hub carrier from behind.

Refitting

8 If removed, refit the bearing and hub flange assembly to the hub carrier and secure with the six bolts.

9 Ensure that the driveshaft joint and hub flange splines are clean and dry, then apply a coat of locking fluid to the driveshaft joint splines.

10 Position the hub carrier over the driveshaft joint splines, tapping it into place if necessary. Engage the upper and lower balljoints with the hub carrier then fit and tighten the retaining nuts. Remember a new nut must be used on the lower balljoint.

11 Reconnect the track rod end to the hub carrier and tighten the retaining nut.

12 Slide on the washer and fit the new driveshaft nut, tightening it by hand only at this stage.

13 Refit the brake disc and securely tighten its retaining screws. Refit the brake caliper assembly and tighten the retaining bolts to the specified torque (see Chapter 9).

14 Insert and tighten two wheel bolts. Tighten the driveshaft nut to the specified torque setting, using the method employed during removal to prevent the hub from rotating.

15 On models with ABS refit or reconnect the wheel sensor.

16 Check that the hub rotates freely, then refit the roadwheel and lower the vehicle to the ground. Tighten the roadwheel bolts to the specified torque.

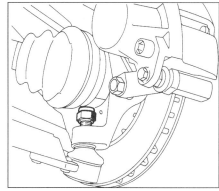

3.4 Using the lower arm balljoint nut to release the balljoint tapered shank

4 Front suspension upper arm - removal and refitting

Removal

1 Chock the rear wheels then jack up the front of the vehicle and support it on axle stands (see *"Jacking and vehicle support"*). Remove the appropriate front roadwheel.

2 Place a jack under the suspension lower arm and just take the weight of the suspension assembly.

3 Release the locknut securing the shock absorber threaded end to the lower mounting **(see illustration)**.

4 Undo the retaining bolt(s) and nut(s) and disconnect the radius rod from the suspension upper arm **(see illustration)**.

5 Undo the retaining nut then disconnect the suspension upper arm balljoint from the hub carrier using a balljoint separator tool.

6 Unscrew the nut from the through-bolt securing the anti-roll bar upper link and shock absorber lower mounting to the suspension upper arm **(see illustration)**. Withdraw the through-bolt from the upper arm.

7 Raise the upper arm slightly and unscrew the lower mounting from the shock absorber threaded end.

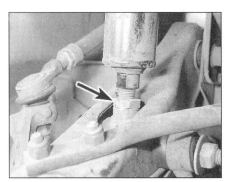

4.3 Shock absorber lower mounting locknut (arrowed)

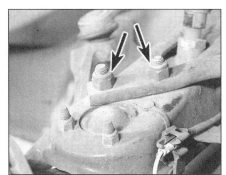

4.4 Radius rod to upper arm retaining nuts (arrowed)

4.6 Anti-roll bar link and shock absorber mounting nut and through bolt

10

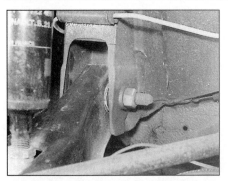

4.8 Upper arm inboard pivot bolt and nut

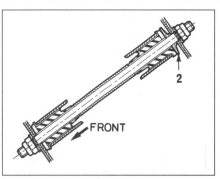

6.3 Lower arm pivot pin and castor control shim (2) (single pivot pin type)

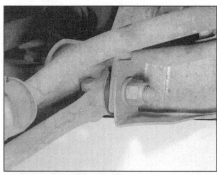

6.4a Lower arm front mounting pivot nut and bolt (separate rear mounting type)

8 Unscrew the upper arm inboard pivot nut and withdraw the bolt **(see illustration)**. Remove the upper arm from the vehicle.

9 If the pivot bush is worn, press it out or use a piece of tubing of suitable diameter, with a bolt, nut and washers to draw out the old bush and refit the new one. Make sure that the new bush is centralised in the arm and protrudes by equal amounts both sides.

Refitting

10 Refitting is a reversal of removal. Tighten the upper arm pivot bolt and the shock absorber bottom mounting pivot bolt moderately tightly initially, then tighten fully to the specified torque when the weight of the vehicle is on the roadwheels.

5 Front suspension upper arm balljoint - renewal

1 Chock the rear wheels then jack up the front of the vehicle and support it on axle stands (see *"Jacking and vehicle support"*). Remove the appropriate front roadwheel.

2 Undo the retaining bolt(s) and nut(s) and disconnect the radius rod from the suspension upper arm.

3 Undo the retaining nut then disconnect the suspension upper arm balljoint from the hub carrier using a balljoint separator tool.

4 Unbolt the balljoint from the upper arm.

6.4b Lower arm rear mounting assembly retaining nuts (arrowed) (separate rear mounting type)

5 Fit the new balljoint, making sure that the retaining bolts have the nuts on top.

6 Reconnect the balljoint and the radius rod, and tighten the nuts and bolts.

7 Refit the roadwheel and lower the vehicle to the ground.

6 Front suspension lower arm - removal and refitting

Removal

1 Chock the rear wheels then jack up the front of the vehicle and support it on axle stands (see *"Jacking and vehicle support"*). Remove the appropriate front roadwheel.

2 Unscrew the suspension lower arm balljoint nut until it makes contact with the driveshaft outer joint. Continue unscrewing it so that it acts as an extractor to release the balljoint tapered shank from of the eye of the hub carrier. Note that a new nut will be required for reassembly.

3 Where the lower arm is secured by a single pivot pin with nuts at each end, unscrew the pivot pin nuts and withdraw the pin towards the front of the vehicle. Note the location of the castor control shim **(see illustration)**.

4 On models where the lower arm rear mounting is a separate assembly, first undo the nut and withdraw the front mounting pivot bolt. Undo the two nuts and bolts securing the

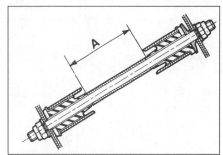

6.5 Lower arm bush setting diagram (single pivot pin type)

A = 181.3 mm (up to December 1987)
A = 112.6 mm (from January 1988)

rear mounting assembly to the body and withdraw the arm from the vehicle **(see illustrations)**.

5 On models with a single pivot pin mounting, worn flexible bushes can be renewed using a press or by using a distance piece, bolt, nut and washers. To maintain the correct fitted dimension between the bushes, remove and refit them one at a time, ensuring that the dimension between their inner ends when fitted, is as shown **(see illustration)**.

6 On models with a separate rear mounting assembly, the bushes at the lower arm front mounting can be renewed as described in the previous paragraph. Note however that a split bush is used with flanged ends and it will be necessary to saw through the flange of one of the bushes to enable them to be removed. Fit the new bushes until their flanges are in contact with the arm. To remove the rear mounting assembly, position it on a press or engage the legs of a puller behind it. Press the pin of the lower arm out of the mounting assembly. Fit the new mounting with reference to the position and dimension shown **(see illustration)**.

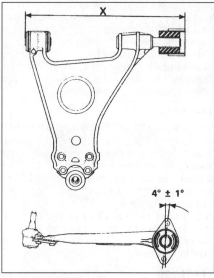

6.6 Lower arm rear mounting setting diagram (separate rear mounting type)

X = 393 ± 0.5 mm

8.3 Radius rod inner mounting

Refitting

7 Refitting is a reversal of removal, noting the following points:

a) Lubricate the pivot pin or front mounting pivot bolt with molybdenum disulphide grease before fitting.

b) Ensure that the castor control shim is fitted between the rear mounting bush and the chassis member.

c) Tighten all nuts and bolts to the specified torque, but leave the pivot pin nuts and rear mounting nuts/bolts until the weight of the vehicle is on the roadwheels.

7 Front suspension lower arm balljoint - renewal
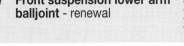

1 Remove the front suspension lower arm as described in Section 6.

2 With the lower arm on the bench, drill out the securing rivets and remove the balljoint. The new balljoint will be supplied with nuts and bolts for refitting.

3 Locate the balljoint on the arm and secure with the new nuts and bolts ensuring that the bolt heads are uppermost.

4 Refit the lower arm as described in Section 6.

8 Front radius rod - removal and refitting

Removal

1 Chock the rear wheels then jack up the front of the vehicle and support it on axle stands (see "Jacking and vehicle support"). Remove the appropriate front roadwheel.

2 Undo the retaining bolt(s) and nut(s) and disconnect the radius rod from the suspension upper arm.

3 Undo the nut and withdraw the pivot bolt from the radius rod inner mounting. Withdraw the inner mounting and remove the radius rod **(see illustration)**.

Refitting

4 Refitting is a reversal of removal. Do not fully tighten the inner mounting nut until the weight of the vehicle is on the roadwheels.

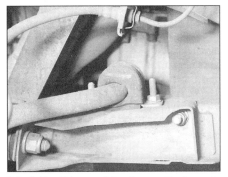

9.3 Anti-roll bar saddle clamp attachments

9 Front anti-roll bar - removal and refitting
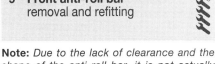

Note: Due to the lack of clearance and the shape of the anti-roll bar, it is not actually possible to remove the bar completely unless the engine is removed first. It is however possible to renew all the mountings with the anti-roll bar installed, as described below. If the anti-roll bar itself is to be renewed, remove the engine as described in Chapter 2C.

Removal

1 Chock the rear wheels then jack up the front of the vehicle and support it on axle stands (see "Jacking and vehicle support"). Remove both front roadwheels.

2 Working on one side at a time, unscrew the nut from the through-bolt securing the anti-roll bar connecting link and shock absorber lower mounting to the suspension upper arm. Withdraw the through-bolt slightly and slide off the link.

3 Unbolt the two saddle clamps which secure the anti-roll bar to the chassis members **(see illustration)**.

4 Extract the circlip and withdraw the connecting link from the end of the anti-roll bar. Collect the washers on each side of the link.

10.3a First version shock absorber upper mounting nut (A)

5 Slide the inner rubber insulators off the end of the anti-roll bar.

6 Repeat the above on the other side of the vehicle. The anti-roll bar can then be withdrawn if the engine has been removed first.

Refitting

7 Refitting is a reversal of removal using new components as necessary. Lubricate the bushes with rubber grease and tighten the nuts to the specified torque when the weight of the vehicle is on its roadwheels.

10 Front coil spring and shock absorber - general information and precautions

General information

1 Two different coil spring and shock absorber upper mounting arrangements may be encountered. On the first version, the shock absorber piston upper mounting is attached directly to the inner wheel arch by rubber bushes, washer and a nut/locknut arrangement. On the second version, the shock absorber piston is attached to an upper mounting plate which also retains the coil spring. This mounting plate is then secured to the inner wheel arch by three or four nuts.

2 Before starting any dismantling of the shock absorber and coil spring components, it is essential to identify the type fitted, and take the necessary precautions detailed below.

3 From within the engine compartment, observe the shock absorber upper mounting at the top of the wheel arch. If only a single nut /locknut can be seen, then the first version is fitted. If three or four nuts are visible, together with the actual shock absorber retaining nut in the centre, then the second version is fitted **(see illustrations)**.

Precautions

4 Due to the need for Renault special tools and jigs to retain the coil spring on the first version, it is essential that any procedures involving the coil spring and/or shock absorber must be carried out by a Renault dealer.

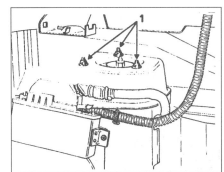

10.3b Second version shock absorber upper mounting nuts (1)

5 The information contained in Sections 11 and 12 is therefore applicable to the second version only, which can be worked on without Renault jigs, although coil spring compressors will still be needed.

 Warning: any attempt to dismantle the first version coil spring and shock absorber without Renault special tools and the knowledge to use them safely could result in damage or personal injury.

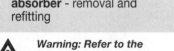
11 Front coil spring and shock absorber - removal and refitting

 Warning: Refer to the information contained in Section 10 before proceeding.
Note: *The following procedures are applicable to the second version coil spring and shock absorber arrangement only (see Section 10).*

Removal

1 Chock the rear wheels then jack up the front of the vehicle and support it on axle stands (see *"Jacking and vehicle support"*). Remove the appropriate front roadwheel.
2 Place a jack under the suspension lower arm and just take the weight of the suspension assembly.
3 Release the locknut securing the shock absorber threaded end to the lower mounting.
4 Unscrew the nut from the through-bolt securing the anti-roll bar upper link and shock absorber lower mounting to the suspension upper arm. Withdraw the through-bolt from the upper arm **(see illustration)**.
5 Raise the upper arm slightly and unscrew the lower mounting from the shock absorber threaded end.
6 Have an assistant support the shock absorber from below. Working in the engine compartment, unscrew the three nuts securing the shock absorber and coil spring upper mounting plate to the inner wheel arch. **Do not** unscrew the centre locknut. Remove the assembly from under the wheel arch.

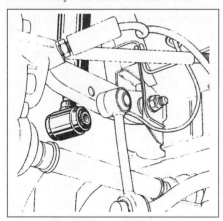
11.4 Separating the shock absorber lower mounting from the upper arm

Refitting

7 Refitting is a reversal of removal. Tighten all nuts and bolts to the specified torque. Tighten the shock absorber bottom mounting pivot bolt moderately tightly initially, then tighten fully when the weight of the vehicle is on the roadwheels.

12 Front coil spring and shock absorber - dismantling, inspection and reassembly

 Warning: Before attempting to dismantle the shock absorber and coil spring assembly, a suitable tool to hold the spring in compression must be obtained. Adjustable coil spring compressors are readily available, and are recommended for this operation. Any attempt at dismantling without such a tool is likely to result in damage or personal injury.

Dismantling

1 Remove the coil spring and shock absorber from the vehicle as described in Section 11.
2 Fit spring compressors to catch at least three coils of the spring. Tighten the compressors to compress the spring by around 10 cm, or until the load is taken off the spring seats. Make sure the compressors are secure.
3 Hold the shock absorber piston rod with an Allen key and unscrew the retaining nut.
4 Remove the washer, spring upper seat, the spring itself, the bump stop (where fitted) and gaiter.

Inspection

5 With the strut assembly now completely dismantled, examine all the components for wear, damage or deformation. Renew any of the components as necessary.
6 Examine the shock absorber for signs of fluid leakage and check the strut piston for signs of pitting along its entire length. Test the operation of the shock absorber, while holding it in an upright position, by moving the piston through a full stroke and then through short strokes of 50 to 100 mm. In both cases the resistance felt should be smooth and continuous. If the resistance is jerky, or uneven, or if there is any visible sign of wear or damage, renewal is necessary.
7 If any doubt exists about the condition of the coil spring, gradually release the spring compressor, and check the spring for distortion and signs of cracking. Since no minimum free length is specified by Renault, the only way to check the tension of the spring is to compare it to a new component. Renew the spring if it is damaged or distorted, or if there is any doubt as to its condition.
8 Inspect all other components for damage or deterioration, and renew any that are suspect.
9 If a new shock absorber is being fitted, hold it vertically and pump the piston a few times to prime it.

Reassembly

10 Reassembly is a reversal of dismantling, however make sure that the spring ends are correctly located in the upper and lower seats and tighten the upper nut to the specified torque.

13 Rear hub bearing - checking and renewal

Drum brake models

Checking and renewal

1 On drum brake models, the rear hub bearings cannot be renewed separately and are supplied with the rear hub as a complete assembly.
2 If the checks described in Chapter 1, indicate that the bearings are worn, remove the brake drum as described in Chapter 9, then undo the hub nut and withdraw the hub and bearing assembly.
3 Fit the new assembly, screw on the hub nut and tighten it to the specified torque. Refit the brake drum as described in Chapter 9.

Disc brake models

Note: *The bearing is a sealed, pre-adjusted and pre-lubricated, double-row ball type, and is intended to last the car's entire service life without maintenance or attention. Do not attempt to remove the bearing unless absolutely necessary, as it will be damaged during the removal operation. Never overtighten the rear hub nut in an attempt to "adjust" the bearing.*
A press will be required to dismantle and rebuild the assembly; if such a tool is not available, a large bench vice and suitable spacers (such as large sockets) will serve as an adequate substitute. The bearing's inner races are an interference fit on the hub flange; if the inner race remains on the hub when it is pressed out of the bearing carrier, a suitable knife-edged bearing puller will be required to remove it.

Checking

4 Chock the front wheels then jack up the rear of the vehicle and support it on axle stands (see *"Jacking and vehicle support"*). Release the handbrake and remove the roadwheel.
5 Wear in the rear hub bearings can be checked by measuring the amount of side play present. To do this, a dial gauge should be fixed so that its probe is in contact with the disc face of the hub. The play should be between 0 and 0.05 mm. If it is greater than this, the bearings are worn excessively, and should be renewed.

Renewal

6 Refit at least two roadwheel bolts to the rear hub, and tighten them securely. Have an assistant firmly depress the brake pedal to prevent the hub from rotating. Using a socket and a long extension bar, slacken and remove the hub nut and washer. This nut is extremely tight. Alternatively, a tool can be fabricated from two lengths of steel strip (one long, one short) and a nut an bolt; the nut and bolt form the pivot of a forked tool. Bolt the tool to the hub using two wheel bolts, and hold the tool to prevent the hub from rotating as the nut is undone (see Chapter 8, Section 2).

7 Refer to Chapter 9 and remove the rear brake pads, caliper carrier bracket and brake disc.

8 Remove the bearing carrier assembly by unscrewing the six retaining bolts using a Torx key inserted through the wheel bolt holes in the hub flange. Withdraw the bearing carrier from the rear axle.

9 Withdraw the stub axle from the hub flange tapping it out with a mallet if necessary.

10 Support the bearing carrier securely on blocks or in a vice. Using a tubular spacer which bears only on the inner end of the hub flange, press the hub flange out of the bearing. If the bearing outboard inner race remains on the hub, remove it using a bearing puller (see note above), then slide the thrustwasher off the hub flange, noting which way round it is fitted.

11 Extract the bearing retaining circlip from the inner end of the bearing carrier.

12 Where necessary, refit the inner race in position over the ball cage, and securely support the inner face of the bearing carrier. Using a tubular spacer which bears only on the inner race, press the complete bearing assembly out of the carrier.

13 Thoroughly clean the hub flange and bearing carrier, removing all traces of dirt and grease. Polish away any burrs or raised edges which might hinder reassembly. Check for cracks or any other signs of wear or damage, and renew the components if necessary. As noted above, the bearing and its circlip must be renewed whenever they are disturbed. A replacement bearing kit, which consists of the bearing, circlip and thrustwasher, is available from Renault dealers.

14 On reassembly, check (if possible) that the new bearing is packed with grease. Apply a light film of oil to the bearing outer race and to the hub flange shaft.

15 Before fitting the new bearing, remove the plastic covers protecting the seals at each end, but leave the inner plastic sleeve in position to hold the inner races together.

16 Securely support the bearing carrier, and locate the bearing in its housing. Press the bearing into position, ensuring that it enters the housing squarely, using a tubular spacer which bears only on the outer race.

17 Once the bearing is correctly seated, secure it with the new circlip and remove the plastic sleeve. Apply a smear of grease to the oil seal lips.

18 Slide the thrustwasher onto the hub flange, ensuring that its flat surface is facing the flange. Securely support the outer face of the hub flange.

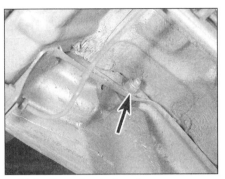

14.3a Rear shock absorber upper . . .

19 Locate the bearing carrier and the bearing inner race over the end of the hub flange. Press the bearing onto the hub flange, using a tubular spacer which bears only on the inner race, until it seats against the thrustwasher. Check that the hub flange rotates freely. Wipe off any excess oil or grease.

20 Refit the stub axle through the hub flange, refit the hub nut and moderately tighten it at this stage.

21 Refit the bearing carrier assembly securing it with the six retaining bolts tightened to the specified torque.

22 Refer to Chapter 9 and refit the rear brake disc, caliper carrier bracket and brake pads.

23 Insert and tighten two wheel bolts. Tighten the hub nut to the specified torque, using the method employed during removal to prevent the hub from rotating.

24 Check that the hub rotates freely, then refit the roadwheel and lower the vehicle to the ground. Tighten the roadwheel bolts to the specified torque.

14 Rear shock absorber - removal, inspection and refitting

Removal

1 Chock the front wheels then jack up the rear of the vehicle and support it on axle stands (see *"Jacking and vehicle support"*). Remove the roadwheel.

2 Place a jack under the rear axle on the side concerned adjacent to the shock absorber lower mounting. Raise the rear axle slightly to take the load off the shock absorber.

3 Remove the shock absorber upper and lower mounting nuts and bolts and remove the unit from under the vehicle **(see illustrations)**.

Inspection

4 Examine the shock absorber for signs of fluid leakage, damage or corrosion. Test the operation of the shock absorber, while holding it in an upright position, by moving the spindle through a full stroke, and then through short strokes of 50 to 100 mm. In both cases, the resistance felt should be smooth and continuous. If the resistance is jerky or

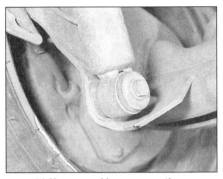

14.3b . . . and lower mountings

uneven, or if there is any visible sign of wear, damage or fluid leakage, renewal is necessary. Also check the condition of the upper and lower mountings, and renew any components as necessary.

5 If a new shock absorber is being fitted, hold it vertically and pump the piston a few times to prime it.

Refitting

6 Refit by reversing the removal operations. Tighten the shock absorber mountings to the specified torque.

15 Rear coil spring - removal and refitting

Removal

1 Chock the front wheels then jack up the rear of the vehicle and support it on axle stands (see *"Jacking and vehicle support"*). Remove the roadwheel.

2 Place a jack under the rear axle on the side concerned beneath the shock absorber lower mounting and just take the weight of the axle assembly.

3 Undo the nut and bolt and release the transverse rod from the axle.

4 Remove the shock absorber lower mounting nuts and bolts.

5 Lower the jack until all tension is relieved from the spring, then lift the spring out of its location.

Refitting

6 Refitting is a reversal of removal, tightening the retaining nuts and bolts to the specified torque.

16 Rear transverse rod - removal and refitting

10

Removal

1 Chock the front wheels then jack up the rear of the vehicle and support it on axle stands (see *"Jacking and vehicle support"*).

2 Accurately mark the position of the brake compensator adjusting nut on the threaded

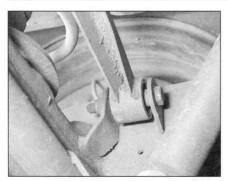

16.3a Rear transverse rod attachment at the rear axle ...

16.3b ... and at the chassis member

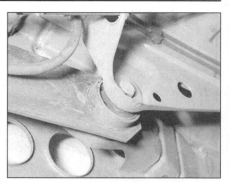

17.10 Rear axle trailing arm front mounting

rod, as an aid to refitting. Unscrew the nut from the end of the compensator threaded rod.

3 Undo the nuts and bolts at each end of the transverse rod and withdraw it from under the vehicle **(see illustrations)**.

4 If necessary the rubber bushes can be renewed using a press or by using a distance piece, bolt, nut and washers.

Refitting

5 Refitting is a reversal of removal, tightening the retaining nuts and bolts to the specified torque. If the set position of the brake compensator was lost, have the adjustment checked by a Renault dealer at the earliest opportunity.

17 Rear axle assembly - removal and refitting

Removal

1 Chock the front wheels then jack up the rear of the vehicle and support it on axle stands (see *"Jacking and vehicle support"*). Remove both rear roadwheels.

2 Unscrew the brake master cylinder reservoir filler cap and place a piece of polythene over the filler neck. Secure the polythene with an elastic band ensuring that an airtight seal is obtained.

3 Disconnect the brake pipes from the axle trailing arms and cover the open unions to prevent dirt entry.

4 On models with drum type rear brakes, remove the brake drums as described in Chapter 9.

5 Disconnect the handbrake cable from the brake shoes or brake caliper levers, referring to Chapter 9 if necessary. Release the cable from the axle trailing arms.

6 Undo the nut and bolt and release the transverse rod from the axle.

7 Place a jack under the centre of the rear axle and just take the weight of the axle assembly.

8 Remove the shock absorber lower mounting nuts and bolts.

9 Lower the jack until all tension is relieved from the coil springs, then lift the springs out of their locations.

10 Undo the trailing arm front mounting nuts and bolts on each side **(see illustration)**.

11 Withdraw the trailing arms from the chassis locations and remove the axle from under the vehicle.

12 Refer to the relevant Chapters and Sections of this manual if further dismantling of the axle is required.

Refitting

13 Refitting is a reversal of removal, but note the following points:

a) Tighten all retaining nuts and bolts to the specified torque.

b) Ensure that all brake fluid line connections are clean before reconnecting them. Refer to the appropriate Sections in Chapter 9 for specific details on reconnecting the brake lines, bleeding the brake hydraulic system, and reconnecting the handbrake cable and brake drums.

18 Steering wheel - removal and refitting

⚠ **Warning: On vehicles equipped with an air bag, DO NOT attempt to remove the steering wheel. Have any work involving steering wheel removal carried out by a Renault dealer. Refer to Chapter 12 for further information.**

Removal

1 Disconnect the battery negative lead.

2 Bring the steering wheel to the straight-ahead position.

3 Prise off the steering wheel centre pad.

4 Undo the steering wheel centre retaining nut.

 HAYNES HiNT *If the wheel is tight, tap it up near the centre, using the palm of your hand, or twist it from side to side whilst pulling, to release it from the column splines.*

5 Make alignment marks between the steering wheel and column, then pull the steering wheel off its splines.

Refitting

6 Refitting is a reversal of removal, observing the alignment marks or the straight-ahead position of the wheel.

19 Steering column - removal and refitting

⚠ **Warning: On vehicles equipped with an air bag, DO NOT attempt to remove the steering wheel. Have any work involving steering wheel removal carried out by a Renault dealer. Refer to Chapter 12 for further information.**

Removal

1 Disconnect the battery negative lead.

2 Remove the steering wheel as described in Section 18.

3 On early models, undo the four screws and remove the parcel shelf below the steering column. Undo the two screws at the top and two screws at the side securing the trim panel under the steering column. Remove the bonnet release handle assembly and lift out the trim panel.

4 On later models, undo the five screws and remove the steering column lower shroud. Disconnect the switch wiring as the shroud is removed. Where fitted, slacken the radio remote control unit mounting bolt on the steering column, then lift off the column upper shroud.

5 Remove the steering column switches, referring to Chapter 12 if necessary. On later models remove the bonnet release control from the steering column.

6 Disconnect the remaining steering column wiring connectors.

7 Where fitted, remove the bulkhead cover plate at the base of the steering column.

8 From the base of the steering column (early models) or from within the engine compartment (later models) undo the clamp bolt securing the

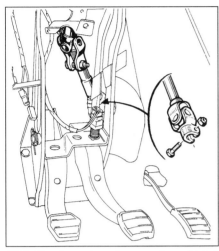

19.8 Steering column lower universal joint clamp details

lower column universal joint to the steering gear pinion shaft **(see illustration)**. On certain models it may be necessary to remove the brake master cylinder and brake servo assembly for access in this area. Refer to Chapter 9 if removal of these components is necessary.

9 Undo the steering column mounting bolts, release the universal joint from the steering gear pinion and remove the column assembly from the vehicle.

Refitting

10 Refitting is a reversal of removal, noting the following points:

a) *Tighten all nuts and bolts to the specified torque.*

b) *Ensure that the roadwheels and the column shaft are in the straight ahead position before connecting the universal joint to the steering gear pinion shaft.*

c) *Align the steering column centrally between the sides of the pedal assembly mounting before tightening the bolts.*

20 Steering gear - removal and refitting

Removal

1 Disconnect the battery negative lead.

2 Chock the rear wheels then jack up the front of the vehicle and support it on axle stands (see *"Jacking and vehicle support"*). Remove the front roadwheels.

3 Disconnect the track rod ends from the steering arms as described in Section 24.

4 On early models, undo the four screws and remove the parcel shelf below the steering column. Undo the two screws at the top and two screws at the side securing the trim panel under the steering column. Remove the bonnet release handle assembly and lift out the trim panel.

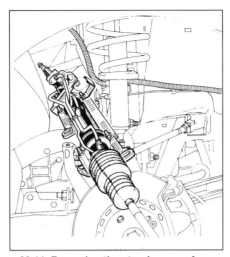

20.11 Removing the steering gear from under the wheel arch

5 On later models, undo the five screws and remove the steering column lower shroud. Disconnect the switch wiring as the shroud is removed. Where fitted, slacken the radio remote control unit mounting bolt on the steering column, then lift off the column upper shroud.

6 Where fitted, remove the bulkhead cover plate at the base of the steering column.

7 Set the steering gear and steering wheel in the straight ahead position.

8 Undo the clamp bolt securing the steering column shaft to the upper universal joint. Pull the steering wheel upwards to free the column shaft from the universal joint.

9 From the base of the steering column (early models) or from within the engine compartment (later models) undo the clamp bolt securing the lower column universal joint to the steering gear pinion shaft. On certain models it may be necessary to remove the brake master cylinder and brake servo assembly for access in this area. Refer to Chapter 9 if removal of these components is necessary.

10 Clean around the fluid supply and return unions, then disconnect them. Be prepared for fluid spillage. Plug or cap open unions to prevent dirt entry.

22.1a Steering reservoir with maximum and minimum level markings

11 Undo the four steering gear retaining bolts and manoeuvre the assembly out from under the wheel arch **(see illustration)**.

Refitting

12 Refitting is a reversal of removal, noting the following points:

a) *Tighten all fastenings to the specified torque.*

b) *Ensure that the steering gear and the column shaft are in the straight ahead position before connecting the universal joints to the steering column and pinion shaft.*

c) *Bleed the steering as described in Section 22.*

d) *Check the front wheel toe setting as described in Section 25.*

21 Steering gear gaiters - renewal

1 Remove the track rod end on the side concerned as described in Section 24.

2 Release the two clips and peel off the gaiter.

3 Clean out any dirt and grit from the inner end of the track rod and (when accessible) the rack.

4 Fit and secure the new gaiter, then refit the track rod end.

22 Steering gear - bleeding

1 The steering gear fluid reservoir is remotely mounted in the engine compartment. Two types of reservoir have been fitted. If the reservoir has maximum and minimum markings on the side, these should be used for reference when filling or topping up. If no markings are visible then the fluid level should be maintained just above the level of the grille **(see illustrations)**.

2 If topping-up is necessary, use clean fluid of the specified type (see *"Weekly checks"*). Check for leaks if frequent topping-up is required. Do not run the pump without fluid in it - remove the drivebelt if necessary.

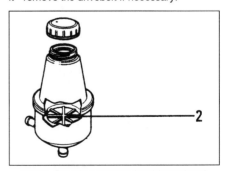

22.1b Steering reservoir without level markings - maintain fluid level just above grille (2)

10

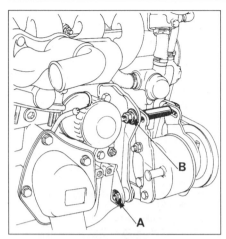

23.1 First version steering pump pivot nut (A) and adjuster nut (B)

3 After component renewal, or if the fluid level has been allowed to fall so low that air has entered the hydraulic system, bleeding must be carried out as follows.

4 Fill the reservoir to the correct level or to the "MAX" mark according to type as described above.

5 Move the steering wheel gently from full lock one way to full lock the other way then return to the straight ahead position. Check the fluid level and top-up if necessary.

6 Start the engine and allow it to idle. Turn the steering wheel from lock to lock a couple of times. Do not hold it on full lock.

7 Top up the fluid again if necessary.

8 Repeat paragraphs 6 and 7 until the fluid level ceases to fall. Stop the engine and refit the reservoir cap.

23 Steering pump - removal and refitting

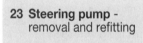

Removal

Note: *Three different pump mounting arrangements may be encountered. Identify the type fitted then proceed according to the relevant sub-heading.*

First version

1 Slacken the pump pivot and adjuster retaining nuts and bolts. Slacken the drivebelt adjuster and slip the drivebelt off the pulley **(see illustration)**.

2 Disconnect the pump hydraulic pipes, either from below or from the back of the pump. Be prepared for fluid spillage and clamp or plug the disconnected unions.

3 Remove the pivot and adjuster nuts and bolts.

4 Lift away the pump. Remove the remote fluid reservoir with the pump, or disconnect the fluid hose from it.

5 If a new pump is to be fitted, transfer the pulley and mounting brackets to it.

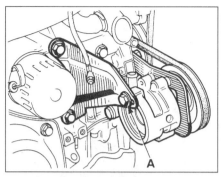

23.6 Second version steering pump rear mounting bolt (A)

Second version

6 At the rear of the pump, slacken the upper mounting bolt **(see illustration)**.

7 At the front of the pump, slacken the four bolts securing the mounting plate to the front of the engine **(see illustration)**. One of these bolts also serves as the alternator adjustment arm retaining bolt. On some models, access to these front bolts may be easier from below. Slip the drivebelt off the pulley.

8 Disconnect the pump hydraulic pipes, either from below or from the back of the pump. Be prepared for fluid spillage and clamp or plug the disconnected unions.

9 Remove the five previously slackened mounting bolts and remove the pump and mounting bracket from below. Remove the remote fluid reservoir with the pump, or disconnect the fluid hose from it.

10 If a new pump is to be fitted, transfer the pulley and mounting brackets to it.

Third version

11 Slacken the alternator tensioner and remove the alternator lower mounting nut **(see illustration)**.

12 Slacken the steering pump tensioner and the three front mounting bolts. Slacken the rear mounting bolt and slip the drivebelt off the pulley. Access to these front bolts may be easier from below.

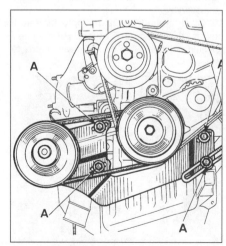

23.7 Second version steering pump front mounting plate bolts (A)

13 Disconnect the pump hydraulic pipes, either from below or from the back of the pump. Be prepared for fluid spillage and clamp or plug the disconnected unions.

14 Remove the previously slackened pump mounting bolts and remove the pump and mounting bracket from below. Remove the remote fluid reservoir with the pump, or disconnect the fluid hose from it.

15 If a new pump is to be fitted, transfer the pulley and mounting brackets to it.

Refitting

16 Refitting is a reversal of removal. Use new seals or copper washers (as applicable) on disconnected unions.

17 Adjust the auxiliary drivebelt tension as described in Chapter 1.

18 Refill the pump reservoir and bleed the system as described in Section 22.

24 Track rod end - removal and refitting

Removal

1 Raise and support the front of the vehicle. Remove the front wheel on the side concerned.

2 Counterhold the track rod and slacken the rod end locknut by half a turn **(see illustration)**.

3 Unscrew the rod end ballpin nut to the end of its threads. Separate the ballpin from the steering arm with a proprietary balljoint separator, then remove the nut and disengage the ballpin from the arm.

4 Unscrew the track rod end from the track rod, counting the number of turns needed to remove it. Record this number.

Refitting

5 Screw the track rod end onto the track rod by the same number of turns noted during removal.

6 Engage the ballpin in the steering arm. Fit the nut and tighten it to the specified torque.

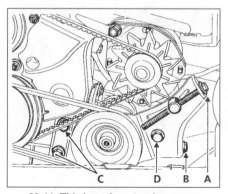

23.11 Third version steering pump attachments

A *Alternator tensioner*
B *Steering pump tensioner*
C *Steering pump front mounting inner bolts*
D *Steering pump front mounting outer bolt*

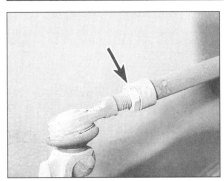

24.2 Track rod end to track rod locknut (arrowed)

7 Counterhold the track rod and tighten the locknut.

8 Refit the front wheel, lower the vehicle and tighten the wheel nuts.

9 Have the front wheel toe setting checked at the first opportunity (Section 25), especially if new components have been fitted.

25 Wheel alignment and steering angles - general information

General

1 A vehicle's steering and suspension geometry is defined in four basic settings - all angles are expressed in degrees (toe settings are also expressed as a measurement); the relevant settings are camber, castor, steering axis inclination, and toe setting. On Espace models, only the castor and front wheel toe settings are adjustable. Castor checking and adjustment must be left to a dealer.

Front wheel toe setting - checking and adjustment

2 Due to the special measuring equipment necessary to accurately check the wheel alignment, and the skill required to use it properly, checking and adjustment is best left to a Renault dealer or similar expert. Note that most tyre fitting shops now posses sophisticated checking equipment. The following is provided as a guide should the owner decide to carry out a DIY check.

3 The front wheel toe setting is checked by measuring the distance between the front and rear inside edges of the roadwheel rims. Proprietary toe measuring gauges are available from accessory shops. Adjustment is made by screwing the track rod ends in or out of their track rods to alter the effective length of the track rod assemblies.

4 For accurate checking, the vehicle must be at kerb weight, ie unladen and with a full tank of fuel.

5 Before starting work, check first that the tyre sizes and types are as specified, then check the tyre pressures and tread wear, the roadwheel run-out, the condition of the wheel bearings, the steering wheel free play, and the condition of the front suspension components (see "Weekly checks" and Chapter 1). Correct any faults found.

6 Park the vehicle on level ground, check that the front roadwheels are in the straight-ahead position, then rock the rear and front ends to settle the suspension. Release the handbrake and roll the vehicle backwards 1 metre, then forwards again, to relieve any stresses in the steering and suspension components.

7 Measure the distance between the front edges of the wheel rims and the rear edges of the rims. Subtract the front measurement from the rear measurement, and check that the result is within the specified range.

8 If adjustment is necessary, apply the handbrake, then jack up and securely support the front of the car. Turn the steering wheel onto full-left lock and record the number of exposed threads on the right-hand track rod. Now turn the steering onto full-right lock, and record the number of threads on the left-hand side. If there are the same number of threads visible on both sides, then subsequent adjustment should be made equally on both sides. If there are more threads visible on one side than the other, it will be necessary to compensate for this during adjustment. **Note:** *It is most important that after adjustment, the same number of threads are visible on each track rod.*

9 First clean the track rod threads; If they are corroded, apply penetrating fluid before starting adjustment. Release the steering rack gaiter outer retaining clips and peel back the bellows; apply a smear of grease to the inside of the gaiters, so that both are free and will not be twisted or strained as their respective track rods are rotated.

10 Use a straight-edge and a scriber or similar to mark the relationship of each track rod to its track rod end then, holding each track rod in turn, unscrew its locknut.

11 Alter the lengths of the track rods, bearing in mind the note made in paragraph 8. Screw them into or out of the track rod ends, rotating the track rods with grips or a similar tool. Shortening the track rods (screwing them into their track rod ends) will increase toe-out/reduce toe-in.

12 When the setting is correct, hold the track rods and securely tighten the track rod end locknuts. Count the number of exposed threads to check the length of both track rods. If they are not the same, then the adjustment has not been made equally, and problems will be encountered with tyre scrubbing in turns; also, the steering wheel spokes will no longer be horizontal when the wheels are in the straight-ahead position.

13 If the track rod lengths are the same, lower the vehicle to the ground and re-check the toe setting; re-adjust if necessary. When the setting is correct, securely tighten the track rod end locknuts. Ensure that the rubber gaiters are seated correctly, and are not twisted or strained, and secure them in position with their retaining clips.

10

Chapter 11
Bodywork and fittings

Contents

Degrees of difficulty

Easy, suitable for novice with little experience	**Fairly easy,** suitable for beginner with some experience	**Fairly difficult,** suitable for competent DIY mechanic	**Difficult,** suitable for experienced DIY mechanic	**Very difficult,** suitable for expert DIY or professional

Specifications

Torque wrench setting	Nm
Seat belt mounting bolts	35

1 General information

All Espace models are of 5 or 7-seat, 5-door multi-purpose vehicle layout. The galvanised steel body/chassis structure features bonded or separate polyester external panels over the entire vehicle. Crumple zones are also incorporated at front and rear which will deform progressively in case of an accident.

Various styling and engineering revisions have taken place since the start of production. Where these revisions affect procedures in this Chapter, reference will be made to "Phase 1", (start of production to 1988), "Phase 2" (1988 to 1991), or "Phase 3" (1991 onward).

2 Maintenance - bodywork and underframe

The general condition of a vehicle's bodywork is the one thing that significantly affects its value. Maintenance is easy but needs to be regular. Neglect, particularly after minor damage, can lead quickly to further deterioration and costly repair bills. It is important also to keep watch on those parts of the vehicle not immediately visible, for instance the underside, inside all the wheel arches and the lower part of the engine compartment.

The basic maintenance routine for the bodywork is washing preferably with a lot of water, from a hose. This will remove all the loose solids which may have stuck to the vehicle. It is important to flush these off in such a way as to prevent grit from scratching the finish. The wheel arches and underframe need washing in the same way to remove any accumulated mud which will retain moisture and tend to encourage rust. Oddly enough, the best time to clean the underframe and wheel arches is in wet weather when the mud is thoroughly wet and soft. In very wet weather the underframe is usually cleaned of large accumulations automatically and this is a good time for inspection.

Periodically, except on vehicles with a wax-based underbody protective coating, it is a good idea to have the whole of the underframe of the vehicle steam cleaned, engine compartment included, so that a thorough inspection can be carried out to see

11

what minor repairs and renovations are necessary. Steam cleaning is available at many garages and is necessary for removal of the accumulation of oily grime which sometimes is allowed to become thick in certain areas. If steam cleaning facilities are not available, there are one or two excellent grease solvents available which can be brush applied; the dirt can then be simply hosed off. Note that these methods should not be used on vehicles with wax-based underbody protective coating or the coating will be removed. Such vehicles should be inspected annually, preferably just prior to winter, when the underbody should be washed down and any damage to the wax coating repaired using underseal. Ideally, a completely fresh coat should be applied. It would also be worth considering the use of such wax-based protection for injection into door panels, sills, box sections, etc, as an additional safeguard against rust damage where such protection is not provided by the vehicle manufacturer.

After washing paintwork, wipe off with a chamois leather to give an unspotted clear finish. A coat of clear protective wax polish will give added protection against chemical pollutants in the air. If the paintwork sheen has dulled or oxidised, use a cleaner/polisher combination to restore the brilliance of the shine. This requires a little effort, but such dulling is usually caused because regular washing has been neglected. Care needs to be taken with metallic paintwork as special non-abrasive cleaner/polisher is required to avoid damage to the finish.

Always check that the door and ventilator opening drain holes and pipes are completely clear so that water can be drained out. Bright work should be treated in the same way as paint work. Windscreens and windows can be kept clear of the smeary film which often appears by the use of a proprietary glass cleaner. Never use any form of wax or other body or chromium polish on glass.

3 Maintenance -
upholstery and carpets

Mats and carpets should be brushed or vacuum cleaned regularly to keep them free of grit. If they are badly stained remove them from the vehicle for scrubbing or sponging and make quite sure they are dry before refitting. Seats and interior trim panels can be kept clean by wiping with a damp cloth and a proprietary upholstery cleaner. If they do become stained (which can be more apparent on light coloured upholstery) use a little liquid detergent and a soft nail brush to scour the grime out of the grain of the material. Do not forget to keep the headlining clean in the same way as the upholstery. When using liquid cleaners inside the vehicle do not over-wet the surfaces being cleaned. Excessive damp could get into the seams and padded interior

causing stains, offensive odours or even rot. If the inside of the vehicle gets wet accidentally it is worthwhile taking some trouble to dry it out properly, particularly where carpets are involved. *Do not leave oil or electric heaters inside the vehicle for this purpose.*

4 Minor body damage - repair

Note: *Although this Section is mainly applicable to vehicles with a metal body panel structure, it includes techniques which are common to all body repair. Repair of Espace external body panelling entails the use of polyester and epoxy resins which must be specially mixed, then preferably oven baked for accelerated hardening. This is a complex process requiring a great deal of skill for satisfactory results. Therefore, any panel damage other than that of a very minor nature should be entrusted to a body repair specialist.*

Repair of minor scratches in bodywork

If the scratch is very superficial, and does not penetrate to the metal of the bodywork, repair is very simple. Lightly rub the area of the scratch with a paintwork renovator, or a very fine cutting paste, to remove loose paint from the scratch, and to clear the surrounding bodywork of wax polish. Rinse the area with clean water.

Apply touch-up paint to the scratch using a fine paint brush; continue to apply fine layers of paint until the surface of the paint in the scratch is level with the surrounding paintwork. Allow the new paint at least two weeks to harden: then blend it into the surrounding paintwork by rubbing the scratch area with a paintwork renovator or a very fine cutting paste. Finally, apply wax polish.

Where the scratch has penetrated right through to the metal of the bodywork, causing the metal to rust, a different repair technique is required. Remove any loose rust from the bottom of the scratch with a penknife, then apply rust-inhibiting paint, to prevent the formation of rust in the future. Using a rubber or nylon applicator fill the scratch with bodystopper paste. If required, this paste can be mixed with cellulose thinners, to provide a very thin paste which is ideal for filling narrow scratches. Before the stopper-paste in the scratch hardens, wrap a piece of smooth cotton rag around the top of a finger. Dip the finger in cellulose thinners, and then quickly sweep it across the surface of the stopper-paste in the scratch; this will ensure that the surface of the stopper-paste is slightly hollowed. The scratch can now be painted over as described earlier in this Section.

Repair of dents in bodywork

When deep denting of the vehicle's bodywork has taken place, the first task is to

pull the dent out, until the affected bodywork almost attains its original shape. There is little point in trying to restore the original shape completely, as the metal in the damaged area will have stretched on impact and cannot be reshaped fully to its original contour. It is better to bring the level of the dent up to a point which is about 3 mm below the level of the surrounding bodywork. In cases where the dent is very shallow anyway, it is not worth trying to pull it out at all. If the underside of the dent is accessible, it can be hammered out gently from behind, using a mallet with a wooden or plastic head. Whilst doing this, hold a suitable block of wood firmly against the outside of the panel to absorb the impact from the hammer blows and thus prevent a large area of the bodywork from being "belled-out".

Should the dent be in a section of the bodywork which has a double skin or some other factor making it inaccessible from behind, a different technique is called for. Drill several small holes through the metal inside the area - particularly in the deeper section. Then screw long self-tapping screws into the holes just sufficiently for them to gain a good purchase in the metal. Now the dent can be pulled out by pulling on the protruding heads of the screws with a pair of pliers.

The next stage of the repair is the removal of the paint from the damaged area, and from an inch or so of the surrounding "sound" bodywork. This is accomplished most easily by using a wire brush or abrasive pad on a power drill, although it can be done just as effectively by hand using sheets of abrasive paper. To complete the preparation for filling, score the surface of the bare metal with a screwdriver or the tang of a file, or alternatively, drill small holes in the affected area. This will provide a really good "key" for the filler paste.

To complete the repair see the Section on filling and re-spraying.

Repair of rust holes or gashes in bodywork

Remove all paint from the affected area and from an inch or so of the surrounding "sound" bodywork, using an abrasive pad or a wire brush on a power drill. If these are not available a few sheets of abrasive paper will do the job just as effectively. With the paint removed you will be able to gauge the severity of the corrosion and therefore decide whether to renew the whole panel (if this is possible) or to repair the affected area. New body panels are not as expensive as most people think and it is often quicker and more satisfactory to fit a new panel than to attempt to repair large areas of corrosion.

Remove all fittings from the affected area except those which will act as a guide to the original shape of the damaged bodywork (eg headlight shells etc). Then, using tin snips or a hacksaw blade, remove all loose metal and any other metal badly affected by corrosion. Hammer the edges of the hole inwards in order to create a slight depression for the filler paste.

Wire brush the affected area to remove the powdery rust from the surface of the remaining metal. Paint the affected area with rust inhibiting paint; if the back of the rusted area is accessible treat this also.

Before filling can take place it will be necessary to block the hole in some way. This can be achieved by the use of aluminium or plastic mesh, or aluminium tape.

Aluminium or plastic mesh or glass fibre matting is probably the best material to use for a large hole. Cut a piece to the approximate size and shape of the hole to be filled, then position it in the hole so that its edges are below the level of the surrounding bodywork. It can be retained in position by several blobs of filler paste around its periphery.

Aluminium tape should be used for small or very narrow holes. Pull a piece off the roll and trim it to the approximate size and shape required, then pull off the backing paper (if used) and stick the tape over the hole; it can be overlapped if the thickness of one piece is insufficient. Burnish down the edges of the tape with the handle of a screwdriver or similar, to ensure that the tape is securely attached to the metal underneath.

Bodywork repairs - filling and re-spraying

Before using this Section, see the Sections on dent, deep scratch, rust holes and gash repairs.

Many types of bodyfiller are available, but generally speaking those proprietary kits which contain a tin of filler paste and a tube of resin hardener are best for this type of repair; some can be used directly from the tube. A wide, flexible plastic or nylon applicator will be found invaluable for imparting a smooth and well contoured finish to the surface of the filler.

Mix up a little filler on a clean piece of card or board - measure the hardener carefully (follow the maker's instructions on the pack) otherwise the filler will set too rapidly or too slowly. Using the applicator, apply the filler paste to the prepared area; draw the applicator across the surface of the filler to achieve the correct contour and to level the filler surface. As soon as a contour that approximates to the correct one is achieved, stop working the paste - if you carry on too long the paste will become sticky and begin to "pick up" on the applicator. Continue to add thin layers of filler paste at twenty-minute intervals until the level of the filler is just proud of the surrounding bodywork.

Once the filler has hardened, excess can be removed using a metal plane or file. From then on, progressively finer grades of abrasive paper should be used, starting with a 40 grade production paper and finishing with 400 grade wet-and-dry paper. Always wrap the abrasive paper around a flat rubber, cork, or wooden block - otherwise the surface of the filler will not be completely flat. During the smoothing of the filler surface the wet-and-dry paper should be periodically rinsed in water. This will ensure that a very smooth finish is imparted to the filler at the final stage.

At this stage the "dent" should be surrounded by a ring of bare metal, which in turn should be encircled by the finely "feathered" edge of the good paintwork. Rinse the repair area with clean water, until all of the dust produced by the rubbing-down operation has gone.

Spray the whole repair area with a light coat of primer - this will show up any imperfections in the surface of the filler. Repair these imperfections with fresh filler paste or bodystopper, and once more smooth the surface with abrasive paper. If bodystopper is used, it can be mixed with cellulose thinners to form a really thin paste which is ideal for filling small holes. Repeat this spray and repair procedure until you are satisfied that the surface of the filler, and the feathered edge of the paintwork are perfect. Clean the repair area with clean water and allow to dry fully.

The repair area is now ready for final spraying. Paint spraying must be carried out in a warm, dry, windless and dust free atmosphere. This condition can be created artificially if you have access to a large indoor working area, but if you are forced to work in the open, you will have to pick your day very carefully. If you are working indoors, dousing the floor in the work area with water will help to settle the dust which would otherwise be in the atmosphere. If the repair area is confined to one body panel, mask off the surrounding panels; this will help to minimise the effects of a slight mis-match in paint colours. Bodywork fittings (eg chrome strips, door handles etc) will also need to be masked off. Use genuine masking tape and several thicknesses of newspaper for the masking operations.

Before commencing to spray, agitate the aerosol can thoroughly, then spray a test area (an old tin, or similar) until the technique is mastered. Cover the repair area with a thick coat of primer; the thickness should be built up using several thin layers of paint rather than one thick one. Using 400 grade wet-and-dry paper, rub down the surface of the primer until it is really smooth. While doing this, the work area should be thoroughly doused with water, and the wet-and-dry paper periodically rinsed in water. Allow to dry before spraying on more paint.

Spray on the top coat, again building up the thickness by using several thin layers of paint. Start spraying in the centre of the repair area and then, with a single side-to-side motion, work outwards until the whole repair area and about 50 mm of the surrounding original paintwork is covered. Remove all masking material 10 to 15 minutes after spraying on the final coat of paint.

Allow the new paint at least two weeks to harden, then, using a paintwork renovator or a very fine cutting paste, blend the edges of the paint into the existing paintwork. Finally, apply wax polish.

Plastic components

With the use of more and more plastic body components by the vehicle manufacturers (eg bumpers, spoilers, and in some cases major body panels), rectification of more serious damage to such items has become a matter of either entrusting repair work to a specialist in this field, or renewing complete components. Repair of such damage by the DIY owner is not really feasible owing to the cost of the equipment and materials required for effecting such repairs. The basic technique involves making a groove along the line of the crack in the plastic using a rotary burr in a power drill. The damaged part is then welded back together by using a hot air gun to heat up and fuse a plastic filler rod into the groove. Any excess plastic is then removed and the area rubbed down to a smooth finish. It is important that a filler rod of the correct plastic is used, as body components can be made of a variety of different types (eg polycarbonate, ABS, polypropylene).

Damage of a less serious nature (abrasions, minor cracks etc) can be repaired by the DIY owner using a two-part epoxy filler repair material. Once mixed in equal proportions, this is used in similar fashion to the bodywork filler used on metal panels. The filler is usually cured in twenty to thirty minutes, ready for sanding and painting.

If the owner is renewing a complete component himself, or if he has repaired it with epoxy filler, he will be left with the problem of finding a suitable paint for finishing which is compatible with the type of plastic used. At one time the use of a universal paint was not possible owing to the complex range of plastics encountered in body component applications. Standard paints, generally speaking, will not bond to plastic or rubber satisfactorily. However, it is now possible to obtain a plastic body parts finishing kit which consists of a pre-primer treatment, a primer and coloured top coat. Full instructions are normally supplied with a kit, but basically the method of use is to first apply the pre-primer to the component concerned and allow it to dry for up to 30 minutes. Then the primer is applied and left to dry for about an hour before finally applying the special coloured top coat. The result is a correctly coloured component where the paint will flex with the plastic or rubber, a property that standard paint does not normally possess.

5 Major body damage - repair

11

Where serious damage has occurred or large areas need renewal due to neglect, completely new sections or panels will need welding in - this is best left to professionals. If the damage is due to impact, it will also be necessary to check completely the alignment of the body shell structure. Due to the principle of construction, the strength and shape of the whole can be affected by damage to a part. In such instances, the services of a Renault agent with specialist checking jigs are essential. If a body is left misaligned, it is first of all dangerous as the car will not handle properly and secondly uneven stresses will be imposed on the steering, engine and transmission, causing abnormal wear or complete failure. Tyre wear may also be excessive.

6 Bonnet - removal and refitting

Removal

1 Disconnect the washer tube and move it to one side.
2 Mark around the hinge bolts with a soft lead pencil for reference when refitting.
3 With the aid of an assistant, support the bonnet and remove the hinge bolts. Lift off the bonnet.

Refitting

4 Fit the bonnet and insert the hinge bolts. Lightly tighten the bolts in their previously marked positions.
5 Reconnect the washer tube.
6 Shut the bonnet and check its fit. The hinge-to-bonnet bolt holes control the fore-and-aft and left-right adjustment. Front height is adjusted by screwing the rubber buffers in or out.
7 Tighten the mounting bolts fully when adjustment is correct.

7 Bonnet lock and release cable - removal and refitting

Removal

Phase 1 and 2 models

1 Open the bonnet and disconnect the battery negative lead.
2 Disconnect the return spring and release the cable from the lock assembly.
3 Undo the two bolts and remove the lock from the front upper crossmember.
4 From inside the vehicle, remove the trim panels as necessary to gain access to the bonnet release handle.
5 Undo the bolt and free the release handle from its location.
6 Tie a long length of string securely to the engine compartment end of the cable.
7 Release the cable from the retaining clips in the engine compartment and pull the cable through into the passenger compartment bringing the string with it. Untie the string, leaving it in position ready for refitting.

Phase 3 models

8 Open the bonnet and disconnect the battery negative lead.
9 Remove the front grille panel as described in Section 29.
10 Disconnect the return spring from the connecting rod then undo the bolts (one each side) securing the two lock units to the front upper crossmember.
11 Move the lock units to the left and remove them from the crossmember. Detach the connecting rod and the release cable from the left-hand lock.
12 From inside the vehicle, undo the five screws and withdraw the steering column lower shroud.
13 Undo the bolt and free the release handle from the steering column.
14 Tie a long length of string securely to the engine compartment end of the cable.
15 Release the cable from the retaining clips in the engine compartment and pull the cable through into the passenger compartment bringing the string with it. Untie the string, leaving it in position ready for refitting.

Refitting

All models

16 Tie the string to the new cable and pull the cable back into the engine compartment, then refit the components using the reversal of removal.

8 Doors - removal and refitting

Removal

Front doors

1 Remove the interior trim panel as described in Section 10.
2 Disconnect the door electrical wiring, then feed the wiring through so that it hangs free.

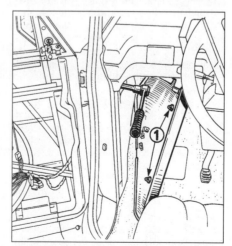

8.6 Remove the trim panel secured by clips (1) then remove the door hinge bolts

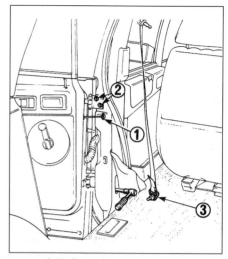

8.13 Rear door attachments

1 *Check strap roll pin*
2 *Upper hinge bolts*
3 *Seat belt lower anchorage*

3 Using a small punch, tap out the single or double roll pin securing the door check strap.
4 Remove the side trim panel in the footwell area for access to the door hinge nuts.
5 Have an assistant support the door.

> **HAYNES HiNT**
>
> *Place a block of wood with rag pads on top beneath the door to help support it as it is removed.*

6 Using a socket and extension bar, unscrew the two nuts securing each hinge to the body pillar **(see illustration)**. A universal joint may be needed to reach the upper nuts.
7 Carefully lift off the door and recover any hinge shims, noting their locations.

Rear doors

8 Remove the interior trim panel as described in Section 11.
9 Disconnect the door electrical wiring, then feed the wiring through so that it hangs free.
10 Using a small punch, tap out the single or double roll pin securing the door check strap.
11 To gain access to the lower hinge nuts, undo the seat belt lower anchorage bolt, and pull away the sealing weatherstrip around the pillar slightly. Partially free the pillar lower trim.
12 Have an assistant support the door.
13 Undo the two upper hinge bolts and two lower hinge nuts and carefully lift off the door. Recover any hinge shims, noting their locations **(see illustration)**.

Refitting

14 Refitting is a reversal of removal. The hinge bolt slots are elongated to allow centralisation of the door in its aperture. To adjust for flush fit with the adjacent panels, add or remove shims from behind the hinges as necessary.

9 Tailgate - removal and refitting

Removal

1 Disconnect the battery negative lead.
2 Remove the tailgate interior trim panel as described in Section 12.
3 Have an assistant support the tailgate. Disconnect the gas struts by removing the wire clips and separating the balljoints.
4 Partially remove the sealing weatherstrip along the tailgate aperture top edge.
5 Release the centre interior light from its location in the headlining.
6 Release the headlining from the roof crossmember and, on Phase 1 models, from the side pillars. On Phase 1 models the headlining is held in place with adhesive and must be carefully released just enough to gain access to the tailgate hinges. On all other models the headlining is secured by clips.
7 Disconnect the wiring connectors from all services in the tailgate making notes for refitting if necessary, and detach the rear screen washer tube.
8 Secure a 2 metre long length of wire to the end of the wiring harness and the washer tube. Release the protective rubber sleeves and pull the wiring out of the tailgate.
9 Unscrew the hinge nuts, washers and spacer plates and withdraw the tailgate from the vehicle **(see illustration)**.

Refitting

10 Refitting is a reversal of removal. The hinge bolt slots are elongated to allow centralisation of the tailgate in its aperture. On early models, to adjust for flush fit with the adjacent panels, add or remove shims from behind the striker pins as necessary. On later models, the striker pins can be screwed in or out after slackening the pin locknut.

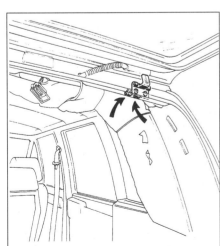

9.9 Tailgate hinge attachments (arrowed)

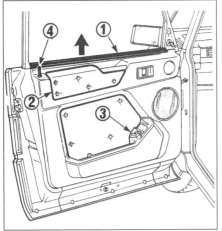

10.3 Door interior trim glass wiper strip (1), upper capping (2), switches (3) and lock button (4) (Phase 1 and 2 models)

10 Front door interior trim - removal and refitting

Removal

Phase 1 and 2 models

1 Disconnect the battery negative lead.
2 Detach the inner trim plate from the door exterior mirror.
3 Carefully prise free the door glass wiper strip from the top of the trim panel **(see illustration)**.
4 Ease off the upper trim capping around the door pull handle which is retained by five clips.
5 Prise out the control switches and disconnect their wiring.
6 Disconnect the electrical control for the door mirror (where applicable).
7 Where fitted, unscrew the door interior lock button.

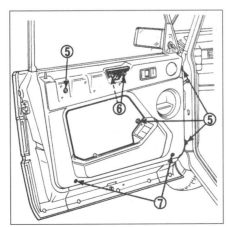

10.8 Door interior trim panel screws (5), pull handle screws (6) and studs (7) (Phase 1 and 2 models)

10.14 Prise out the control switches . . .

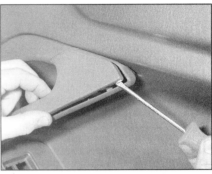

10.15a . . . prise up the door handle trim . . .

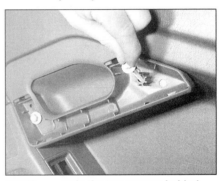

10.15b . . . undo the two screws behind . . .

8 Undo the four trim panel retaining screws **(see illustration)**.
9 Undo the door pull handle screw(s).
10 Release the plastic sheeting from the trim panel upper stiffener and withdraw the panel from the door, releasing the additional retaining studs as necessary.
11 From behind the panel, release the door latch operating rod, disconnect the speaker wiring, then lift away the trim panel.
12 If the panel has been removed for access to the door internal components, peel off the plastic condensation barrier and store it flat, adhesive side up, ready for refitting.

Phase 3 models

13 Disconnect the battery negative lead.
14 Prise out the control switches and disconnect their wiring **(see illustration)**.
15 Carefully prise up the trim over the door pull handle and undo the two screws behind **(see illustrations)**.

11

10.16 . . . undo the screws at the base and remove the trim (Phase 3 models)

11.1 Removing a rear door manual window handle

12.1 Undo the tailgate interior handle screws . . .

16 Undo the panel retaining screws at the base of the door **(see illustration)**.
17 Ease off the quarter trim at the lower front corner of the window glass.
18 Withdraw the panel from the door, releasing the additional retaining studs as necessary.
19 From behind the panel, release the door latch operating rod and disconnect the speaker wiring then lift away the trim panel.
20 If the panel has been removed for access to the door internal components, peel off the plastic condensation barrier and store it flat, adhesive side up, ready for refitting.

Refitting

21 In all cases, refitting is a reversal of removal.

11 Rear door interior trim - removal and refitting

The removal and refitting procedures are virtually identical to those for the front door (Section 10) except that where manually operated window regulators are fitted, carefully prise off the handles using a forked tool inserted from behind **(see illustration)**. Take care to protect the panel as this is done.

12 Tailgate interior trim - removal and refitting

Removal

1 Open the tailgate, lift up the plastic caps and unscrew the interior handle retaining screws **(see illustration)**.
2 Prise out the retaining clip and detach the plastic cover over the wiper motor **(see illustrations)**.
3 Ease the trim panel away from the tailgate to release the retaining studs, and remove the panel from the tailgate **(see illustration)**.

Refitting

4 Refitting is a reversal of removal.

13 Windscreen, tailgate and fixed window glass - general information

These areas of glass are secured by the tight fit of the weatherstrip in the body aperture, and are bonded in position with a special adhesive. Renewal of such fixed glass is a difficult, messy and time-consuming task, which is considered beyond the scope of the home mechanic. It is difficult, unless one has plenty of practice, to obtain a secure, waterproof fit. Furthermore, the task carries a high risk of breakage; this applies especially to the laminated glass windscreen. In view of this, owners are strongly advised to have this sort of work carried out by one of the many specialist windscreen fitters.

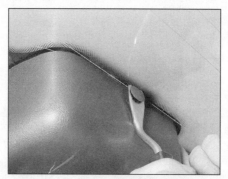

12.2a . . . prise out the retaining clip . . .

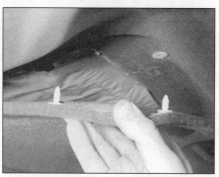

12.3 . . . then release the studs and remove the trim panel

14 Front door window - removal and refitting

Removal

1 Remove the door interior trim (Section 10).
2 Remove the inner and outer rubbing strips from the top of the door panel.
3 Position the window so the two bolts securing the window bottom frame to the lifting channel are accessible. On later models two holes in the door allow access for a socket **(see illustration)**. Unscrew the two bolts.
4 Lift the rear upper corner of the glass and manipulate it up and out of the door.
5 If new glass is being fitted, check whether or not it is supplied with the bottom frame

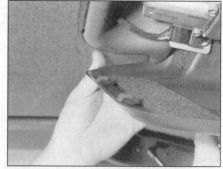

12.2b . . . and detach the plastic cover . . .

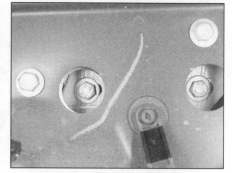

14.3 Undo the window frame bolts through the holes in the door

attached. If not, it will be necessary to transfer the frame and fit it to the new glass. When doing this make sure that the rear edge of the frame is positioned 200 mm (Phase 1 and 2 models) or 225 mm (Phase 3 models) from the trailing edge of the glass.

Refitting

6 Refitting is a reversal of removal.

15 Rear door window - removal and refitting

Removal

Phase 1 and 2 models

1 Remove the door interior trim (Section 11).
2 Raise the window then undo the screw below the door latch and the screw at the base of the window rear frame. Withdraw the rear slide and guide lower section from inside the door.
3 Lower the window fully.
4 On models with a quadrant type window lift mechanism, remove the lift mechanism as described in Section 17.
5 On models with a worm type window lift mechanism, undo the two bolts securing the window bottom frame to the lifting channel.
6 Pull out the window guide channel from the window rear frame.
7 Undo the screw on the window rear frame and lift out the rear corner piece by moving it in at the top, then lifting upwards.
8 Withdraw the window by lifting it up and out of the frame.
9 If a new window is being fitted, check whether or not it is supplied with the bottom frame attached. If not, it will be necessary to transfer the frame and fit it to the new window. When doing this make sure that the rear edge of the frame is positioned 200 mm (models with a worm type lift mechanism) or 180 mm (models with a quadrant type lift mechanism) from the trailing edge of the glass.

Phase 3 models

10 Remove the door interior trim (Section 11).

11 Remove the inner and outer rubbing strips from the top of the door panel.
12 Position the window so that the two bolts securing the window bottom frame to the lifting channel are accessible through the two holes in the door for this purpose. Unscrew the two bolts.
13 Undo the two bolts securing the movable guide mounting to the door and window rear frame.
14 Withdraw the window by lifting it up and out of the frame.
15 If a new window is being fitted, check whether or not it is supplied with the bottom frame attached. If not, it will be necessary to transfer the frame and fit it to the new window. When doing this make sure that the front edge of the frame is positioned 195 mm from the leading edge of the glass.

Refitting

All models

16 Refitting is a reversal of removal.

16 Front window lift mechanism - removal and refitting

Removal

1 Disconnect the battery negative lead.
2 Proceed as for door window removal (Section 14 paragraphs 1 to 3), but do not remove the window completely. Tape or wedge it in the fully raised position.
3 Disconnect the motor wiring electrical connector (see illustration)
4 Undo the three bolts securing the motor and lift mechanism assembly to the door.
5 Undo the two bolts at the top, and single bolt at the bottom securing the lifting channel to the door (see illustrations).
6 Tilt the assembly and manipulate it out through the door opening.

Refitting

7 Refitting is a reversal of removal. Adjust as follows during installation. Centralise the window in its guide channels before tightening the two bolts securing the window

bottom frame to the lifting channel. With the lifting channel mounting bolts slackened, raise the window fully and tighten one of the upper bolts. Lower the window and tighten the lower bolt and the remaining upper bolt. Operate the window and check for smooth movement, making fine adjustments as necessary.

17 Rear window lift mechanism - removal and refitting

Removal

Phase 1 and 2 models

Worm type lift mechanism
1 Remove the door interior trim (Section 11).
2 Tape or wedge the window in the fully raised position.
3 Undo the two bolts securing the window bottom frame to the lifting channel.
4 Undo the bolt securing the winder mechanism to the door.
5 Undo the two bolts at the top, and single bolt at the bottom securing the lifting channel to the door.
6 Remove the rack guide tube.
7 Tilt the assembly towards the door lock and manipulate it out through the door opening.
Quadrant type lift mechanism
8 Remove the door interior trim (Section 11).
9 Tape or wedge the window in the fully raised position.
10 Undo the three lift mechanism bolts.
11 Slide the lifting arms rearwards off the window lift channels.
12 Remove the assembly by tilting it downwards and out of the door opening.

Phase 3 models

13 Where electric windows are fitted, disconnect the battery negative lead.
14 Remove the door interior trim (Section 11).
15 Position the window so that the two bolts securing the window bottom frame to the lifting channel are accessible through the two holes in the door for this purpose. Unscrew the two bolts.
16 Tape or wedge the window in the fully raised position.

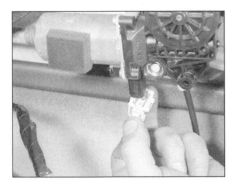

16.3 Disconnect the window lift motor wiring connector

16.5a Undo the window lifting channel upper bolts . . .

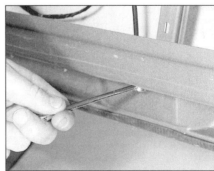

16.5b . . . and the lower bolt

11

17.18 Rear door manual window lift mechanism retaining bolts

17 Disconnect the motor wiring electrical connector.

18 Undo the three bolts securing the lift mechanism (and where applicable, the motor) assembly to the door **(see illustration)**.

19 Undo the two bolts at the top, and single bolt at the bottom securing the lifting channel to the door.

20 Tilt the assembly and manipulate it out through the door opening.

Refitting

All models

21 Refitting is a reversal of removal. Adjust the position of the window bottom frame and lifting channel so that the window opens and closes smoothly without binding or excessive side movement.

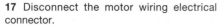

18 Door handles, locks and latches - removal and refitting

Removal

1 Remove the door interior trim (Section 10 or 11). Ensure that the window is fully closed.

Lock barrel

2 Withdraw the lock barrel retaining clip. On Phase 3 models it will be necessary to extract the blanking plug from the side of the door and pull the clip out using a hooked piece of wire **(see illustration)**.

18.7 Door latch retaining screws

18.2 Using a wire hook to remove the lock barrel retaining clip

3 Detach the operating rod and remove the lock barrel.

Exterior handle

4 On Phase 1 and 2 models, remove the two screws which secure the handle. Detach the operating rod at the handle end and remove the handle.

5 On Phase 3 models, detach the operating rod at the latch end. Undo the nut and remove the handle retaining plate **(see illustration)**. Withdraw the handle and operating rod.

Latch mechanism

6 Disconnect the lock barrel and exterior handle operating rods from the latch.

7 Undo the three screws on the edge of the door and lower the latch assembly into the door **(see illustration)**.

8 Disconnect the central locking wiring connector and the interior handle operating rod. Remove the latch assembly from the door.

9 If required, the central locking motor can be removed from the latch after undoing the retaining screw.

Refitting

10 In all cases, refitting is a reversal of removal. Check for correct operation before refitting the door trim.

19.3 Detach the threaded rods from the tailgate latch levers

18.5 Door exterior handle retaining plate

19 Tailgate lock - removal and refitting

Removal

1 Remove the tailgate interior trim panel (Section 12).

2 Disconnect the battery negative lead.

Latch mechanisms

3 To remove the two latch mechanisms, detach the operating rods from the latch levers. This is done either by releasing the clips or by simply prising the threaded end of the rods out of the retainers on the latch levers **(see illustration)**. Undo the two bolts on each latch and remove the relevant latch.

Locking motor

4 Disconnect the motor wiring connector.

5 Extract the clip securing the motor plunger to the exterior handle **(see illustration)**.

6 Undo the two mounting bolts, tilt the motor downward and remove it from the tailgate.

Exterior handle

7 Remove the locking motor as described previously.

8 Disconnect the operating rods from the exterior handle either by unscrewing the adjusting nuts at the quadrant or by simply prising the threaded end of the rods out of the retainers on the quadrant **(see illustration)**.

9 Undo the mounting bolts and remove the handle from the tailgate.

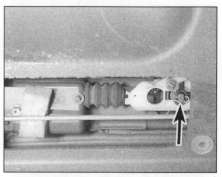

19.5 Tailgate locking motor plunger retaining clip (arrowed)

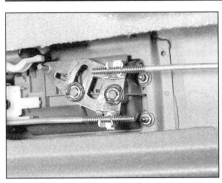

19.8 Detach the threaded rods from the tailgate exterior handle quadrant

Lock barrel

10 Remove the exterior handle as described previously.
11 Extract the roll pin then remove the control finger and blade assembly.
12 Withdraw the retaining clip and remove the lock barrel from the handle.

Refitting

13 Refitting is a reversal of removal. Adjust the operating rods by means of the adjusting nuts or by repositioning their threaded ends so that the latch mechanism levers just start to move as the exterior handle is operated.

20 Exterior mirror - removal and refitting

Removal

Phase 1 and 2 models

1 If the mirror is electrically operated, disconnect the battery negative lead then remove the door interior trim (Section 10). With the trim removed disconnect the wiring at the mirror control switch.
2 If the mirror is manually operated, unscrew the mirror control lever retaining nut.
3 Undo the screw and remove the interior trim plate.
4 Undo the three screws securing the mirror to the door **(see illustration)**.
5 From the outside, gently pull the mirror off the door - it will be initially tight due to the mastic seal.
6 Release the grommet and remove the mirror complete with control and cables or wiring harness.
7 No further dismantling can be carried out. The mirror is supplied as an assembly and individual parts are not available.

Phase 3 models

8 If the mirror is electrically operated, disconnect the battery negative lead.
9 Carefully prise up the speaker grille from the top corner of the facia. Where fitted, disconnect the speaker wiring and remove the grille **(see illustration)**.

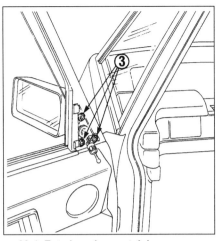

20.4 Exterior mirror retaining screws (Phase 1 and 2 models)

10 Undo the four screws, disconnect the wiring and remove the main speaker.
11 Remove the facia side panel by undoing the screw at the front which is located behind a plastic cap **(see illustration)**. Pull the side panel rearward to free it.
12 Disconnect the electric mirror control switch wiring from the switch in the side panel. If a manual mirror is fitted, pull off the grommet, unscrew the nut and withdraw the control from the side panel **(see illustrations)**.
13 Release the side demister vent and hose from their location.
14 Undo the mirror bolt adjacent to the speaker aperture in the facia **(see illustration)**.

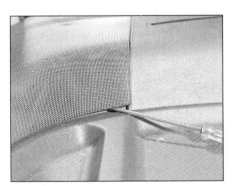

20.9 Prise up and remove the speaker grille

20.11 Undo the side panel screw under the plastic cap

20.12a Pull off the grommet on the manual mirror control . . .

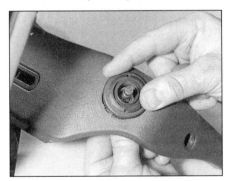

20.12b . . . unscrew the retaining nut . . .

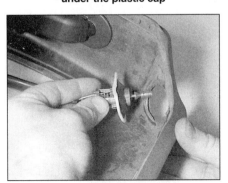

20.12c . . . and withdraw the control from the panel

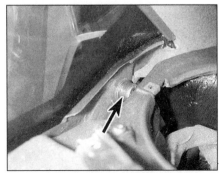

20.14 Undo the bolt adjacent to the speaker aperture (arrowed)

11

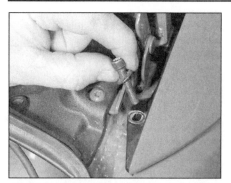

20.15 Undo the bolt at the forward end of the mirror cowl

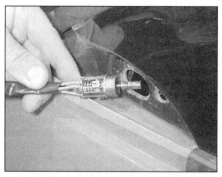

20.16 Remove the mirror and feed the controls through the body opening

21.3 Locating the mirror glass spring on the back of the glass

15 Open the bonnet and undo the bolt at the forward end of the mirror cowl **(see illustration)**.
16 Withdraw the mirror from its location, feeding the wiring or the control cables through the opening in the bodywork **(see illustration)**.

Refitting

17 In all cases, refitting is a reversal of removal. On Phase 1 and 2 models, apply a bead of mastic to the mirror contact area on the door.

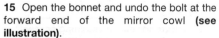

21 Exterior mirror glass and motor - removal and refitting

Note: *The following procedure is applicable to Phase 3 models only. It would appear that individual components are not available separately for the mirror assembly fitted to earlier models.*

Mirror glass

Removal

1 Insert a thin, flat, screwdriver between the bottom of the glass and the surround, and release the retaining spring wire by pushing it inwards off the lugs on the back of the glass.
2 Withdraw the mirror glass from its location.

Refitting

3 Locate the spring wire behind the lugs on

the back of the glass **(see illustration)**. Place the mirror in position and push on the glass to clip it into place.

Motor and/or control cables

Removal

4 Remove the mirror from the vehicle as described in Section 20.
5 Remove the mirror glass as described previously.
6 On manually operated mirrors, undo the four screws securing the mechanism, unfasten the control cables noting their locations for refitting then remove the mechanism **(see illustration)**.
7 On electrically operated mirrors, undo the three screws, disconnect the wiring connections and remove the motor.
8 To dismantle the mirror shell, undo the five screws from the interior of the mirror shell and lift off the front surround. Undo the four screws now exposed and the seven screws from fixed shell. Separate the components.

Refitting

9 Refitting is a reversal of removal.

22 Seats - removal and refitting

⚠️ **Warning: Vehicles for certain markets may be equipped with mechanical front seat belt**

tensioners. **DO NOT attempt to remove the front seats on vehicles so equipped. Have any work involving front seat removal carried out by a Renault dealer.**

Front seat

Removal

1 Move the seat fully forwards. Remove the single screw from the rear of each track **(see illustration)**.
2 Move the seat fully rearwards. Remove the single screw from the front of each track **(see illustration)**.
3 Remove the seat and tracks together.

Refitting

4 Refit by reversing the removal operations.

Rear seat

Removal

5 If fitted, remove the head restraint then lift the lever on the side of the seat and fold down the backrest.
6 Pull the strap at the base of the seat and lift the seat up and tilt it forwards.
7 Lift the bar at the bottom front of the seat to release the front hooks then lift away the seat.

Refitting

8 With the seat in the folded position engage the front hooks in their mountings and push down firmly to lock.
9 Move the seat to its original position and push down to lock the rear mountings.
10 Lift up the backrest if wished.

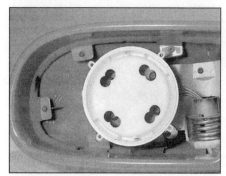

21.6 Mirror control mechanism screws are reached through the holes in the plate

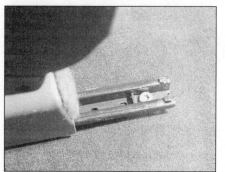

22.1 Front seat track rear retaining screw

22.2 Front seat track front retaining screw

23.1 Seat belt lower anchorage bolt

23.3 Seat belt upper anchorage bolt

23.5 Seat belt inertia reel mounting

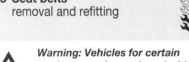

23 Seat belts -
removal and refitting

⚠ *Warning: Vehicles for certain markets may be equipped with mechanical front seat belt tensioners. DO NOT attempt to remove the front seat belts on vehicles so equipped. Have any work involving front seat belt removal carried out by a Renault dealer.*

Note: *Take note of the positions of any washers and spacers on the seat belt anchors, and ensure that they are refitted in their original positions.*

Front seat belt

Removal

1 Prise off the trim cap then unscrew the bolt securing the lower seat belt anchor to the body pillar **(see illustration)**.
2 At the belt exit point on the door pillar, undo the screw and remove the trim cover by pulling it downward to free the internal clips.
3 Prise off the trim cap from the upper seat belt anchor bolt on the body pillar **(see illustration)**.
4 Unscrew the upper anchor bolt, and release the anchor plate from the pillar.
5 Unscrew the inertia reel securing bolt, then withdraw the seat belt assembly **(see illustration)**.

Refitting

6 Refitting is a reversal of removal. Ensure that all washers and/or spacers are positioned as noted before removal, and tighten all mounting bolts to the specified torque.

Front seat belt stalk

Removal

7 Each stalk is secured either to the front seat frame or to the floor or floor bracket by a bolt and washer.
8 Prise off the trim cap (where applicable) from the floor mounted stalk, undo the bolt and remove the stalk. Working at the lower rear inner corner of the front seat, undo the bolt and remove the seat mounted stalk.

Refitting

9 Refitting is a reversal of removal, but tighten the retaining bolts to the specified torque.

Rear seat belt

Removal

10 Remove the wheel arch interior trim panel which is secured by screws and internal clips.
11 Prise off the trim cap from the upper seat belt anchor bolt on the body panel. Unscrew the upper anchor bolt, and release the anchor plate **(see illustration)**.
12 Unscrew the inertia reel securing bolt, then withdraw the seat belt assembly.

Refitting

13 Refitting is a reversal of removal, but tighten the retaining bolts to the specified torque.

Rear seat belt stalk

Removal

14 Prise off the trim cover around the stalk location on the rear seat.
15 Undo the retaining bolt and remove the stalk from the seat.

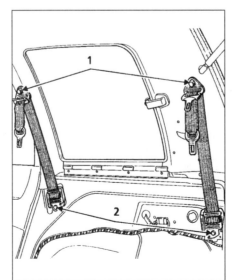

23.11 Rear seat belt upper anchorage (1) and inertia reel attachment (2)

Refitting

16 Refitting is a reversal of removal, but tighten the bolts to the specified torque.

24 Centre console -
removal and refitting

Removal

1 Release the gear lever gaiter from the base of the console by easing it out of its location **(see illustration)**. The gaiter can be left attached to the gear lever and pushed down through its opening as the console is removed.
2 Prise up the plastic strip at the front of the handbrake lever base and undo the screw now revealed **(see illustration)**.

24.1 Release the gear lever gaiter from the centre console

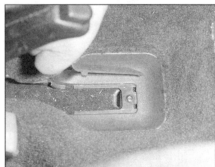

24.2 Prise up the plastic strip for access to the console front screw

11

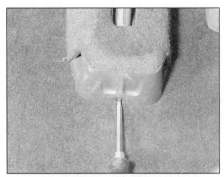

24.3 Undo the screw at the rear of the console base

3 Undo the screw at the centre rear of the console base **(see illustration)**.

4 Slide the console rearward to disengage the locating clip under the facia. When sufficient clearance exists, manoeuvre the console up over the handbrake lever and gear lever and remove from the vehicle.

Refitting

5 Refitting is a reversal of removal.

25 Roof console - removal and refitting

Removal

1 Carefully prise out the trim cover around the two lower switches and the blanking plate in the centre between the two light units.

2 Undo the three screws now revealed and withdraw the console from the roof.

3 Disconnect the wiring connectors, noting their locations and remove the console.

Refitting

4 Refitting is a reversal of removal.

26 Facia - removal and refitting
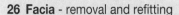

Phase 1 and 2 models

Removal

1 Disconnect the battery negative lead.

2 Remove the steering wheel, the steering column switches and the instrument panel. See Chapters 10 and 12.

3 Undo the two screws each side and remove the parcel shelf under the steering column.

4 Undo the remaining two screws on the right-hand side of the pedal cover trim and withdraw the trim. Disconnect the wiring connector at the light switch rheostat and, on later models, remove the bonnet release handle. Remove the pedal cover trim.

5 On early models, undo the two screws securing the bonnet release handle to the footwell side panel.

6 Undo the four nuts securing the steering column to the mounting frame and lower the column as far as the universal joint will allow.

7 From within the instrument panel aperture undo the four screws, two at the top and two from the front centre and withdraw the instrument panel lower casing.

8 Open the fuse box by turning the two knobs and lowering it at the front. Using a screwdriver, disengage the spindle and pull the fuse box out until it is clear of the facia.

9 Undo the two screws securing the right-hand parcel shelf to the footwell side panel.

10 On early models, undo the four screws each side and remove the right-hand and left-hand side panels from the facia lower centre section. On later models, remove the cover and undo the two screws each side, then remove the two side panels from the facia lower centre section after releasing the clips at the rear.

11 Identify the location of the two heater control cables to aid refitting. Disconnect the control cables from the flap levers by releasing the retaining clip and sliding the inner cable ends off the lever pegs.

12 Undo the two screws each side securing the facia lower mounting brackets to the right-hand and left-hand door pillars **(see illustration)**.

13 Carefully prise out the demister vents on each side of the facia.

14 Undo the securing screw under the centre of the facia lower centre section.

15 Undo the screw behind the facia centre trim section on each side.

16 Lift the facia to free the front mounting lugs from the crossmember.

17 With the facia released, disconnect all wiring and cable connections at the rear, marking each for reassembly. Check that all attachments have been disconnected, then carefully withdraw the facia and remove it from the vehicle.

18 With the facia removed, the front parcel shelf can be removed after undoing the retaining screws at the base of the windscreen and along the top edge of the crossmember.

Refitting

19 Refitting is a reversal of removal, bearing in mind the following points:

a) *Ensure that all wiring is connected as noted before removal.*

b) *Adjust the heater control cables as follows. Move the temperature control lever to the "cold" position and ensure that the hot air/cold air flap in the heater unit is closed. Engage the control inner cable end with the flap lever then secure the outer cable with the retaining clip. Adjustment is made by slightly repositioning the outer cable in its clip as necessary. Move the air distribution control lever to its lowest "face only" position and ensure that the two distribution flaps in the heater unit are closed. Connect and adjust the cable as just described.*

c) *Refit the steering wheel as described in Chapter 10, and the instrument panel and switches as described in Chapter 12.*

Phase 3 models

Removal

Warning: On vehicles equipped with an air bag, some of the following operations will entail disturbing some of the air bag components. Have any work involving removal of the air bag components carried out by a Renault dealer.

20 Disconnect the battery negative lead.

21 Remove the steering wheel and the instrument panel as described in Chapters 10 and 12.

22 Carefully prise up the speaker grille from the top corner of the facia. Where fitted,

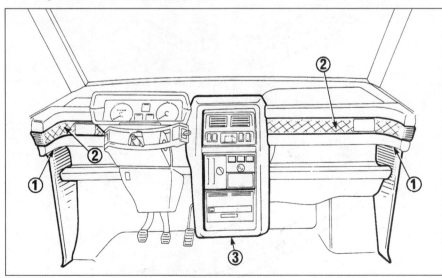

26.12 Location of facia attachments on Phase 1 and 2 models

1 Door pillar screws   2 Centre trim screws   3 Lower centre section screw

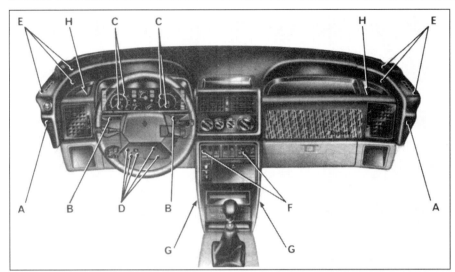

26.22 Location of facia attachments on Phase 3 models

A Side panel screws
B Instrument panel surround screws
C Instrument panel mounting screws
D Steering column lower shroud screws

E Upper section screws under speaker grilles
F Centre section upper screws
G Centre section lower screws in vent grilles
H Facia-to-crossmember bolts

disconnect the speaker wiring and remove the grille **(see illustration)**.

23 Undo the four screws, disconnect the wiring and remove the main speaker.

24 Remove the facia side panel by undoing the screw at the front which is located behind a plastic cap. Pull the side panel rearward to free it.

25 Disconnect the exterior mirror control switch wiring from the switch in the side panel. If a manual mirror is fitted, pull off the grommet, unscrew the retaining nut and withdraw the control from the side panel.

26 Undo the four screws and remove the instrument panel mounting from within the panel aperture.

27 Pull off the headlight height adjustment switch knob.

28 Undo the five screws securing the steering column lower shroud. Slacken the radio remote control assembly mounting bolt (where fitted) and lower the shroud at the top. Disengage the two lower lugs and lift off the shroud. Disconnect the wiring connector at the light switch rheostat and pull out the illumination bulbholder from the headlight height adjustment switch. Remove the height adjustment switch face plate, undo the two screws now visible, and withdraw the switch body from the surround. Remove the lower shroud.

29 Lift off the steering column upper shroud.

30 Undo the three screws each side securing the facia upper section. Lift the upper section and release the heater control unit by pushing it inward to release the retaining clips. Remove the facia upper section from the vehicle.

31 Remove the radio (see Chapter 12).

32 Disconnect all the switch and accessory wiring at the rear of the facia centre section, making careful notes for reassembly.

33 Undo the two screws, securing the facia centre section at the top.

34 Undo the screw at each lower side of the centre section in the footwell vent grille.

35 Open the glovebox then lower the fuse box by pressing the two tabs at the side. Separate the fuse box from the facia by

undoing the two retaining nuts and disengaging the locating peg.

36 Undo the three bolts each side securing the facia to the crossmember. Check that all wiring, cables and connections have been disconnected then withdraw the facia centre section from its location. Remove the centre section from the vehicle.

37 Refitting is a reversal of removal, bearing in mind the following points:

a) Ensure that all wiring is connected as noted before removal.

b) Refit the steering wheel as described in Chapter 10, and the instrument panel, switches and radio as described in Chapter 12.

27 Front bumper -
removal and refitting

Phase 1 and 2 models

Removal

1 Drill out the securing rivets and remove the mud baffles from both wheel arches **(see illustration)**

2 From within the engine compartment, undo the two bolts each side securing the bumper side brackets to the body.

3 Remove the bolt each side securing the bumper front brackets to the headlight supports.

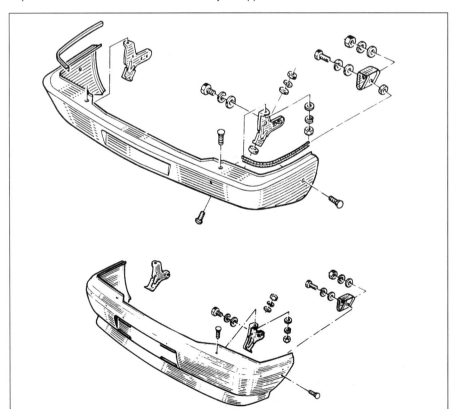

27.1 Front bumper components (Phase 1 and 2 models)

11

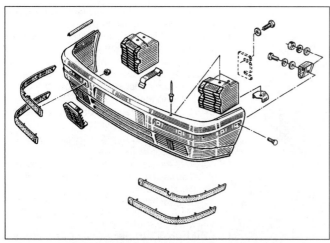

27.8 Front bumper components (Phase 3 models)

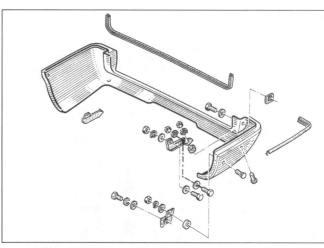

28.1 Rear bumper components (Phase 1 and 2 models)

4 Withdraw the bumper and disconnect the foglight wiring (where fitted).

5 On models with a separate spoiler, this can be removed from the bumper by undoing the seven screws.

Refitting

6 Refitting is a reversal of removal. Secure the mud baffles by re-riveting them into place.

Phase 3 models

Removal

7 The bumper side mounting bolts are located in the engine compartment on the lower inner wing panels. To gain access it will be necessary to remove any components in that area which will impede access. Component locations vary considerably according to engine type and equipment, but it is likely that the following will have to be removed:

   a) *Air cleaner assembly.*
   b) *Wiring multi-plug holder.*
   c) *Relay carrier.*
   d) *Fuel injection system ECU case.*

It will not be necessary to disconnect any of these components, just undo their mountings and move them to one side.

8 With access gained, undo the two side mounting bolts **(see illustration)**.

9 Undo the two front mounting bolts located on the headlight support uprights.

10 Withdraw the bumper from its location and where applicable, disconnect the fog light wiring.

11 If required the impact absorbers can be removed after drilling out the single rivet on each.

12 Note the number of packing pieces behind the impact absorbers and ensure that the same number are used when refitting.

Refitting

13 Refitting is a reversal of removal, but apply a thread locking compound to the threads of the side mounting bolts.

28 Rear bumper - removal and refitting

Phase 1 and 2 models

Removal

1 From under the rear of the vehicle undo the single bolt each side securing the bumper to the outer chassis member **(see illustration)**. Also undo the single bolt (Phase 1 models) or two bolts (Phase 2 models) securing the bumper to the inner chassis member.

2 Open the tailgate and undo the bolt on each side securing the bumper to the tailgate pillar.

3 Carefully withdraw the bumper from its location.

Refitting

4 Refitting is a reversal of removal.

Phase 3 models

Removal

5 Remove the rear light unit (see Chapter 12).

6 Drill out the rivet securing the bumper to the impact absorber. This is located on the bumper upper face now visible by removal of the light unit **(see illustration)**.

7 From under the rear of the vehicle undo the single bolt each side securing the bumper to the outer chassis member.

8 Carefully withdraw the bumper.

9 To remove the impact absorbers, remove the wheel arch trim at the rear or open the access cover (where fitted).

10 Undo the two bolts each side and remove the impact absorbers.

Refitting

11 Refitting is a reversal of removal, but apply a thread locking compound to the threads of the side mounting bolts.

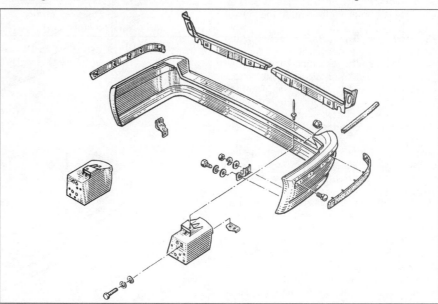

28.6 Rear bumper components (Phase 3 models)

29 Front grille panel - removal and refitting

Phase 1 and 2 models

Removal

1 Open the bonnet and undo the four screws along the grille panel top edge (Phase 1 models) or the four screws on the panel front face (Phase 2 models).

29.4 Remove the bonnet sealing weatherstrip from the grille panel

29.6a Undo the screws at the upper corner . . .

2 Undo the nuts each side securing the panel to the headlight support uprights and remove the grille panel.

Refitting

3 Refitting is a reversal of removal.

Phase 3 models

Removal

4 Open the bonnet and pull off the bonnet sealing weatherstrip **(see illustration)**.
5 Undo the two screws each side and lift off the grille end plates **(see illustration)**.

29.5 Undo the grille end plate screws (arrowed)

29.6b . . . and at the lower corner of each headlight . . .

6 Undo the screws at the upper and lower inner corners of each headlight and the remaining screw at each upper end **(see illustrations)**. Withdraw the grille from its location.

Refitting

7 Refitting is a reversal of removal.

30 Sunroof - general information

A mechanically or electrically operated sunroof is available as standard or optional equipment according to model.

The sunroof is maintenance-free, but any adjustment or removal and refitting of the component parts should be entrusted to a Renault dealer, due to the complexity of the unit and the need to remove much of the interior trim and headlining to gain access. The latter operation is involved, and requires care and specialist knowledge to avoid damage.

29.6c . . . and the remaining screw at each upper corner

11

Chapter 12
Body electrical systems

Contents

Degrees of difficulty

Easy, suitable for novice with little experience	**Fairly easy,** suitable for beginner with some experience 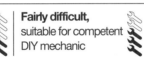	**Fairly difficult,** suitable for competent DIY mechanic 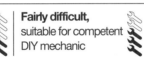	**Difficult,** suitable for experienced DIY mechanic	**Very difficult,** suitable for expert DIY or professional

Specifications

Fuses - Phase 1 and 2 models

No	Rating (amps)	Circuit(s) protected
1	7.5	Rear foglight
2	7.5	Windscreen and tailgate wiper "park"
3	15	Cigar lighter/clock/interior lights
4	20	Heated rear window
5	7.5	Windscreen wash/wipe, tailgate wiper
6	7.5	Reversing lights, windscreen wiper delay
7	5	Right-hand sidelights, instrument lighting rheostat
8	5	Left-hand sidelights, number plate lights
9	3	Instrument panel supply
10	15	Stop lights
11	10	Direction indicator flasher
12	15	Heater blower motor
13	3/10	Radio, radio/cassette player
14	2	Automatic transmission
15	15	Central locking
16	25	Air conditioning, electric sun roof
17	25	Left-hand window lift motor
18	25	Right-hand window lift motor, electric exterior mirror
19	15	Front foglights

12

Fuses - Phase 3 models

No	Rating (amps)	Circuit(s) protected
1	20	Heated rear window, electric exterior mirrors, instrument panel warning lights
2	5	Right-hand side lights, number plate lights
3	5	Fuel pump, fuel injection, air conditioning, diesel preheating, emission control solenoids
4	10	Facia and passenger compartment switch lighting
5	20	Windscreen/tailgate wipers, tailgate wiper delay, reversing lights, automatic transmission selector quadrant lighting
6	20	Seat belt pre-tensioners, instrument panel warning lights, courtesy light delay, windscreen wiper delay, windscreen washer pump
7	15	Radio/cassette player, remote control, courtesy light delay, clock and interior lighting
8	25	Headlight main beam
9	15	Radio remote control unit
10	15	Heating and controls, anti-theft alarm, direction indicators
11	5	Left-hand sidelights
12	10	Cigar lighter, accessory supply
13	20	Heater blower motor, car phone supply
14	30	Front electric window lift motors
15	10	Radiator fan thermostatic switch, horn relay, air conditioning, automatic transmission mode control
16	5	Automatic transmission ECU
17	7.5	Stop lights, "lights on" warning buzzer, anti-theft alarm, clock
18	25	Windscreen/tailgate wiper "park", central locking
19	10	Hazard warning lights, electric exterior mirrors

Light bulbs (typical)

	Wattage
Headlight main/dipped beam	60/55
Front sidelights	5
Direction indicators	21
Front foglights	55
Combined stop and tail light	21/5
Rear foglights	21
Reversing lights	21
Number plate light	5
Interior lights	10
Instrument panel lights	1.2 or 2

---

1 General information and precautions

General information

The electrical system is of 12-volt negative earth type. Power for the lights and all electrical accessories is supplied by a lead/acid battery which is charged by the alternator.

This Chapter covers repair and service procedures for the various electrical components and systems not associated with the engine. Information on the battery, ignition system, alternator, and starter motor can be found in Chapter 5.

Precautions

Warning: Before carrying out any work on the electrical system, read through the precautions given in "Safety first!" at the beginning of this manual and in Chapter 5A.

Caution: Prior to working on any component in the electrical system, the battery negative lead should first be disconnected, to prevent the possibility of electrical short-circuits and/or fires. If a radio/cassette player with anti-theft security code is fitted, refer to the information given in the reference sections of this manual before disconnecting the battery.

2 Electrical fault finding - general information

Note: *Refer to the precautions given in "Safety first!" and in Section 1 of this Chapter before starting work. The following tests relate to testing of the main electrical circuits, and should not be used to test delicate electronic circuits, particularly where an electronic control unit is used.*

General

1 A typical electrical circuit consists of an electrical component, any switches, relays, motors, fuses, fusible links or circuit breakers related to that component, and the wiring and connectors which link the component to both the battery and the chassis. To help to pinpoint a problem in an electrical circuit, wiring diagrams are included at the end of this manual.

2 Before attempting to diagnose an electrical fault, first study the appropriate wiring diagram, to obtain a complete understanding of the components included in the particular circuit concerned. The possible sources of a fault can be narrowed down by noting if other components related to the circuit are operating properly. If several components or circuits fail at one time, the problem is likely to be related to a shared fuse or earth connection.

3 Electrical problems usually stem from simple causes, such as loose or corroded connections, a faulty earth connection, a blown fuse, a melted fusible link, or a faulty relay. Visually inspect the condition of all fuses, wires and connections in a problem circuit before testing the components. Use the wiring diagrams to determine which terminal connections will need to be checked in order to pinpoint the trouble-spot.

4 The basic tools required for electrical fault-finding include a circuit tester or voltmeter (a 12-volt bulb with a set of test leads can also be used for certain tests); an ohmmeter (to measure resistance and check for continuity); a battery and set of test leads; and a jumper wire, preferably with a circuit breaker or fuse incorporated, which can be used to bypass suspect wires or electrical components. Before attempting to locate a problem with test instruments, use the wiring diagram to determine where to make the connections.

5 To find the source of an intermittent wiring fault (usually due to a poor or dirty connection, or damaged wiring insulation), a "wiggle" test can be performed on the wiring. This involves wiggling the wiring by hand to see if the fault occurs as the wiring is moved. It should be possible to narrow down the source of the fault to a particular section of wiring. This method of testing can be used in conjunction with any of the tests described in the following sub-Sections.

6 Apart from problems due to poor connections, two basic types of fault can occur in an electrical circuit - open-circuit, or short-circuit.

7 Open-circuit faults are caused by a break somewhere in the circuit, which prevents current from flowing. An open-circuit fault will prevent a component from working.

8 Short-circuit faults are caused by a "short" somewhere in the circuit, which allows the current flowing in the circuit to "escape" along an alternative route, usually to earth. Short-circuit faults are normally caused by a breakdown in wiring insulation, which allows a feed wire to touch either another wire, or an earthed component such as the bodyshell. A short-circuit fault will normally cause the relevant circuit fuse to blow.

Finding an open-circuit

9 To check for an open-circuit, connect one lead of a circuit tester or the negative lead of a voltmeter either to the battery negative terminal or to a known good earth.

10 Connect the other lead to a connector in the circuit being tested, preferably nearest to the battery or fuse. At this point, battery voltage should be present, unless the lead from the battery or the fuse itself is faulty (bearing in mind that some circuits are live only when the ignition switch is moved to a particular position).

11 Switch on the circuit, then connect the tester lead to the connector nearest the circuit switch on the component side.

12 If voltage is present (indicated either by the tester bulb lighting or a voltmeter reading, as applicable), this means that the section of the circuit between the relevant connector and the switch is problem-free.

13 Continue to check the remainder of the circuit in the same fashion.

14 When a point is reached at which no voltage is present, the problem must lie between that point and the previous test point with voltage. Most problems can be traced to a broken, corroded or loose connection.

Finding a short-circuit

15 To check for a short-circuit, first disconnect the load(s) from the circuit (loads are the components which draw current from a circuit, such as bulbs, motors, heating elements, etc).

16 Remove the relevant fuse from the circuit, and connect a circuit tester or voltmeter to the fuse connections.

17 Switch on the circuit, bearing in mind that some circuits are live only when the ignition switch is moved to a particular position.

18 If voltage is present (indicated either by the tester bulb lighting or a voltmeter reading, as applicable), this means that there is a short-circuit.

19 If no voltage is present during this test, but the fuse still blows with the load(s) reconnected, this indicates an internal fault in the load(s).

Finding an earth fault

20 The battery negative terminal is connected to "earth" - the metal of the engine/transmission and the vehicle body - and many systems are wired so that they only receive a positive feed, the current returning via the metal of the car body. This means that the component mounting and the body form part of that circuit. Loose or corroded mountings can therefore cause a range of electrical faults, ranging from total failure of a circuit, to a puzzling partial failure. In particular, lights may shine dimly (especially when another circuit sharing the same earth point is in operation), motors (eg wiper motors or the radiator cooling fan motor) may run slowly, and the operation of one circuit may have an apparently-unrelated effect on another. Note that on many vehicles, earth straps are used between certain components, such as the engine/transmission and the body, usually where there is no metal-to-metal contact between components, due to flexible rubber mountings, etc.

21 To check whether a component is properly earthed, disconnect the battery and connect one lead of an ohmmeter to a known good earth point. Connect the other lead to the wire or earth connection being tested. The resistance reading should be zero; if not, check the connection as follows.

22 If an earth connection is thought to be faulty, dismantle the connection, and clean both the bodyshell and the wire terminal (or the component earth connection mating surface) back to bare metal. Be careful to remove all traces of dirt and corrosion, then use a knife to trim away any paint, so that a clean metal-to-metal joint is made. On reassembly, tighten the joint fasteners securely; if a wire terminal is being refitted, use serrated washers between the terminal and the bodyshell, to ensure a clean and secure connection. When the connection is remade, prevent the onset of corrosion in the future by applying a coat of petroleum jelly or silicone-based grease, or by spraying on (at regular intervals) a proprietary ignition sealer, or a water-dispersant lubricant.

3 Fuses and relays - general information

Fuses

1 The fuses are located on the accessory plate (fusebox), which is situated below the glove box on Phase 1 and 2 models, or in the roof of the glove box on Phase 3 models. Access is gained by turning the two knobs and lowering the accessory plate, or by opening the glove box, pressing the tabs on each side of the accessory plate and lowering it at the front **(see illustration)**.

2 If a fuse blows, the electrical circuit(s) protected by that fuse will cease to operate. Lists of the circuits protected are given in the *Specifications*, and the fuse arrangement is shown on these pages **(see illustrations)**.

3 To check for a blown fuse, either remove the fuse and inspect its wire link, or (with the power on) connect a 12 volt test light between earth and each of the fuse pegs. If the test light comes on at both pegs, the fuse is OK; if it comes on at one peg only, the fuse is blown.

4 To renew a blown fuse, pull out the old fuse either with the fingers or with the special tool provided. Press in a new fuse of the correct rating (indicated by colour and by a number on the fuse). Spare fuses are provided at various locations in the fusebox.

5 Never fit a fuse of a higher rating than that specified, nor bypass a blown fuse with wire or metal foil. Serious damage or fire could result.

6 Persistent blowing of a particular fuse indicates a fault in the circuit(s) protected. Where more than one circuit is involved, switch on one item at a time until the fuse blows, so showing in which circuit the fault lies.

7 Besides a fault in the electrical component concerned, a blown fuse can also be caused

3.1 Fusebox location in the glove box roof on Phase 3 models

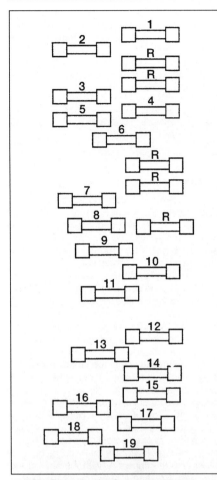

3.2b Fuse numbering arrangement on Phase 3 models

by a short-circuit in the wiring to the component. Look for trapped or frayed wires allowing a live wire to touch vehicle metal, and for loose or damaged connectors.

Relays - general

8 A relay is an electrically-operated switch, which is used for the following reasons:

a) *A relay can switch a heavy current remotely from the circuit in which the current is flowing, allowing the use of lighter gauge wiring and switch contacts.*

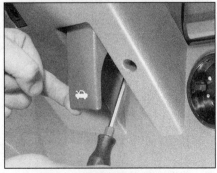

4.7b ...and lower screws...

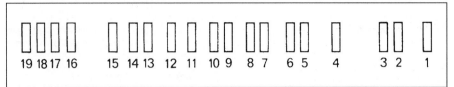

3.2a Fuse numbering arrangement on Phase 1 and 2 models

b) *A relay can receive more than one control input, unlike a mechanical switch.*

c) *A relay can have a timer function - for example an intermittent wiper delay.*

9 If a circuit which includes a relay develops a fault, remember that the relay itself could be faulty. Testing is by substitution of a known good relay. Do not assume that relays which look similar are necessarily identical for purposes of substitution.

10 Most relays are located on the accessory plate, together with the fuses. Additional relays relating to the fuel and ignition systems and various accessories are located in the engine compartment.

4 Switches - removal and refitting

Steering column switches

Phase 1 and 2 models

1 Disconnect the battery negative lead.

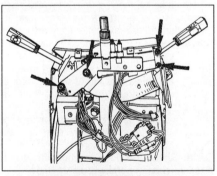

4.3 Steering column switch attachments (arrowed) on Phase 1 and 2 models

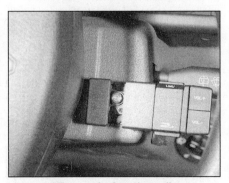

4.7c ...slacken the radio remote control unit screw...

2 Undo the three screws and remove the steering column upper and lower shrouds.
3 Undo the two screws securing the relevant switch to the steering column bracket **(see illustration)**. Withdraw the switch, disconnect the wiring connector and remove the switch.
4 Refit by reversing the removal operations.

Phase 3 models

5 Disconnect the battery negative lead.
6 Remove the steering wheel (Chapter 10).
7 Undo the five screws securing the steering column lower shroud. Slacken the radio remote control assembly mounting screw (where fitted) and lower the shroud at the top. Disengage the two lower lugs and move the shroud to one side without disconnecting the switch wiring or controls **(see illustrations)**.
8 Lift off the steering column upper shroud.
9 Slacken the retaining screw on the top of the switch holder. Disconnect the switch wiring connectors and withdraw the switch holder off the steering column.
10 Undo the two screws and remove the relevant switch from the holder.
11 Refit by reversing the removal operations.

4.7a Undo the upper screws ...

4.7d ...and lift off the steering column shroud after disengaging the lower lugs

Ignition/starter switch

Phase 1 and 2 models

12 Disconnect the battery negative lead.
13 Undo the three screws and remove the steering column upper and lower shrouds.
14 Disconnect the wiring connector from the switch.
15 Turn the ignition key to the "Garage" position and remove the key.
16 Undo the retaining screw on the side of the lock barrel.
17 Using a small pointed tool such as a punch or thin nail, depress the retaining notch, push on the rear of the switch and remove it from the steering column.
18 Refit by reversing the removal operations.

Phase 3 models

19 Disconnect the battery negative lead.
20 Set the steering wheel and roadwheels in the straight-ahead position.
21 Undo the five screws securing the steering column lower shroud. Slacken the radio remote control assembly mounting bolt (where fitted) and lower the shroud at the top. Disengage the two lower lugs and move the shroud to one side without disconnecting the switch wiring or controls.
22 Lift off the steering column upper shroud.
23 Disconnect the two ignition switch wiring connectors.
24 Turn the ignition key to position "A", depress the retaining lugs and withdraw the switch from the steering column.
25 Refit by reversing the removal operations.

Facia switches

26 Disconnect the battery negative lead.
27 All the facia switches are a push fit in their locations and can be removed by carefully prising them out with a small screwdriver, or by pushing them out from behind after removing an adjacent switch **(see illustration)**. Once the switch is released, disconnect the wiring connector and remove the switch.
28 Refit by reversing the removal operations.

Window/mirror control switches

29 Disconnect the battery negative lead.
30 Carefully prise the switch from its location in the door switch panel **(see illustration)**.

4.27 Removing a facia switch

31 Disconnect the wiring connector and remove the switch
32 Refit by reversing the removal operations.

Door/tailgate switches

33 Disconnect the battery negative lead.
34 Open the door or tailgate and either prise the switch from its location or remove the retaining screw, according to type.
35 Secure the wires with a clothes peg before disconnecting them so that they are not lost in the door pillar.
36 Refit by reversing the removal operations.

Brake stop light switch

37 Disconnect the battery negative lead.
38 On Phase 1 and 2 models, undo the three screws and remove the steering column upper and lower shrouds. Undo the two screws each side and remove the parcel shelf under the steering column. Undo the remaining two screws on the right-hand side of the pedal cover trim and withdraw the trim, without disconnecting the switch wiring.
39 On Phase 3 models, undo the five screws securing the steering column lower shroud. Slacken the radio remote control assembly mounting bolt (where fitted) and lower the shroud at the top. Disengage the two lower lugs and move the shroud to one side without disconnecting the switch wiring or controls.
40 Disconnect the wiring from the switch. Undo the locknut and unscrew the switch.
41 When refitting, screw the switch in so that it operates after 8 to 14 mm movement of the brake pedal. Reconnect the wires and tighten the locknut.
42 Check for correct operation, then refit the disturbed trim.

Handbrake warning switch

43 Disconnect the battery negative lead.
44 Remove the centre console (where fitted) as described in Chapter 11.
45 Disconnect the switch wiring, undo the switch securing screw and remove the switch.
46 Refit by reversing the removal operations. Check for correct operation of the switch before refitting the console.

Instrument lighting rheostat

47 Disconnect the battery negative lead.

4.30 Removing a door switch

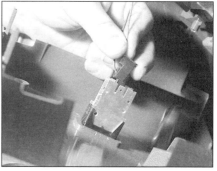

4.49 **Disconnect the wiring from the instrument panel rheostat**

48 Remove the pedal cover trim (paragraph 38) or the steering column lower shroud (paragraph 39) according to model.
49 Disconnect the wiring connector **(see illustration)**.
50 Prise the rheostat from its location using a small screwdriver.
51 Refit by reversing the removal operations.

Roof console switches

52 Disconnect the battery negative lead.
53 Carefully prise out the trim cover around the two lower switches and the blanking plate in the centre between the two light units.
54 Undo the three screws now revealed and withdraw the console from the roof.
55 Disconnect the wiring connectors, and push out the relevant switch from its location.
56 Refit by reversing the removal operations.

Radio/cassette player remote control switch

57 Disconnect the battery negative lead.
58 Remove the radio/cassette player, as described in Section 19.
59 Disconnect the remote control switch wiring from the rear of the radio/cassette unit.
60 Remove the steering column shrouds (paragraph 39).
61 Slide the switch from its bracket, then feed the wiring through from behind the facia, noting its routing.
62 Refit by reversing the removal operations noting the following points:

a) Refit the radio/cassette player as described in Section 19.
b) Ensure that the wiring is routed as noted before removal.
c) Do not fully tighten the switch clamp screw until the steering column shrouds have been refitted.

5 Clock - removal and refitting

Removal

1 Disconnect the battery negative lead.
2 Carefully prise the clock from the facia and disconnect the wiring plug **(see illustration)**.

12

5.2 Carefully prise out the clock with a screwdriver

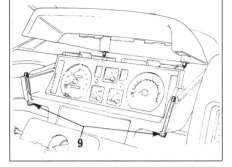

7.2 Undo the two lower screws (9) to release the instrument panel surround

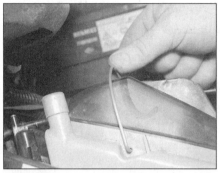

9.4 Release the clip and remove the cover from the rear of the headlight

The clock is retained by plastic clips which are pushed aside as the clock is removed.

Refitting

3 Refitting is a reversal of removal.

6 Speedometer drive cable - removal and refitting

Removal

1 Refer to Section 7 and remove the instrument panel sufficiently to allow the speedometer cable to be disconnected.
2 Chock the rear wheels then jack up the front of the vehicle and support it on axle stands (see "Jacking and vehicle support").
3 Disconnect the speedometer cable from the transmission by gripping the retaining pin with a pair of pliers and pulling it outwards to release the cable.
4 Withdraw the speedometer cable into the passenger compartment through the bulkhead, noting its routing.

Refitting

5 Refitting is a reversal of removal.

7 Instrument panel - removal and refitting

Removal

1 Disconnect the battery negative lead.
2 Undo the two screws at the bottom of the instrument panel surround, then lift off the surround upper section (Phase 1 and 2 models) or the complete surround (Phase 3 models) **(see illustration)**.
3 Disconnect the speedometer cable and wiring connectors then remove the instrument panel from its location. On Phase 3 models lift the instrument panel upwards first to disengage the three clips.

Refitting

4 Refit by reversing the removal operations.

8 Instrument panel components - removal and refitting

Note: *Various different instrument panel layouts may be encountered depending on model specification. Although the details may differ from those described, the following paragraphs can be used as a guide for all models.*

Removal

1 Remove the instrument panel as described in Section 7.
2 Prise the plastic hooks outwards and remove the front cover.
3 To remove the speedometer extract the two screws from the front and/or rear of the unit.
4 To remove the coolant temperature indicator extract the printed circuit nuts and the two retaining screws.
5 To remove the fuel gauge extract the printed circuit nuts and the two retaining screws.
6 To remove the tachometer extract the single rear screw and the two front screws.
7 To remove the oil level indicator, first remove the tachometer, then extract the printed circuit nuts and the two retaining screws.

Refitting

8 Refitting is a reversal of removal.

9 Bulbs (exterior lights) - renewal

General

1 With all light bulbs, remember that if they have just been in use, they may be very hot. Switch off the power before renewing a bulb.
2 With quartz halogen bulbs (headlights and similar applications), do not touch the bulb glass with the fingers. Even small quantities of grease from the fingers will cause blackening and premature failure. If a bulb is accidentally touched, clean it with methylated spirit and a clean rag.

3 Unless otherwise stated, fit the new bulb by reversing the removal operations.

Bulb renewal

Headlight

4 On Phase 3 models, release the clip and remove the cover from the rear of the headlight **(see illustration)**.
5 Pull the wiring connector from the rear of the headlight bulb(s) **(see illustration)**. Phase 1 and 2 models have a single dipped beam/main beam bulb; Phase 3 models may have a single dipped beam/main beam, or a separate dipped beam and main beam.
6 Release the spring clip and pivot the clip clear.
7 Withdraw the bulb from its location in the headlight **(see illustration)**.

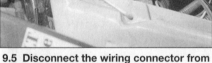

9.5 Disconnect the wiring connector from the rear of the headlight bulb

9.7 Withdraw the bulb from the headlight unit

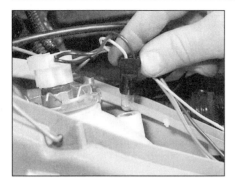

9.11 Removing the sidelight bulbholder

9.13 Removing the front direction indicator bulbholder

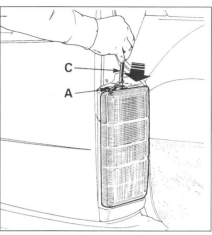

9.27 On Phase 1 models release the rear light cluster catches (A) using a screwdriver (C)

9.15 Release the direction indicator repeater lens with a screwdriver

9.16 Pull out the repeater bulbholder from the light unit

8 Fit the new bulb using a reversal of the removal procedure, but make sure that the tabs on the bulb support are correctly located in the cut-outs in the light unit.

Sidelight

9 On Phase 1 models, carefully squeeze the retaining lugs on the rear of the light unit and withdraw the sidelight and direction indicator bulbholder. Remove the bulb from the holder.
10 On Phase 2 and 3 models, release the clip and remove the cover from the rear of the headlight (Phase 3).
11 Withdraw the bulb from the holder, fit a new bulb and reassemble **(see illustration)**.

Front direction indicator

12 On Phase 1 models, proceed as described in paragraph 9.
13 On Phase 2 and 3 models, turn the bulbholder a quarter turn and withdraw it from the light unit **(see illustration)**.
14 Withdraw the bulb from the holder, fit a new bulb and reassemble.

Front direction indicator repeater

15 Release the lens by inserting a small screwdriver into the slot and prising out **(see illustration)**.
16 Withdraw the light unit, pull out the bulbholder and remove the bulb **(see illustration)**.
17 Fit the new bulb and reassemble.

Front fog light

Phase 1 and 2 models
18 Undo the two screws and withdraw the light unit.
19 Disconnect the wiring connectors then unhook the spring and remove the bulbholder.
20 Withdraw the bulb from the holder, fit a new bulb and reassemble.
Phase 3 models
21 Unclip the plastic trim around the light unit.
22 Undo the two screws and withdraw the light unit.
23 Disconnect the wiring connector then undo the four screws and remove the rear cover.
24 Disconnect the wiring at the bulb then release the spring clip and remove the bulb.
25 Fit the new bulb and reassemble.

Rear light cluster

Phase 1 models
26 With the tailgate open, remove the cover over the light cluster, then insert a screwdriver through the opening.
27 Press down on the screwdriver to release the internal catches and withdraw the assembly from the wing **(see illustration)**.
28 Spread the four tongues on the rear of the unit and separate the lens from the bulbholder. Remove the relevant bayonet fitting bulb from the holder.
29 Fit the new bulb and reassemble.
Phase 2 models
30 Undo the two screws and lift off the lens.
31 Press the four tabs and withdraw the bulbholder from the rear wing. Remove the relevant bayonet fitting bulb from the holder.
32 Fit the new bulb and reassemble.
Phase 3 models
33 With the tailgate open, undo the two screws at the top and withdraw the light cluster **(see illustration)**.
34 Press the two tongues at the rear and separate the lens from the bulbholder **(see illustration)**. Remove the relevant bayonet fitting bulb from the holder.
35 Fit the new bulb and reassemble.

9.33 Undoing the rear light cluster screws on Phase 3 models

9.34 With the cluster released, press the tongues and remove the bulbholder

12

9.36 Removing the number plate light unit from the tailgate

9.37 Withdraw the bulbholder from the number plate light unit

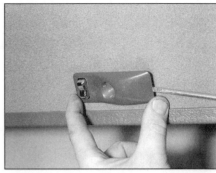

10.3 Release the interior courtesy lights by carefully prising them from their locations

Number plate light

36 Undo the screw (where fitted) or alternatively prise the light unit from the tailgate **(see illustration)**.
37 Withdraw the bulbholder from the lens and remove the bulb **(see illustration)**.
38 Fit the new bulb and reassemble.

---

10 Bulbs (interior lights) - renewal

General

1 See Section 9, paragraphs 1 and 3.
2 Some switch illumination/pilot bulbs are integral with their switches and cannot be renewed separately.

Bulb renewal

Courtesy lights

3 Pull or prise the light unit from its mountings **(see illustration)**.
4 Renew the bulb(s), which may be bayonet or end clip fitting **(see illustration)**.

Switch/accessory illumination bulbs

5 Where these are renewable individually, the bulbholders simply pull out after removal of the relevant switch or accessory **(see illustrations)**.
6 Renew the bulb by pulling from the

bulbholder. These are separable from the switch, they simply pull out.

Instrument panel bulbs

7 Remove the instrument panel as described in Section 7.
8 Turn the bulbholder a quarter turn to align the shoulders with the slots, then remove the bulbholders.
9 The bulbs are a push-fit in the bulbholders.
10 Fit the new bulb and reassemble.

---

11 Exterior light units - removal and refitting

Note: *Ensure that all lights are switched off before disconnecting any wiring connectors.*

Headlight unit

Phase 1 and 2 models

1 Remove the direction indicator light.
2 Depending on model, it may be beneficial to remove the battery or air cleaner unit (according to side) if clearance is insufficient.
3 Disconnect the wiring connectors from the headlight and where applicable, the sidelight bulbs.
4 Undo the four screws and remove the headlight unit from the body.
5 Refit by reversing the removal operations. Have the headlight beam alignment checked on completion.

Phase 3 models

6 Remove the direction indicator light.
7 Depending on model, it may be beneficial to remove the battery or air cleaner unit (according to side) if clearance is insufficient.
8 Refer to Chapter 11 and remove the front grille panel.
9 Remove the cover at the rear of the headlight then disconnect the wiring connectors from the headlight and the sidelight bulbs.
10 Undo the four nuts and remove the headlight unit from the body. Note the location of any spacer shims that may be fitted **(see illustrations)**.
11 Refit by reversing the removal operations. Have the headlight beam alignment checked on completion.

Direction indicator

Phase 1 models

12 Squeeze the retaining lugs on the rear of the light unit and withdraw the sidelight and direction indicator bulbholder.
13 Slacken the two screws securing the unit to the body side panel, then pull the unit forward to disengage it from the headlight.
14 Refit by reversing the removal operations.

Phase 2 models

15 Turn the bulbholder a quarter turn and withdraw it from the light unit.

10.4 Renew the bulb after freeing the light unit

10.5a Removing the bulbholder from the rear of the clock . . .

10.5b . . . and from the headlight height adjustment control

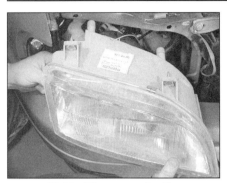

11.10a When removing the headlight unit . . .

16 Unhook the tension spring from the headlight and direction indicator units.

17 Depress the retaining tab on the side of the headlight and withdraw the direction indicator unit forward to release.

18 Refit by reversing the removal operations.

Phase 3 models

19 Turn the bulbholder a quarter turn and withdraw it from the light unit.

20 Depress the retaining tab on the side of the headlight and withdraw the direction indicator unit forward to release **(see illustration)**.

21 Refit by reversing the removal operations.

Front foglight

22 The light units are removed as part of the bulb renewal procedure described in Section 9.

23 Beam adjustment is carried out by turning the adjustment screw on the upper corner of the unit.

Rear light cluster

24 The light units are removed as part of the bulb renewal procedure described in Section 9.

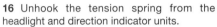

12 Headlight beam alignment - checking and adjusting

Beam alignment should be carried out by a Renault dealer or other specialist heaving the necessary optical alignment equipment.

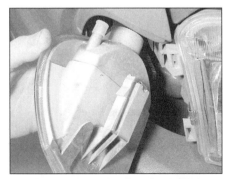

11.20 Removing the direction indicator light unit

11.10b . . . recover any shims that may be fitted

In an emergency, adjustment may be carried out on a trial and error basis, using the two adjustment screws on the rear, at diagonally opposite corners of each headlight unit.

13 Washer system components - removal and refitting

Removal

1 The reservoir is located on the left-hand side of the engine compartment on Phase 1 and 2 models and at the front of the engine compartment alongside the radiator on Phase 3 models. For access to the reservoir and pump(s) it may be necessary to remove the air cleaner unit or battery (as applicable) according to model.

2 Disconnect the battery negative lead.

3 Unscrew the mounting screw(s) and lift the reservoir from its location.

4 Disconnect the wiring and fluid hoses from the pump(s).

5 To remove the pump(s), empty the reservoir of any remaining fluid then pull the pump(s) from the rubber grommet.

Refitting

6 Refitting is a reversal of removal.

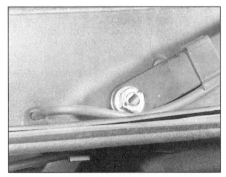

14.4a Windscreen wiper arm retaining nut . . .

14 Wiper arms - removal and refitting

Removal

1 Remove the wiper blades as described in "*Weekly checks*".

2 Make sure that the wiper is in its parked position, and note this position for correct refitting. If necessary, switch the wipers on and off in order to allow them to return to the "park" position.

3 On Phase 3 models disconnect the washer hose by unclipping it from the arm.

4 Lift up the cover (where applicable), unscrew the retaining nut and pull the arm from the spindle **(see illustrations)**. If necessary use a screwdriver to prise off the arm, being careful not to damage the paintwork. On the tailgate wiper it will help if the arm is moved to its fully raised position before removing it from the spindle.

Refitting

5 Fit the new arm using a reversal of the removal procedure.

6 Refit the wiper blades on completion.

15 Windscreen wiper motor and linkage - removal and refitting

Removal

1 Prior to removal, operate the wipers, then switch off so that the motor and linkage are in the parked position.

2 Disconnect the battery negative lead.

3 Remove the windscreen wiper arms.

4 Undo the nuts at the base of the wiper arm spindles and remove the spindle seals.

5 Disconnect the wiper motor wiring connector.

6 On Phase 1 and 2 models, undo the two bolts securing the motor mounting plate to the support bracket. On Phase 3 models, undo the two mounting bolts each side securing the mechanism to the body **(see illustration)**.

14.4b . . . and tailgate wiper arm retaining nut under plastic cover

12

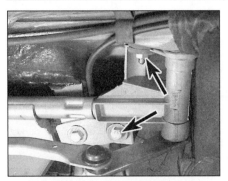

15.6 Windscreen wiper and linkage mechanism side attachment (arrowed) on Phase 3 models

7 Push the wiper spindles out of their apertures then manipulate the assembly from the engine compartment.
8 The motor may be removed from the linkage by undoing the spindle nut and the three securing bolts **(see illustration)**. Withdraw off the crank arm then remove the motor. Do not attempt to dismantle the motor; spares are unlikely to be available.
9 Other components of the linkage may be renewed as necessary.

Refitting

10 If the motor has been removed, attach the crank arm so that it forms a straight run with the linkage fully extended.
11 Refit by reversing the removal operations. Before refitting the wiper arms, switch the wipers on and off to bring the motor into the parked position.

16 Tailgate wiper motor - removal and refitting

Removal

1 Remove the tailgate interior trim (Chapter 11).
2 Remove the wiper arm (Section 14).
3 Withdraw the cover over the spindle and undo the spindle retaining nut **(see illustration)**.
4 Disconnect the motor wiring connector.
5 Remove the two bolts which secure the motor, then remove the motor from the tailgate **(see illustration)**.

Refitting

6 Refit by reversing the removal operations. Check the operation of the motor before refitting the trim.

17 Heated rear window - general information

1 All models are equipped with a heated rear window. Heating is achieved by passing current through a resistive grid bonded to the inside of the rear window.

15.8 Windscreen wiper motor spindle retaining nut and motor securing bolts

2 Do not allow hard or sharp items of luggage to rub against the heating grid. Use a soft cloth or chamois to clean the inside of the window, working along the lines of the grid.

 HAYNES HiNT *Small breaks in the heated rear window grid can be repaired using special conductive paint, obtainable from motor accessory shops. Use the paint as directed by its manufacturer.*

3 The heated rear window draws a high current, so it should not be left switched on longer than necessary. On some models a so-called "delay relay" is incorporated into the circuit in order to switch the window off after a few minutes.

16.3 Withdraw the cover for access to the tailgate wiper spindle nut

18.2a Remove the screw from the remote control door locking transmitter . . .

18 Remote control door locking system - general

1 The ignition key incorporates an infra-red remote control door locking transmitter. The transmitter signal is decoded by a receiver mounted on the roof console and this activates the electro-mechanical system to lock or unlock the doors.
2 The transmitter is powered by two 1.5 volt alkaline type batteries which have a life of approximately 12 months. The batteries can be renewed after unscrewing the transmitter case screw and opening the case to gain access **(see illustrations)**.
3 In the event of a fault occurring in the system it is recommended that you seek the advice of a Renault dealer as specialist knowledge and equipment are necessary for accurate fault diagnosis.

19 Radio/cassette player - removal and refitting

Note: *Various players may be fitted, according to model, territory and optional equipment. Removal and refitting procedures for one of the common types are as follows.*

Removal

1 Disconnect the battery negative lead. If the

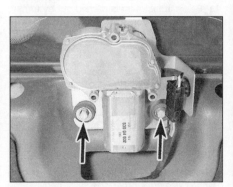

16.5 Tailgate wiper motor securing bolts (arrowed)

18.2b . . . and separate the covers

19.3 Insert the removal tools in the side of the radio/cassette unit . . .

19.4 . . . and withdraw the radio/cassette player from the facia

radio/cassette player is equipped with an anti-theft security code, refer to the information given in the reference sections of this manual before disconnecting the battery.

2 In order to release the radio retaining clips, two U-shaped rods must be inserted into the special holes on each side of the radio. If possible, it is preferable to obtain purpose made rods from an audio specialist as these have cut-outs which snap firmly into the clips so that the radio can be pulled out. On some models, it will be necessary to remove the two side bezels first, to allow access to the holes for insertion of the U-shaped removal tools.

3 Insert the removal tools into each pair of holes at the edge of the unit, and push the tools fully home to engage the radio retaining clips **(see illustration)**.

4 Move the tools outward to depress the retaining clips, and withdraw the radio from the facia sufficiently to gain access to the wiring at the rear **(see illustration)**.

5 Note the location of the speaker wiring by recording cable colours and their positions, then disconnect the speaker leads, aerial lead and wiring connectors. Remove the unit from the car.

6 Disengage the removal tools from the side of the radio, and remove the tools.

Refitting

7 Refitting is a reversal of removal.

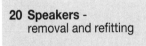

20 Speakers -
removal and refitting

Removal

1 To remove the front speakers located on the top of the facia panel, prise out the speaker grille panel, disconnect the wiring and remove the small speaker from the panel. To remove the main speaker, undo the securing screws, then lift out the speaker and disconnect the wiring **(see illustrations)**.

2 Access to the rear speakers is gained by removing the trim panel around the speaker. Remove the screws, withdraw the speaker and disconnect the wiring **(see illustrations)**.

3 To remove a door speaker, remove the door interior trim as described in Chapter 11. Remove the screws and withdraw the speaker, then disconnect the wiring.

Refitting

4 Refitting is a reversal of removal.

21 Anti-theft alarm system -
general

Certain models are fitted with an anti-theft alarm and/or engine immobiliser system as standard or optional equipment.

Various systems may be fitted, some operating in conjunction with the remote control central door locking system.

20.1a Disconnect the wiring and remove the small speaker from the grille panel

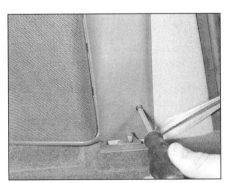

20.2a Access to the rear speakers is gained by removing the trim panel . . .

Some systems have a self-diagnosis function, which can be used to detect faults in conjunction with Renault dedicated test equipment.

No specific details were available for the anti-theft systems at the time of writing. Consult a Renault dealer for further information.

22 Air bag - general information and precautions

General information

Certain models are fitted with a driver's side air bag, located in the steering wheel boss.

The system consists of the air bag unit and gas cartridge incorporated in the steering wheel, an electronic unit, two batteries, and a warning light.

In the event of a severe frontal impact, the air bag inflates (in approximately 30 milliseconds), softening the impact of the driver's head with the steering wheel. The air bag then deflates.

The instrument panel warning light, illuminates to indicate that the air bag battery charge is low, or there is a fault with the system.

In addition to the air bag, certain models may also be fitted with seat belt pre-tensioners, to tighten the seat belts in the event of frontal impact.

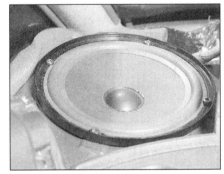

20.1b Undo the four screws to remove the main speaker

20.2b . . . then undo the screws and remove the speaker

12

Precautions

The following precautions **must** be observed when working on models equipped with an air bag or seat belt pre-tensioners.

Do not, under any circumstances, attempt to carry out any work on the steering wheel, the air bag system itself or the seat belt pre-tensioners. Consult a Renault dealer if any work involving these components is to be carried out.

Do not cover the steering wheel hub.

If the air bag warning light illuminates, take the vehicle to a Renault dealer as soon as possible to have the system checked.

If the vehicle is involved in an accident, have the air bag system and seat belt pre-tensioners checked by a Renault dealer as soon as possible.

In the event of the vehicle being scrapped, contact a Renault dealer first to have the gas cartridge removed from the steering wheel.

If the vehicle is stolen, or an attempt is made to steal the vehicle, have the system checked by a Renault dealer as a precaution.

If you sell the vehicle, inform the new owner that these components are fitted.

Key to wiring diagrams

Not all items are fitted to all models

1	Driving school unit	48	RH main beam headlight	142	Electric boot lid lock
2	Battery isolating switch	49	LH main beam headlight	143	Washer bottle minimum level sensor
3	Tachograph	50	RH dipped beam headlight	144	Coolant minimum level sensor
4	RH door lock switch	51	LH dipped beam headlight	145	Wash/wipe combination switch
5	LH door lock switch	52	Alarm electronic key (jack)	146	Pinking sensor
6	AC fan unit electronic module	53	Cooling fan motor assembly diode	147	Atmospheric pressure sensor
7	Module control resistance unit	54	Windscreen wiper motor filter (radio)	148	Oil pressure sensor
8	Line pressure sensor (Autatron)	55	Retractable headlights relay	149	Top dead centre sensor
9	Torque limited solenoid switch	56	Lighting rheostat switch	150	Rear RH wheel sensor
10	First speed switch	57	Fan motor assembly relay via accessories central unit (UCA)	151	Rear LH wheel sensor
11	Transmission engagement switch			152	Front RH wheel sensor
12	Dipped running light earth relay	101	Cigar lighter	153	Front LH wheel sensor
13	Warning cancellation switch	102	Distributor	154	Boot lid switch
14	Rear door locking switch	103	Alternator	155	Reversing light switch
15	Rear door locking warning light	104	Anti-theft switch	156	Handbrake switch
16	Injection pump (KSB) advance solenoid valve relay	105	Electro-magnetic horn	157	Brake pedal switch
		106	Electro-pneumatic horn	158	Full throttle switch
17	Injection pump (KSB) advance solenoid valve temperature switch	107	Battery	159	No throttle switch
		108	Ignition coil	160	Stop light switch
18	Blown air temperature sensor	109	Trip computer unit	161	Glove compartment switch
19	Electronic thermostat	110	Brake pressure control unit	162	Flow sensor
20	Front ashtray light	111	Ignition assistance unit	163	Starter
21	Alarm display diode	112	Rear screen wiper timer	164	Cold air blower
22	Tailgate gas strut	113	Windscreen wiper timer	165	Boot light
23	Door and lid decoding relay	114	Dim/dip unit	166	RH number plate light
24	Transverse acceleration sensor (ABS)	115	Electric pump regulator unit	167	LH number plate light
25	RH door opening motor	116	Headlight wiper timer unit	168	Glove compartment light
26	LH door opening motor	117	"Lights on" warning buzzer	169	Gas recycling solenoid valve
27	Engine compartment cooling fan switch off relay	118	ABS computer	170	Power steering solenoid valve
		119	Automatic transmission computer	171	Air conditioning clutch
28	RH door lock relay	120	Injection computer	172	RH rear light
29	LH door lock relay	121	Rear fog light switch	173	LH rear light
30	Door/lid warning diode	122	Front fog light switch	174	Rear RH fog light
31	Rear fog light diode	123	Electric door lock control switch	175	Rear LH fog light
32	Canister diode	124	Heater switch	176	Front RH fog light
33	Electronic fuel gauge unit timer relay	125	Hazard warning light switch	177	Front LH fog light
34	Roof lights	126	Cold air blower switch	178	Rear RH door switch
35	Suspension height sensor	127	Rear screen wiper switch	179	Rear LH door switch
36	Suspension height correction compressor unit	128	Heated rear screen switch	180	Driver's door switch
		129	Transmission shift speed control switch	181	Passenger door switch
37	Central accessory control unit	130	Rear RH window winder switch	182	RH reversing light
38	Retracting headlight electronic unit	131	Rear LH window winder switch	183	LH reversing light
39	RH retracting headlight motor	132	Driver's window winder switch	184	RH side light
40	LH retracting headlight motor	133	Passenger's window winder switch	185	LH side light
41	Suspension height correction computer	134	Electric rear view mirror switch	186	Power steering electric pump unit
42	Gas recirculation control computer	135	Rear window winder locking switch	187	Heater blower
43	Cold starting warning light	136	Choke control	188	Cooling fan unit
44	Heated seat warning light	137	Flasher unit	189	Rear RH speaker
45	Cold starting control computer	138	Rear RH electric door lock	190	Rear LH speaker
46	Cold start solenoid valve (diesel fuel inlet)	139	Rear LH electric door lock	191	Front RH speaker
		140	Driver's electric door lock	192	Front LH speaker
47	Oil level computer	141	Passenger's electric door lock	193	Injector 1

Key to wiring diagrams (continued)

Not all items are fitted to all models

194	Injector 2	255	RH direction indication light	318	Carburettor base heater
195	Injector 3	256	LH direction indication light	319	Air conditioning control panel
196	Injector 4	257	Pre-heater unit	320	Basic/air conditioned fan unit
197	Injector 5	258	Pre-heater plugs	321	Air conditioning fan unit resistance
198	Injector 6	259	Temperature switch	322	Power steering/air conditioning diode
199	Fuel gauge	260	Fuse box	323	Power steering/air conditioning
200	Heated rear screen	261	Radio		solenoid valve
201	Rear RH window winder	262	AC cooling fan unit	324	Overspeed relay
202	Rear LH window winder	263	Rear screen wash/wipe switch	325	Radio control satellite
203	Driver's window winder	264	Electric door lock timer	326	Overspeed warning
204	Passenger's window winder	265	Map reading/interior light console	327	Electronic fuel gauge
205	Pressure switch	266	Full throttle/no throttle switch	328	Front LH interior light
206	Air conditioning three function	267	RH repeater	329	Front RH interior light
	pressure switch	268	LH repeater	330	Rear cigar light
207	Minimum brake fluid level	269	Idling shut out	331	Cruise control
208	Integral electronic ignition unit	270	8° temperature switch	332	Window winder "one touch" switch
209	Horn and lighting switch	271	Thermistor	333	Seat belt switch
210	Clock	272	Air temperature sensor	334	Thermal circuit breaker
211	Rear screen wiper motor	273	Speed threshold sensor	335	Fan unit first speed relay
212	Windscreen wiper motor	274	Air conditioning solenoid valve	336	Fan unit second speed relay
213	Front interior light	275	Additional fuel pump timer	337	Fan unit third speed relay
214	Rear RH interior light	276	"One touch" window winder	338	Turbo pressure regulator
215	Rear LH interior light		control unit	339	Cold starting injector
216	Front RH brake pad	277	Filament failure warning light	340	Timed temperature switch
217	Front LH brake pad	278	Number 2 pinking sensor	341	Idling regulator valve
218	Fuel pump	279	Anti-percolation relay	342	Turbo safety pressure switch
219	Headlight washer pump	280	Integral electronic ignition shut off relay	343	Oil temperature sensor
220	Rear screen washer pump	281	Dipped beam relay	344	Cruise control compressor
221	Windscreen washer pump	282	Electric fuel filler lock	345	Cruise control safety valve
222	Throttle potentiometer	283	Additional fuel pump	346	Cruise control pump solenoid valve
223	Idling speed potentiometer	284	RH headlight wiper motor	347	Radio power supply
224	Power steering pressure switch	285	LH headlight wiper motor	348	"One touch" switch upper plate
225	Diagnostic plug	286	Rear screen washer switch	349	Ignition distributor
226	RH headlight	287	Ballast coil relay	350	Rear LH brake pad
227	LH headlight	288	Main running light relay	351	Rear RH brake pad
228	Idling speed regulator	289	Side running light relay	352	Front LH seat back motor 1
229	Horn relay	290	Dipped beam running light relay	353	Front LH seat back motor 2
230	Rear fog light relay	291	Carburettor solenoid valve	354	Front LH raise/lower motor
231	Front fog light relay	292	Lighting rheostat relay	355	Front LH seat/cushion motor
232	Starter relay	293	Main current supply	356	Front RH seat back motor 1
233	Cold air blower relay	294	Heated rear screen timer	357	Front RH seat back motor 2
234	Electric fan relay	295	Warning light unit	358	Front RH seat raise/lower motor
235	Heated rear screen relay	296	Fog light shunt relay	359	Front RH seat cushion motor
236	Fuel pump relay	297	Front fog light shunt	360	Speech synthesiser control
237	Twin headlight relay	298	Heater	361	ABS hydraulic unit
238	Injection locking relay	299	Accessory connection plate	362	Battery + terminal plate
239	Electric rear view mirror, driver side	300	Rear cross member interior light	363	Speech synthesiser unit
240	Electric rear view mirror,	301	ABS electric pump relay	364	Speech synthesiser speaker
	passenger side	302	Variable rate power steering relay	365	RH speaker tweeter
241	Lighting rheostat or shunt	303	Automatic transmission selector light	366	LH speaker tweeter
242	Oxygen sensor	304	Sun roof	367	RH bonnet open switch
243	Oil level sensor	305	Advance correction solenoid valve	368	LH bonnet open switch
244	Coolant temperature sensor	306	Advance correction temperature switch	369	Turbo bearing coolant pump
245	External temperature sensor	307	Accessory plate earth shunt	370	Dim/dip resistance
246	Electric shut off	308	Degassing system timer	371	Fuel vapour absorption canister
247	Instrument panel	309	Multi function buzzer	372	Boot open/close unit
248	Fan unit temperature switch	310	Injection power module	373	Cruise control unit
249	Infra red transmitter	311	Interior light timer	374	Front LH seat back control switch
250	Speed sensor	312	Consumption shut off relay	375	Front RH seat back control switch
251	Coolant dual function	313	Tachometer relay	376	Front LH seat control switch
	temperature switch	314	Headlight wiper relay	377	Front RH seat control switch
252	Radio telephone filter	315	Windscreen wiper second speed relay	378	Front LH seat raise/lower switch
253	Front RH speaker	316	Ignition 4° relay	379	Fast idling relay
254	Front LH speaker	317	Sun roof switch	380	Trip computer conversion unit

12

Key to wiring diagrams (continued)

Not all items are fitted to all models

381	Carburettor	443	Automatic transmission solenoid valve	506	Accessory plug
382	Inlet manifold relay	444	Map reading light	507	Front and rear fog and hazard warning light switch
383	Inlet manifold temperature switch	445	Fuel pump ballast resistance	508	RH boot light
384	Manifold heater	446	Headlight adjustment control light	509	LH boot light
385	Heated driver seat	447	Rear fog light switch relay	510	Memory seat sensors
386	Heated passenger seat	448	Junction plate after ignition switch	511	Central interior light switch
387	2 bar oil pressure sensor	449	Fuel heater resistance	512	Map reading light switch
388	4 x 4 warning light	450	Fuel heater relay	513	Ergonomic seat inflation switch
389	Central speaker	451	Fuel heater temperature switch	514	Ergonomic seat inflation pump
390	Rear fog light shunt	452	Peripheral detector unit	515	Seat memory unit
391	Rear screen wiper timer	453	Volumetric detector unit	516	Seat memory programme unit
392	Trip computer run through control switch (ADAC)	454	Volumetric transmitter/receiver	517	Seat memory programme and control keyboard
393	Power steering/air conditioning solenoid valve	455	Emission control solenoid valve diode	518	Pulse generator
		456	Fuel pump ballast relay	519	Front LH door edge light
394	Electric aerial	457	Door first position switch	520	Front RH door edge light
395	Aut. trans. shut off switch	458	Fog and reversing light	521	Rear RH door edge light
396	Full throttle switch	459	Rear screen wiper timer	522	Rear LH door edge light
397	Anti percolation fan unit	460	Rear axle switch	523	Driver door light
398	Exhaust gas recycling solenoid valve	461	ABS overload protection relay	524	Passenger door light
399	Emission control relay	462	Tailgate number plate light	525	Rear RH door light
400	Anti pollution diode	463	Light on quarter panel	526	Rear LH door light
401	Anti pollution solenoid valve	464	Interior light switch	527	Driver switch for rear LH window winder
402	Oil temperature switch	465	Turbo bearing coolant pump timer		
403	Secondary electromagnetic horn	466	Shunt unit	528	Driver switch for rear RH window winder
404	Injection pump advance solenoid valve	467	Dipped/side light relay		
405	Load lever switch	468	Driving school dipped beam diode	529	Central interior light
406	Pre-heater temperature switch	469	Instructor control unit	530	Cruise control stop switch
407	Air recycling flap control	470	Driving school windscreen wiper high speed relay	531	Cruise control clutch switch
408	Evaporator sensor			532	Driver switch for front passenger window winder
409	Power steering pump unit relay	471	Electric window winder control relay		
410	Idling shut off relay	472	Radio shut off relay	533	Suspension height corrector switch
411	Air conditioning pressure switch	473	Speed synthesiser test switch	534	Control suspension switch
412	Fast idling solenoid valve	474	Air conditioning compressor control relay	535	Shift threshold indicator light
413	Heated seat identifier unit			536	Jack plug for head set
414	Water in fuel sensor	475	Recycling motor	537	LH headlight correction motor
415	Headlight wiper solenoid valve	476	Quadra transmission unit	538	RH headlight correction motor
416	Idling shut off capacitor	477	First position switch	539	Engine compartment light switch
417	Air conditioning recycling relay	478	Heater accelerator pump	540	Variable rate power steering motor
418	Passenger compartment temperature sensor fan	479	Heater accelerator temperature switch	541	Illuminated courtesy mirror
		480	Hot air extractor sensor	542	Suspension height correction computer
419	Air conditioning monitoring unit	481	Hot air extractor	543	Variable rate shock absorber computer
420	Mixing flap	482	Transmission engagement valve	544	Suspension height correction unit relay
421	Clutch pedal switch	483	Acceleration sensor	545	Suspension height correction safety relay
422	Cruise control column switch 1	484	4 x 4 transmission solenoid valve		
423	Cruise control column switch 2	485	Multi function switch	546	Suspension correction compression unit
424	Cruise control overspeed relay	486	Passenger seat belt switch		
425	ABS connection plate	487	Enrichener solenoid valve	547	Rear LH shock absorber solenoid valve
426	Turbo charger opening solenoid valve	488	Enrichener temperature switch	548	Rear RH shock absorber solenoid valve
427	Alarm unit	489	Rear LH first position switch	549	Front LH shock absorber solenoid valve
428	Bosch ABS main relay	490	Front RH first position switch	550	Front RH shock absorber solenoid valve
429	Bosch ABS auxiliary relay	491	Front LH first position switch		
430	Bosch ABS diode unit	492	Radio telephone	551	Front RH vehicle level sensor
431	Tip computer initialisation switch	493	Rear LH seat	552	Front LH vehicle level sensor
432	Main ABS solenoid valve	494	Rear RH seat	553	Rear RH vehicle level sensor
433	Alarm detector unit	495	Front RH seat	554	Rear LH vehicle level sensor
434	ABS shut off pressure switch	496	Front LH seat	555	Suspension correction solenoid valve
435	ABS solenoid valve unit	497	ABS 4 x 4 accelerometer	556	Tailgate position switch
436	Turbo regulator control	498	Vertical accelerometer	557	Tailgate closing assistance motor
437	Throttle unit heater	499	Longitudinal accelerometer	558	Tailgate closing on/off switch
438	Bonnet switch	500	Transverse accelerometer	559	Tailgate closing assistance unit
439	ABS computer relay	501	Seat and rear view mirror memory unit	560	Tailgate opening switch
440	Heated seat switch	502	Variable rate steering electronic unit	561	Horn compressor
441	Automatic transmission	503	Electronic de-coder	562	Headlight adjustment switch
442	Self fed alarm siren	504	Rear RH reading light		
		505	Rear LH reading light		

Key to wiring diagrams (continued)

Not all items are fitted to all models

563 Oil cooler fan unit
564 Oil cooler fan unit relay
565 Anti percolation timer temperature switch
567 Electric coolant pump
568 Electric coolant pump timer
569 4 speed transmission kick-down switch
572 Power steering diode
573 Timer retaining relay
574 Electric coolant pump diode
575 Engine adjustment connector
576 Anti percolation authorisation relay
577 Radio telephone electronic unit
579 Gas recycling solenoid valve switch
580 Turbo bearing coolant pump authorisation relay
581 Air conditioning/coolant pump separator diode
582 Coolant pump temperature switch
583 Flywheel position sensor
584 Air conditioning compressor clutch relay
585 Pneumatic pressure sensor
586 Hazard warning light switch
587 ABS longitudinal accelerator
588 Driver courtesy mirror light
589 Injection pump
590 Alarm switch
591 Catalytic converter temperature sensor
592 Catalytic converter temperature electronic unit
593 Variable rate power steering safety relay
594 Catalytic converter temperature warning light

595 Pump unit authorisation relay
596 ABS separation diode
597 Engine fuse box
598 Torque reducer solenoid valve
599 Coolant pump retainer relay
600 Heater fan motor
601 Heater water temperature switch
602 Reversing light relay
603 Steering column memory adjustment control
604 Memory steering column motor
605 Carburettor base heater authorisation relay
606 Carburettor base heater relay
607 Carburettor base temperature switch
608 Anti percolation fan unit sensor
609 Coolant temperature electronic unit
610 ABS diagnostic switch
611 LH electric windscreen
612 LH electric windscreen defroster relay
613 Windscreen defroster switch unit
614 "One touch" electric window winder switch
615 Heated driver seat switch
616 Heated passenger seat switch
617 Attenuation resistance
620 Twin throttle potentiometer
621 Coolant temperature switch shunt relay
622 Anti percolation timer
623 Degassing solenoid valve
624 Rear RH seat back
625 Rear LH seat back
626 Aut. transmission selector light switch
627 Cruise control on/off

628 Variable rate power steering speed sensor
629 RH windscreen defroster relay
630 RH electric windscreen
631 External temperature module
632 Pre-heater plugs 1 and 3
633 Pre-heater plugs 2 and 4
634 Clutch sensor
635 AC compressor blocking time switch
636 Stop light separator diode
637 Stop light/clutch separator diode
638 Driving school warning light/buzzer relay
639 Upper stop light
640 Starter relay assistance relay
641 Cooling/timer separator diode
642 Diesel pre-heat/AC separator diode
643 Anti-percolation resistance
644 Controlled suspension computer
645 Passenger compartment inter-connection box
646 Heated windscreen relay
647 Heated windscreen
648 Injection diode
649 Stepping motor
650 Heated seat warning light relay
651 Panel
652 Air conditioning control relay via aut. transmission
653 Combined clock/external temperature/RT display unit
654 Alarm key and equipment locking key
684 Compact disc player

How to read the wiring diagrams

A Connection bar number
B Connection bar
C Connection bar colour
D Fuse rating
E Routing used
F Unit number
G Connector colour
H Function symbol
I Routing used
J Modular terminal block number
K Connector colour
L Connector symbol
M Wire number
N Wire colour
O Wire joint
P Wire joint reference
Q Earthing point number

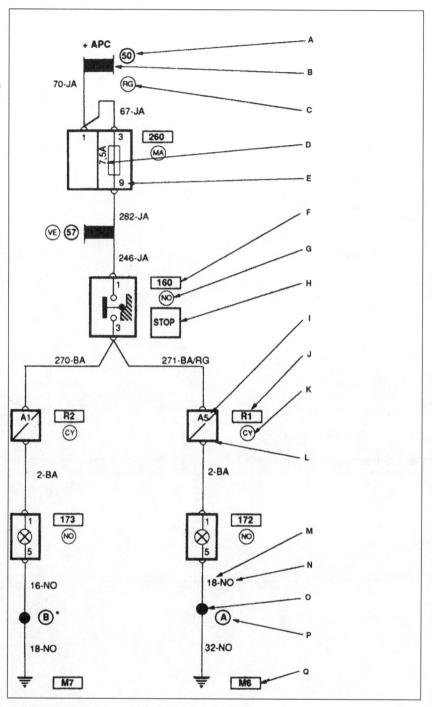

Wire/connector colours

Code	Colour		Code	Colour
BA	White		NO	Black
BE	Blue		OR	Orange
BJ	Beige		RG	Red
CY	Clear		SA	Salmon
GR	Grey		VE	Green
JA	Yellow		VI	Violet
MA	Brown			

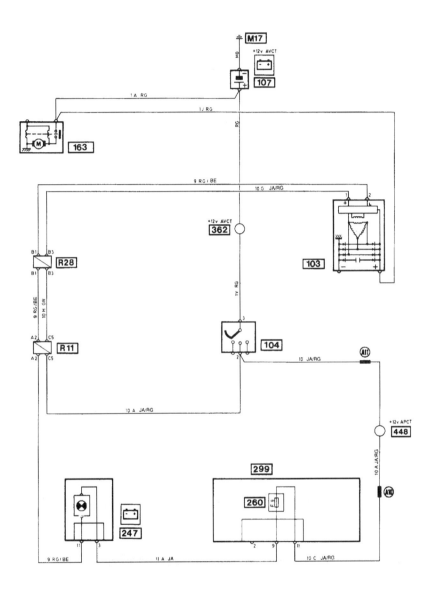

Typical fuel system

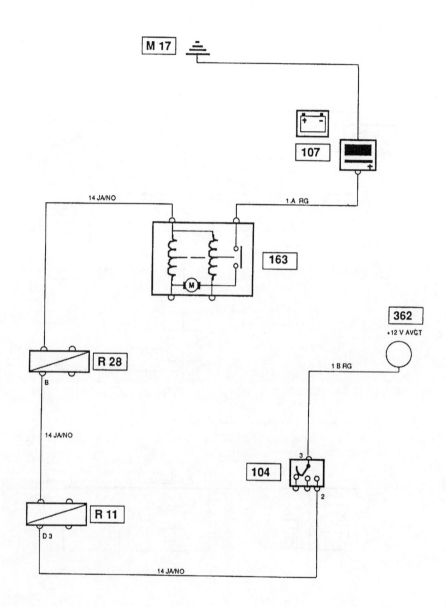

Typical starting system

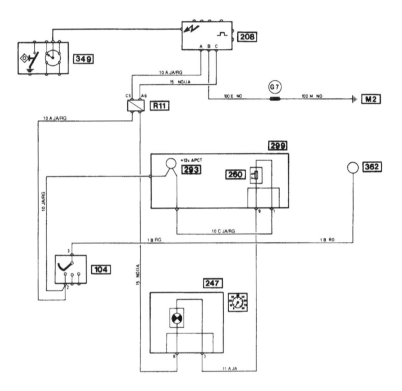

Typical electronic ignition system

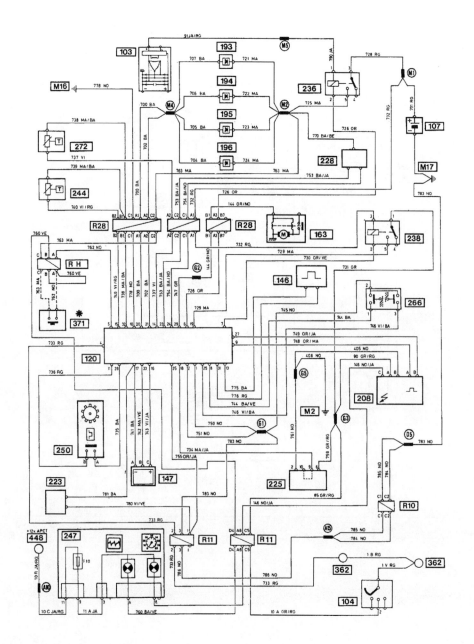

Typical fuel injection system - petrol

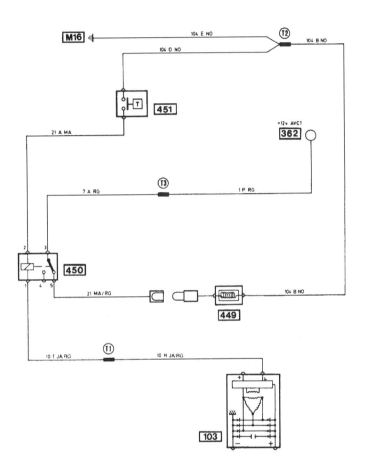

Typical fuel heating system - diesel

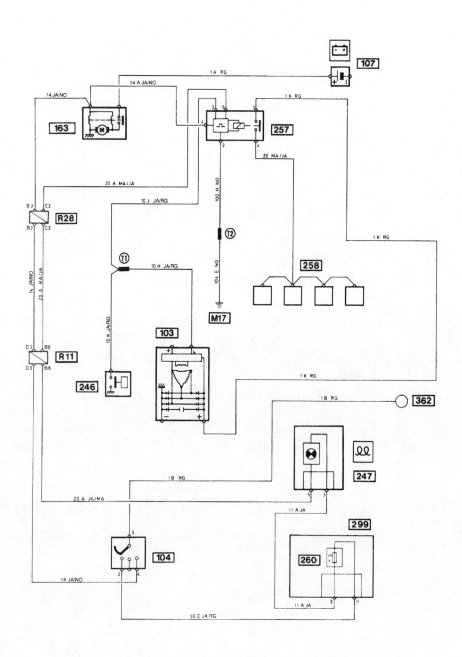

Typical pre-heating system - diesel engines

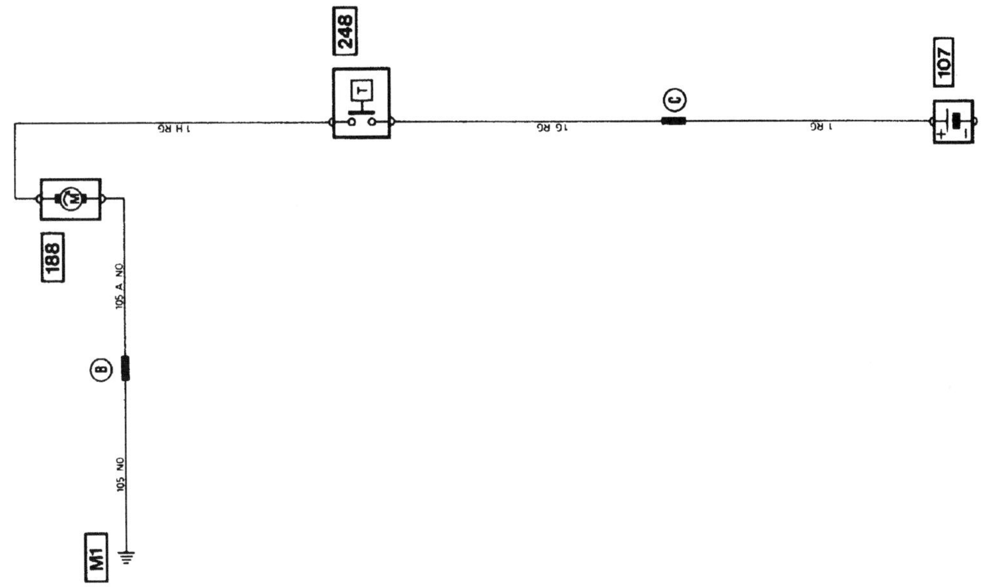

Typical cooling fan - petrol engines

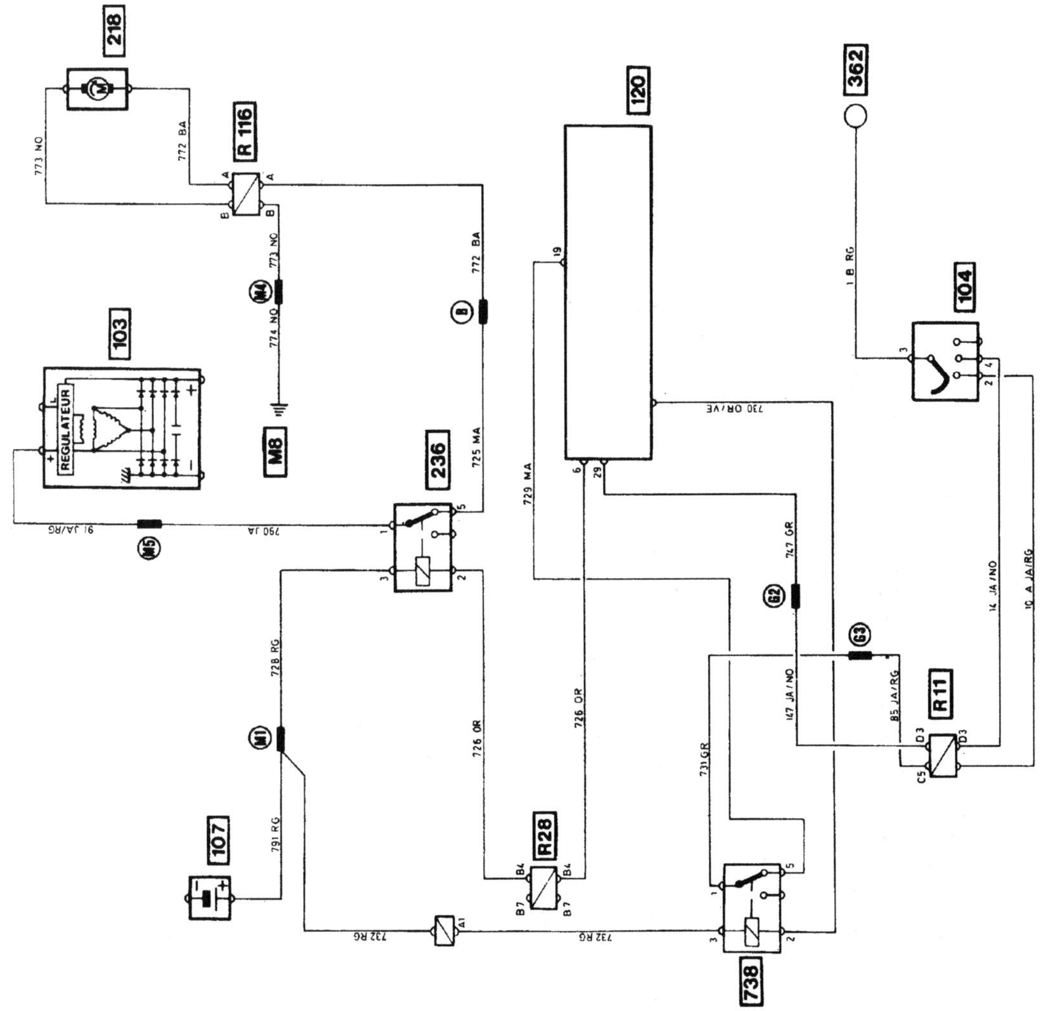

Typical fuel pump

12

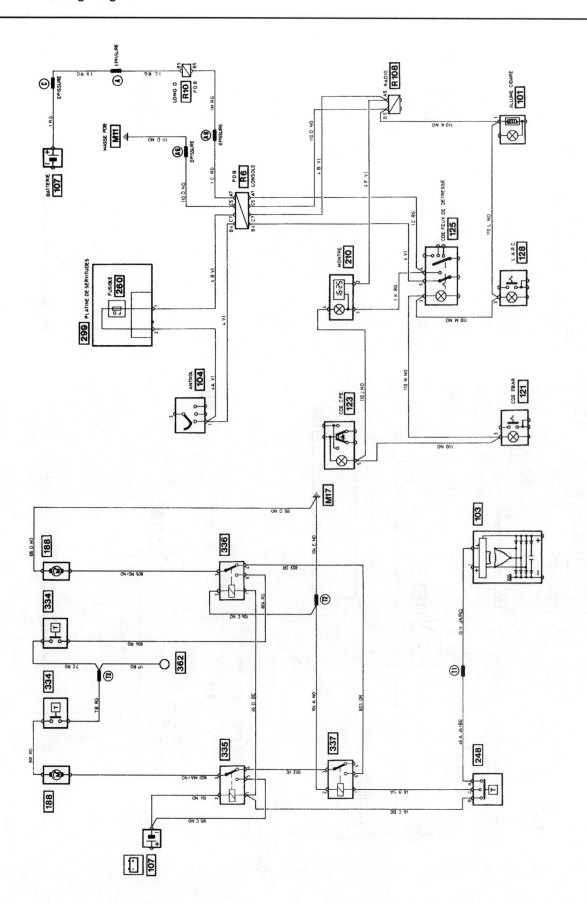

Typical clock

Typical cooling fan - diesel engines

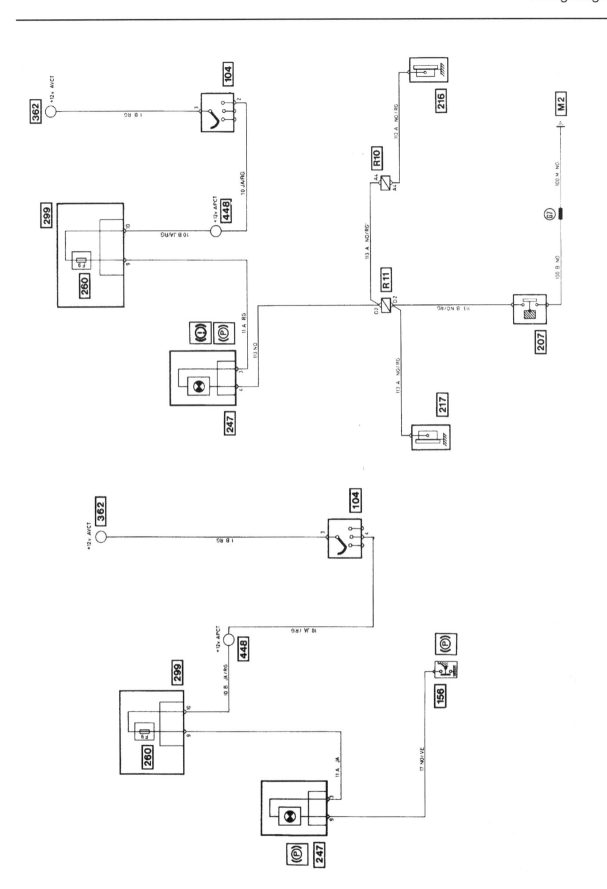

Typical braking system warning light

Typical "handbrake-on" warning light

12

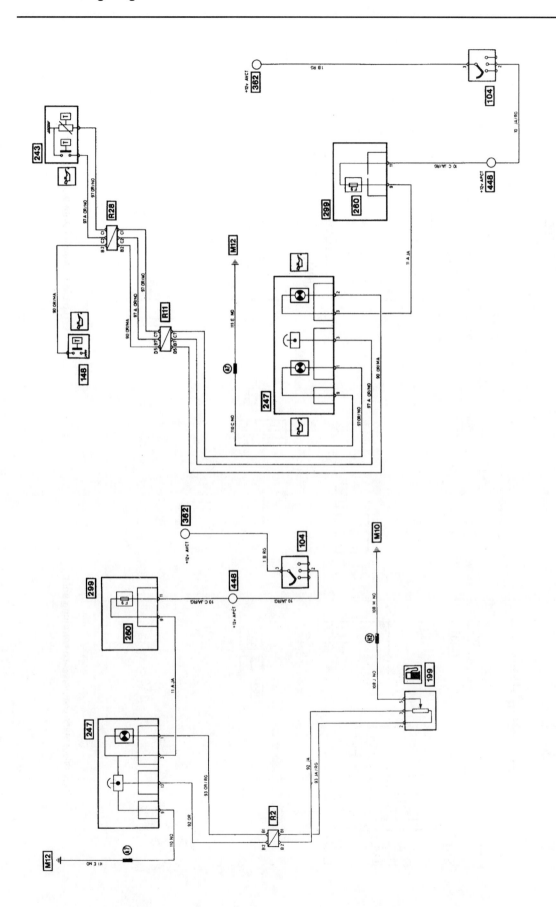

Typical oil pressure gauge-warning light

Typical oil level gauge

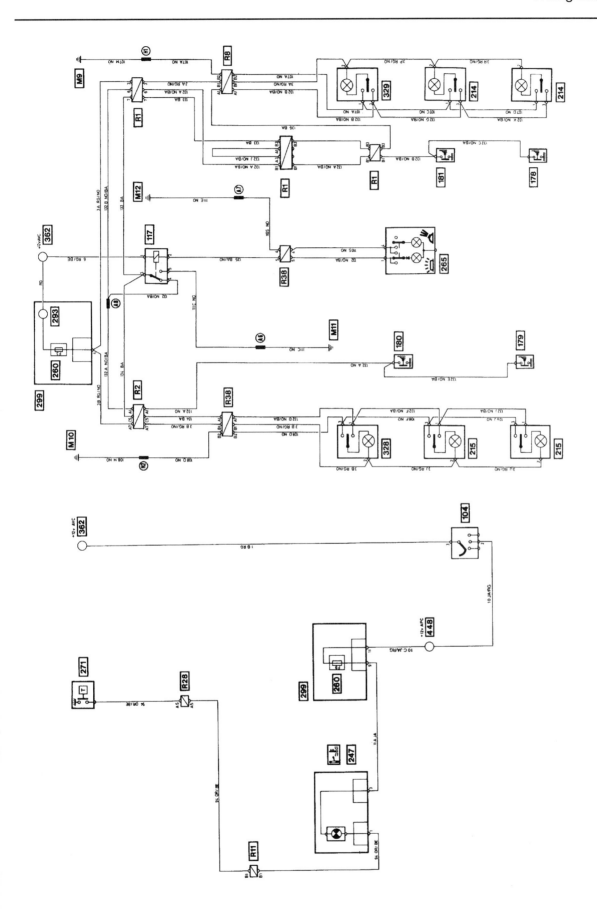

Typical interior lighting

Typical coolant temperature warning light

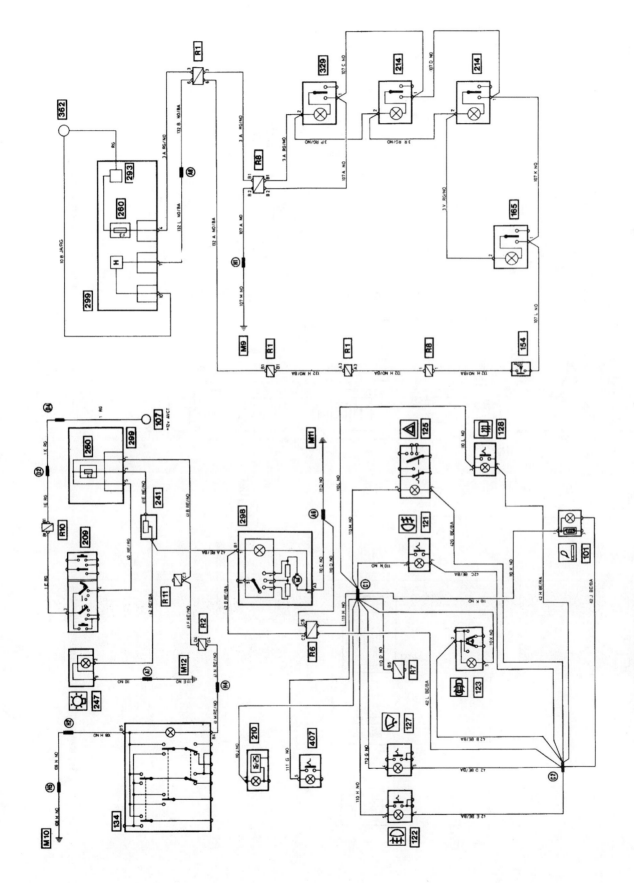

Typical luggage compartment lighting

Typical lighting switches

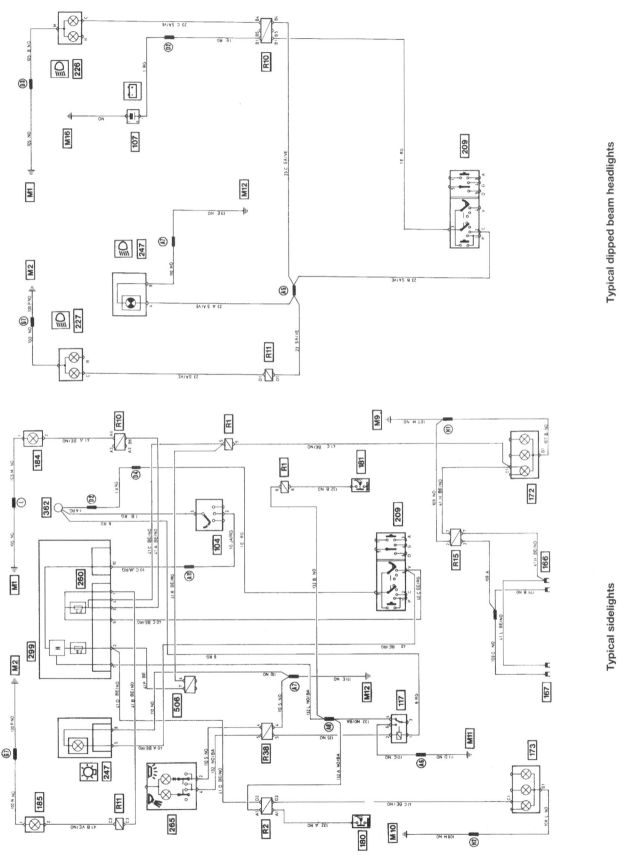

Typical dipped beam headlights

Typical sidelights

12

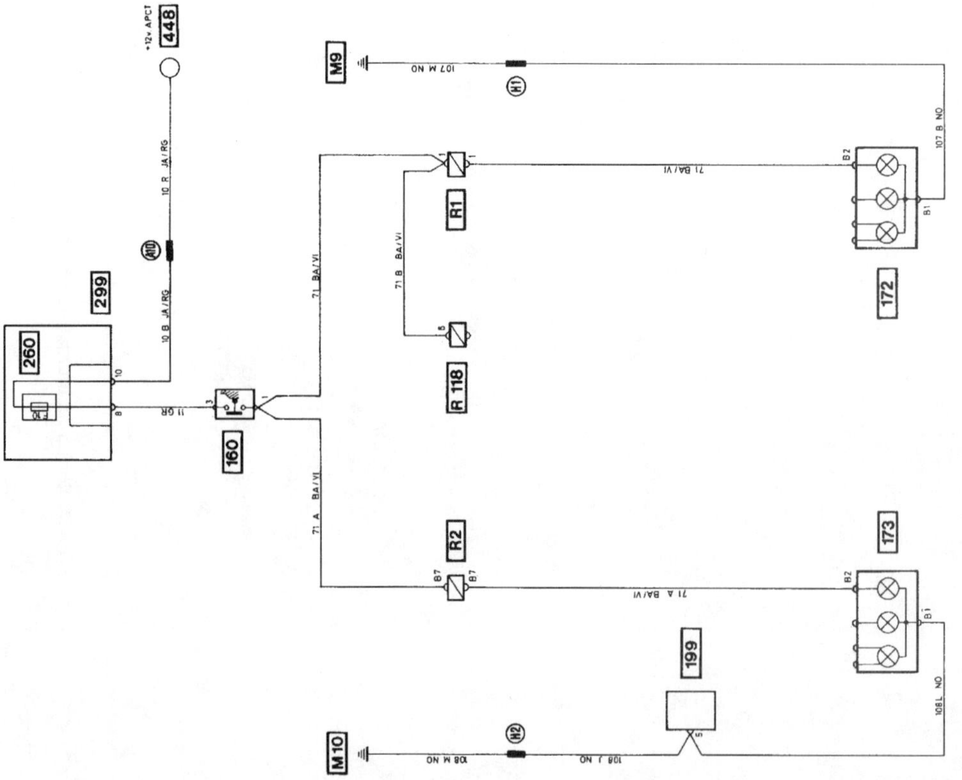

Typical stop lights

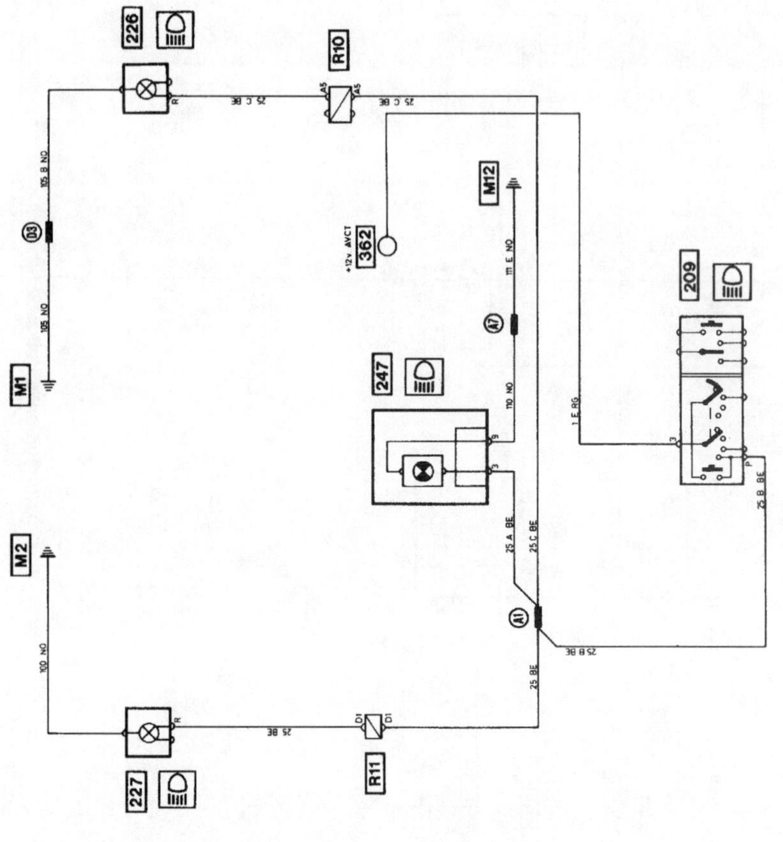

Typical main beam headlights

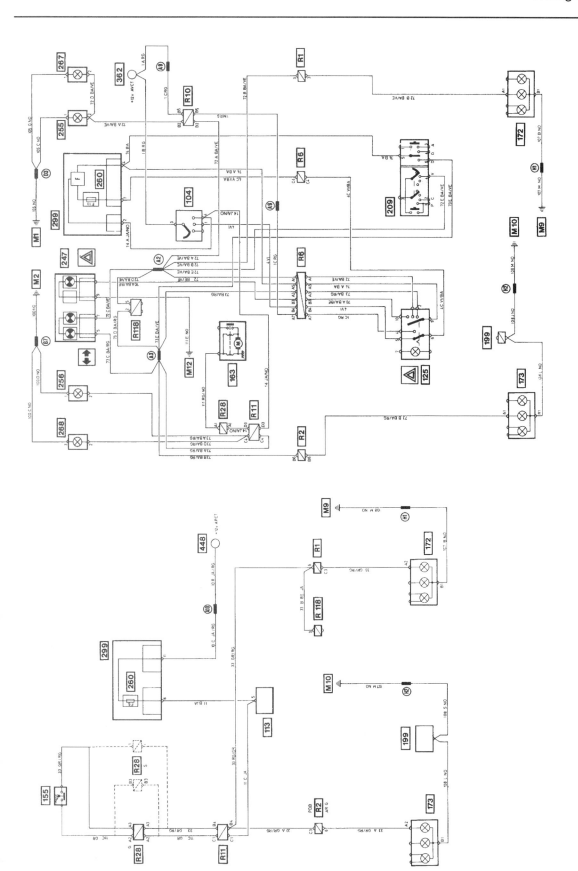

Typical direction indicators

Typical reversing lights

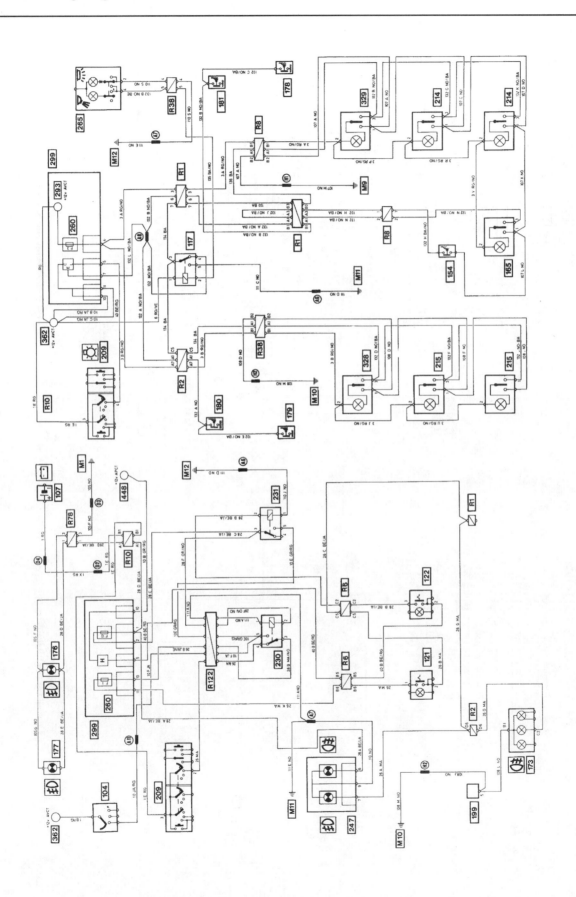

Typical "lights-on" warning buzzer

Typical foglights

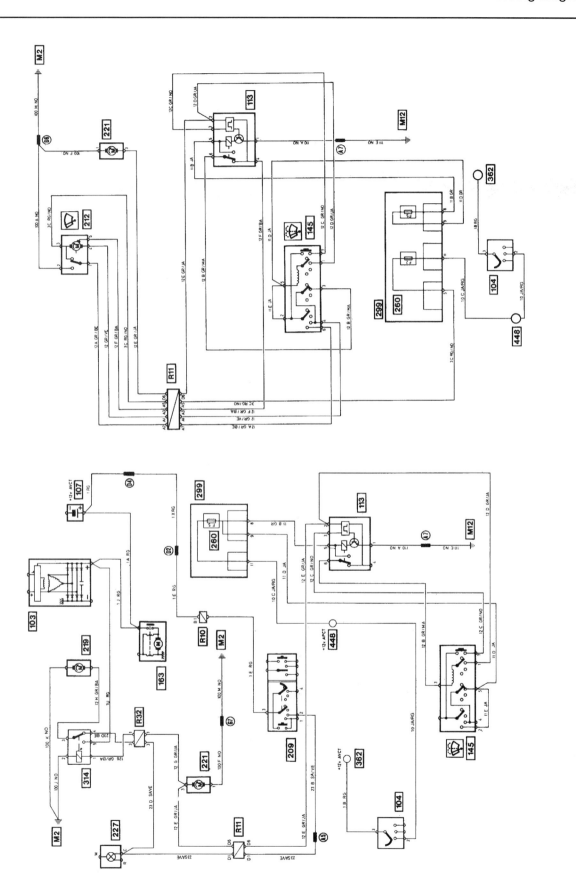

Typical windscreen washer

Typical headlight washer

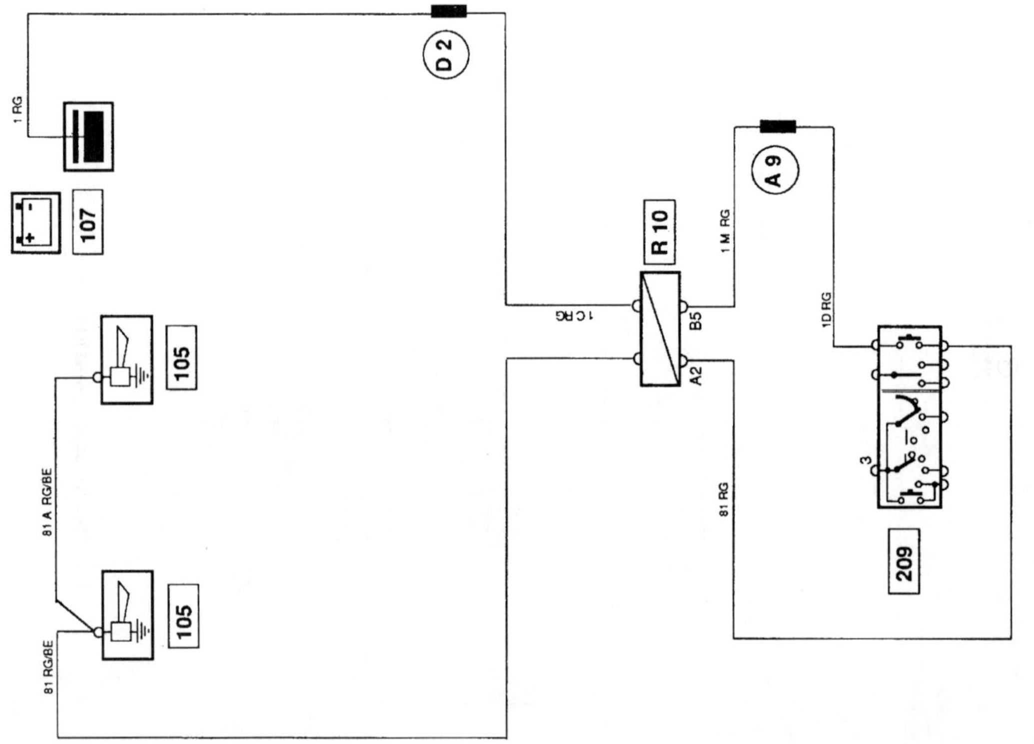

Typical horn

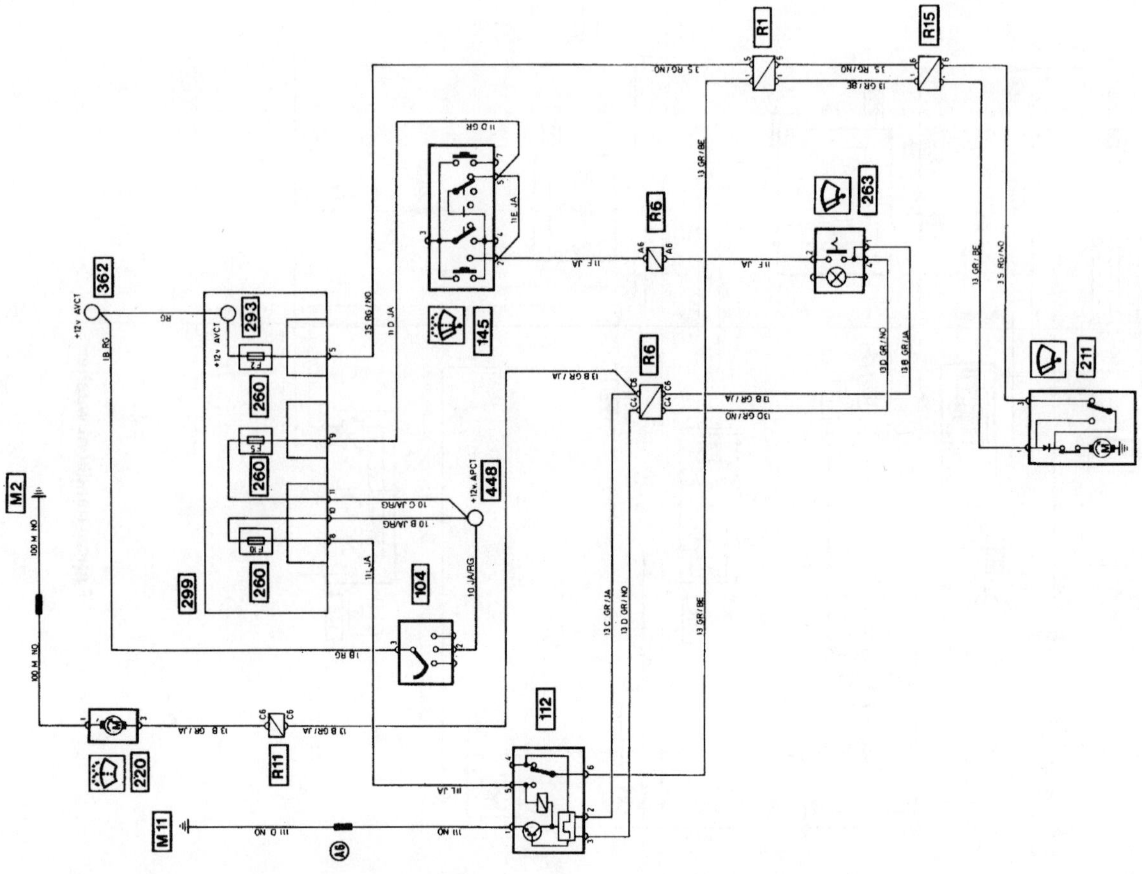

Typical tailgate washer

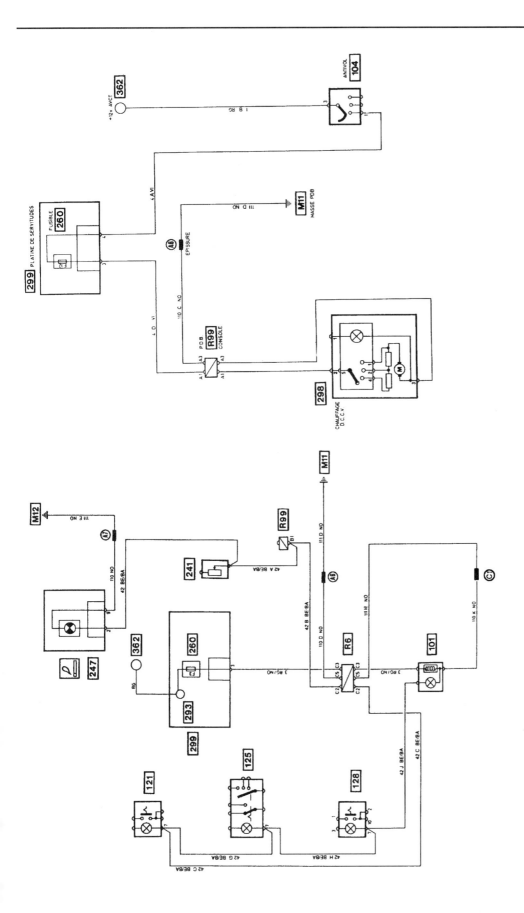

Typical heater blower

Typical cigar lighter

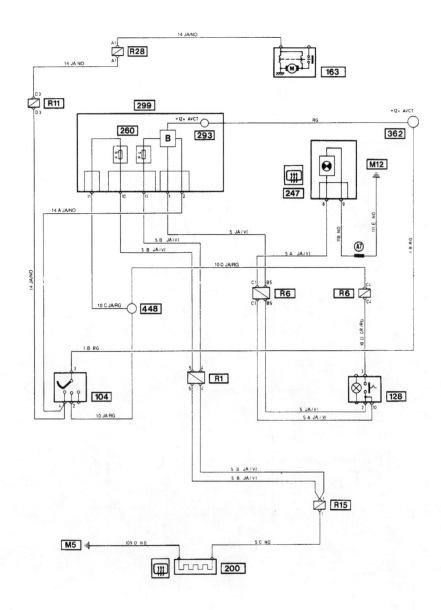

Typical heated rear screen

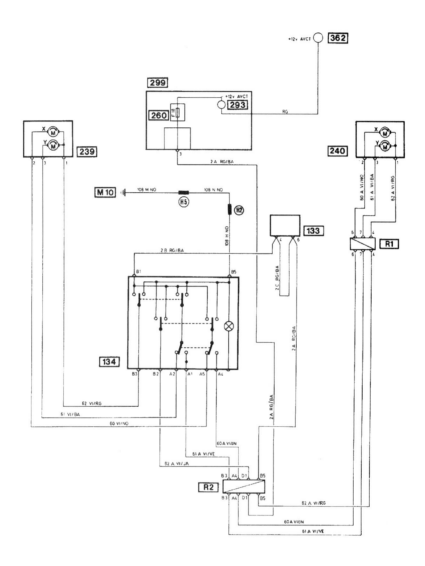

Typical electric mirrors

12

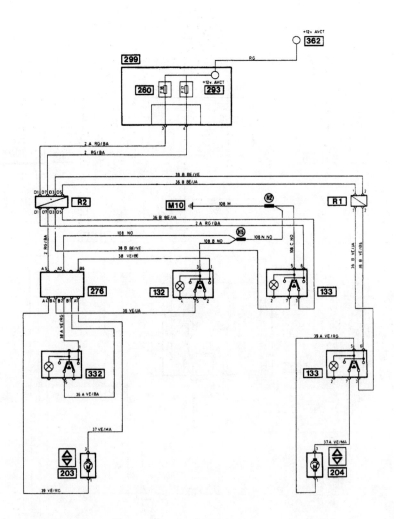

Typical electric windows

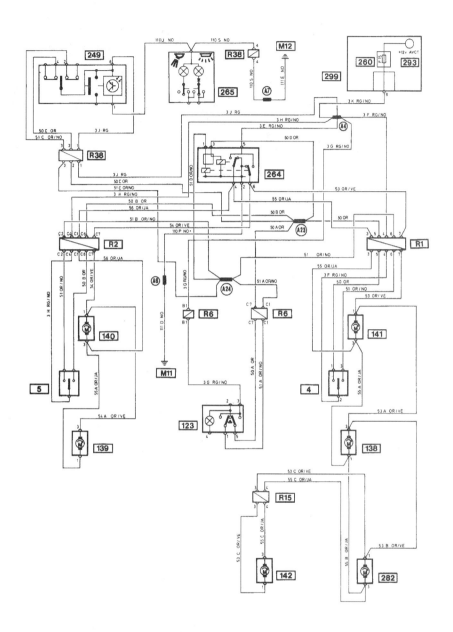

Typical central locking

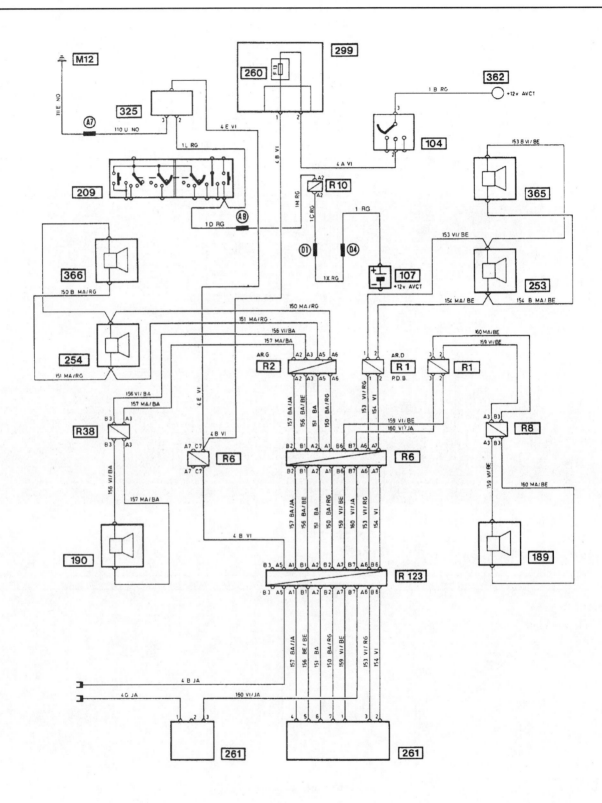

Typical radio/cassette

Reference

Dimensions and weights

Note: *All figures are approximate, and may vary according to model. Refer to manufacturer's data for exact figures.*

Dimensions

Phase 1 and 2 models
Overall length . . . .   4250 to 4300 mm
Overall width (excluding mirrors) . . . .   1777 mm
Overall height (unladen) . . . .   1660 mm

Phase 3 models
Overall length . . . .   4429 to 4464 mm
Overall width (excluding mirrors) . . . .   1795 mm
Overall height (unladen) . . . .   1705 mm

Weights

Phase 1 and 2 models
Kerb weight . . . .   1176 to 1260 kg*
Maximum gross vehicle weight . . . .   1480 to 1665 kg*
Maximum roof rack load . . . .   75 kg

Phase 3 models
Kerb weight . . . .   1330 to 1430 kg*
Maximum gross vehicle weight . . . .   2000 to 2230 kg*
Maximum roof rack load . . . .   60 kg
Depending on model and specification.

Length (distance)

Inches (in)	x 25.4	= Millimetres (mm)	x 0.0394	=	Inches (in)
Feet (ft)	x 0.305	= Metres (m)	x 3.281	=	Feet (ft)
Miles	x 1.609	= Kilometres (km)	x 0.621	=	Miles

Volume (capacity)

Cubic inches (cu in; in^3)	x 16.387	= Cubic centimetres (cc; cm^3)	x 0.061	=	Cubic inches (cu in; in^3)
Imperial pints (Imp pt)	x 0.568	= Litres (l)	x 1.76	=	Imperial pints (Imp pt)
Imperial quarts (Imp qt)	x 1.137	= Litres (l)	x 0.88	=	Imperial quarts (Imp qt)
Imperial quarts (Imp qt)	x 1.201	= US quarts (US qt)	x 0.833	=	Imperial quarts (Imp qt)
US quarts (US qt)	x 0.946	= Litres (l)	x 1.057	=	US quarts (US qt)
Imperial gallons (Imp gal)	x 4.546	= Litres (l)	x 0.22	=	Imperial gallons (Imp gal)
Imperial gallons (Imp gal)	x 1.201	= US gallons (US gal)	x 0.833	=	Imperial gallons (Imp gal)
US gallons (US gal)	x 3.785	= Litres (l)	x 0.264	=	US gallons (US gal)

Mass (weight)

Ounces (oz)	x 28.35	= Grams (g)	x 0.035	=	Ounces (oz)
Pounds (lb)	x 0.454	= Kilograms (kg)	x 2.205	=	Pounds (lb)

Force

Ounces-force (ozf; oz)	x 0.278	= Newtons (N)	x 3.6	=	Ounces-force (ozf; oz)
Pounds-force (lbf; lb)	x 4.448	= Newtons (N)	x 0.225	=	Pounds-force (lbf; lb)
Newtons (N)	x 0.1	= Kilograms-force (kgf; kg)	x 9.81	=	Newtons (N)

Pressure

Pounds-force per square inch (psi; lbf/in^2; lb/in^2)	x 0.070	= Kilograms-force per square centimetre (kgf/cm^2; kg/cm^2)	x 14.223	=	Pounds-force per square inch (psi; lbf/in^2; lb/in^2)
Pounds-force per square inch (psi; lbf/in^2; lb/in^2)	x 0.068	= Atmospheres (atm)	x 14.696	=	Pounds-force per square inch (psi; lbf/in^2; lb/in^2)
Pounds-force per square inch (psi; lbf/in^2; lb/in^2)	x 0.069	= Bars	x 14.5	=	Pounds-force per square inch (psi; lbf/in^2; lb/in^2)
Pounds-force per square inch (psi; lbf/in^2; lb/in^2)	x 6.895	= Kilopascals (kPa)	x 0.145	=	Pounds-force per square inch (psi; lbf/in^2; lb/in^2)
Kilopascals (kPa)	x 0.01	= Kilograms-force per square centimetre (kgf/cm^2; kg/cm^2)	x 98.1	=	Kilopascals (kPa)
Millibar (mbar)	x 100	= Pascals (Pa)	x 0.01	=	Millibar (mbar)
Millibar (mbar)	x 0.0145	= Pounds-force per square inch (psi; lbf/in^2; lb/in^2)	x 68.947	=	Millibar (mbar)
Millibar (mbar)	x 0.75	= Millimetres of mercury (mmHg)	x 1.333	=	Millibar (mbar)
Millibar (mbar)	x 0.401	= Inches of water (inH$_2$O)	x 2.491	=	Millibar (mbar)
Millimetres of mercury (mmHg)	x 0.535	= Inches of water (inH$_2$O)	x 1.868	=	Millimetres of mercury (mmHg)
Inches of water (inH$_2$O)	x 0.036	= Pounds-force per square inch (psi; lbf/in^2; lb/in^2)	x 27.68	=	Inches of water (inH$_2$O)

Torque (moment of force)

Pounds-force inches (lbf in; lb in)	x 1.152	= Kilograms-force centimetre (kgf cm; kg cm)	x 0.868	=	Pounds-force inches (lbf in; lb in)
Pounds-force inches (lbf in; lb in)	x 0.113	= Newton metres (Nm)	x 8.85	=	Pounds-force inches (lbf in; lb in)
Pounds-force inches (lbf in; lb in)	x 0.083	= Pounds-force feet (lbf ft; lb ft)	x 12	=	Pounds-force inches (lbf in; lb in)
Pounds-force feet (lbf ft; lb ft)	x 0.138	= Kilograms-force metres (kgf m; kg m)	x 7.233	=	Pounds-force feet (lbf ft; lb ft)
Pounds-force feet (lbf ft; lb ft)	x 1.356	= Newton metres (Nm)	x 0.738	=	Pounds-force feet (lbf ft; lb ft)
Newton metres (Nm)	x 0.102	= Kilograms-force metres (kgf m; kg m)	x 9.804	=	Newton metres (Nm)

Power

Horsepower (hp)	x 745.7	= Watts (W)	x 0.0013	=	Horsepower (hp)

Velocity (speed)

Miles per hour (miles/hr; mph)	x 1.609	= Kilometres per hour (km/hr; kph)	x 0.621	=	Miles per hour (miles/hr; mph)

Fuel consumption*

Miles per gallon (mpg)	x 0.354	= Kilometres per litre (km/l)	x 2.825	=	Miles per gallon (mpg)

Temperature

Degrees Fahrenheit = (°C x 1.8) + 32   Degrees Celsius (Degrees Centigrade; °C) = (°F - 32) x 0.56

It is common practice to convert from miles per gallon (mpg) to litres/100 kilometres (l/100km), where mpg x l/100 km = 282

Buying spare parts

Spare parts are available from many sources, including maker's appointed garages, accessory shops, and motor factors. To be sure of obtaining the correct parts, it will sometimes be necessary to quote the vehicle identification number. If possible, it can also be useful to take the old parts along for positive identification. Items such as starter motors and alternators may be available under a service exchange scheme - any parts returned should always be clean.

Our advice regarding spare part sources is as follows.

Officially-appointed garages

This is the best source of parts which are peculiar to your car, and which are not otherwise generally available (eg badges, interior trim, certain body panels, etc). It is also the only place at which you should buy parts if the vehicle is still under warranty.

Accessory shops

These are very good places to buy materials and components needed for the maintenance of your car (oil, air and fuel filters, spark plugs, light bulbs, drivebelts, oils and greases, brake pads, touch-up paint, etc). Components of this nature sold by a reputable shop are of the same standard as those used by the car manufacturer.

Besides components, these shops also sell tools and general accessories, usually have convenient opening hours, charge lower prices, and can often be found not far from home. Some accessory shops have parts counters where the components needed for almost any repair job can be purchased or ordered.

Motor factors

Good factors will stock all the more important components which wear out comparatively quickly, and can sometimes supply individual components needed for the overhaul of a larger assembly (eg brake seals and hydraulic parts, bearing shells, pistons, valves, alternator brushes). They may also handle work such as cylinder block reboring, crankshaft regrinding and balancing, etc.

Tyre and exhaust specialists

These outlets may be independent, or members of a local or national chain. They frequently offer competitive prices when compared with a main dealer or local garage, but it will pay to obtain several quotes before making a decision. When researching prices, also ask what "extras" may be added - for instance, fitting a new valve and balancing the wheel are both commonly charged on top of the price of a new tyre.

Other sources

Beware of parts or materials obtained from market stalls, car boot sales or similar outlets. Such items are not invariably sub-standard, but there is little chance of compensation if they do prove unsatisfactory. In the case of safety-critical components such as brake pads, there is the risk not only of financial loss but also of an accident causing injury or death.

Second-hand components or assemblies obtained from a car breaker can be a good buy in some circumstances, but this sort of purchase is best made by the experienced DIY mechanic.

Vehicle identification

Modifications are a continuing and unpublicised process in vehicle manufacture, quite apart from major model changes. Spare parts manuals and lists are compiled upon a numerical basis, the individual vehicle identification numbers being essential to correct identification of the component concerned.

When ordering spare parts, always give as much information as possible. Quote the type number, year of manufacture, chassis and engine numbers as appropriate.

On Phase 1 and 2 models two separate *vehicle identification plates* are riveted to the engine compartment bulkhead on the right-hand side (see illustration). The oval plate contains the vehicle type number, the equipment number and fabrication number. The manufacturer's plate contains the vehicle type number, chassis number and additional information on vehicle and axle weights.

On Phase 3 models the *vehicle identification plate* is located on the front face of the right-hand front door pillar (see illustration).

All the information described above for Phase 1 and 2 models is incorporated into a single plate.

The *chassis number* appears on the manufacturer's plate described previously.

The *engine number* is stamped on a plate riveted to the front right-hand side of the cylinder block below the thermostat housing (see illustration).

The *paint code* is stamped on the oval plate and may also be shown on a label next to the manufacturer's plate.

Vehicle identification number plate (Phase 1 and 2 models)

A Oval plate
C Vehicle identification number plate
D Vehicle paint code

Vehicle identification number plate (Phase 3 model)

Engine number plate (arrowed)

Whenever servicing, repair or overhaul work is carried out on the car or its components, it is necessary to observe the following procedures and instructions. This will assist in carrying out the operation efficiently and to a professional standard of workmanship.

Joint mating faces and gaskets

When separating components at their mating faces, never insert screwdrivers or similar implements into the joint between the faces in order to prise them apart. This can cause severe damage which results in oil leaks, coolant leaks, etc upon reassembly. Separation is usually achieved by tapping along the joint with a soft-faced hammer in order to break the seal. However, note that this method may not be suitable where dowels are used for component location.

Where a gasket is used between the mating faces of two components, ensure that it is renewed on reassembly, and fit it dry unless otherwise stated in the repair procedure. Make sure that the mating faces are clean and dry, with all traces of old gasket removed. When cleaning a joint face, use a tool which is not likely to score or damage the face, and remove any burrs or nicks with an oilstone or fine file.

Make sure that tapped holes are cleaned with a pipe cleaner, and keep them free of jointing compound, if this is being used, unless specifically instructed otherwise.

Ensure that all orifices, channels or pipes are clear, and blow through them, preferably using compressed air.

Oil seals

Oil seals can be removed by levering them out with a wide flat-bladed screwdriver or similar tool. Alternatively, a number of self-tapping screws may be screwed into the seal, and these used as a purchase for pliers or similar in order to pull the seal free.

Whenever an oil seal is removed from its working location, either individually or as part of an assembly, it should be renewed.

The very fine sealing lip of the seal is easily damaged, and will not seal if the surface it contacts is not completely clean and free from scratches, nicks or grooves. If the original sealing surface of the component cannot be restored, and the manufacturer has not made provision for slight relocation of the seal relative to the sealing surface, the component should be renewed.

Protect the lips of the seal from any surface which may damage them in the course of fitting. Use tape or a conical sleeve where possible. Lubricate the seal lips with oil before fitting and, on dual-lipped seals, fill the space between the lips with grease.

Unless otherwise stated, oil seals must be fitted with their sealing lips toward the lubricant to be sealed.

Use a tubular drift or block of wood of the appropriate size to install the seal and, if the seal housing is shouldered, drive the seal down to the shoulder. If the seal housing is unshouldered, the seal should be fitted with its face flush with the housing top face (unless otherwise instructed).

Screw threads and fastenings

Seized nuts, bolts and screws are quite a common occurrence where corrosion has set in, and the use of penetrating oil or releasing fluid will often overcome this problem if the offending item is soaked for a while before attempting to release it. The use of an impact driver may also provide a means of releasing such stubborn fastening devices, when used in conjunction with the appropriate screwdriver bit or socket. If none of these methods works, it may be necessary to resort to the careful application of heat, or the use of a hacksaw or nut splitter device.

Studs are usually removed by locking two nuts together on the threaded part, and then using a spanner on the lower nut to unscrew the stud. Studs or bolts which have broken off below the surface of the component in which they are mounted can sometimes be removed using a stud extractor. Always ensure that a blind tapped hole is completely free from oil, grease, water or other fluid before installing the bolt or stud. Failure to do this could cause the housing to crack due to the hydraulic action of the bolt or stud as it is screwed in.

When tightening a castellated nut to accept a split pin, tighten the nut to the specified torque, where applicable, and then tighten further to the next split pin hole. Never slacken the nut to align the split pin hole, unless stated in the repair procedure.

When checking or retightening a nut or bolt to a specified torque setting, slacken the nut or bolt by a quarter of a turn, and then retighten to the specified setting. However, this should not be attempted where angular tightening has been used.

For some screw fastenings, notably cylinder head bolts or nuts, torque wrench settings are no longer specified for the latter stages of tightening, "angle-tightening" being called up instead. Typically, a fairly low torque wrench setting will be applied to the bolts/nuts in the correct sequence, followed by one or more stages of tightening through specified angles.

Locknuts, locktabs and washers

Any fastening which will rotate against a component or housing during tightening should always have a washer between it and the relevant component or housing.

Spring or split washers should always be renewed when they are used to lock a critical component such as a big-end bearing retaining bolt or nut. Locktabs which are folded over to retain a nut or bolt should always be renewed.

Self-locking nuts can be re-used in non-critical areas, providing resistance can be felt when the locking portion passes over the bolt or stud thread. However, it should be noted that self-locking stiffnuts tend to lose their effectiveness after long periods of use, and should be renewed as a matter of course.

Split pins must always be replaced with new ones of the correct size for the hole.

When thread-locking compound is found on the threads of a fastener which is to be re-used, it should be cleaned off with a wire brush and solvent, and fresh compound applied on reassembly.

Special tools

Some repair procedures in this manual entail the use of special tools such as a press, two or three-legged pullers, spring compressors, etc. Wherever possible, suitable readily-available alternatives to the manufacturer's special tools are described, and are shown in use. In some instances, where no alternative is possible, it has been necessary to resort to the use of a manufacturer's tool, and this has been done for reasons of safety as well as the efficient completion of the repair operation. Unless you are highly-skilled and have a thorough understanding of the procedures described, never attempt to bypass the use of any special tool when the procedure described specifies its use. Not only is there a very great risk of personal injury, but expensive damage could be caused to the components involved.

Environmental considerations

When disposing of used engine oil, brake fluid, antifreeze, etc, give due consideration to any detrimental environmental effects. Do not, for instance, pour any of the above liquids down drains into the general sewage system, or onto the ground to soak away. Many local council refuse tips provide a facility for waste oil disposal, as do some garages. If none of these facilities are available, consult your local Environmental Health Department, or the National Rivers Authority, for further advice.

With the universal tightening-up of legislation regarding the emission of environmentally-harmful substances from motor vehicles, most current vehicles have tamperproof devices fitted to the main adjustment points of the fuel system. These devices are primarily designed to prevent unqualified persons from adjusting the fuel/air mixture, with the chance of a consequent increase in toxic emissions. If such devices are encountered during servicing or overhaul, they should, wherever possible, be renewed or refitted in accordance with the vehicle manufacturer's requirements or current legislation.

OIL CARE
OIL BANK LINE
0800 66 33 66

Note: It is antisocial and illegal to dump oil down the drain. To find the location of your local oil recycling bank, call this number free.

The jack supplied with the vehicle tool kit should only be used for changing the roadwheels - see *"Wheel changing"* at the front of this manual. When carrying out any other kind of work, raise the vehicle using a hydraulic (or "trolley") jack, and always supplement the jack with axle stands positioned under the vehicle jacking points.

When using a hydraulic jack or axle stands, always position the jack head or axle stand head under one of the relevant jacking points.

To raise the front of the vehicle, use a stout wooden beam, or similar steel item, long enough to contact the chassis rails on each side of the vehicle. Locate the beam behind the front crossmember, then place the jack head beneath the centre of the beam **(see illustration)**. **Do not** jack the vehicle under the sump, or any of the steering or suspension components. With the front raised, position axle stands under the strengtheners at the vehicle jack locating points on each side **(see illustration)**.

To raise the rear of the vehicle, raise one side at a time with the jack head positioned under the rear axle, at the shock absorber lower mountings **(see illustration)**. With the rear raised, position axle stands under the strengtheners at the vehicle jack locating points on each side.

The jack supplied with the vehicle locates in the jacking points in the reinforced area on the inside of the sills. Ensure that the jack head is correctly engaged before attempting to raise the vehicle.

Never work under, around, or near a raised vehicle, unless it is adequately supported in at least two places.

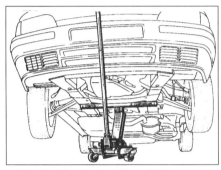

To raise the front of the vehicle, use a beam long enough to contact the chassis rails at each side. Locate the beam behind the front crossmember, then jack under the centre of the beam

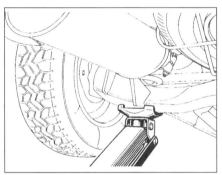

To raise the rear of the vehicle, raise one side at a time with the jack head positioned under the rear axle, at the shock absorber lower mountings

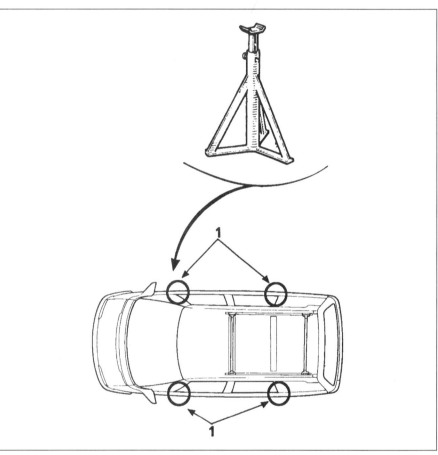

Axle stand location points (1)

Radio/cassette unit anti-theft system - precaution

The radio/cassette unit fitted as standard equipment by Renault may be equipped with a built-in security code, to deter thieves. If the power source to the unit is cut, the anti-theft system will activate. Even if the power source is immediately reconnected, the radio/cassette unit will not function until the correct security code has been entered. Therefore, if you do not know the correct security code for the radio/cassette unit **do not** disconnect either of the battery terminals, or remove the radio/cassette unit from the vehicle.

To enter the security code, follow the instructions in the radio/cassette handbook.

If an incorrect code is entered, the unit will become locked, and cannot be operated.

If this happens, or if the security code is lost or forgotten, seek the advice of your dealer.

Introduction

A selection of good tools is a fundamental requirement for anyone contemplating the maintenance and repair of a motor vehicle. For the owner who does not possess any, their purchase will prove a considerable expense, offsetting some of the savings made by doing-it-yourself. However, provided that the tools purchased meet the relevant national safety standards and are of good quality, they will last for many years and prove an extremely worthwhile investment.

To help the average owner to decide which tools are needed to carry out the various tasks detailed in this manual, we have compiled three lists of tools under the following headings: *Maintenance and minor repair, Repair and overhaul*, and *Special*. Newcomers to practical mechanics should start off with the *Maintenance and minor repair* tool kit, and confine themselves to the simpler jobs around the vehicle. Then, as confidence and experience grow, more difficult tasks can be undertaken, with extra tools being purchased as, and when, they are needed. In this way, a *Maintenance and minor repair* tool kit can be built up into a *Repair and overhaul* tool kit over a considerable period of time, without any major cash outlays. The experienced do-it-yourselfer will have a tool kit good enough for most repair and overhaul procedures, and will add tools from the *Special* category when it is felt that the expense is justified by the amount of use to which these tools will be put.

Maintenance and minor repair tool kit

The tools given in this list should be considered as a minimum requirement if routine maintenance, servicing and minor repair operations are to be undertaken. We recommend the purchase of combination spanners (ring one end, open-ended the other); although more expensive than open-ended ones, they do give the advantages of both types of spanner.

☐ *Combination spanners:*
   Metric - 8 to 19 mm inclusive
☐ *Adjustable spanner - 35 mm jaw (approx.)*
☐ *Spark plug spanner (with rubber insert) - petrol models*
☐ *Spark plug gap adjustment tool - petrol models*
☐ *Set of feeler blades*
☐ *Brake bleed nipple spanner*
☐ *Screwdrivers:*
   Flat blade - 100 mm long x 6 mm dia
   Cross blade - 100 mm long x 6 mm dia
☐ *Combination pliers*
☐ *Hacksaw (junior)*
☐ *Tyre pump*
☐ *Tyre pressure gauge*
☐ *Oil can*
☐ *Oil filter removal tool*
☐ *Fine emery cloth*
☐ *Wire brush (small)*
☐ *Funnel (medium size)*

Repair and overhaul tool kit

These tools are virtually essential for anyone undertaking any major repairs to a motor vehicle, and are additional to those given in the *Maintenance and minor repair* list. Included in this list is a comprehensive set of sockets. Although these are expensive, they will be found invaluable as they are so versatile - particularly if various drives are included in the set. We recommend the half-inch square-drive type, as this can be used with most proprietary torque wrenches.

The tools in this list will sometimes need to be supplemented by tools from the *Special* list:

☐ *Sockets (or box spanners) to cover range in previous list (including Torx sockets)*
☐ *Reversible ratchet drive (for use with sockets)*
☐ *Extension piece, 250 mm (for use with sockets)*
☐ *Universal joint (for use with sockets)*
☐ *Torque wrench (for use with sockets)*
☐ *Self-locking grips*
☐ *Ball pein hammer*
☐ *Soft-faced mallet (plastic/aluminium or rubber)*
☐ *Screwdrivers:*
   Flat blade - long & sturdy, short (chubby), and narrow (electrician's) types
   Cross blade – Long & sturdy, and short (chubby) types
☐ *Pliers:*
   Long-nosed
   Side cutters (electrician's)
   Circlip (internal and external)
☐ *Cold chisel - 25 mm*
☐ *Scriber*
☐ *Scraper*
☐ *Centre-punch*
☐ *Pin punch*
☐ *Hacksaw*
☐ *Brake hose clamp*
☐ *Brake/clutch bleeding kit*
☐ *Selection of twist drills*
☐ *Steel rule/straight-edge*
☐ *Allen keys (inc. splined/Torx type)*
☐ *Selection of files*
☐ *Wire brush*
☐ *Axle stands*
☐ *Jack (strong trolley or hydraulic type)*
☐ *Light with extension lead*

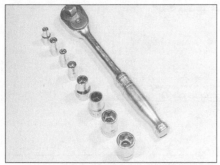

Sockets and reversible ratchet drive

Valve spring compressor

Spline bit set

Piston ring compressor

Clutch plate alignment set

Special tools

The tools in this list are those which are not used regularly, are expensive to buy, or which need to be used in accordance with their manufacturers' instructions. Unless relatively difficult mechanical jobs are undertaken frequently, it will not be economic to buy many of these tools. Where this is the case, you could consider clubbing together with friends (or joining a motorists' club) to make a joint purchase, or borrowing the tools against a deposit from a local garage or tool hire specialist. It is worth noting that many of the larger DIY superstores now carry a large range of special tools for hire at modest rates.

The following list contains only those tools and instruments freely available to the public, and not those special tools produced by the vehicle manufacturer specifically for its dealer network. You will find occasional references to these manufacturers' special tools in the text of this manual. Generally, an alternative method of doing the job without the vehicle manufacturers' special tool is given. However, sometimes there is no alternative to using them. Where this is the case and the relevant tool cannot be bought or borrowed, you will have to entrust the work to a dealer.

☐ Valve spring compressor
☐ Valve grinding tool
☐ Piston ring compressor
☐ Piston ring removal/installation tool
☐ Cylinder bore hone
☐ Balljoint separator
☐ Coil spring compressors (where applicable)
☐ Two/three-legged hub and bearing puller
☐ Impact screwdriver
☐ Micrometer and/or vernier calipers
☐ Dial gauge
☐ Stroboscopic timing light
☐ Dwell angle meter/tachometer
☐ Universal electrical multi-meter
☐ Cylinder compression gauge
☐ Hand-operated vacuum pump and gauge
☐ Clutch plate alignment set
☐ Brake shoe steady spring cup removal tool
☐ Bush and bearing removal/installation set
☐ Stud extractors
☐ Tap and die set
☐ Lifting tackle
☐ Trolley jack

Buying tools

Reputable motor accessory shops and superstores often offer excellent quality tools at discount prices, so it pays to shop around.

Remember, you don't have to buy the most expensive items on the shelf, but it is always advisable to steer clear of the very cheap tools. Beware of 'bargains' offered on market stalls or at car boot sales. There are plenty of good tools around at reasonable prices, but always aim to purchase items which meet the relevant national safety standards. If in doubt, ask the proprietor or manager of the shop for advice before making a purchase.

Care and maintenance of tools

Having purchased a reasonable tool kit, it is necessary to keep the tools in a clean and serviceable condition. After use, always wipe off any dirt, grease and metal particles using a clean, dry cloth, before putting the tools away. Never leave them lying around after they have been used. A simple tool rack on the garage or workshop wall for items such as screwdrivers and pliers is a good idea. Store all normal spanners and sockets in a metal box. Any measuring instruments, gauges, meters, etc, must be carefully stored where they cannot be damaged or become rusty.

Take a little care when tools are used. Hammer heads inevitably become marked, and screwdrivers lose the keen edge on their blades from time to time. A little timely attention with emery cloth or a file will soon restore items like this to a good finish.

Working facilities

Not to be forgotten when discussing tools is the workshop itself. If anything more than routine maintenance is to be carried out, a suitable working area becomes essential.

It is appreciated that many an owner-mechanic is forced by circumstances to remove an engine or similar item without the benefit of a garage or workshop. Having done this, any repairs should always be done under the cover of a roof.

Wherever possible, any dismantling should be done on a clean, flat workbench or table at a suitable working height.

Any workbench needs a vice; one with a jaw opening of 100 mm is suitable for most jobs. As mentioned previously, some clean dry storage space is also required for tools, as well as for any lubricants, cleaning fluids, touch-up paints etc, which become necessary.

Another item which may be required, and which has a much more general usage, is an electric drill with a chuck capacity of at least 8 mm. This, together with a good range of twist drills, is virtually essential for fitting accessories.

Last, but not least, always keep a supply of old newspapers and clean, lint-free rags available, and try to keep any working area as clean as possible.

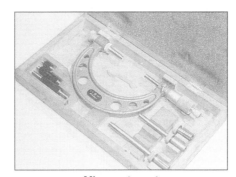
Micrometer set

Dial test indicator ("dial gauge")

Stroboscopic timing light

Compression tester

Stud extractor set

This is a guide to getting your vehicle through the MOT test. Obviously it will not be possible to examine the vehicle to the same standard as the professional MOT tester. However, working through the following checks will enable you to identify any problem areas before submitting the vehicle for the test.

Where a testable component is in borderline condition, the tester has discretion in deciding whether to pass or fail it. The basis of such discretion is whether the tester would be happy for a close relative or friend to use the vehicle with the component in that condition. If the vehicle presented is clean and evidently well cared for, the tester may be more inclined to pass a borderline component than if the vehicle is scruffy and apparently neglected.

It has only been possible to summarise the test requirements here, based on the regulations in force at the time of printing. Test standards are becoming increasingly stringent, although there are some exemptions for older vehicles. For full details obtain a copy of the Haynes publication Pass the MOT! (available from stockists of Haynes manuals).

An assistant will be needed to help carry out some of these checks.

The checks have been sub-divided into four categories, as follows:

1 Checks carried out **FROM THE DRIVER'S SEAT**

2 Checks carried out **WITH THE VEHICLE ON THE GROUND**

3 Checks carried out **WITH THE VEHICLE RAISED AND THE WHEELS FREE TO TURN**

4 Checks carried out on **YOUR VEHICLE'S EXHAUST EMISSION SYSTEM**

---

1 Checks carried out **FROM THE DRIVER'S SEAT**

Handbrake

☐ Test the operation of the handbrake. Excessive travel (too many clicks) indicates incorrect brake or cable adjustment.

☐ Check that the handbrake cannot be released by tapping the lever sideways. Check the security of the lever mountings.

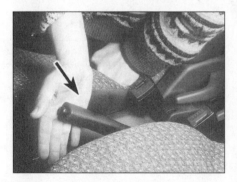

Footbrake

☐ Depress the brake pedal and check that it does not creep down to the floor, indicating a master cylinder fault. Release the pedal, wait a few seconds, then depress it again. If the pedal travels nearly to the floor before firm resistance is felt, brake adjustment or repair is necessary. If the pedal feels spongy, there is air in the hydraulic system which must be removed by bleeding.

☐ Check that the brake pedal is secure and in good condition. Check also for signs of fluid leaks on the pedal, floor or carpets, which would indicate failed seals in the brake master cylinder.

☐ Check the servo unit (when applicable) by operating the brake pedal several times, then keeping the pedal depressed and starting the engine. As the engine starts, the pedal will move down slightly. If not, the vacuum hose or the servo itself may be faulty.

Steering wheel and column

☐ Examine the steering wheel for fractures or looseness of the hub, spokes or rim.

☐ Move the steering wheel from side to side and then up and down. Check that the steering wheel is not loose on the column, indicating wear or a loose retaining nut. Continue moving the steering wheel as before, but also turn it slightly from left to right.

☐ Check that the steering wheel is not loose on the column, and that there is no abnormal

movement of the steering wheel, indicating wear in the column support bearings or couplings.

Windscreen and mirrors

☐ The windscreen must be free of cracks or other significant damage within the driver's field of view. (Small stone chips are acceptable.) Rear view mirrors must be secure, intact, and capable of being adjusted.

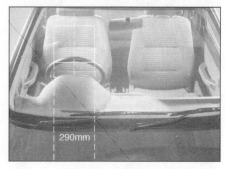

Seat belts and seats

Note: *The following checks are applicable to all seat belts, front and rear.*

☐ Examine the webbing of all the belts (including rear belts if fitted) for cuts, serious fraying or deterioration. Fasten and unfasten each belt to check the buckles. If applicable, check the retracting mechanism. Check the security of all seat belt mountings accessible from inside the vehicle.

☐ The front seats themselves must be securely attached and the backrests must lock in the upright position.

Doors

☐ Both front doors must be able to be opened and closed from outside and inside, and must latch securely when closed.

2 Checks carried out WITH THE VEHICLE ON THE GROUND

Vehicle identification

☐ Number plates must be in good condition, secure and legible, with letters and numbers correctly spaced – spacing at (A) should be twice that at (B).

☐ The VIN plate and/or homologation plate must be legible.

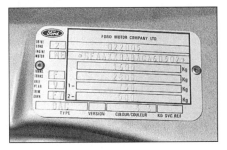

Electrical equipment

☐ Switch on the ignition and check the operation of the horn.

☐ Check the windscreen washers and wipers, examining the wiper blades; renew damaged or perished blades. Also check the operation of the stop-lights.

☐ Check the operation of the sidelights and number plate lights. The lenses and reflectors must be secure, clean and undamaged.

☐ Check the operation and alignment of the headlights. The headlight reflectors must not be tarnished and the lenses must be undamaged.

☐ Switch on the ignition and check the operation of the direction indicators (including the instrument panel tell-tale) and the hazard warning lights. Operation of the sidelights and stop-lights must not affect the indicators - if it does, the cause is usually a bad earth at the rear light cluster.

☐ Check the operation of the rear foglight(s), including the warning light on the instrument panel or in the switch.

Footbrake

☐ Examine the master cylinder, brake pipes and servo unit for leaks, loose mountings, corrosion or other damage.

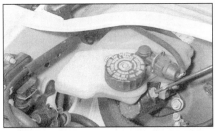

☐ The fluid reservoir must be secure and the fluid level must be between the upper (**A**) and lower (**B**) markings.

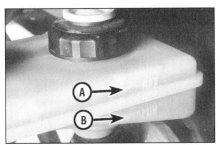

☐ Inspect both front brake flexible hoses for cracks or deterioration of the rubber. Turn the steering from lock to lock, and ensure that the hoses do not contact the wheel, tyre, or any part of the steering or suspension mechanism. With the brake pedal firmly depressed, check the hoses for bulges or leaks under pressure.

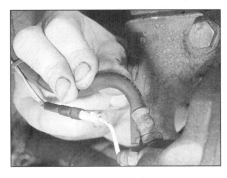

Steering and suspension

☐ Have your assistant turn the steering wheel from side to side slightly, up to the point where the steering gear just begins to transmit this movement to the roadwheels. Check for excessive free play between the steering wheel and the steering gear, indicating wear or insecurity of the steering column joints, the column-to-steering gear coupling, or the steering gear itself.

☐ Have your assistant turn the steering wheel more vigorously in each direction, so that the roadwheels just begin to turn. As this is done, examine all the steering joints, linkages, fittings and attachments. Renew any component that shows signs of wear or damage. On vehicles with power steering, check the security and condition of the steering pump, drivebelt and hoses.

☐ Check that the vehicle is standing level, and at approximately the correct ride height.

Shock absorbers

☐ Depress each corner of the vehicle in turn, then release it. The vehicle should rise and then settle in its normal position. If the vehicle continues to rise and fall, the shock absorber is defective. A shock absorber which has seized will also cause the vehicle to fail.

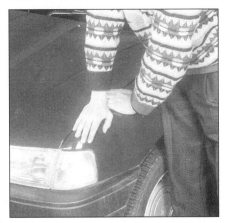

Exhaust system

☐ Start the engine. With your assistant holding a rag over the tailpipe, check the entire system for leaks. Repair or renew leaking sections.

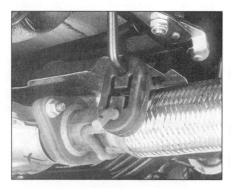

3 Checks carried out
**WITH THE VEHICLE RAISED
AND THE WHEELS FREE TO
TURN**

Jack up the front and rear of the vehicle, and securely support it on axle stands. Position the stands clear of the suspension assemblies. Ensure that the wheels are clear of the ground and that the steering can be turned from lock to lock.

Steering mechanism

☐ Have your assistant turn the steering from lock to lock. Check that the steering turns smoothly, and that no part of the steering mechanism, including a wheel or tyre, fouls any brake hose or pipe or any part of the body structure.

☐ Examine the steering rack rubber gaiters for damage or insecurity of the retaining clips. If power steering is fitted, check for signs of damage or leakage of the fluid hoses, pipes or connections. Also check for excessive stiffness or binding of the steering, a missing split pin or locking device, or severe corrosion of the body structure within 30 cm of any steering component attachment point.

Front and rear suspension and wheel bearings

☐ Starting at the front right-hand side, grasp the roadwheel at the 3 o'clock and 9 o'clock positions and shake it vigorously. Check for free play or insecurity at the wheel bearings, suspension balljoints, or suspension mountings, pivots and attachments.

☐ Now grasp the wheel at the 12 o'clock and 6 o'clock positions and repeat the previous inspection. Spin the wheel, and check for roughness or tightness of the front wheel bearing.

☐ If excess free play is suspected at a component pivot point, this can be confirmed by using a large screwdriver or similar tool and levering between the mounting and the component attachment. This will confirm whether the wear is in the pivot bush, its retaining bolt, or in the mounting itself (the bolt holes can often become elongated).

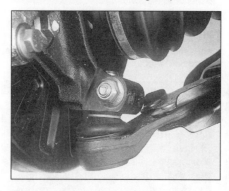

☐ Carry out all the above checks at the other front wheel, and then at both rear wheels.

Springs and shock absorbers

☐ Examine the suspension struts (when applicable) for serious fluid leakage, corrosion, or damage to the casing. Also check the security of the mounting points.

☐ If coil springs are fitted, check that the spring ends locate in their seats, and that the spring is not corroded, cracked or broken.

☐ If leaf springs are fitted, check that all leaves are intact, that the axle is securely attached to each spring, and that there is no deterioration of the spring eye mountings, bushes, and shackles.

☐ The same general checks apply to vehicles fitted with other suspension types, such as torsion bars, hydraulic displacer units, etc. Ensure that all mountings and attachments are secure, that there are no signs of excessive wear, corrosion or damage, and (on hydraulic types) that there are no fluid leaks or damaged pipes).

☐ Inspect the shock absorbers for signs of serious fluid leakage. Check for wear of the mounting bushes or attachments, or damage to the body of the unit.

Driveshafts
(fwd vehicles only)

☐ Rotate each front wheel in turn and inspect the constant velocity joint gaiters for splits or damage. Also check that each driveshaft is straight and undamaged.

Braking system

☐ If possible without dismantling, check brake pad wear and disc condition. Ensure that the friction lining material has not worn excessively, (A) and that the discs are not fractured, pitted, scored or badly worn (B).

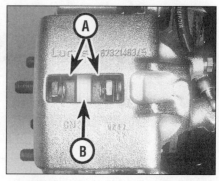

☐ Examine all the rigid brake pipes underneath the vehicle, and the flexible hose(s) at the rear. Look for corrosion, chafing or insecurity of the pipes, and for signs of bulging under pressure, chafing, splits or deterioration of the flexible hoses.

☐ Look for signs of fluid leaks at the brake calipers or on the brake backplates. Repair or renew leaking components.

☐ Slowly spin each wheel, while your assistant depresses and releases the footbrake. Ensure that each brake is operating and does not bind when the pedal is released.

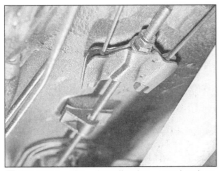

□ Examine the handbrake mechanism, checking for frayed or broken cables, excessive corrosion, or wear or insecurity of the linkage. Check that the mechanism works on each relevant wheel, and releases fully, without binding.

□ It is not possible to test brake efficiency without special equipment, but a road test can be carried out later to check that the vehicle pulls up in a straight line.

Fuel and exhaust systems

□ Inspect the fuel tank (including the filler cap), fuel pipes, hoses and unions. All components must be secure and free from leaks.

□ Examine the exhaust system over its entire length, checking for any damaged, broken or missing mountings, security of the retaining clamps and rust or corrosion.

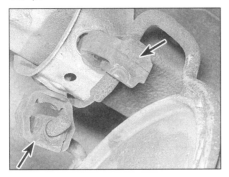

Wheels and tyres

□ Examine the sidewalls and tread area of each tyre in turn. Check for cuts, tears, lumps, bulges, separation of the tread, and exposure of the ply or cord due to wear or damage. Check that the tyre bead is correctly seated on the wheel rim, that the valve is sound and

properly seated, and that the wheel is not distorted or damaged.

□ Check that the tyres are of the correct size for the vehicle, that they are of the same size and type on each axle, and that the pressures are correct.

□ Check the tyre tread depth. The legal minimum at the time of writing is 1.6 mm over at least three-quarters of the tread width. Abnormal tread wear may indicate incorrect front wheel alignment.

Body corrosion

□ Check the condition of the entire vehicle structure for signs of corrosion in load-bearing areas. (These include chassis box sections, side sills, cross-members, pillars, and all suspension, steering, braking system and seat belt mountings and anchorages.) Any corrosion which has seriously reduced the thickness of a load-bearing area is likely to cause the vehicle to fail. In this case professional repairs are likely to be needed.

□ Damage or corrosion which causes sharp or otherwise dangerous edges to be exposed will also cause the vehicle to fail.

4 Checks carried out on YOUR VEHICLE'S EXHAUST EMISSION SYSTEM

Petrol models

□ Have the engine at normal operating temperature, and make sure that it is in good tune (ignition system in good order, air filter element clean, etc).

□ Before any measurements are carried out, raise the engine speed to around 2500 rpm, and hold it at this speed for 20 seconds. Allow

the engine speed to return to idle, and watch for smoke emissions from the exhaust tailpipe. If the idle speed is obviously much too high, or if dense blue or clearly-visible black smoke comes from the tailpipe for more than 5 seconds, the vehicle will fail. As a rule of thumb, blue smoke signifies oil being burnt (engine wear) while black smoke signifies unburnt fuel (dirty air cleaner element, or other carburettor or fuel system fault).

□ An exhaust gas analyser capable of measuring carbon monoxide (CO) and hydrocarbons (HC) is now needed. If such an instrument cannot be hired or borrowed, a local garage may agree to perform the check for a small fee.

CO emissions (mixture)

□ At the time of writing, the maximum CO level at idle is 3.5% for vehicles first used after August 1986 and 4.5% for older vehicles. From January 1996 a much tighter limit (around 0.5%) applies to catalyst-equipped vehicles first used from August 1992. If the CO level cannot be reduced far enough to pass the test (and the fuel and ignition systems are otherwise in good condition) then the carburettor is badly worn, or there is some problem in the fuel injection system or catalytic converter (as applicable).

HC emissions

□ With the CO emissions within limits, HC emissions must be no more than 1200 ppm (parts per million). If the vehicle fails this test at idle, it can be re-tested at around 2000 rpm; if the HC level is then 1200 ppm or less, this counts as a pass.

□ Excessive HC emissions can be caused by oil being burnt, but they are more likely to be due to unburnt fuel.

Diesel models

□ The only emission test applicable to Diesel engines is the measuring of exhaust smoke density. The test involves accelerating the engine several times to its maximum unloaded speed.

Note: *It is of the utmost importance that the engine timing belt is in good condition before the test is carried out.*

□ Excessive smoke can be caused by a dirty air cleaner element. Otherwise, professional advice may be needed to find the cause.

Engine 1
- ☐ Engine fails to rotate when attempting to start
- ☐ Engine rotates, but will not start
- ☐ Engine difficult to start when cold
- ☐ Engine difficult to start when hot
- ☐ Starter motor noisy or excessively-rough in engagement
- ☐ Engine starts, but stops immediately
- ☐ Engine idles erratically
- ☐ Engine misfires at idle speed
- ☐ Engine misfires throughout the driving speed range
- ☐ Engine hesitates on acceleration
- ☐ Engine stalls
- ☐ Engine lacks power
- ☐ Engine backfires
- ☐ Oil pressure warning light illuminated with engine running
- ☐ Engine runs-on after switching off
- ☐ Engine noises

Cooling system 2
- ☐ Overheating
- ☐ Overcooling
- ☐ External coolant leakage
- ☐ Internal coolant leakage
- ☐ Corrosion

Fuel and exhaust systems 3
- ☐ Excessive fuel consumption
- ☐ Fuel leakage and/or fuel odour
- ☐ Excessive noise or fumes from exhaust system

Clutch 4
- ☐ Pedal travels to floor - no pressure or very little resistance
- ☐ Clutch fails to disengage (unable to select gears)
- ☐ Clutch slips (engine speed increases, with no increase in vehicle speed)
- ☐ Judder as clutch is engaged
- ☐ Noise when depressing or releasing clutch pedal

Manual transmission 5
- ☐ Noisy in neutral with engine running
- ☐ Noisy in one particular gear
- ☐ Difficulty engaging gears
- ☐ Jumps out of gear
- ☐ Vibration
- ☐ Lubricant leaks

Driveshafts 6
- ☐ Clicking or knocking noise on turns (at slow speed on full-lock)
- ☐ Vibration when accelerating or decelerating

Braking system 7
- ☐ Vehicle pulls to one side under braking
- ☐ Noise (grinding or high-pitched squeal) when brakes applied
- ☐ Excessive brake pedal travel
- ☐ Brake pedal feels spongy when depressed
- ☐ Excessive brake pedal effort required to stop vehicle
- ☐ Judder felt through brake pedal or steering wheel when braking
- ☐ Brakes binding
- ☐ Rear wheels locking under normal braking

Suspension and steering 8
- ☐ Vehicle pulls to one side
- ☐ Wheel wobble and vibration
- ☐ Excessive pitching and/or rolling around corners, or during braking
- ☐ Wandering or general instability
- ☐ Excessively-stiff steering
- ☐ Excessive play in steering
- ☐ Lack of power assistance
- ☐ Tyre wear excessive

Electrical system 9
- ☐ Battery will not hold a charge for more than a few days
- ☐ Ignition/no-charge warning light remains illuminated with engine running
- ☐ Ignition/no-charge warning light fails to come on
- ☐ Lights inoperative
- ☐ Instrument readings inaccurate or erratic
- ☐ Horn inoperative, or unsatisfactory in operation
- ☐ Windscreen/tailgate wipers inoperative, or unsatisfactory in operation
- ☐ Windscreen/tailgate washers inoperative, or unsatisfactory in operation
- ☐ Electric windows inoperative, or unsatisfactory in operation
- ☐ Central locking system inoperative, or unsatisfactory in operation

Introduction

The vehicle owner who does his or her own maintenance according to the recommended service schedules should not have to use this section of the manual very often. Modern component reliability is such that, provided those items subject to wear or deterioration are inspected or renewed at the specified intervals, sudden failure is comparatively rare. Faults do not usually just happen as a result of sudden failure, but develop over a period of time. Major mechanical failures in particular are usually preceded by characteristic symptoms over hundreds or even thousands of miles. Those components which do occasionally fail without warning are often small and easily carried in the vehicle.

With any fault-finding, the first step is to decide where to begin investigations. Sometimes this is obvious, but on other occasions, a little detective work will be necessary. The owner who makes half a dozen haphazard adjustments or replacements may be successful in curing a fault (or its symptoms), but will be none the wiser if the fault recurs, and ultimately may have spent more time and money than was necessary. A calm and logical approach will be found to be more satisfactory in the long run. Always take into account any warning signs or abnormalities that may have been noticed in the period preceding the fault - power loss, high or low gauge readings, unusual smells, etc - and remember that failure of components such as fuses or spark plugs may only be pointers to some underlying fault.

The pages which follow provide an easy-reference guide to the more common problems which may occur during the operation of the vehicle. These problems and their possible causes are grouped under headings denoting various components or systems, such as Engine, Cooling system, etc. The Chapter and/or Section which deals with the problem is also shown in brackets. Whatever the fault, certain basic principles apply. These are as follows:

Verify the fault. This is simply a matter of being sure that you know what the symptoms are before starting work. This is particularly important if you are investigating a fault for someone else, who may not have described it very accurately.

Don't overlook the obvious. For example, if the vehicle won't start, is there petrol in the tank? (Don't take anyone else's word on this particular point, and don't trust the fuel gauge either!) If an electrical fault is indicated, look for loose or broken wires before digging out the test gear.

Cure the disease, not the symptom. Substituting a flat battery with a fully-charged one will get you off the hard shoulder, but if the underlying cause is not attended to, the new battery will go the same way. Similarly, changing oil-fouled spark plugs (petrol models) for a new set will get you moving again, but remember that the reason for the fouling (if it wasn't simply an incorrect grade of plug) will have to be established and corrected.

Don't take anything for granted. Particularly, don't forget that a "new" component may itself be defective (especially if it's been rattling around in the boot for months), and don't leave components out of a fault diagnosis sequence just because they are new or recently-fitted. When you do finally diagnose a difficult fault, you'll probably realise that all the evidence was there from the start.

1 Engine

Engine fails to rotate when attempting to start

- [ ] Battery terminal connections loose or corroded ("*Weekly checks*").
- [ ] Battery discharged or faulty (Chapter 5A).
- [ ] Broken, loose or disconnected wiring in the starting circuit (Chapter 5A).
- [ ] Defective starter solenoid or switch (Chapter 5A).
- [ ] Defective starter motor (Chapter 5A).
- [ ] Starter pinion or flywheel ring gear teeth loose or broken (Chapters 2A, 2B, 2C and 5A).
- [ ] Engine earth strap broken or disconnected (Chapter 5A).

Engine rotates, but will not start

- [ ] Fuel tank empty.
- [ ] Battery discharged (engine rotates slowly) (Chapter 5A).
- [ ] Battery terminal connections loose or corroded ("*Weekly checks*").
- [ ] Ignition components damp or damaged - petrol models (Chapters 1 and 5B).
- [ ] Broken, loose or disconnected wiring in the ignition circuit - petrol models (Chapters 1 and 5B).
- [ ] Worn, faulty or incorrectly-gapped spark plugs - petrol models (Chapter 1).
- [ ] Preheating system faulty - diesel models (Chapter 5C).
- [ ] Fuel system fault - petrol models (Chapter 4A or 4B).
- [ ] Stop solenoid faulty - diesel models (Chapter 4C).
- [ ] Air in fuel system - diesel models (Chapter 4C).
- [ ] Major mechanical failure (eg camshaft drive) (Chapter 2A, 2B or 2C).

Engine difficult to start when cold

- [ ] Battery discharged (Chapter 5A).
- [ ] Battery terminal connections loose or corroded ("*Weekly checks*").
- [ ] Worn, faulty or incorrectly-gapped spark plugs - petrol models (Chapter 1).
- [ ] Preheating system faulty - diesel models (Chapter 5C).
- [ ] Fuel system fault - petrol models (Chapter 4A or 4B).
- [ ] Other ignition system fault - petrol models (Chapters 1 and 5B).
- [ ] Low cylinder compressions (Chapter 2A or 2B).

Engine difficult to start when hot

- [ ] Air filter element dirty or clogged (Chapter 1).
- [ ] Fuel system fault - petrol models (Chapter 4A or 4B).
- [ ] Low cylinder compressions (Chapter 2A or 2B).

Starter motor noisy or excessively-rough in engagement

- [ ] Starter pinion or flywheel ring gear teeth loose or broken (Chapters 2A, 2B and 5A).
- [ ] Starter motor mounting bolts loose or missing (Chapter 5A).
- [ ] Starter motor internal components worn or damaged (Chapter 5A).

Engine starts, but stops immediately

- [ ] Loose or faulty electrical connections in the ignition circuit - petrol models (Chapters 1 and 5B).
- [ ] Vacuum leak at the throttle body or inlet manifold - petrol models (Chapter 4A or 4B).
- [ ] Blocked injector/jet or other fuel system fault - petrol models (Chapter 4A or 4B).

Engine idles erratically

- [ ] Air filter element clogged (Chapter 1).
- [ ] Vacuum leak at the throttle body, inlet manifold or associated hoses - petrol models (Chapter 4A or 4B).
- [ ] Worn, faulty or incorrectly-gapped spark plugs - petrol models (Chapter 1).
- [ ] Uneven or low cylinder compressions (Chapter 2A or 2B).
- [ ] Camshaft lobes worn (Chapter 2A or 2B).
- [ ] Valve clearances incorrect (Chapter 2A or 2B).
- [ ] Timing belt incorrectly tensioned (Chapter 2A or 2B).
- [ ] Blocked injector/jet or other fuel system fault - petrol models (Chapter 4A or 4B).
- [ ] Faulty injector(s) - diesel models (Chapter 4C).

Engine misfires at idle speed

- [ ] Worn, faulty or incorrectly-gapped spark plugs - petrol models (Chapter 1).
- [ ] Faulty spark plug HT leads - petrol models (Chapter 1).
- [ ] Vacuum leak at the throttle body, inlet manifold or associated hoses - petrol models (Chapter 4A or 4B).
- [ ] Blocked injector/jet or other fuel system fault - petrol models (Chapter 4A or 4B).
- [ ] Faulty injector(s) - diesel models (Chapter 4C).
- [ ] Valve clearances incorrect (Chapter 2A or 2B).
- [ ] Distributor cap cracked or tracking internally - petrol models (where applicable) (Chapter 1).
- [ ] Uneven or low cylinder compressions (Chapter 2A or 2B).
- [ ] Disconnected, leaking, or perished crankcase ventilation hoses (Chapter 4D).

1 Engine (continued)

Engine misfires throughout the driving speed range

☐ Fuel filter choked (Chapter 1).
☐ Fuel pump faulty, or delivery pressure low - petrol models (Chapter 4A or 4B).
☐ Fuel tank vent blocked, or fuel pipes restricted (Chapter 4A, 4B or 4C).
☐ Vacuum leak at the throttle body, inlet manifold or associated hoses - petrol models (Chapter 4A or 4B).
☐ Worn, faulty or incorrectly-gapped spark plugs - petrol models (Chapter 1).
☐ Valve clearances incorrect (Chapter 2A or 2B).
☐ Faulty spark plug HT leads - petrol models (Chapter 1).
☐ Faulty injector(s) - diesel models (Chapter 4C).
☐ Distributor cap cracked or tracking internally - petrol models (where applicable) (Chapter 1).
☐ Faulty ignition coil - petrol models (Chapter 5B).
☐ Uneven or low cylinder compressions (Chapter 2A or 2B).
☐ Blocked injector/jet or other fuel system fault - petrol models (Chapter 4A or 4B).

Engine hesitates on acceleration

☐ Worn, faulty or incorrectly-gapped spark plugs - petrol models (Chapter 1).
☐ Vacuum leak at the throttle body, inlet manifold or associated hoses - petrol models (Chapter 4A or 4B).
☐ Valve clearances incorrect (Chapter 2A or 2B).
☐ Blocked injector/jet or other fuel system fault - petrol models (Chapter 4A or 4B).
☐ Faulty injector(s) - diesel models (Chapter 4C).

Engine stalls

☐ Vacuum leak at the throttle body, inlet manifold or associated hoses - petrol models (Chapter 4A or 4B).
☐ Fuel filter choked (Chapter 1).
☐ Fuel pump faulty, or delivery pressure low - petrol models (Chapter 4A or 4B).
☐ Fuel tank vent blocked, or fuel pipes restricted (Chapter 4A, 4B or 4C).
☐ Blocked injector/jet or other fuel system fault - petrol models (Chapter 4A or 4B).
☐ Faulty injector(s) - diesel models (Chapter 4C).

Engine lacks power

☐ Timing belt incorrectly fitted or tensioned (Chapter 2A or 2B).
☐ Fuel filter choked (Chapter 1).
☐ Fuel pump faulty, or delivery pressure low - petrol models (Chapter 4A or 4B).
☐ Valve clearances incorrect (Chapter 2A or 2B).
☐ Uneven or low cylinder compressions (Chapter 2A or 2B).
☐ Worn, faulty or incorrectly-gapped spark plugs - petrol models (Chapter 1).
☐ Vacuum leak at the throttle body, inlet manifold or associated hoses - petrol models (Chapter 4A or 4B).
☐ Blocked injector/jet or other fuel system fault - petrol models (Chapter 4A or 4B).
☐ Faulty injector(s) - diesel models (Chapter 4C).
☐ Injection pump timing incorrect - diesel models (Chapter 4C).
☐ Brakes binding (Chapters 1 and 9).
☐ Clutch slipping (Chapter 6).

Engine backfires

☐ Timing belt incorrectly fitted or tensioned (Chapter 2A or 2B).
☐ Vacuum leak at the throttle body, inlet manifold or associated hoses - petrol models (Chapter 4A or 4B).
☐ Blocked injector/jet or other fuel system fault - petrol models (Chapter 4A or 4B).

Oil pressure warning light illuminated with engine running

☐ Low oil level, or incorrect oil grade ("Weekly checks").
☐ Faulty oil pressure sensor (Chapter 5A).
☐ Worn engine bearings and/or oil pump (Chapter 2C).
☐ High engine operating temperature (Chapter 3).
☐ Oil pressure relief valve defective (Chapter 2A or 2B).
☐ Oil pick-up strainer clogged (Chapter 2A or 2B).

Engine runs-on after switching off

☐ Excessive carbon build-up in engine (Chapter 2C).
☐ High engine operating temperature (Chapter 3).
☐ Fuel injection system fault - petrol models (Chapter 4A or 4B).
☐ Faulty stop solenoid - diesel models (Chapter 4C).

Engine noises

Pre-ignition (pinking) or knocking during acceleration or under load

☐ Ignition timing incorrect/ignition system fault - petrol models (Chapters 1 and 5B).
☐ Incorrect grade of spark plug - petrol models (Chapter 1).
☐ Incorrect grade of fuel (Chapter 1).
☐ Vacuum leak at the throttle body, inlet manifold or associated hoses - petrol models (Chapter 4A or 4B).
☐ Excessive carbon build-up in engine (Chapter 2C).
☐ Blocked injector/jet or other fuel system fault - petrol models (Chapter 4A or 4B).

Whistling or wheezing noises

☐ Leaking inlet manifold or throttle body gasket - petrol models (Chapter 4A or 4B).
☐ Leaking exhaust manifold gasket or pipe-to-manifold joint (Chapter 4A, 4B or 4C).
☐ Leaking vacuum hose (Chapters 4A, 4B, 4C, 5B and 9).
☐ Blowing cylinder head gasket (Chapter 2A or 2B).

Tapping or rattling noises

☐ Worn valve gear or camshaft (Chapter 2A or 2B).
☐ Valve clearances incorrect (Chapter 2A or 2B).
☐ Ancillary component fault (water pump, alternator, etc) (Chapters 3, 5A, etc).

Knocking or thumping noises

☐ Worn big-end bearings (regular heavy knocking, perhaps less under load) (Chapter 2C).
☐ Worn main bearings (rumbling and knocking, perhaps worsening under load) (Chapter 2C).
☐ Piston slap (most noticeable when cold) (Chapter 2C).
☐ Ancillary component fault (water pump, alternator, etc) (Chapters 3, 5A, etc).

2 Cooling system

Overheating

- ☐ Insufficient coolant in system ("*Weekly checks*").
- ☐ Thermostat faulty (Chapter 3).
- ☐ Radiator core blocked, or grille restricted (Chapter 3).
- ☐ Electric cooling fan or thermoswitch faulty (Chapter 3).
- ☐ Valve clearances incorrect (Chapter 2A or 2B).
- ☐ Pressure cap faulty (Chapter 3).
- ☐ Ignition timing incorrect/ignition system fault - petrol models (Chapters 1 and 5B).
- ☐ Inaccurate temperature gauge sender unit (Chapter 3).
- ☐ Airlock in cooling system (Chapter 1).

Overcooling

- ☐ Thermostat faulty (Chapter 3).
- ☐ Inaccurate temperature gauge sender unit (Chapter 3).

External coolant leakage

- ☐ Deteriorated or damaged hoses or hose clips (Chapter 1).
- ☐ Radiator core or heater matrix leaking (Chapter 3).
- ☐ Pressure cap faulty (Chapter 3).
- ☐ Water pump seal leaking (Chapter 3).
- ☐ Boiling due to overheating (Chapter 3).
- ☐ Core plug leaking (Chapter 2C).

Internal coolant leakage

- ☐ Leaking cylinder head gasket (Chapter 2A or 2B).
- ☐ Cracked cylinder head or cylinder bore (Chapter 2A or 2B).

Corrosion

- ☐ Infrequent draining and flushing (Chapter 1).
- ☐ Incorrect coolant mixture or inappropriate coolant type (Chapter 1).

3 Fuel and exhaust systems

Excessive fuel consumption

- ☐ Air filter element dirty or clogged (Chapter 1).
- ☐ Fuel injection system fault - petrol models (Chapter 4A or 4B).
- ☐ Faulty injector(s) - diesel models (Chapter 4C).
- ☐ Ignition timing incorrect/ignition system fault - petrol models (Chapters 1 and 5B).
- ☐ Valve clearances incorrect (Chapter 2A or 2B).
- ☐ Tyres under-inflated ("*Weekly checks*").

Fuel leakage and/or fuel odour

- ☐ Damaged or corroded fuel tank, pipes or connections (Chapter 4A, 4B, 4C or 4D).

Excessive noise or fumes from exhaust system

- ☐ Leaking exhaust system or manifold joints (Chapters 1 and 4A, 4B or 4C).
- ☐ Leaking, corroded or damaged silencers or pipe (Chapters 1 and 4A, 4B or 4C).
- ☐ Broken mountings causing body or suspension contact (Chapter 1).

4 Clutch

Pedal travels to floor - no pressure or very little resistance

- ☐ Broken clutch cable (Chapter 6).
- ☐ Incorrect clutch cable adjustment (Chapter 6).
- ☐ Broken clutch release bearing or fork (Chapter 6).
- ☐ Broken diaphragm spring in clutch pressure plate (Chapter 6).

Clutch fails to disengage (unable to select gears)

- ☐ Incorrect clutch cable adjustment (Chapter 6).
- ☐ Clutch disc sticking on gearbox primary shaft splines (Chapter 6).
- ☐ Clutch disc sticking to flywheel or pressure plate (Chapter 6).
- ☐ Faulty pressure plate assembly (Chapter 6).
- ☐ Clutch release mechanism worn or poorly assembled (Chapter 6).

Clutch slips (engine speed increases, with no increase in vehicle speed)

- ☐ Incorrect clutch cable adjustment (Chapter 6).
- ☐ Clutch disc linings excessively worn (Chapter 6).
- ☐ Clutch disc linings contaminated with oil or grease (Chapter 6).
- ☐ Faulty pressure plate or weak diaphragm spring (Chapter 6).

Judder as clutch is engaged

- ☐ Clutch disc linings contaminated with oil or grease (Chapter 6).
- ☐ Clutch disc linings excessively worn (Chapter 6).
- ☐ Clutch cable sticking or frayed (Chapter 6).
- ☐ Faulty or distorted pressure plate or diaphragm spring (Chapter 6).
- ☐ Worn or loose engine or gearbox mountings (Chapter 2A or 2B).
- ☐ Clutch disc hub or gearbox primary shaft splines worn (Chapter 6).

Noise when depressing or releasing clutch pedal

- ☐ Worn clutch release bearing (Chapter 6).
- ☐ Worn or dry clutch pedal bushes (Chapter 6).
- ☐ Faulty pressure plate assembly (Chapter 6).
- ☐ Pressure plate diaphragm spring broken (Chapter 6).
- ☐ Broken clutch disc cushioning springs (Chapter 6).

5 Manual transmission

Noisy in neutral with engine running

☐ Primary shaft bearings worn (noise apparent with clutch pedal released, but not when depressed) (Chapter 7).*
☐ Clutch release bearing worn (noise apparent with clutch pedal depressed, possibly less when released) (Chapter 6).

Noisy in one particular gear

☐ Worn, damaged or chipped gear teeth (Chapter 7).*

Difficulty engaging gears

☐ Clutch fault (Chapter 6).
☐ Worn or damaged gearchange linkage/cable (Chapter 7).
☐ Incorrectly-adjusted gearchange linkage/cable (Chapter 7).
☐ Worn synchroniser units (Chapter 7).*

Jumps out of gear

☐ Worn or damaged gearchange linkage/cable (Chapter 7).
☐ Incorrectly-adjusted gearchange linkage/cable (Chapter 7).
☐ Worn synchroniser units (Chapter 7).*
☐ Worn selector forks (Chapter 7).*

Vibration

☐ Lack of oil (Chapter 1).
☐ Worn bearings (Chapter 7).*

Lubricant leaks

☐ Leaking differential output oil seal (Chapter 7).
☐ Leaking housing joint (Chapter 7).*
☐ Leaking primary shaft oil seal (Chapter 7).*

Although the corrective action necessary to remedy the symptoms described is beyond the scope of the home mechanic, the above information should be helpful in isolating the cause of the condition, so that the owner can communicate clearly with a professional mechanic.

6 Driveshafts

Clicking or knocking noise on turns (at slow speed on full-lock)

☐ Lack of constant velocity joint lubricant, possibly due to damaged gaiter (Chapter 8).
☐ Worn outer constant velocity joint (Chapter 8).

Vibration when accelerating or decelerating

☐ Worn inner constant velocity joint (Chapter 8).
☐ Bent or distorted driveshaft (Chapter 8).

7 Braking system

Note: *Before assuming that a brake problem exists, make sure that the tyres are in good condition and correctly inflated, that the front wheel alignment is correct, and that the vehicle is not loaded with weight in an unequal manner. Apart from checking the condition of all pipe and hose connections, any faults occurring on the anti-lock braking system should be referred to a VW dealer for diagnosis.*

Vehicle pulls to one side under braking

☐ Worn, defective, damaged or contaminated brake pads/shoes on one side (Chapters 1 and 9).
☐ Seized or partially-seized front brake caliper/wheel cylinder piston (Chapters 1 and 9).
☐ A mixture of brake pad/shoe lining materials fitted between sides (Chapters 1 and 9).
☐ Brake caliper or backplate mounting bolts loose (Chapter 9).
☐ Worn or damaged steering or suspension components (Chapters 1 and 10).

Noise (grinding or high-pitched squeal) when brakes applied

☐ Brake pad or shoe friction lining material worn down to metal backing (Chapters 1 and 9).
☐ Excessive corrosion of brake disc or drum. (May be apparent after the vehicle has been standing for some time (Chapters 1 and 9).
☐ Foreign object (stone chipping, etc) trapped between brake disc and shield (Chapters 1 and 9).

Excessive brake pedal travel

☐ Inoperative rear brake self-adjust mechanism - drum brakes (Chapters 1 and 9).
☐ Faulty master cylinder (Chapter 9).
☐ Air in hydraulic system (Chapters 1 and 9).
☐ Faulty vacuum servo unit (Chapter 9).

Brake pedal feels spongy when depressed

☐ Air in hydraulic system (Chapters 1 and 9).
☐ Deteriorated flexible rubber brake hoses (Chapters 1 and 9).
☐ Master cylinder mounting nuts loose (Chapter 9).
☐ Faulty master cylinder (Chapter 9).

Excessive pedal effort required to stop vehicle

☐ Faulty vacuum servo unit (Chapter 9).
☐ Faulty vacuum pump - diesel models (Chapter 9).
☐ Disconnected, damaged or insecure brake servo vacuum hose (Chapter 9).
☐ Primary or secondary hydraulic circuit failure (Chapter 9).
☐ Seized brake caliper or wheel cylinder piston(s) (Chapter 9).
☐ Brake pads or brake shoes incorrectly fitted (Chapters 1 and 9).
☐ Incorrect grade of brake pads or shoes fitted (Chapters 1 and 9).
☐ Brake pads or brake shoe linings contaminated (Chapters 1 and 9).

Judder felt through brake pedal or steering wheel when braking

☐ Excessive run-out or distortion of discs/drums (Chapters 1 and 9).
☐ Brake pad or brake shoe linings worn (Chapters 1 and 9).
☐ Brake caliper or brake backplate mounting bolts loose (Chapter 9).
☐ Wear in suspension or steering components or mountings (Chapters 1 and 10).

Brakes binding

☐ Seized brake caliper or wheel cylinder piston(s) (Chapter 9).
☐ Incorrectly-adjusted handbrake mechanism (Chapter 9).
☐ Faulty master cylinder (Chapter 9).

Rear wheels locking under normal braking

☐ Rear brake shoe linings contaminated (Chapters 1 and 9).
☐ Faulty brake pressure regulator (Chapter 9).

8 Suspension and steering

Note: *Before diagnosing suspension or steering faults, be sure that the trouble is not due to incorrect tyre pressures, mixtures of tyre types, or binding brakes.*

Vehicle pulls to one side

- ☐ Defective tyre (*"Weekly checks"*).
- ☐ Excessive wear in suspension or steering components (Chapters 1 and 10).
- ☐ Incorrect front wheel alignment (Chapter 10).
- ☐ Accident damage to steering or suspension components (Chapter 1).

Wheel wobble and vibration

- ☐ Front roadwheels out of balance (vibration felt mainly through the steering wheel) (Chapters 1 and 10).
- ☐ Rear roadwheels out of balance (vibration felt throughout the vehicle) (Chapters 1 and 10).
- ☐ Roadwheels damaged or distorted (Chapters 1 and 10).
- ☐ Faulty or damaged tyre (*"Weekly checks"*).
- ☐ Worn steering or suspension joints, bushes or components (Chapters 1 and 10).
- ☐ Wheel bolts loose (Chapters 1 and 10).

Excessive pitching and/or rolling around corners, or during braking

- ☐ Defective shock absorbers (Chapters 1 and 10).
- ☐ Broken or weak spring and/or suspension component (Chapters 1 and 10).
- ☐ Worn or damaged anti-roll bar or mountings (Chapter 10).

Wandering or general instability

- ☐ Incorrect front wheel alignment (Chapter 10).
- ☐ Worn steering or suspension joints, bushes or components (Chapters 1 and 10).
- ☐ Roadwheels out of balance (Chapters 1 and 10).
- ☐ Faulty or damaged tyre (*"Weekly checks"*).
- ☐ Wheel bolts loose (Chapters 1 and 10).
- ☐ Defective shock absorbers (Chapters 1 and 10).

Excessively-stiff steering

- ☐ Lack of steering gear lubricant (Chapter 10).
- ☐ Seized track rod end balljoint or suspension balljoint (Chapters 1 and 10).
- ☐ Broken or incorrectly-adjusted power steering drivebelt (Chapter 1).
- ☐ Incorrect front wheel alignment (Chapter 10).
- ☐ Steering rack or column bent or damaged (Chapter 10).

Excessive play in steering

- ☐ Worn steering column intermediate shaft universal joint (Chapter 10).
- ☐ Worn steering track rod end balljoints (Chapters 1 and 10).
- ☐ Worn rack-and-pinion steering gear (Chapter 10).
- ☐ Worn steering or suspension joints, bushes or components (Chapters 1 and 10).

Lack of power assistance

- ☐ Broken or incorrectly-adjusted auxiliary drivebelt (Chapter 1).
- ☐ Incorrect power steering fluid level (*"Weekly checks"*).
- ☐ Restriction in power steering fluid hoses (Chapter 1).
- ☐ Faulty power steering pump (Chapter 10).
- ☐ Faulty rack-and-pinion steering gear (Chapter 10).

Tyre wear excessive

Tyres worn on inside or outside edges

- ☐ Tyres under-inflated (wear on both edges) (*"Weekly checks"*).
- ☐ Incorrect camber or castor angles (wear on one edge only) (Chapter 10).
- ☐ Worn steering or suspension joints, bushes or components (Chapters 1 and 10).
- ☐ Excessively-hard cornering.
- ☐ Accident damage.

Tyre treads exhibit feathered edges

- ☐ Incorrect toe setting (Chapter 10).

Tyres worn in centre of tread

- ☐ Tyres over-inflated (*"Weekly checks"*).

Tyres worn on inside and outside edges

- ☐ Tyres under-inflated (*"Weekly checks"*).

Tyres worn unevenly

- ☐ Tyres/wheels out of balance (Chapter 1).
- ☐ Excessive wheel or tyre run-out (Chapter 1).
- ☐ Worn shock absorbers (Chapters 1 and 10).
- ☐ Faulty tyre (*"Weekly checks"*).

9 Electrical system

Note: *For problems associated with the starting system, refer to the faults listed under "Engine" earlier in this Section.*

Battery will not hold a charge for more than a few days

- ☐ Battery defective internally (Chapter 5A).
- ☐ Battery terminal connections loose or corroded (*"Weekly checks"*).
- ☐ Auxiliary drivebelt worn or incorrectly adjusted (Chapter 1).
- ☐ Alternator not charging at correct output (Chapter 5A).
- ☐ Alternator or voltage regulator faulty (Chapter 5A).
- ☐ Short-circuit causing continual battery drain (Chapters 5A and 12).

Ignition/no-charge warning light remains illuminated with engine running

- ☐ Auxiliary drivebelt broken, worn, or incorrectly adjusted (Chapter 1).
- ☐ Alternator brushes worn, sticking, or dirty (Chapter 5A).
- ☐ Alternator brush springs weak or broken (Chapter 5A).
- ☐ Internal fault in alternator or voltage regulator (Chapter 5A).
- ☐ Broken, disconnected, or loose wiring in charging circuit (Chapter 5A).

Ignition/no-charge warning light fails to come on

- ☐ Warning light bulb blown (Chapter 12).
- ☐ Broken, disconnected, or loose wiring in warning light circuit (Chapter 12).
- ☐ Alternator faulty (Chapter 5A).

9 Electrical system (continued)

Lights inoperative

☐ Bulb blown (Chapter 12).
☐ Corrosion of bulb or bulbholder contacts (Chapter 12).
☐ Blown fuse (Chapter 12).
☐ Faulty relay (Chapter 12).
☐ Broken, loose, or disconnected wiring (Chapter 12).
☐ Faulty switch (Chapter 12).

Instrument readings inaccurate or erratic

Instrument readings increase with engine speed

☐ Faulty voltage regulator (Chapter 12).

Fuel or temperature gauges give no reading

☐ Faulty gauge sender unit (Chapters 3 and 4A, 4B or 4C).
☐ Wiring open-circuit (Chapter 12).
☐ Faulty gauge (Chapter 12).

Fuel or temperature gauges give continuous maximum reading

☐ Faulty gauge sender unit (Chapters 3 and 4A, 4B or 4C).
☐ Wiring short-circuit (Chapter 12).
☐ Faulty gauge (Chapter 12).

Horn inoperative, or unsatisfactory in operation

Horn operates all the time

☐ Horn push either earthed or stuck down (Chapter 12).
☐ Horn cable-to-horn push earthed (Chapter 12).

Horn fails to operate

☐ Blown fuse (Chapter 12).
☐ Cable or cable connections loose, broken or disconnected (Chapter 12).

Horn emits intermittent or unsatisfactory sound

☐ Cable connections loose (Chapter 12).
☐ Horn mountings loose (Chapter 12).

Windscreen/tailgate wipers inoperative, or unsatisfactory in operation

Wipers fail to operate, or operate very slowly

☐ Wiper blades stuck to screen, or linkage seized or binding (Chapters 1 and 12).
☐ Blown fuse (Chapter 12).
☐ Cable or cable connections loose, broken or disconnected (Chapter 12).
☐ Faulty relay (Chapter 12).
☐ Faulty wiper motor (Chapter 12).

Wiper blades sweep over too large or too small an area of the glass

☐ Wiper arms incorrectly positioned on spindles (Chapter 1).
☐ Excessive wear of wiper linkage (Chapter 12).
☐ Wiper motor or linkage mountings loose or insecure (Chapter 12).

Wiper blades fail to clean the glass effectively

☐ Wiper blade rubbers worn or perished ("Weekly checks").
☐ Wiper arm tension springs broken, or arm pivots seized (Chapter 12).
☐ Insufficient windscreen washer additive to adequately remove road film ("Weekly checks").

Windscreen/tailgate washers inoperative, or unsatisfactory in operation

One or more washer jets inoperative

☐ Blocked washer jet (Chapter 1).
☐ Disconnected, kinked or restricted fluid hose (Chapter 12).
☐ Insufficient fluid in washer reservoir ("Weekly checks").

Washer pump fails to operate

☐ Broken or disconnected wiring or connections (Chapter 12).
☐ Blown fuse (Chapter 12).
☐ Faulty washer switch (Chapter 12).
☐ Faulty washer pump (Chapter 12).

Washer pump runs for some time before fluid is emitted from jets

☐ Faulty one-way valve in fluid supply hose (Chapter 12).

Electric windows inoperative, or unsatisfactory in operation

Window glass will only move in one direction

☐ Faulty switch (Chapter 12).

Window glass slow to move

☐ Regulator seized or damaged, or in need of lubrication (Chapter 11).
☐ Door internal components or trim fouling regulator (Chapter 11).
☐ Faulty motor (Chapter 11).

Window glass fails to move

☐ Blown fuse (Chapter 12).
☐ Faulty relay (Chapter 12).
☐ Broken or disconnected wiring or connections (Chapter 12).
☐ Faulty motor (Chapter 11).

Central locking system inoperative, or unsatisfactory in operation

Complete system failure

☐ Blown fuse (Chapter 12).
☐ Faulty relay (Chapter 12).
☐ Broken or disconnected wiring or connections (Chapter 12).

Latch locks but will not unlock, or unlocks but will not lock

☐ Faulty master switch (Chapter 12).
☐ Broken or disconnected latch operating rods or levers (Chapter 11).
☐ Faulty relay (Chapter 12).

One solenoid/motor fails to operate

☐ Broken or disconnected wiring or connections (Chapter 12).
☐ Faulty operating assembly (Chapter 11).
☐ Broken, binding or disconnected latch operating rods or levers (Chapter 11).
☐ Fault in door latch (Chapter 11).